INUYASHA™

VOL. 31

VIZ Media Edition

STORY AND ART BY
RUMIKO TAKAHASHI

CONTENTS

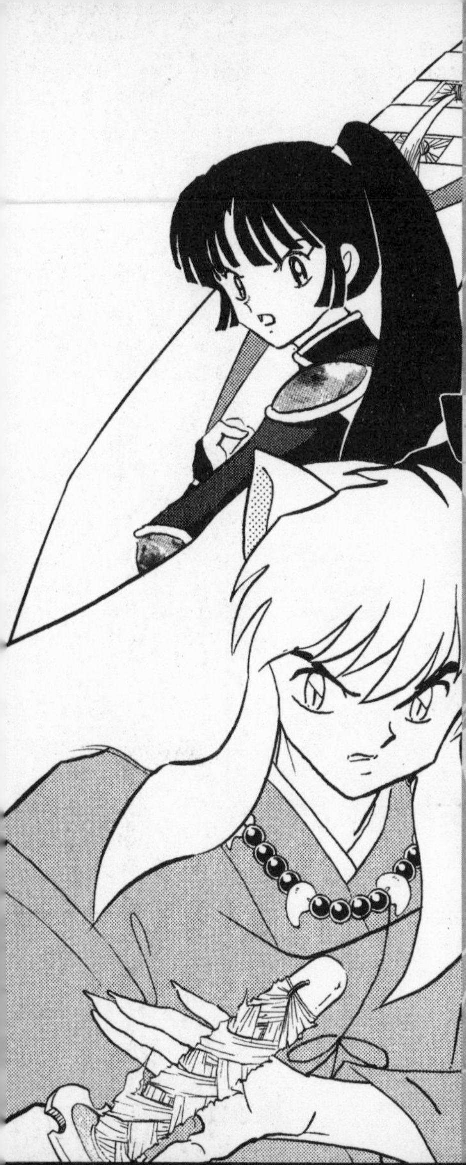

Long ago, in the "Warring States" era of Japan's Muromachi period (*Sengoku-jidai*, approximately 1467-1568 CE), a legendary dog-like half-demon called "Inuyasha" attempted to steal the Shikon Jewel—or "Jewel of Four Souls"—from a village, but was stopped by the enchanted arrow of the village priestess, Kikyo. Inuyasha fell into a deep sleep, pinned to a tree by Kikyo's arrow, while the mortally wounded Kikyo took the Shikon Jewel with her into the fires of her funeral pyre. Years passed.

Fast-forward to the present day. Kagome, a Japanese high school girl, is pulled into a well one day by a mysterious centipede monster and finds herself transported into the past—only to come face to face with the trapped Inuyasha. She frees him, and Inuyasha easily defeats the centipede monster.

The residents of the village, now 50 years older, readily accept Kagome as the reincarnation of their deceased priestess Kikyo, a claim supported by the fact that the Shikon Jewel emerges from a cut on Kagome's body. Unfortunately, the jewel's rediscovery means that the village is soon under attack by a variety of demons in search of this treasure. Then, the jewel is accidentally shattered into many shards, each of which may have the fearsome power of the entire jewel.

Although Inuyasha says he hates Kagome because of her resemblance to Kikyo, the woman who "killed" him, he is forced to team up with her when Kaede, the village leader, binds him to Kagome with a powerful spell. Now the two grudging companions must fight to reclaim and reassemble the shattered shards of the Shikon Jewel before they fall into the wrong hands...

THIS VOLUME The search for the final shard of the Shikon Jewel leads Inuyasha and the gang to a mountain fortress. But the gate is guarded by two giant statues and a force that will only allow the dead to enter! In the meantime, Naraku is seeking a path to the underworld and teams up with a demon, Abi Hime, who hunts the blood of innocent villagers to heal her mother. Inuyasha and friends step in to stop them when

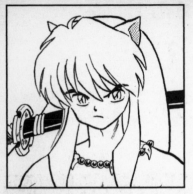

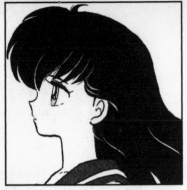

INUYASHA
Half-demon hybrid, son of a human mother and demon father. His necklace is enchanted, allowing Kagome to control him with a word.

KAGOME
Modern-day Japanese schoolgirl who can travel back and forth between the past and present through an enchanted well.

NARAKU
Enigmatic demon-mastermind behind the miseries of nearly everyone in the story.

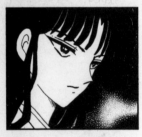

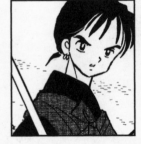

MIROKU
Lecherous Buddhist priest cursed with a mystical "hellhole" in his hand that's slowly killing him.

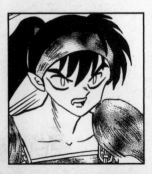

KOGA
Leader of the Wolf Clan, Koga is himself a Wolf Demon and, because of several Shikon shards in his legs, possesses super speed. Enamored of Kagome, he quarrels with Inuyasha frequently.

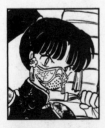

SANGO
"Demon Exterminator" or slayer from the village where the Shikon Jewel was first born.

SCROLL 1

THE GATEKEEPERS

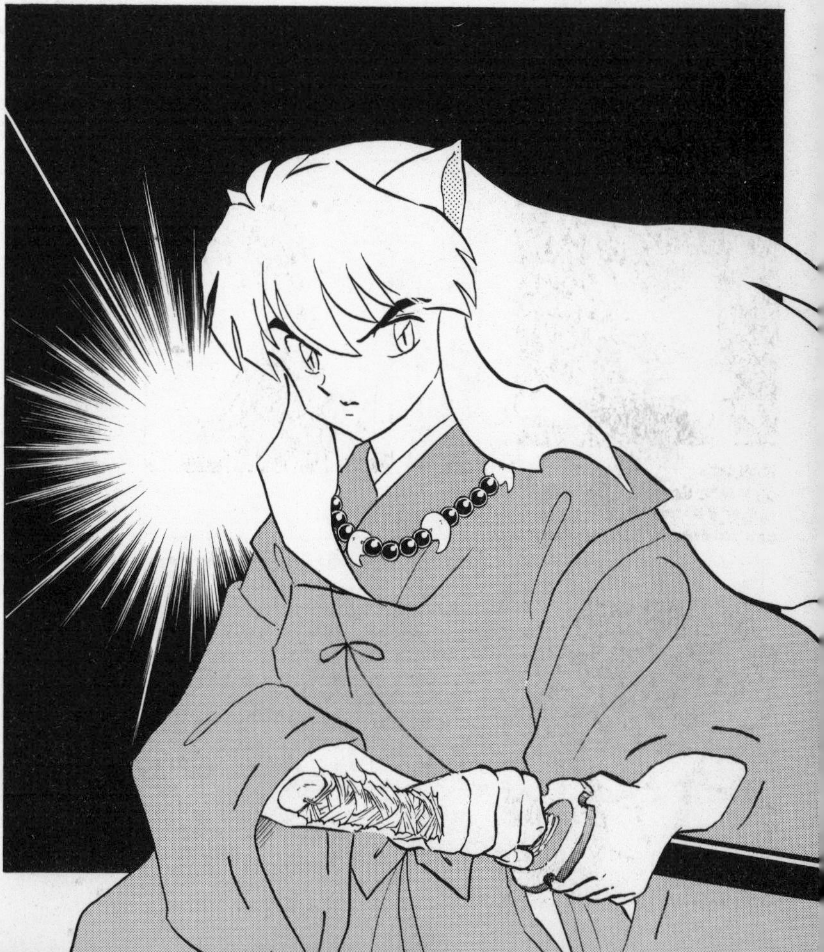

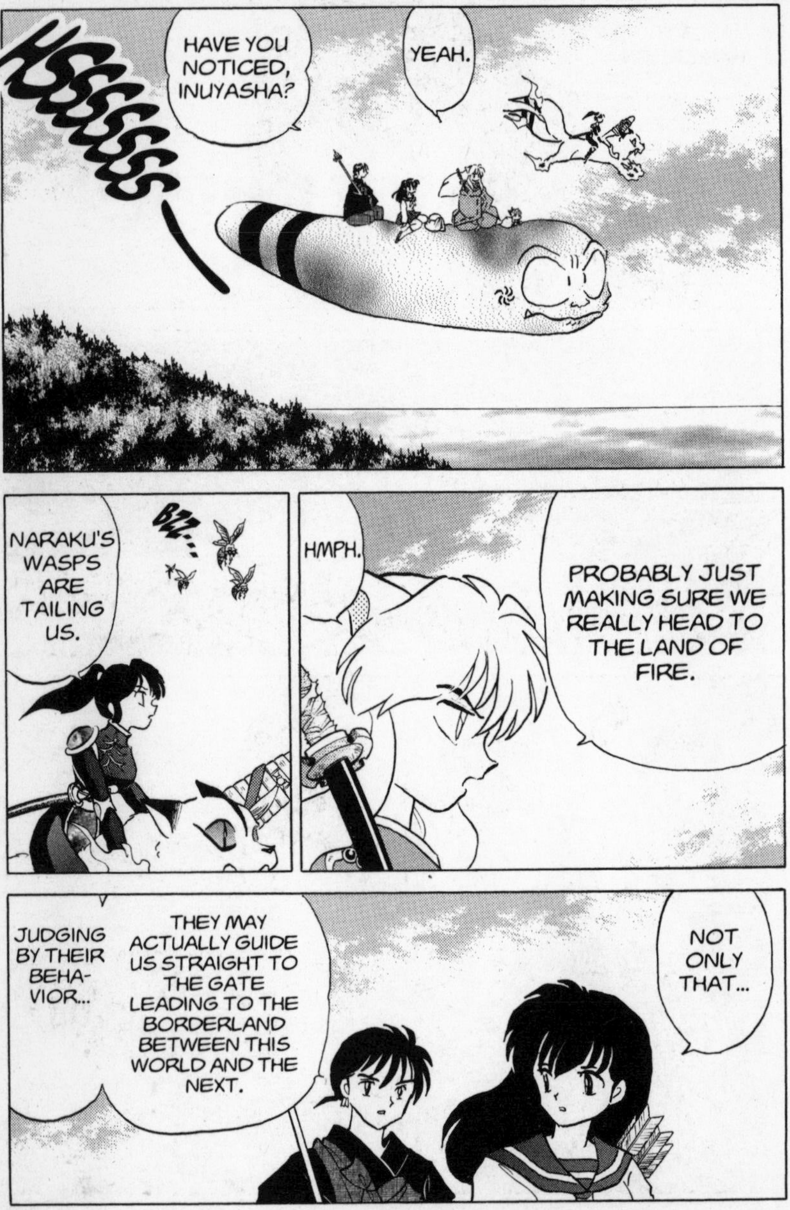
HSSSSSS
HAVE YOU NOTICED, INUYASHA?
YEAH.
NARAKU'S WASPS ARE TAILING US.
BZZ...
HMPH.
PROBABLY JUST MAKING SURE WE REALLY HEAD TO THE LAND OF FIRE.
JUDGING BY THEIR BEHA-VIOR...
THEY MAY ACTUALLY GUIDE US STRAIGHT TO THE GATE LEADING TO THE BORDERLAND BETWEEN THIS WORLD AND THE NEXT.
NOT ONLY THAT...

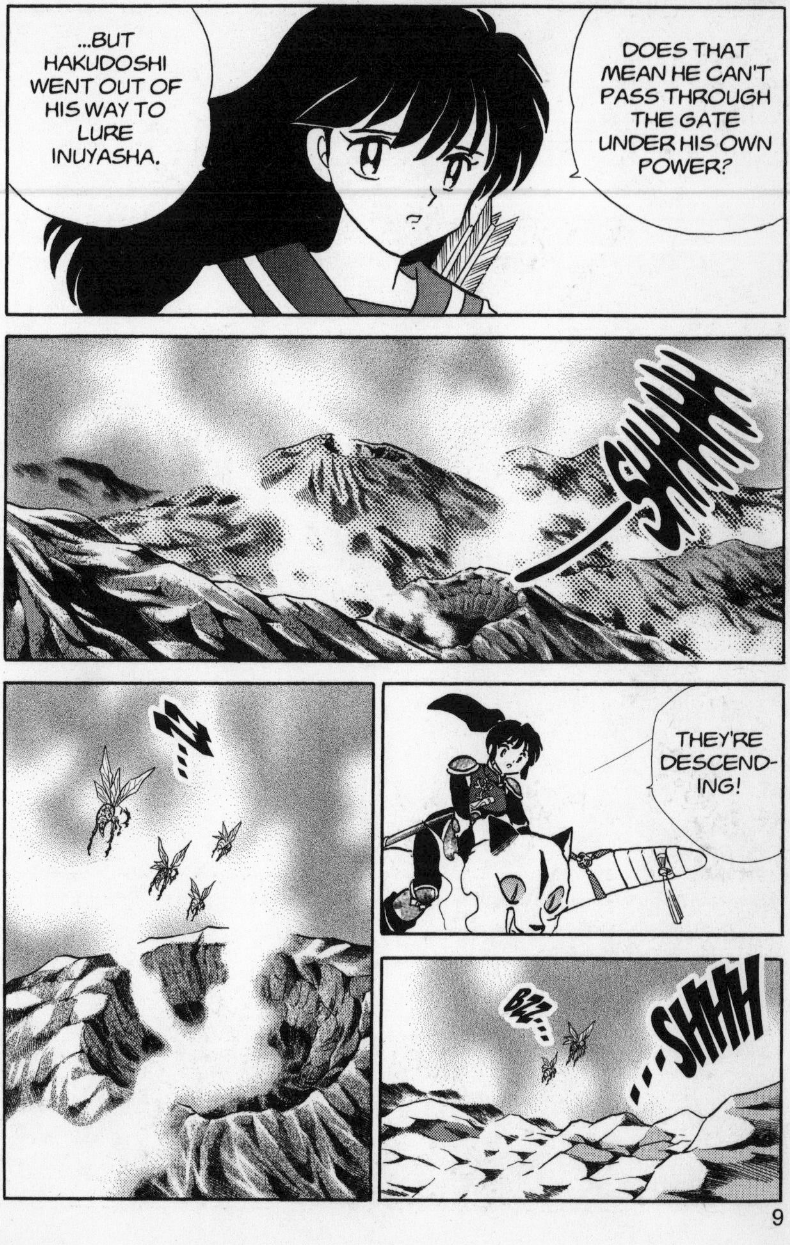
...BUT HAKUDOSHI WENT OUT OF HIS WAY TO LURE INUYASHA.
DOES THAT MEAN HE CAN'T PASS THROUGH THE GATE UNDER HIS OWN POWER?
SHHHH
ZZ...
THEY'RE DESCENDING!
BZZ...
...SHHHH

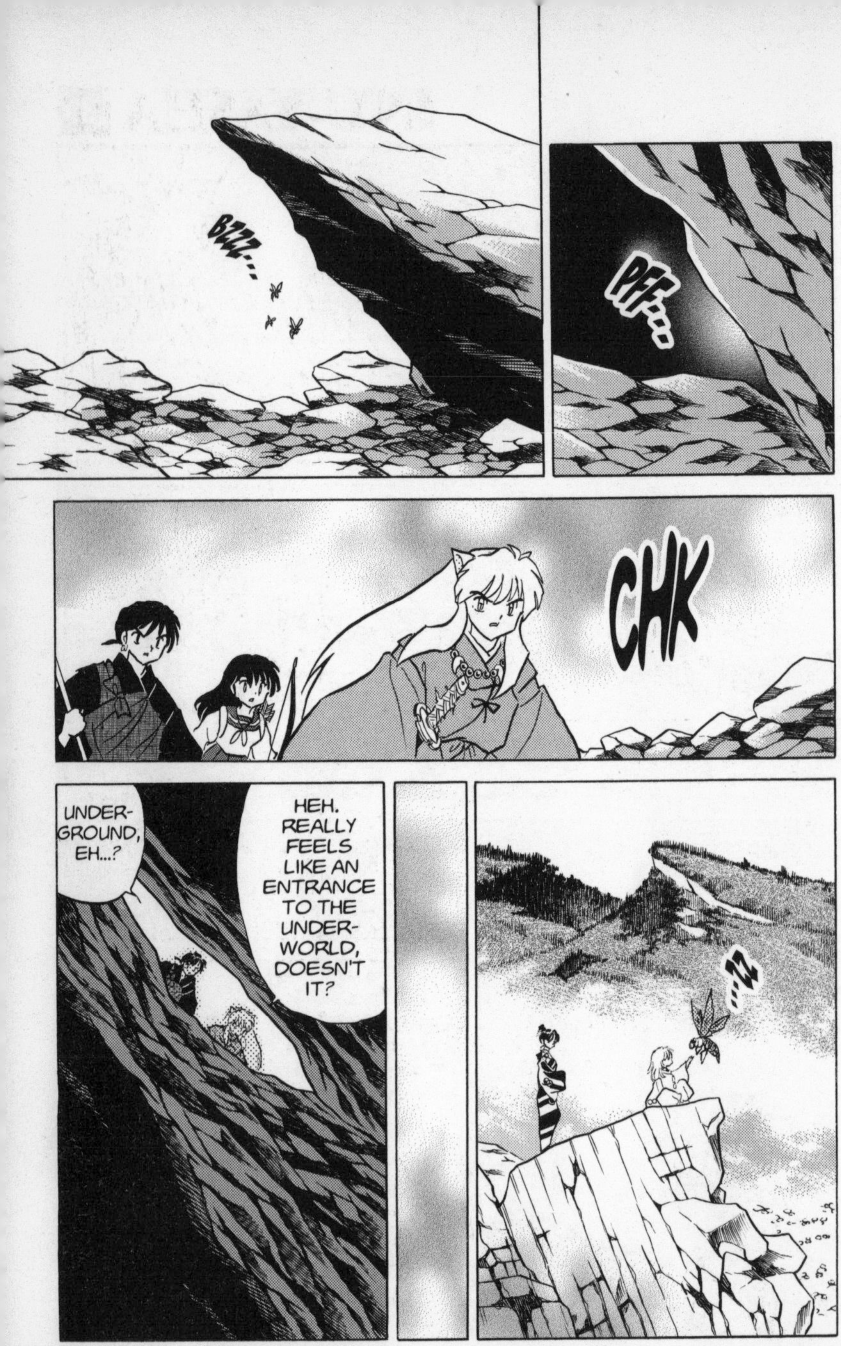
BZZZ...
PFF...
CHK
UNDER-GROUND, EH...?
HEH. REALLY FEELS LIKE AN ENTRANCE TO THE UNDER-WORLD, DOESN'T IT?

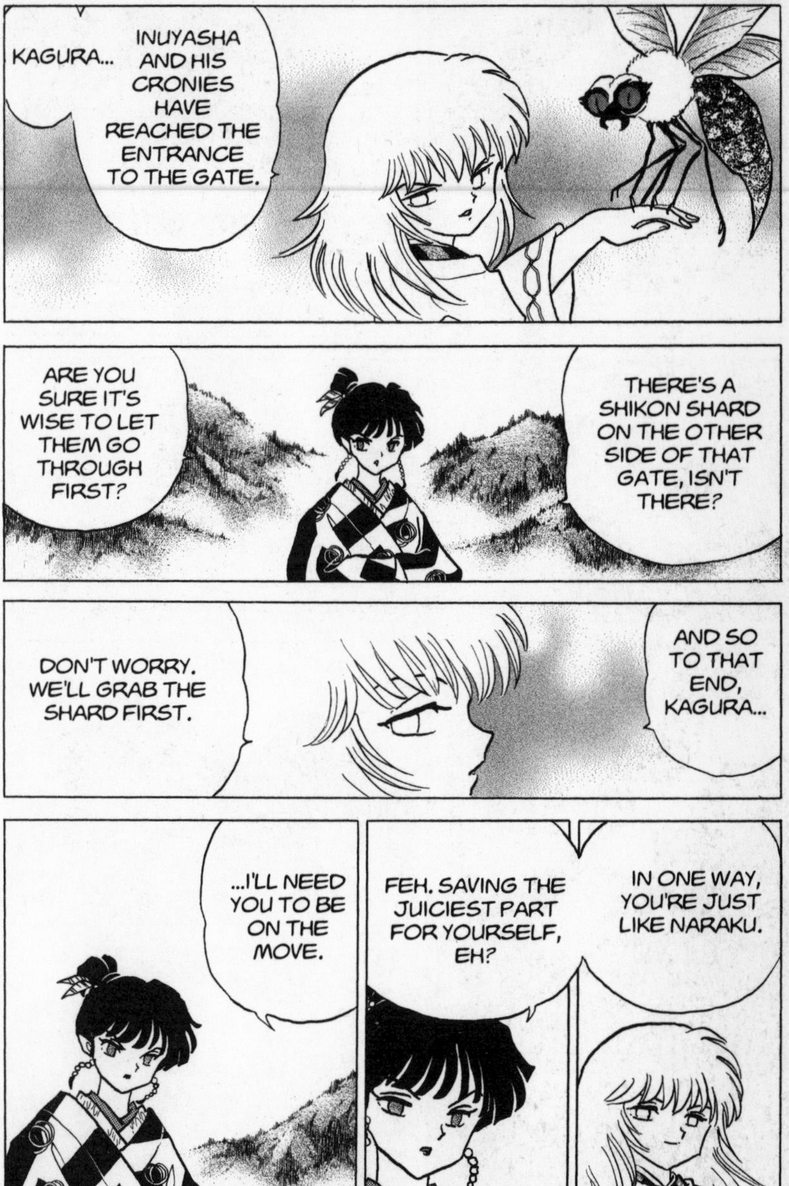
KAGURA...
INUYASHA AND HIS CRONIES HAVE REACHED THE ENTRANCE TO THE GATE.
ARE YOU SURE IT'S WISE TO LET THEM GO THROUGH FIRST?
THERE'S A SHIKON SHARD ON THE OTHER SIDE OF THAT GATE, ISN'T THERE?
DON'T WORRY. WE'LL GRAB THE SHARD FIRST.
AND SO TO THAT END, KAGURA...
...I'LL NEED YOU TO BE ON THE MOVE.
FEH. SAVING THE JUICIEST PART FOR YOURSELF, EH?
IN ONE WAY, YOU'RE JUST LIKE NARAKU.

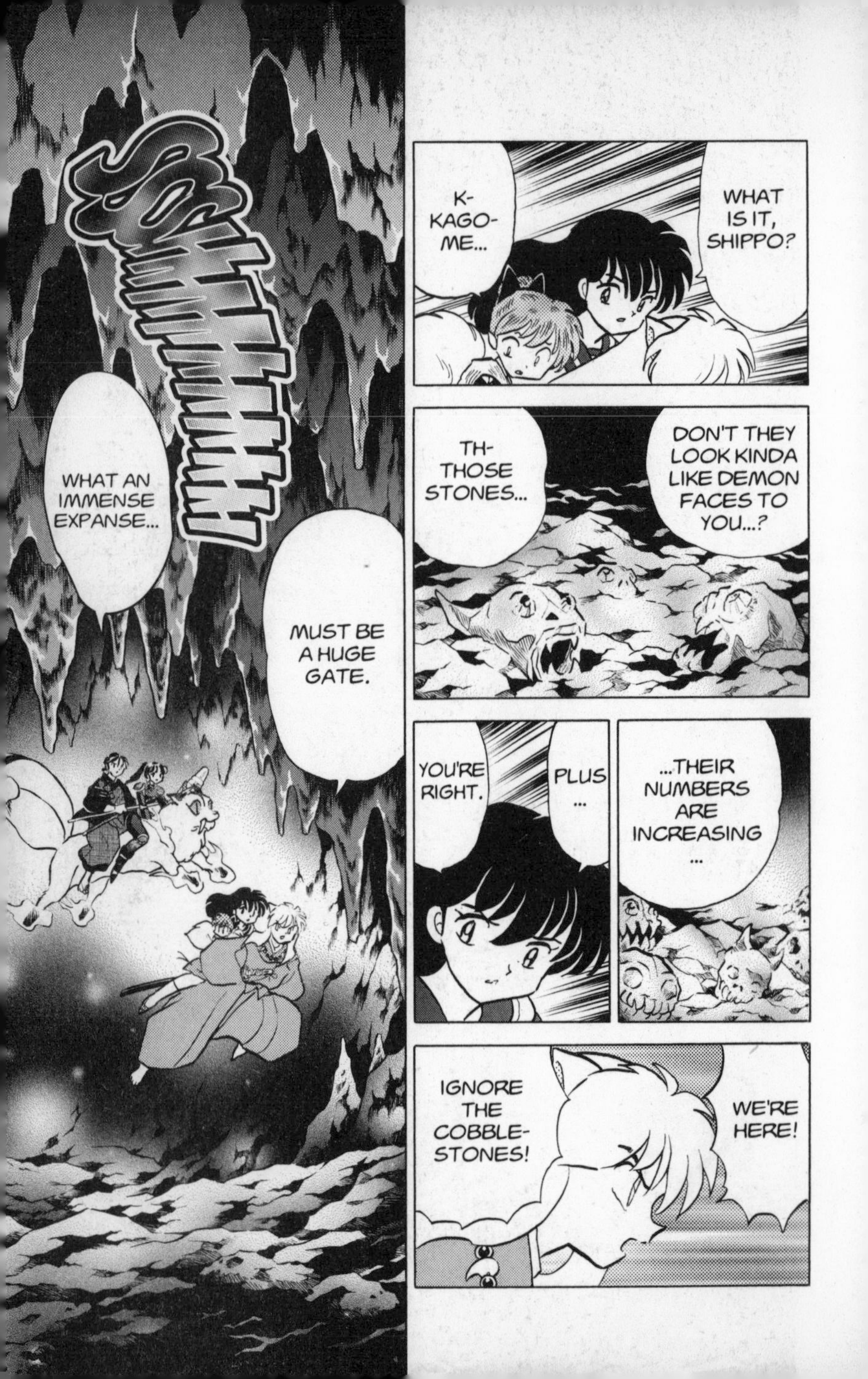
WHAT AN IMMENSE EXPANSE...
MUST BE A HUGE GATE.
K-KAGOME...
WHAT IS IT, SHIPPO?
TH-THOSE STONES...
DON'T THEY LOOK KINDA LIKE DEMON FACES TO YOU...?
YOU'RE RIGHT.
PLUS ...
...THEIR NUMBERS ARE INCREASING ...
IGNORE THE COBBLESTONES!
WE'RE HERE!

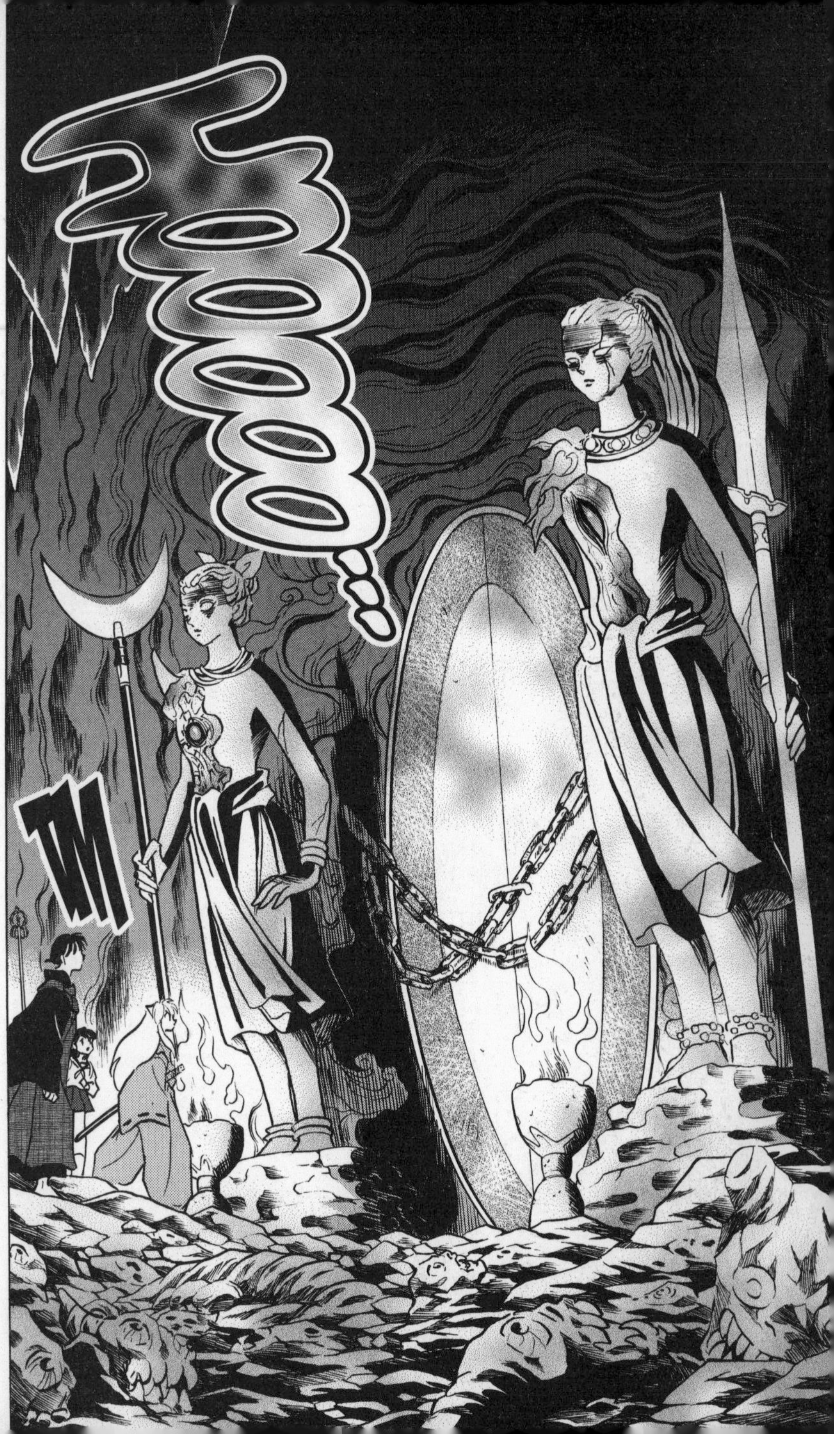
FOOOOO....
TM

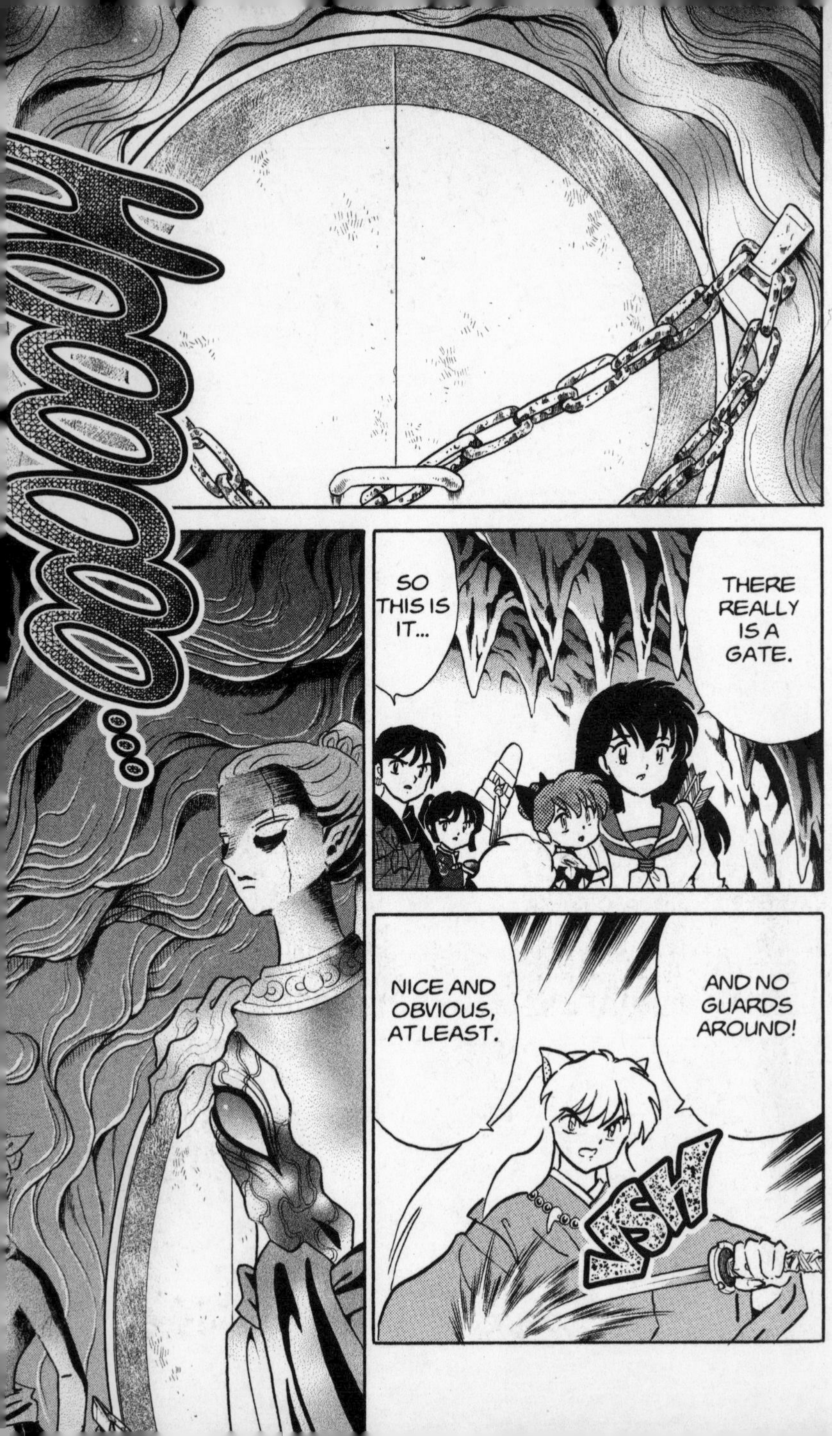
HWOOOO...
SO THIS IS IT...
THERE REALLY IS A GATE.
NICE AND OBVIOUS, AT LEAST.
AND NO GUARDS AROUND!
KSH

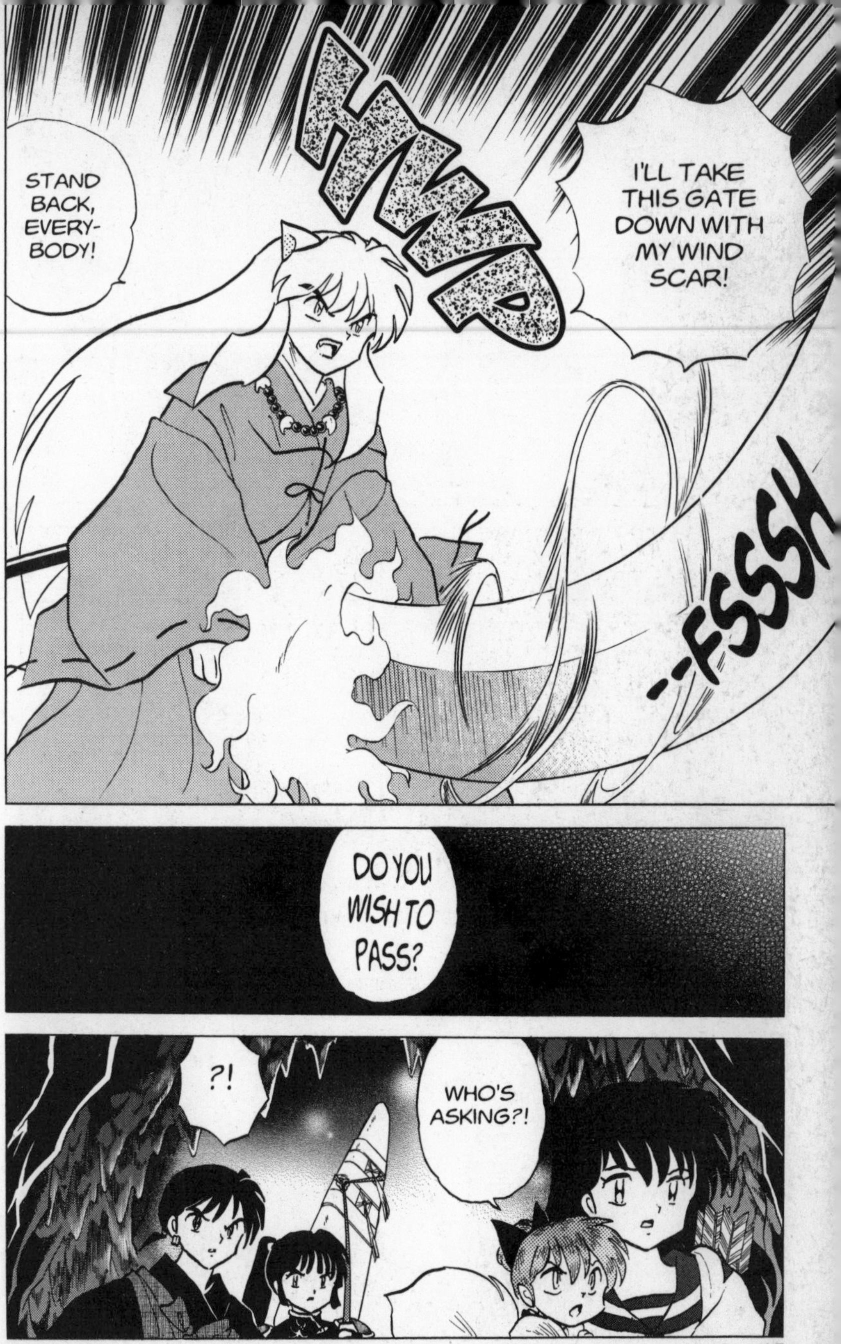
STAND BACK, EVERY-BODY!
HWMP
I'LL TAKE THIS GATE DOWN WITH MY WIND SCAR!
--FSSSH
DO YOU WISH TO PASS?
?!
WHO'S ASKING?!

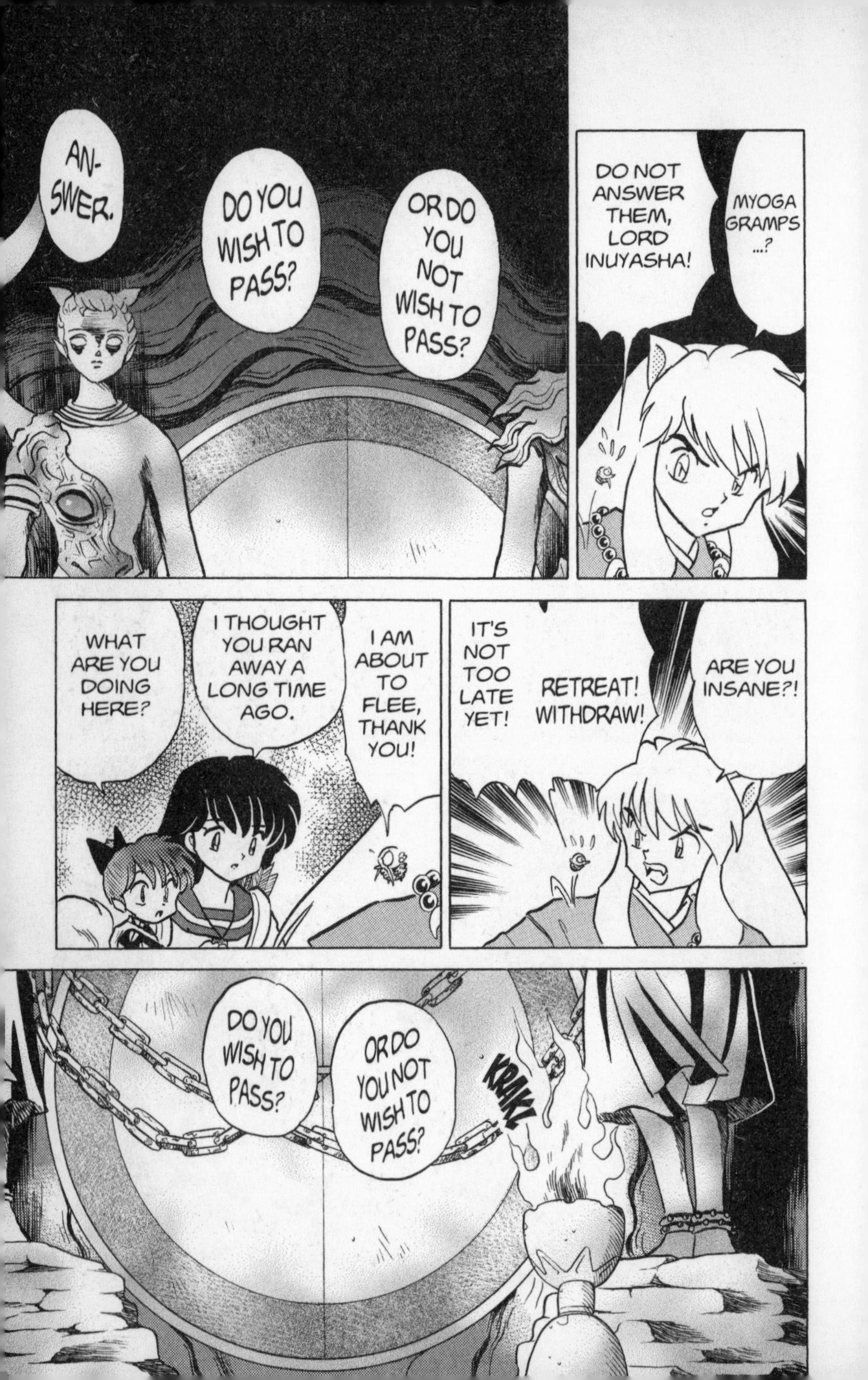
AN-SWER.
DO YOU WISH TO PASS?
OR DO YOU NOT WISH TO PASS?
DO NOT ANSWER THEM, LORD INUYASHA!
MYOGA GRAMPS ...?
WHAT ARE YOU DOING HERE?
I THOUGHT YOU RAN AWAY A LONG TIME AGO.
I AM ABOUT TO FLEE, THANK YOU!
IT'S NOT TOO LATE YET!
RETREAT! WITHDRAW!
ARE YOU INSANE?!
DO YOU WISH TO PASS?
OR DO YOU NOT WISH TO PASS?
KRAK!

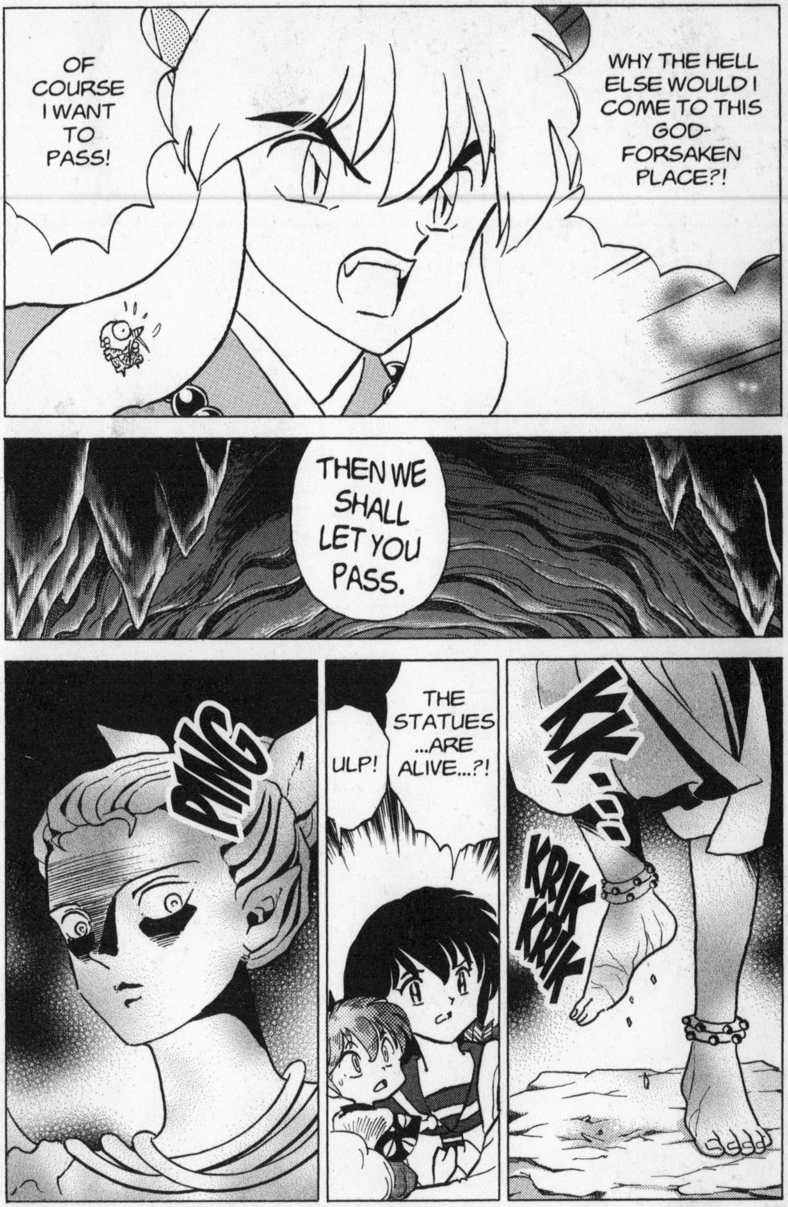
OF COURSE I WANT TO PASS!
WHY THE HELL ELSE WOULD I COME TO THIS GOD-FORSAKEN PLACE?!
THEN WE SHALL LET YOU PASS.
PING
ULP!
THE STATUES ...ARE ALIVE...?!
KK...
KRIK KRIK

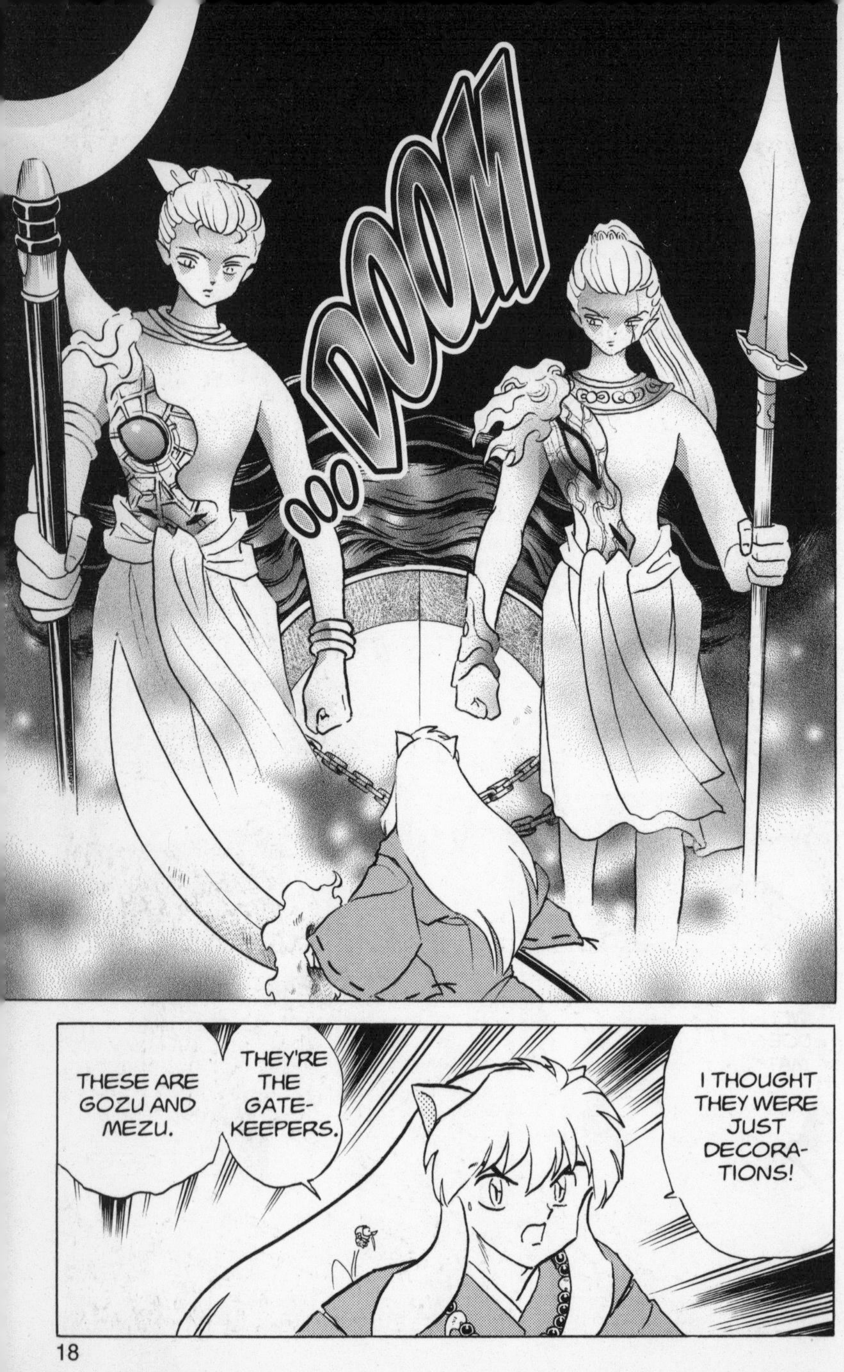
...DOOM
THESE ARE GOZU AND MEZU.
THEY'RE THE GATE-KEEPERS.
I THOUGHT THEY WERE JUST DECORA-TIONS!

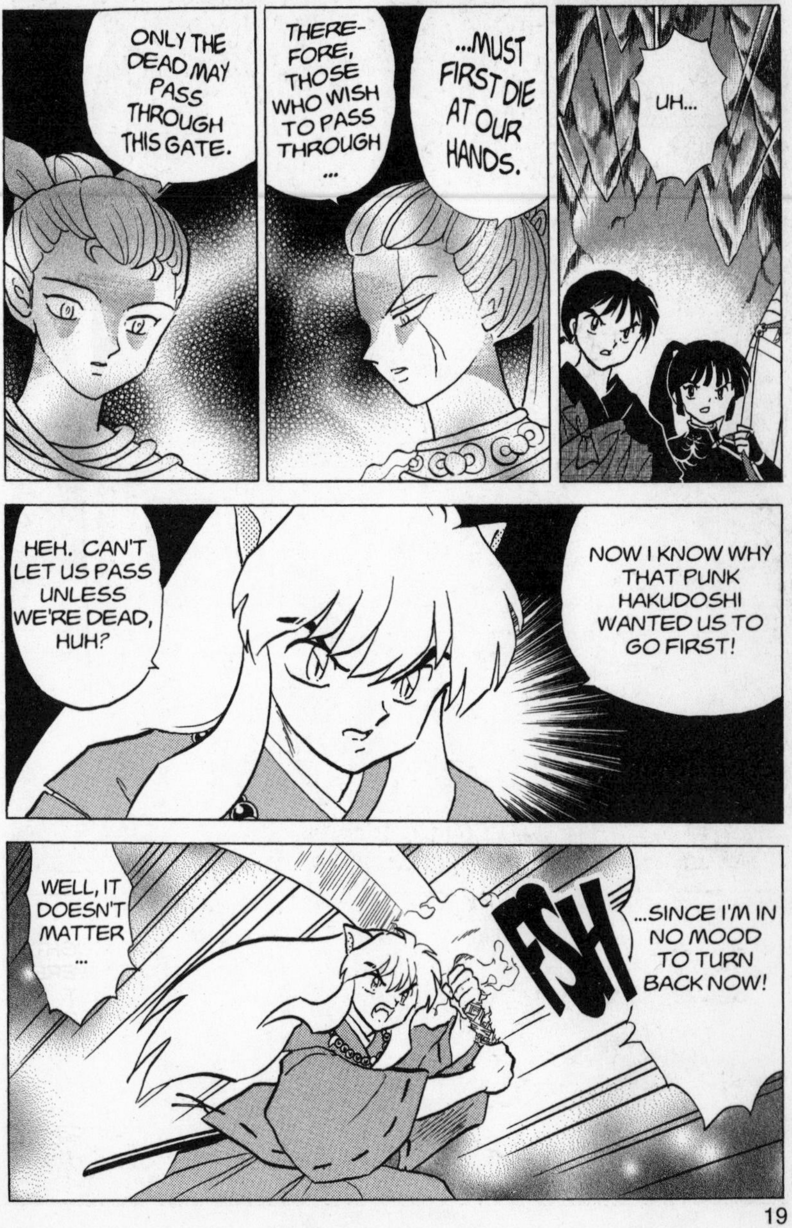
ONLY THE DEAD MAY PASS THROUGH THIS GATE.
THEREFORE, THOSE WHO WISH TO PASS THROUGH ...
...MUST FIRST DIE AT OUR HANDS.
UH...
HEH. CAN'T LET US PASS UNLESS WE'RE DEAD, HUH?
NOW I KNOW WHY THAT PUNK HAKUDOSHI WANTED US TO GO FIRST!
WELL, IT DOESN'T MATTER ...
FSH
...SINCE I'M IN NO MOOD TO TURN BACK NOW!

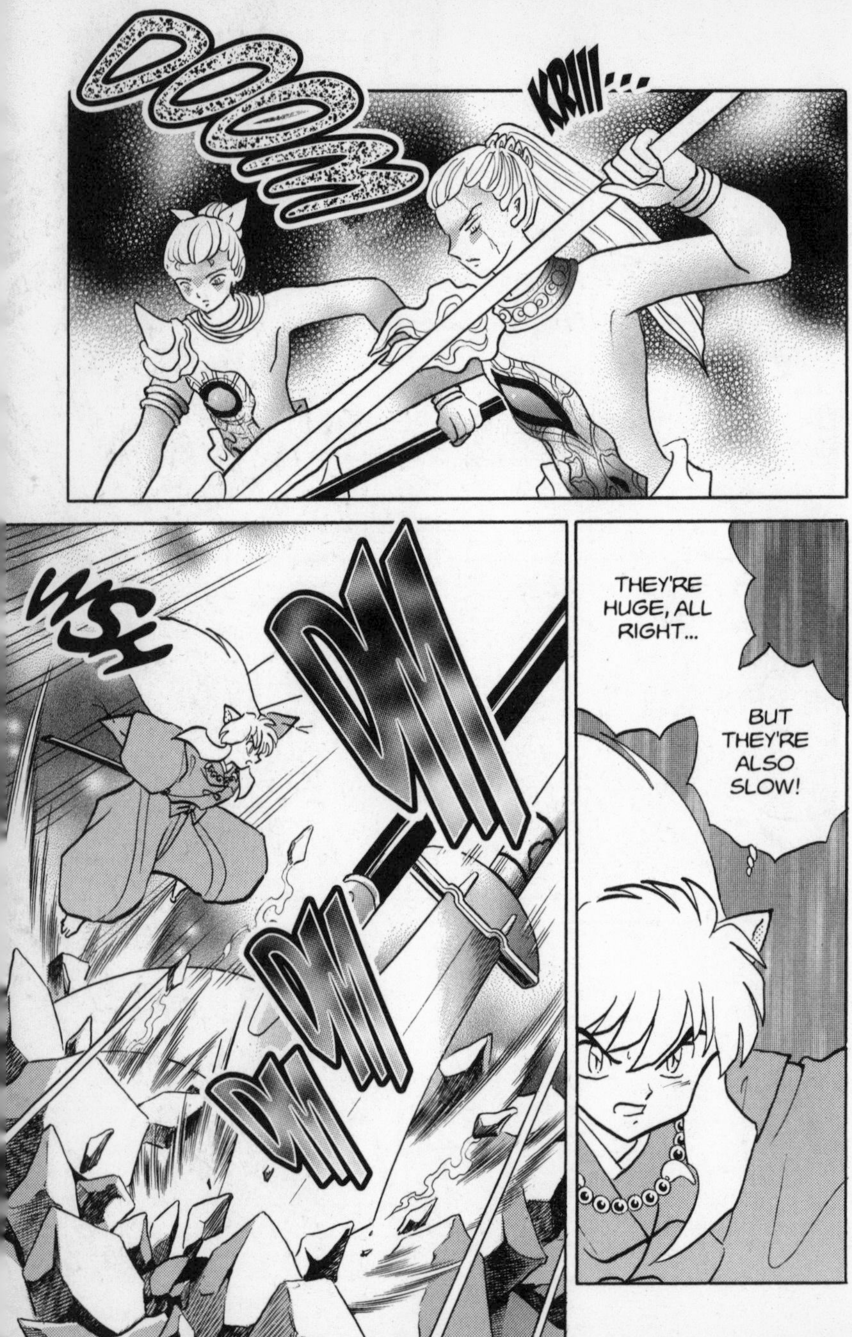
DOOOM
KRIII...
WSH
THEY'RE HUGE, ALL RIGHT...
BUT THEY'RE ALSO SLOW!

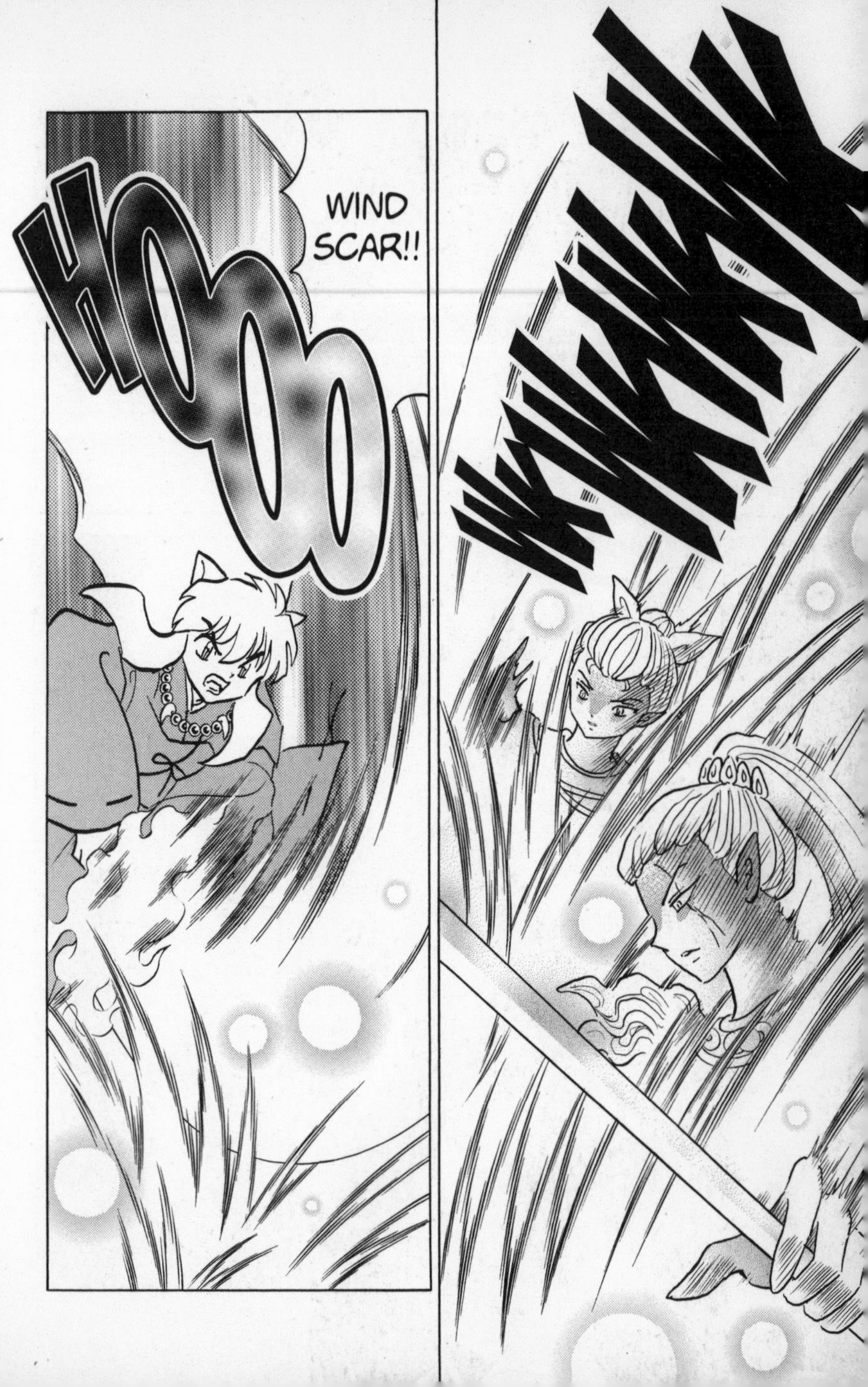
WIND
SCAR!!

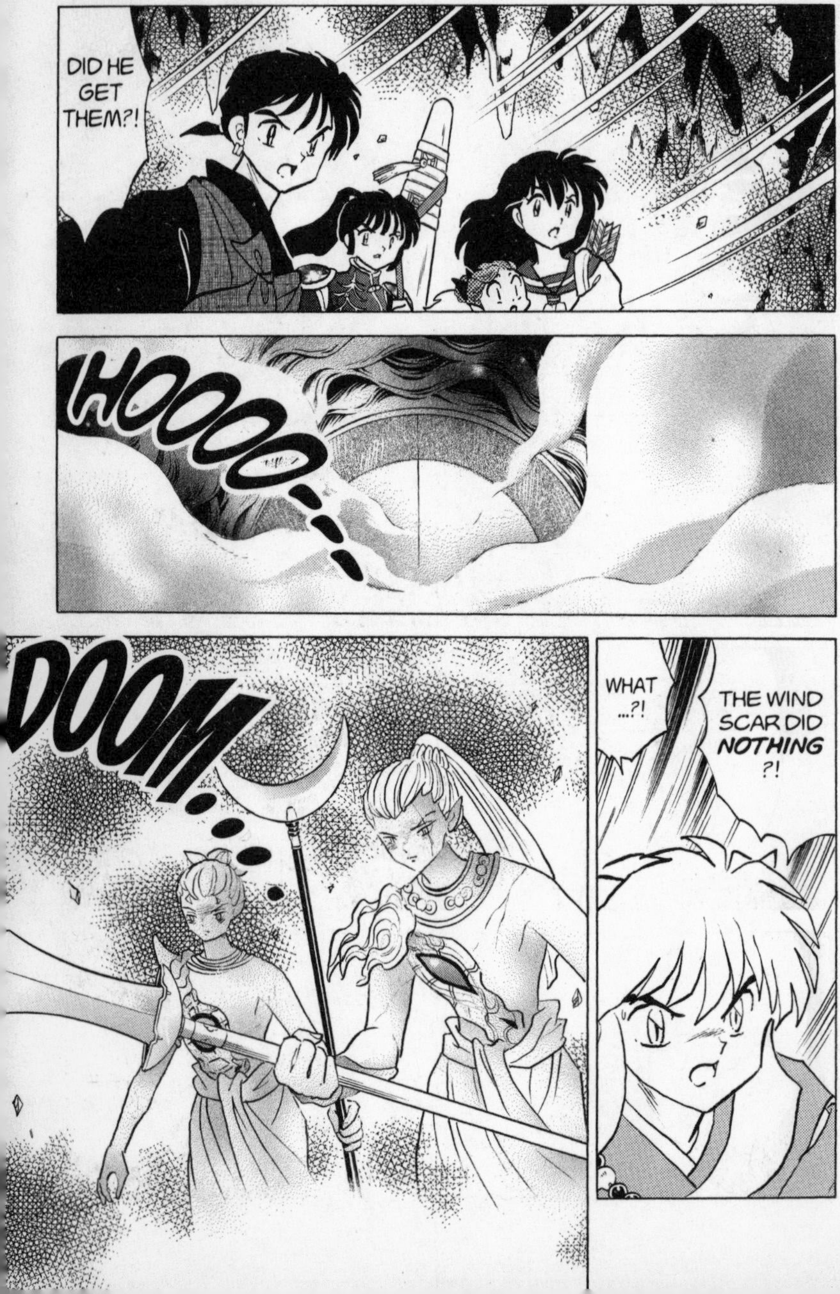
DID HE GET THEM?!
HOOOO...
DOOM...
WHAT ...?!
THE WIND SCAR DID NOTHING ?!

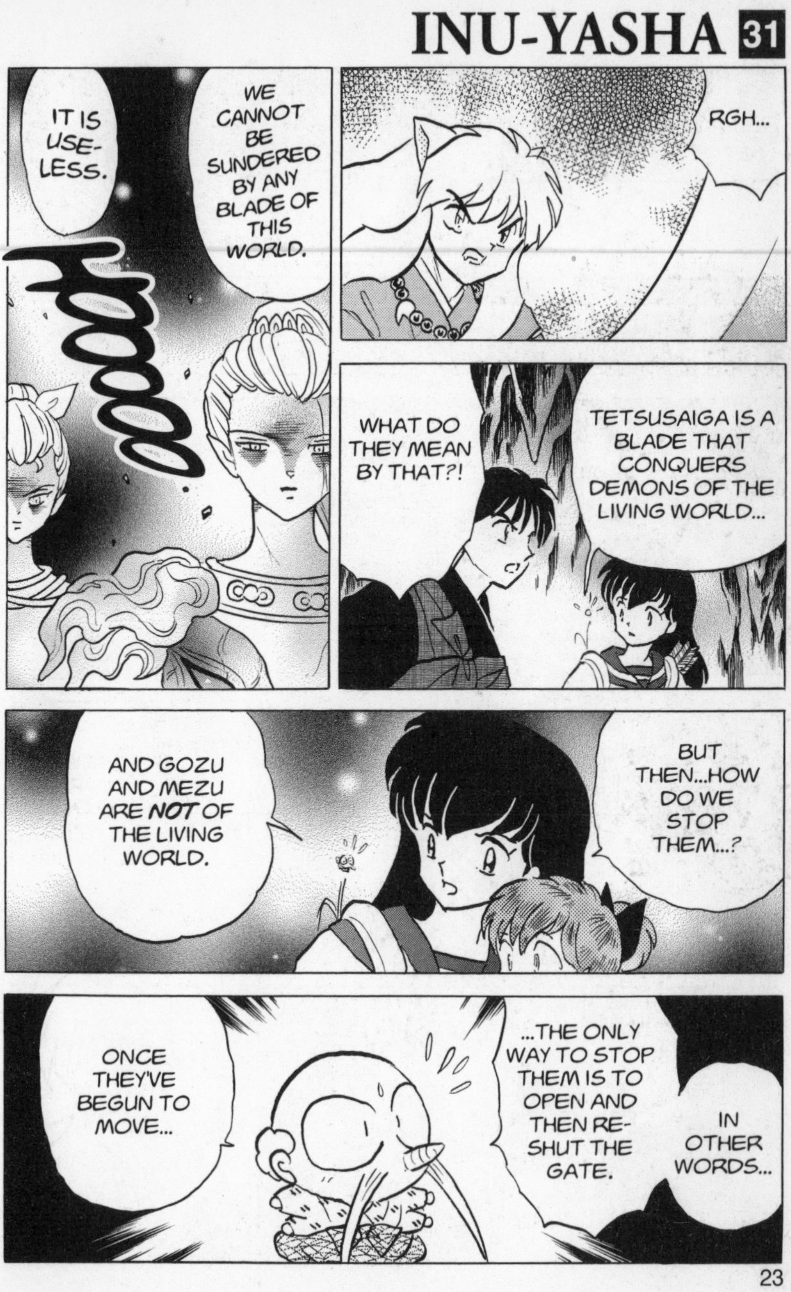
IT IS USE-LESS.
WE CANNOT BE SUNDERED BY ANY BLADE OF THIS WORLD.
RGH...
WHAT DO THEY MEAN BY THAT?!
TETSUSAIGA IS A BLADE THAT CONQUERS DEMONS OF THE LIVING WORLD...
AND GOZU AND MEZU ARE ***NOT*** OF THE LIVING WORLD.
BUT THEN...HOW DO WE STOP THEM...?
ONCE THEY'VE BEGUN TO MOVE...
...THE ONLY WAY TO STOP THEM IS TO OPEN AND THEN RE-SHUT THE GATE.
IN OTHER WORDS...

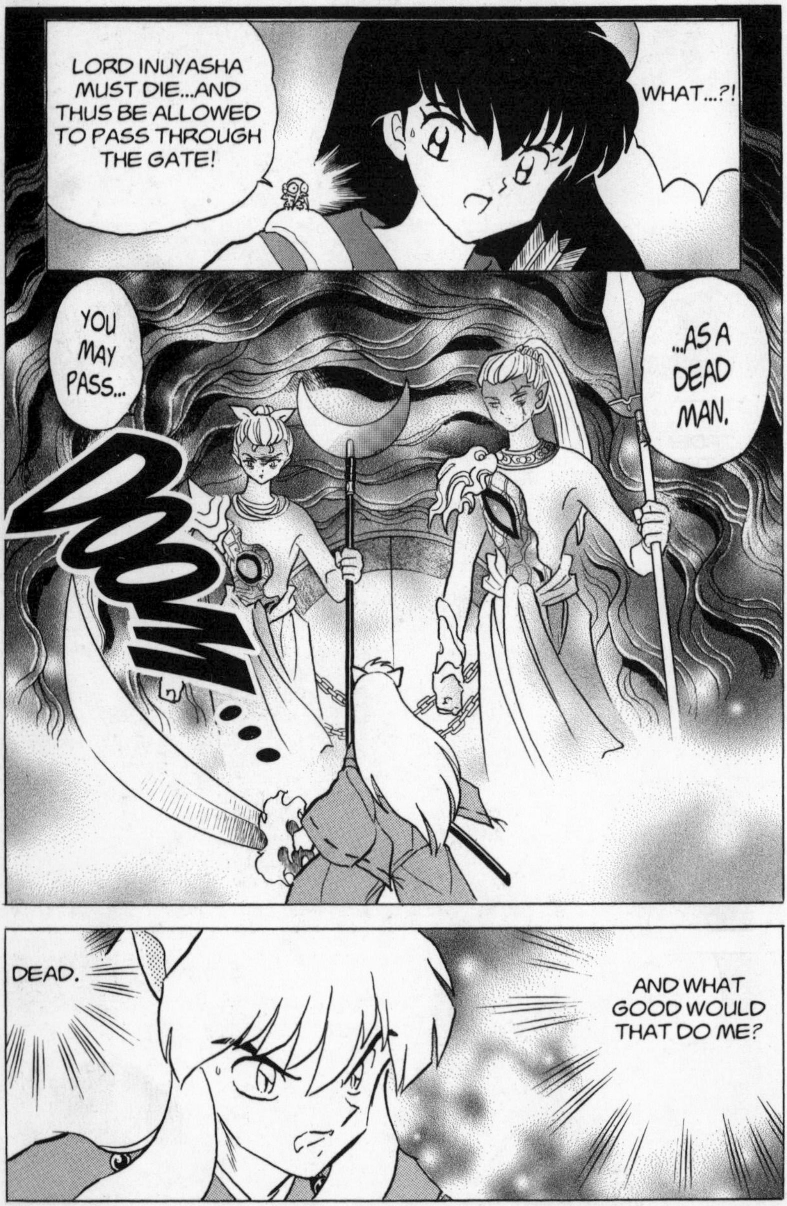
LORD INUYASHA MUST DIE...AND THUS BE ALLOWED TO PASS THROUGH THE GATE!
WHAT...?!
YOU MAY PASS...
VOOOM...
...AS A DEAD MAN.
DEAD.
AND WHAT GOOD WOULD THAT DO ME?

SCROLL 2 : THE OPENED GATE

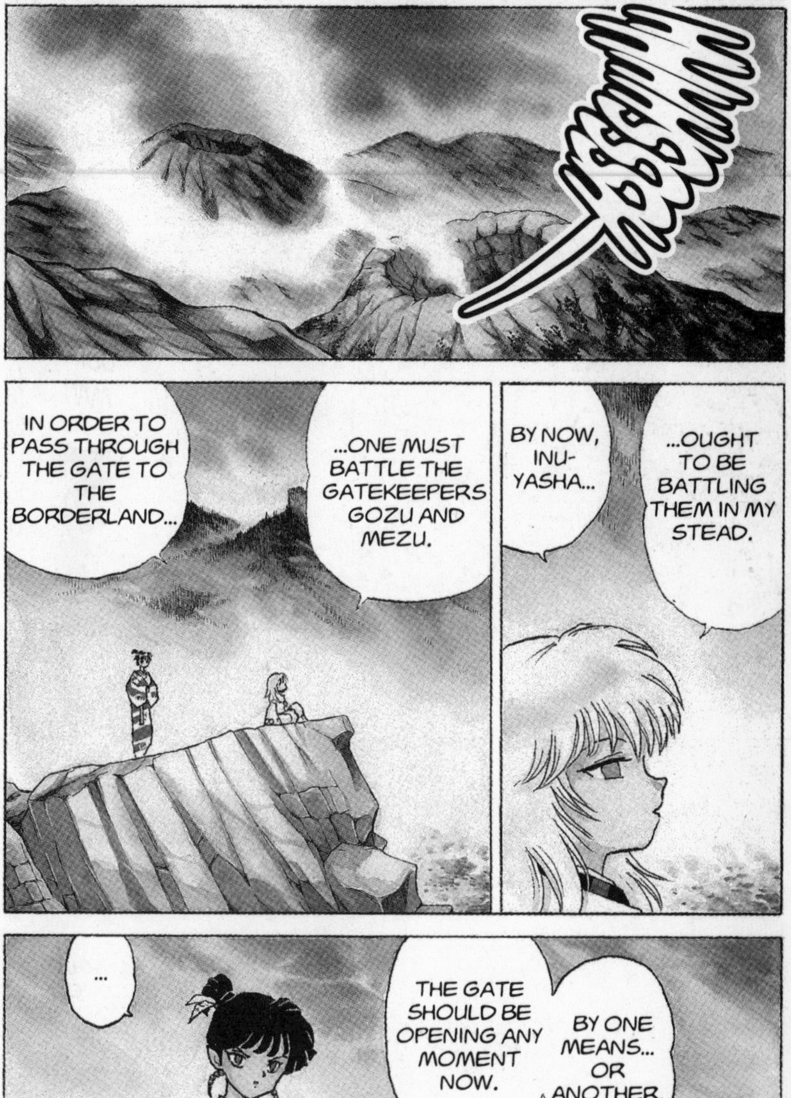
IN ORDER TO PASS THROUGH THE GATE TO THE BORDERLAND...
...ONE MUST BATTLE THE GATEKEEPERS GOZU AND MEZU.
BY NOW, INU-YASHA...
...OUGHT TO BE BATTLING THEM IN MY STEAD.
...
THE GATE SHOULD BE OPENING ANY MOMENT NOW.
BY ONE MEANS... OR ANOTHER.

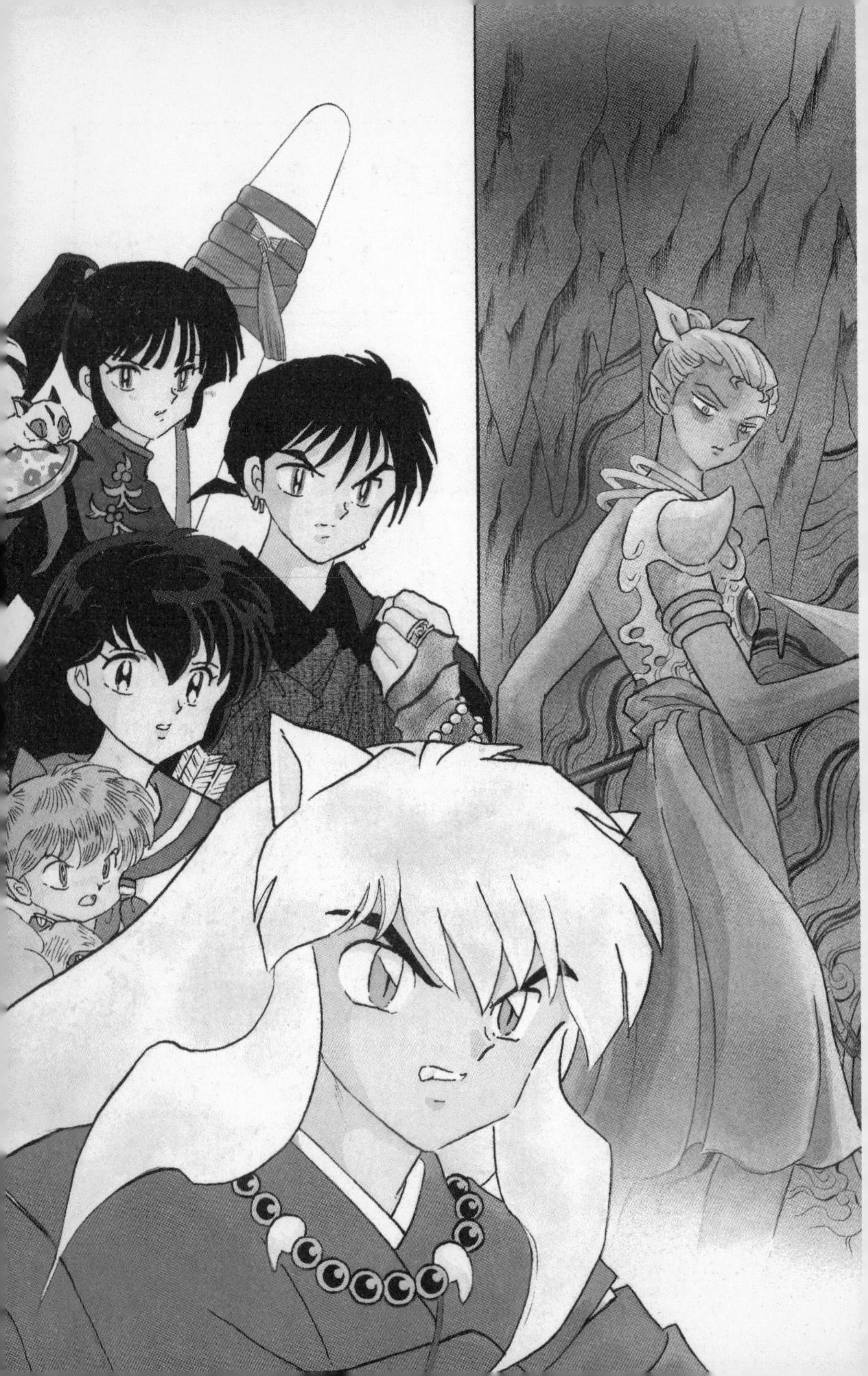

SCROLL 2
THE OPENED GATE

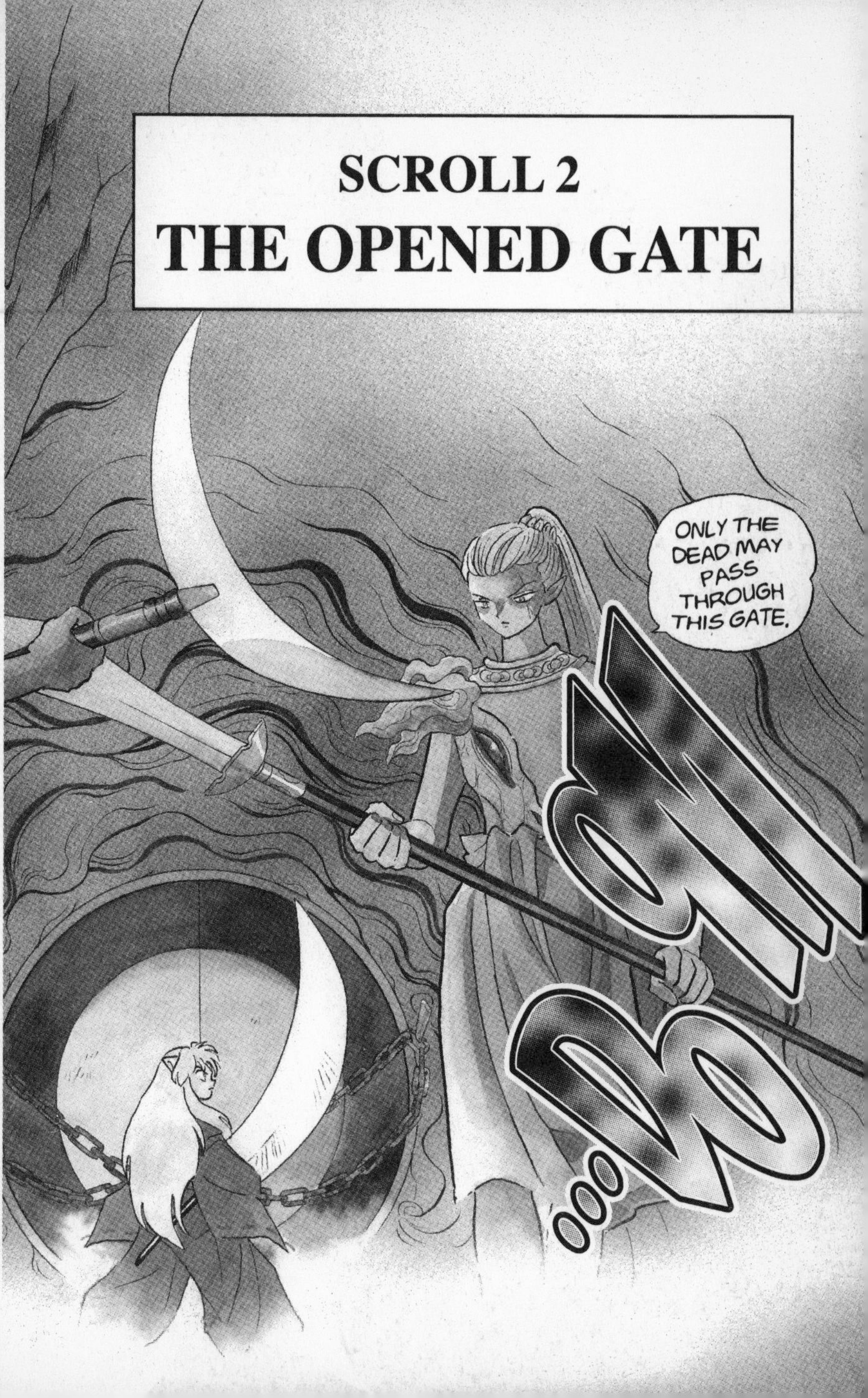
ONLY THE DEAD MAY PASS THROUGH THIS GATE.

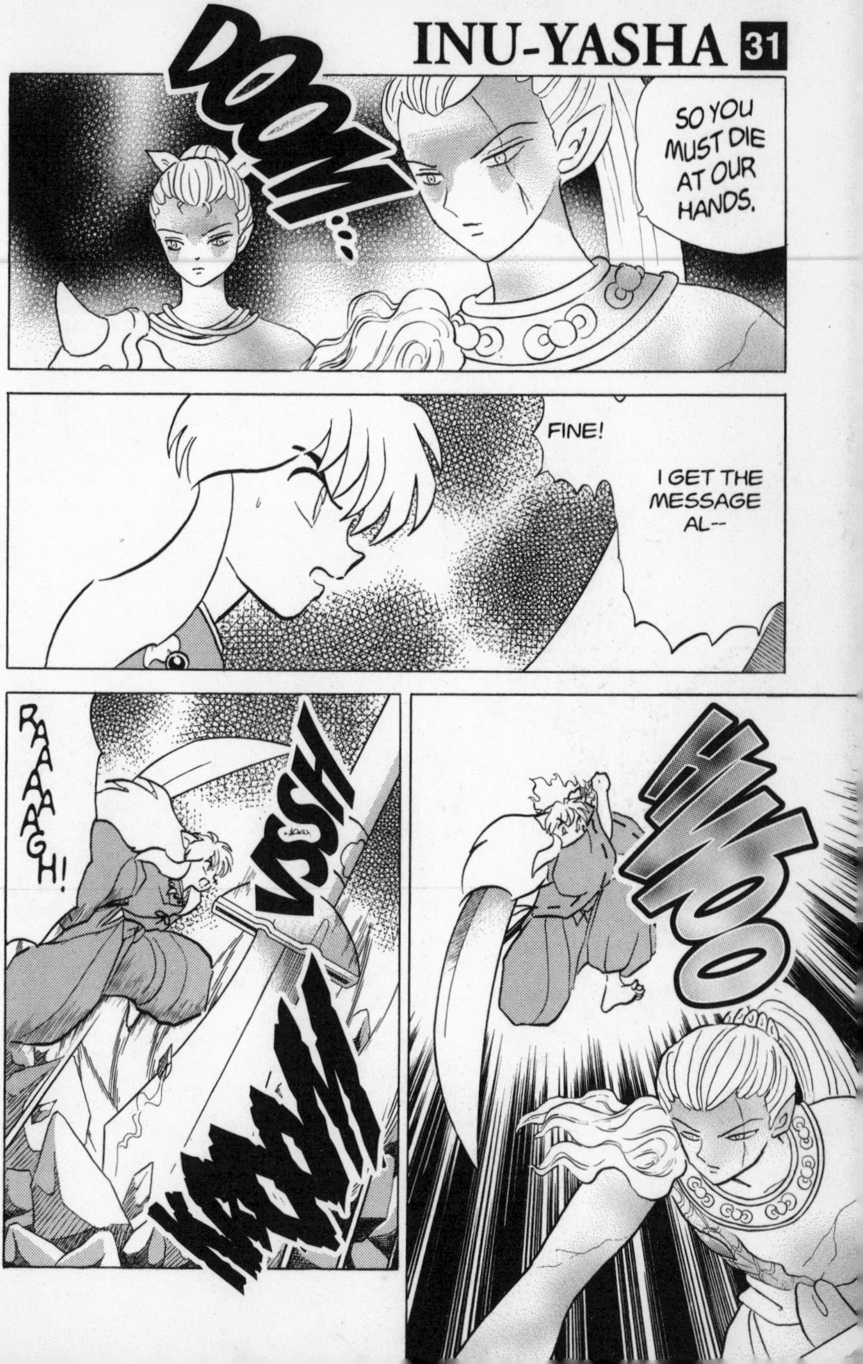
DOOM...
SO YOU MUST DIE AT OUR HANDS.
FINE!
I GET THE MESSAGE AL--
RAAAAAGH!
VOSH
HWOO

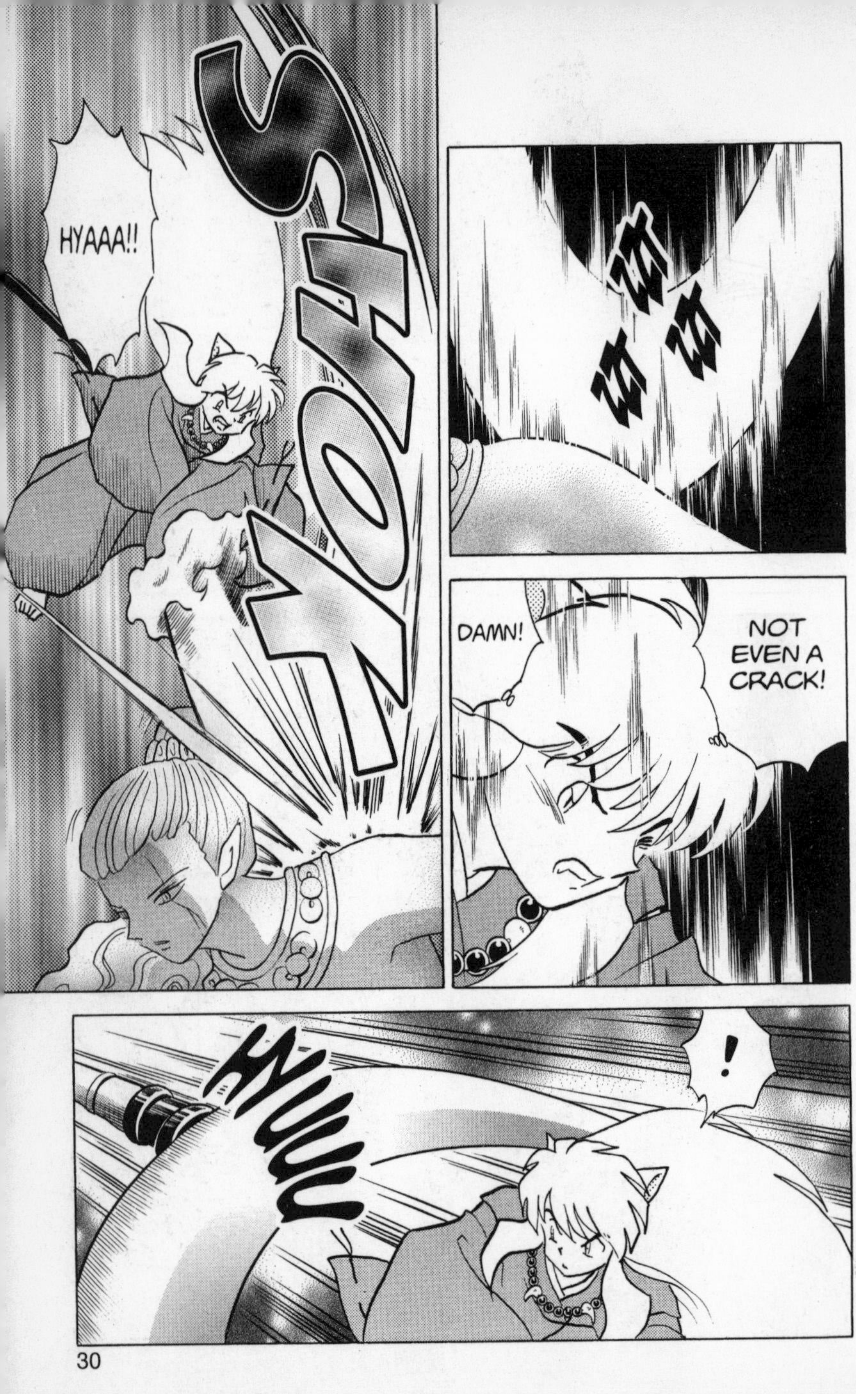
HYAAA!!
DAMN!
NOT EVEN A CRACK!
HYUUU
!

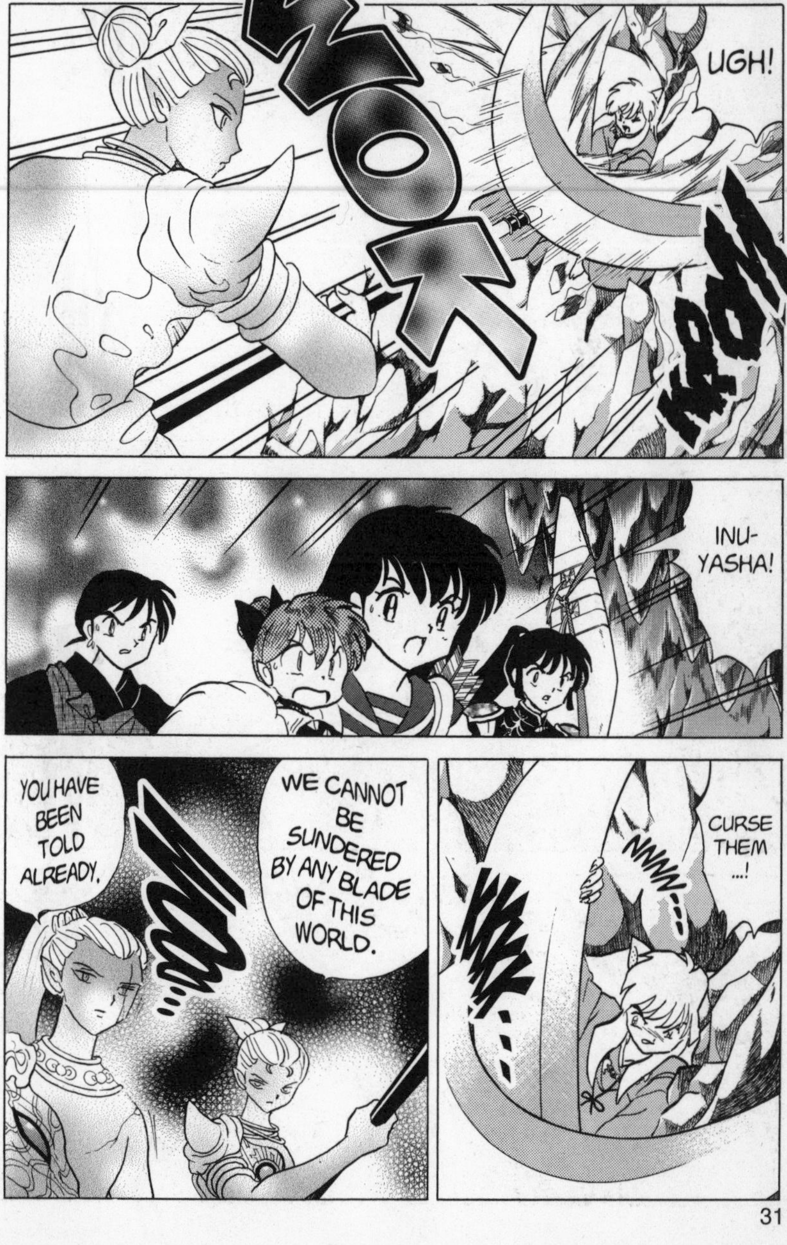
WOK
UGH!
INU-YASHA!
YOU HAVE BEEN TOLD ALREADY.
WE CANNOT BE SUNDERED BY ANY BLADE OF THIS WORLD.
CURSE THEM ...!
NNNN...

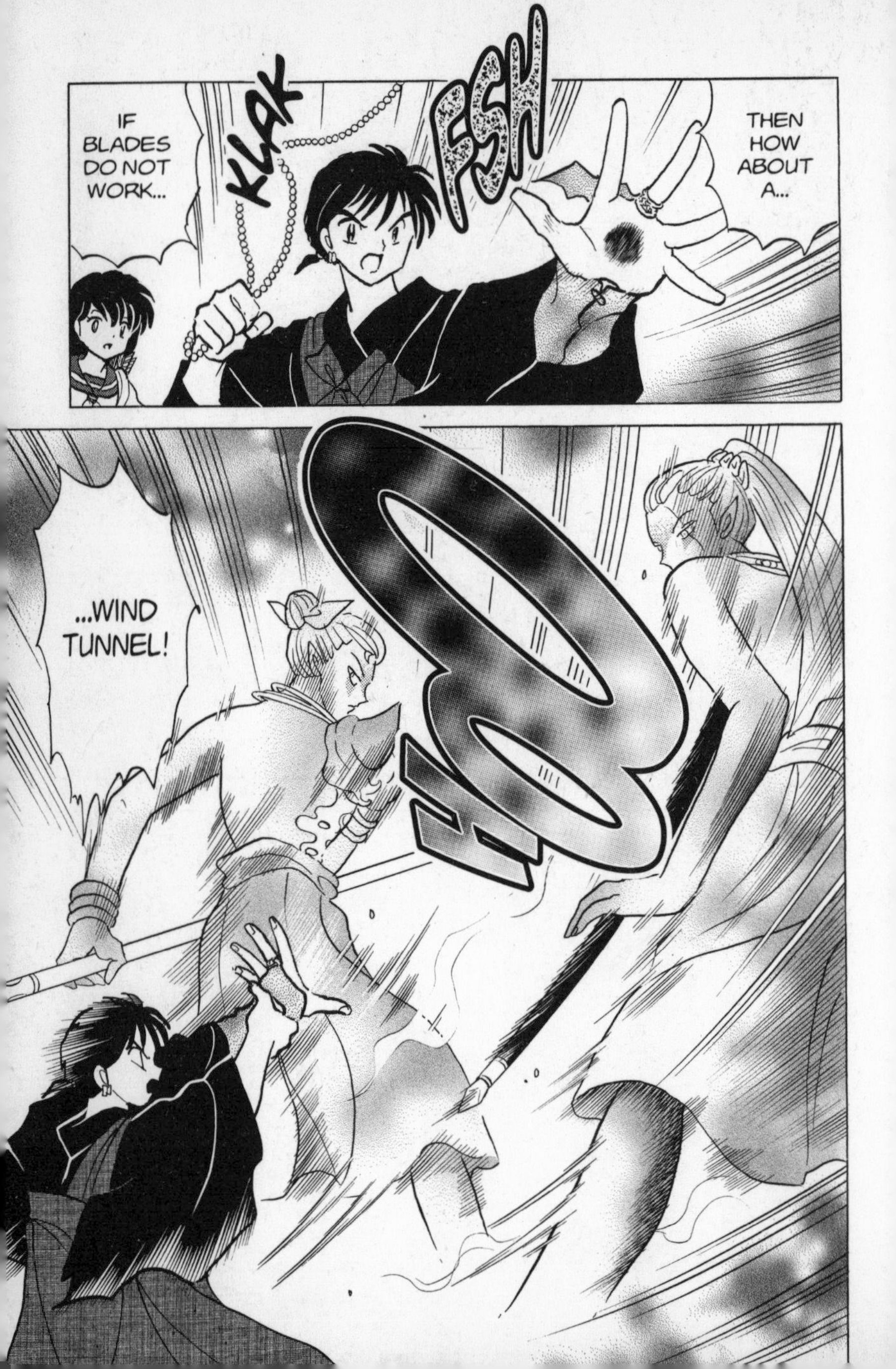
IF BLADES DO NOT WORK...
KLAK
FSH
THEN HOW ABOUT A...
...WIND TUNNEL!
FSH

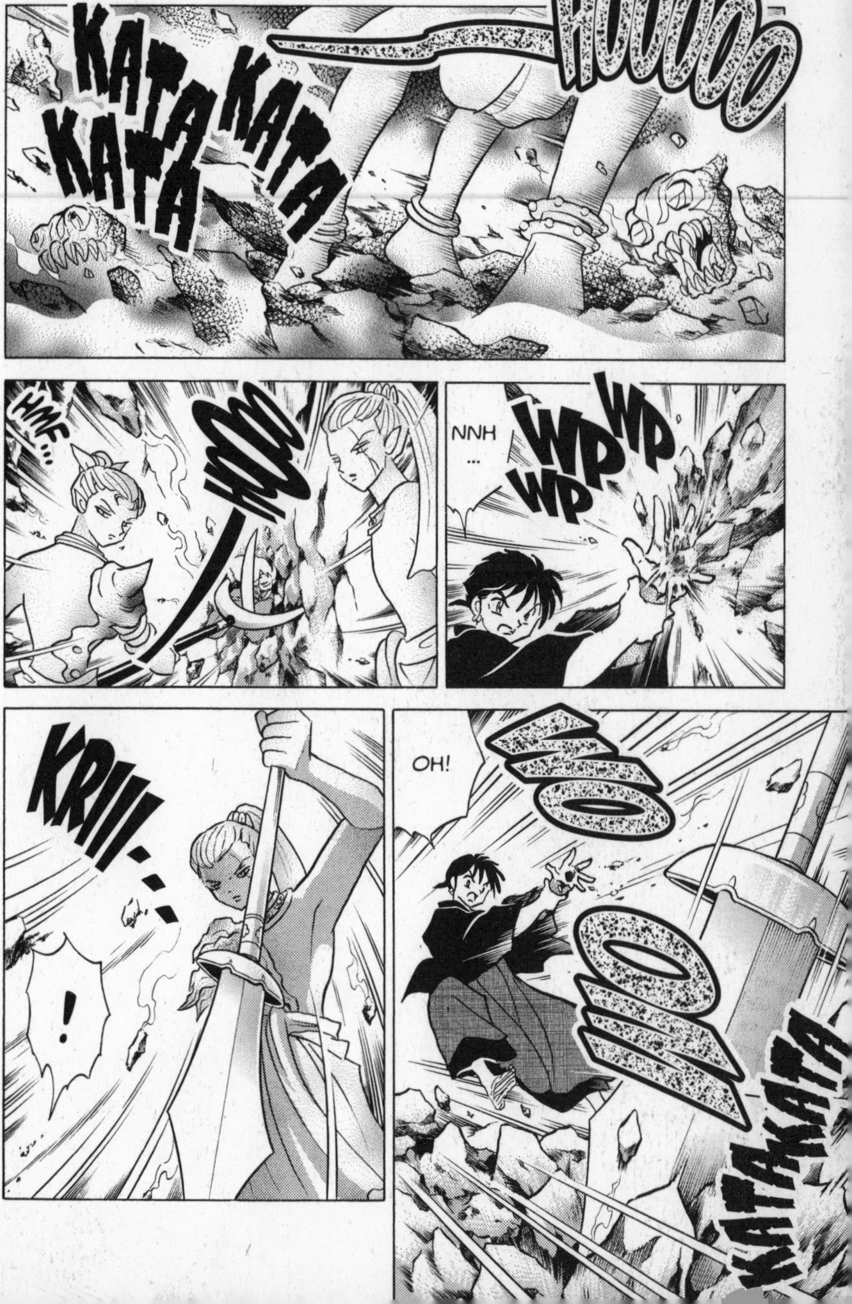
KATA KATA
KATA KATA
HOOOOOO
HMF...
WOOO
NNH...
WP WP
WP WP
KRIII...
!
OH!
WOO
OOOO
KATAKATA

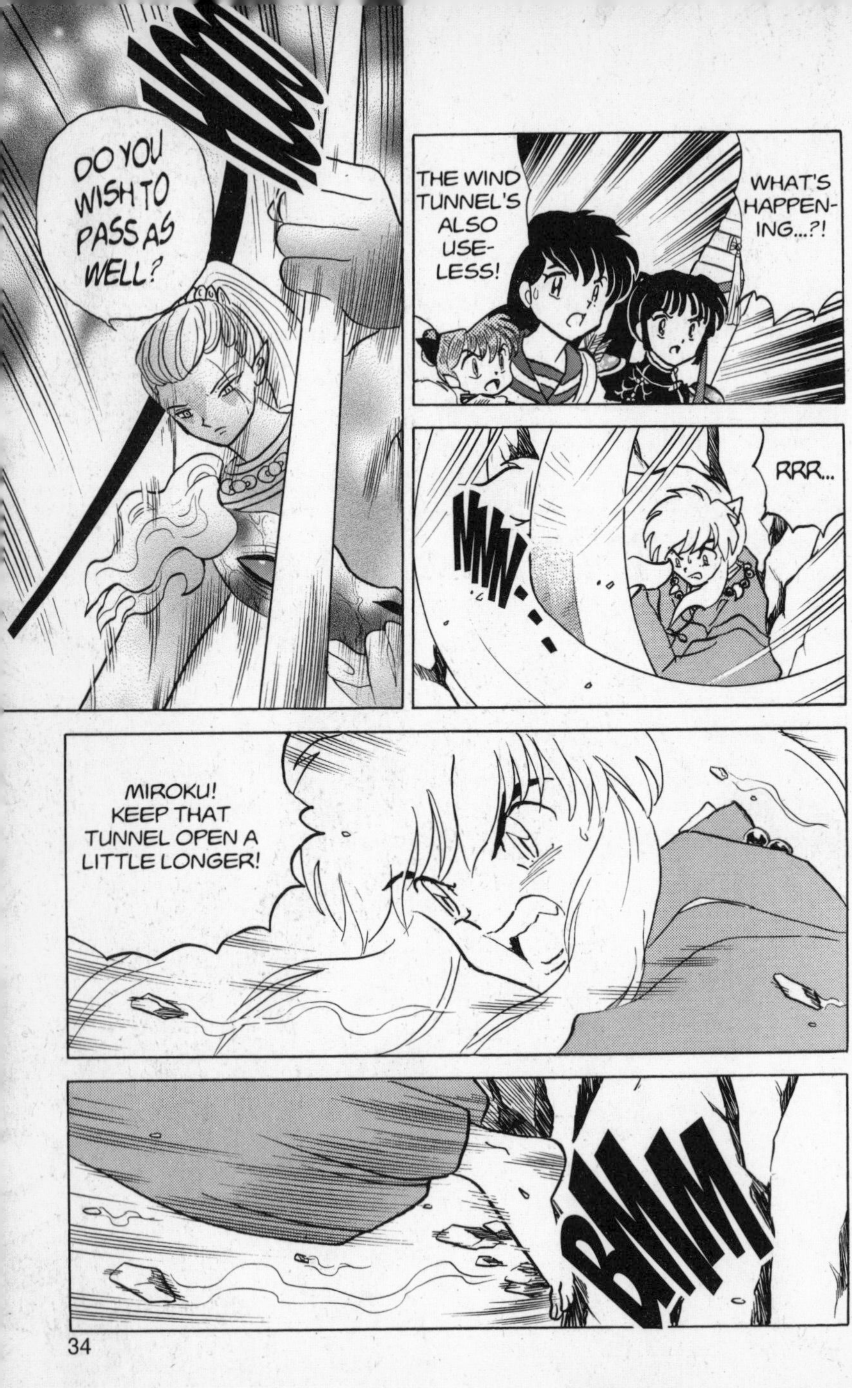
DO YOU WISH TO PASS AS WELL?
THE WIND TUNNEL'S ALSO USE-LESS!
WHAT'S HAPPEN-ING...?!
MMN...
RRR...
MIROKU! KEEP THAT TUNNEL OPEN A LITTLE LONGER!
BAM

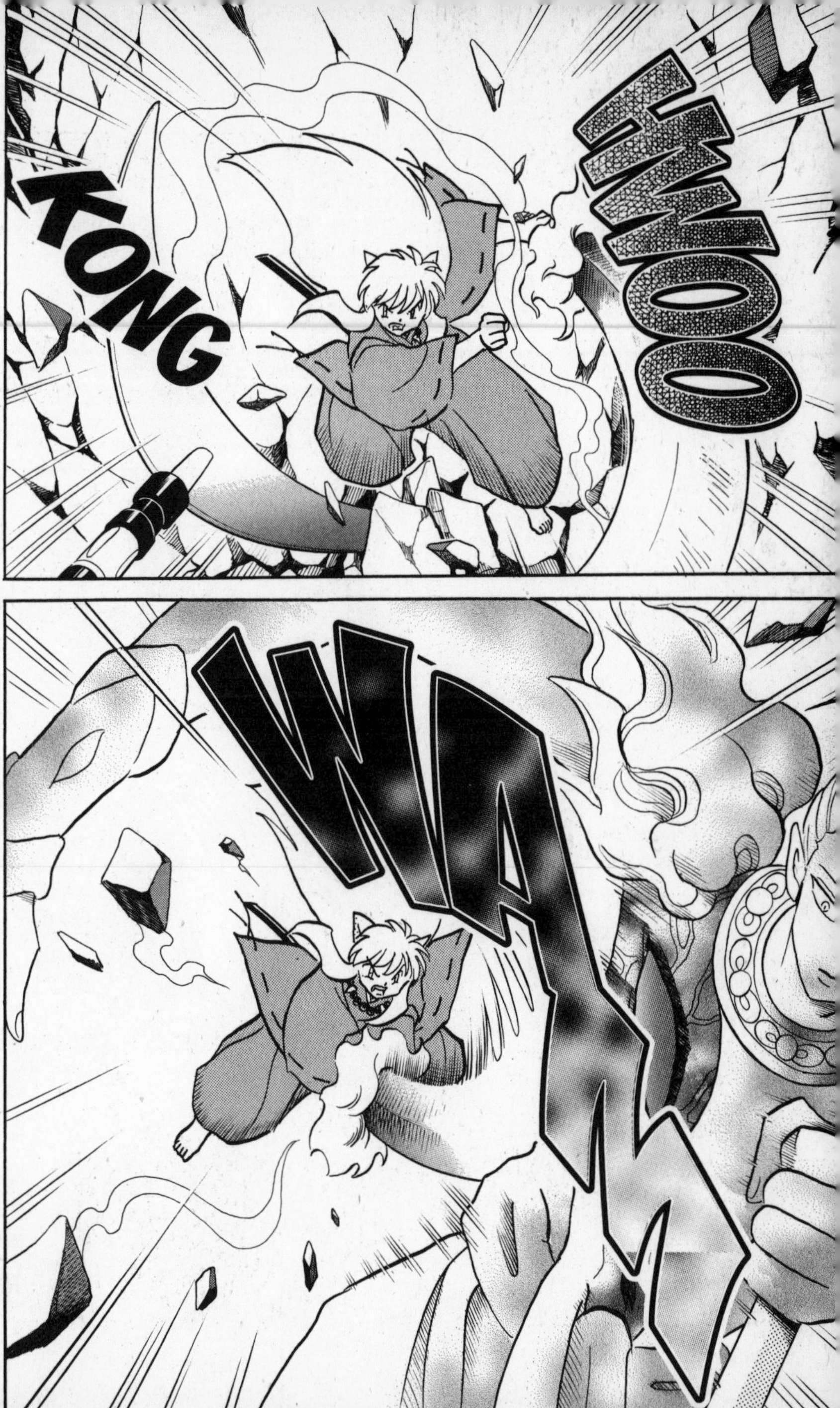
KONG
FWOOO
WAM

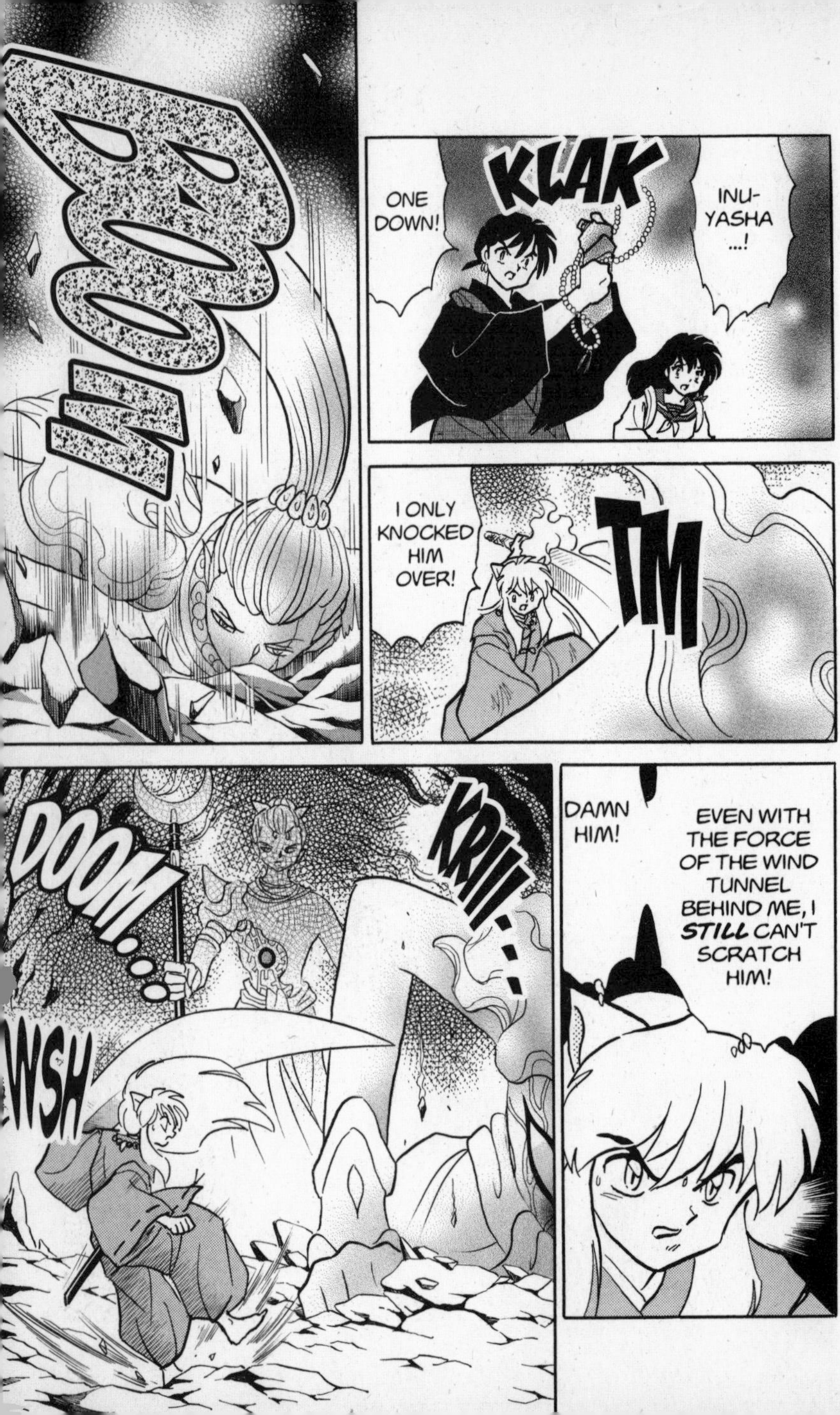
BOOOM!!
ONE DOWN!
KLAK
INU-YASHA ...!
I ONLY KNOCKED HIM OVER!
TM
DOOM...
KRIII...
WSH
DAMN HIM!
EVEN WITH THE FORCE OF THE WIND TUNNEL BEHIND ME, I *STILL* CAN'T SCRATCH HIM!

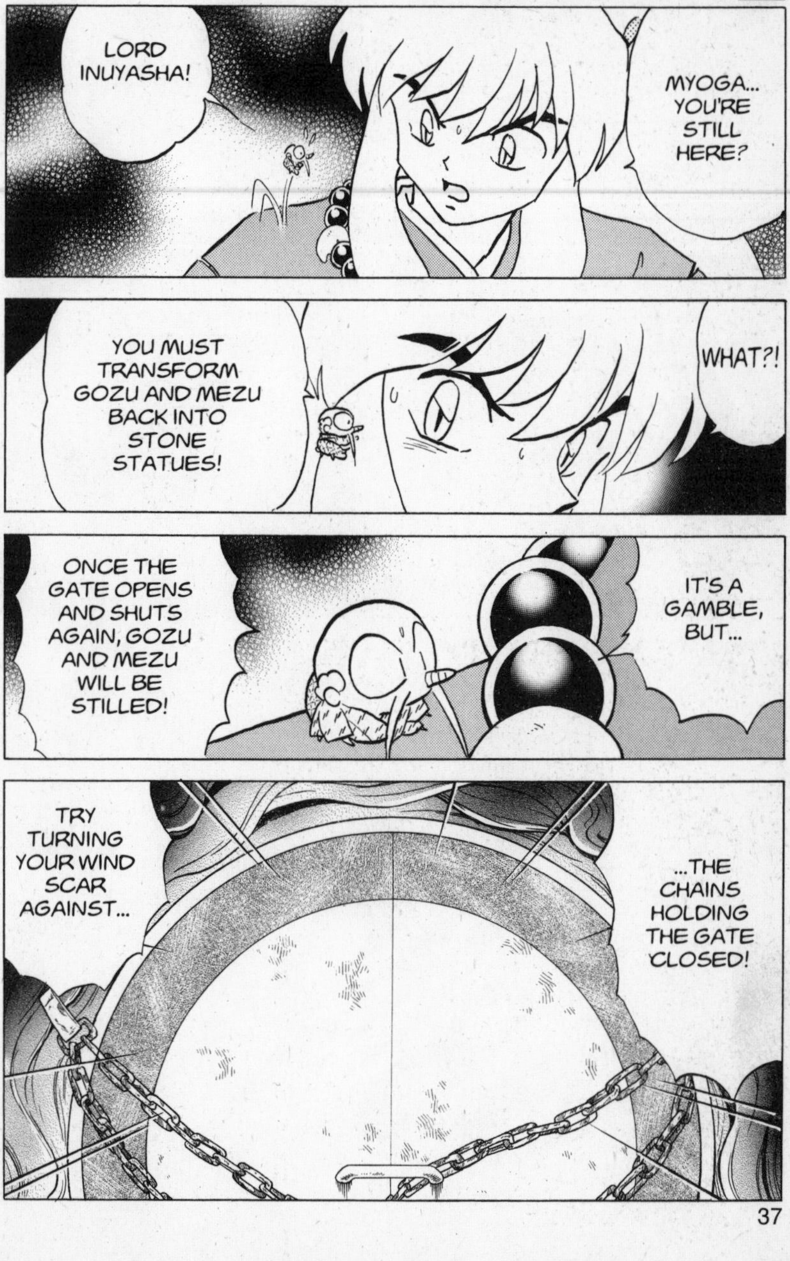
LORD INUYASHA!
MYOGA... YOU'RE STILL HERE?
YOU MUST TRANSFORM GOZU AND MEZU BACK INTO STONE STATUES!
WHAT?!
ONCE THE GATE OPENS AND SHUTS AGAIN, GOZU AND MEZU WILL BE STILLED!
IT'S A GAMBLE, BUT...
TRY TURNING YOUR WIND SCAR AGAINST...
...THE CHAINS HOLDING THE GATE CLOSED!

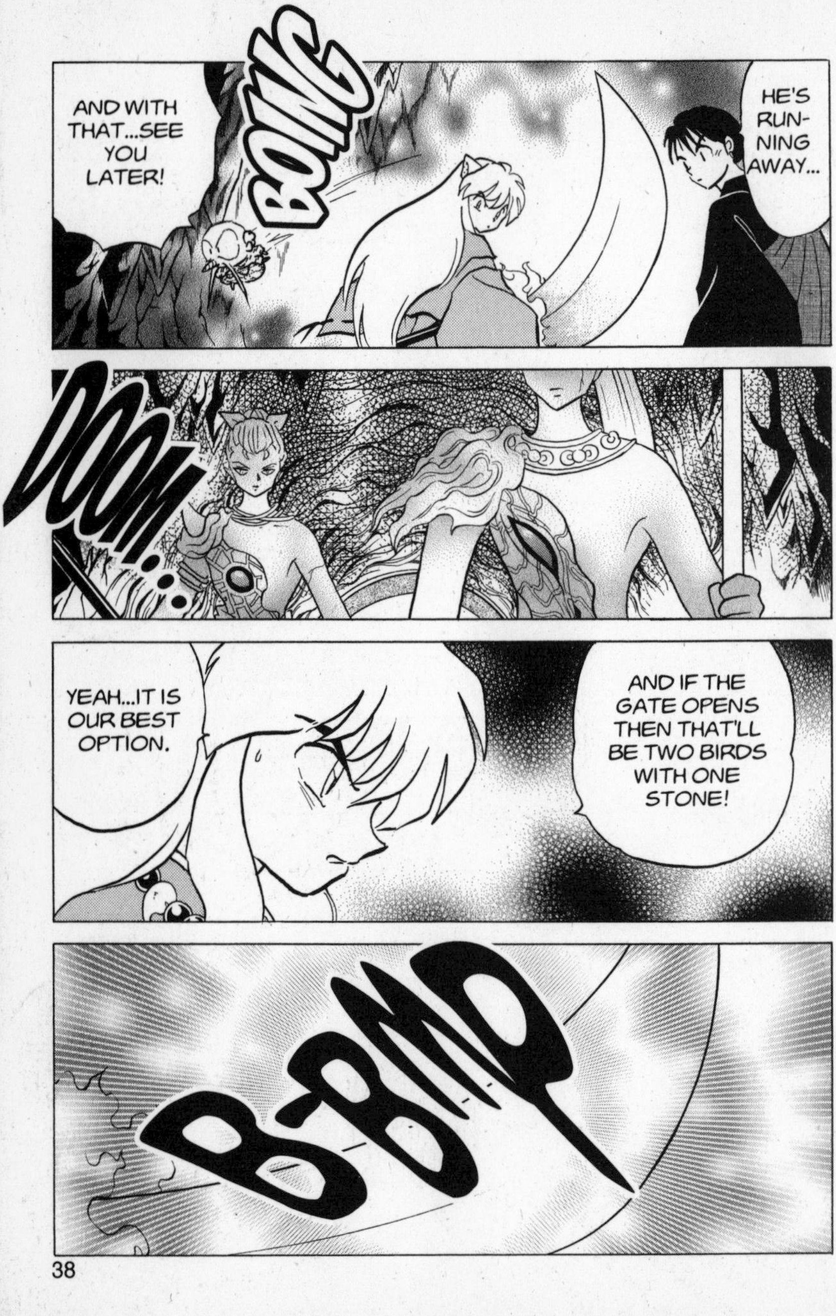
AND WITH THAT...SEE YOU LATER!
BOING
HE'S RUN-NING AWAY...
DOOM!...
YEAH...IT IS OUR BEST OPTION.
AND IF THE GATE OPENS THEN THAT'LL BE TWO BIRDS WITH ONE STONE!
B-BMP

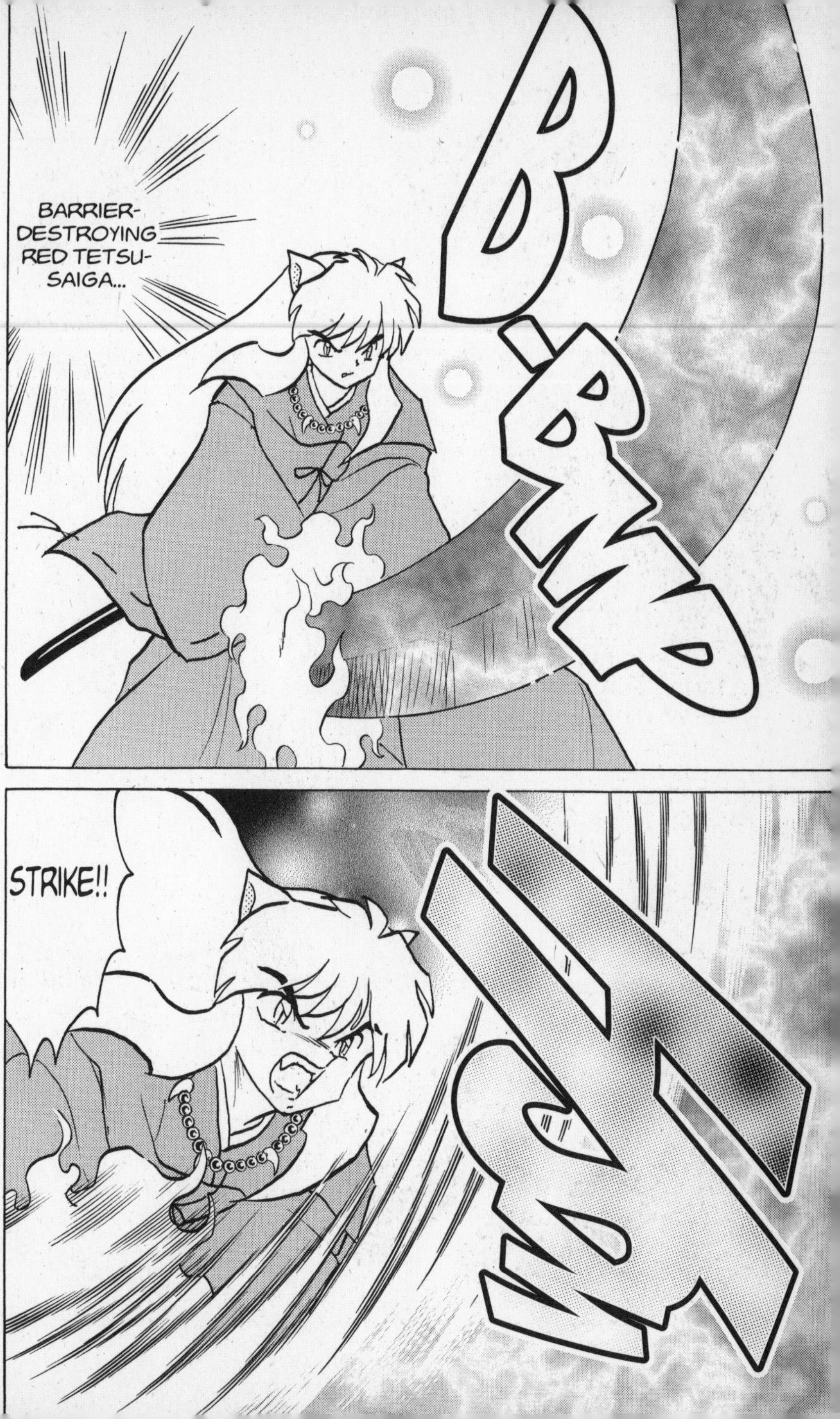
BARRIER-DESTROYING RED TETSU-SAIGA...
B-BMP
STRIKE!!

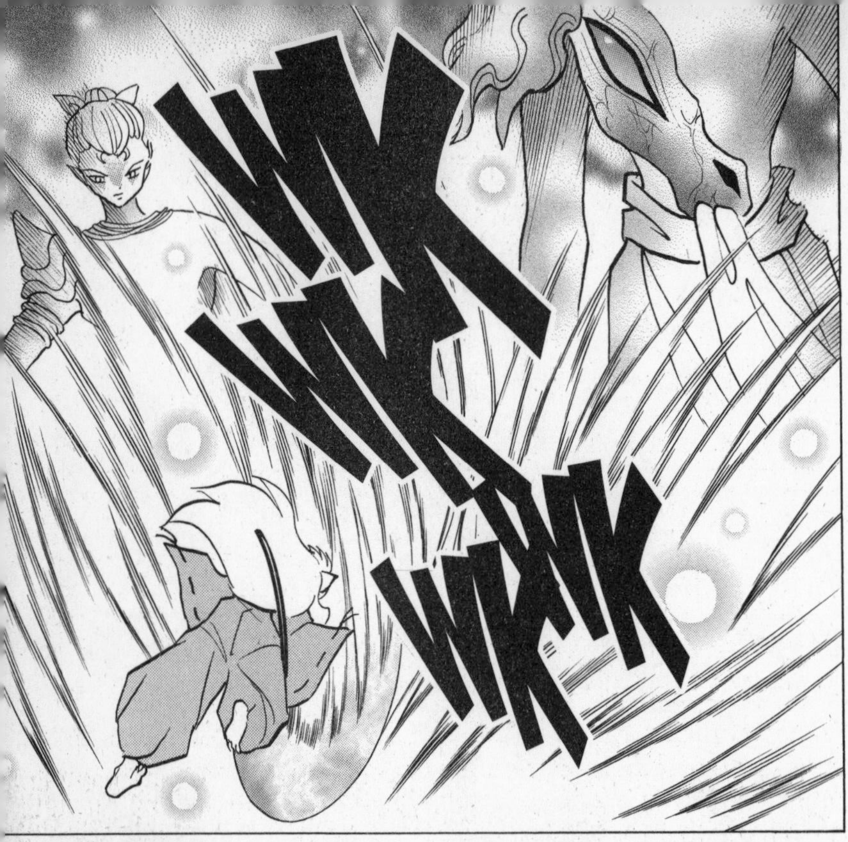

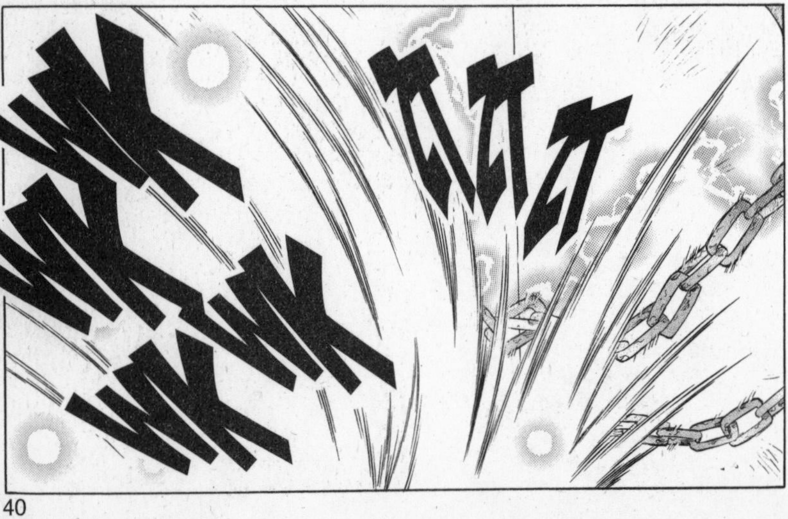

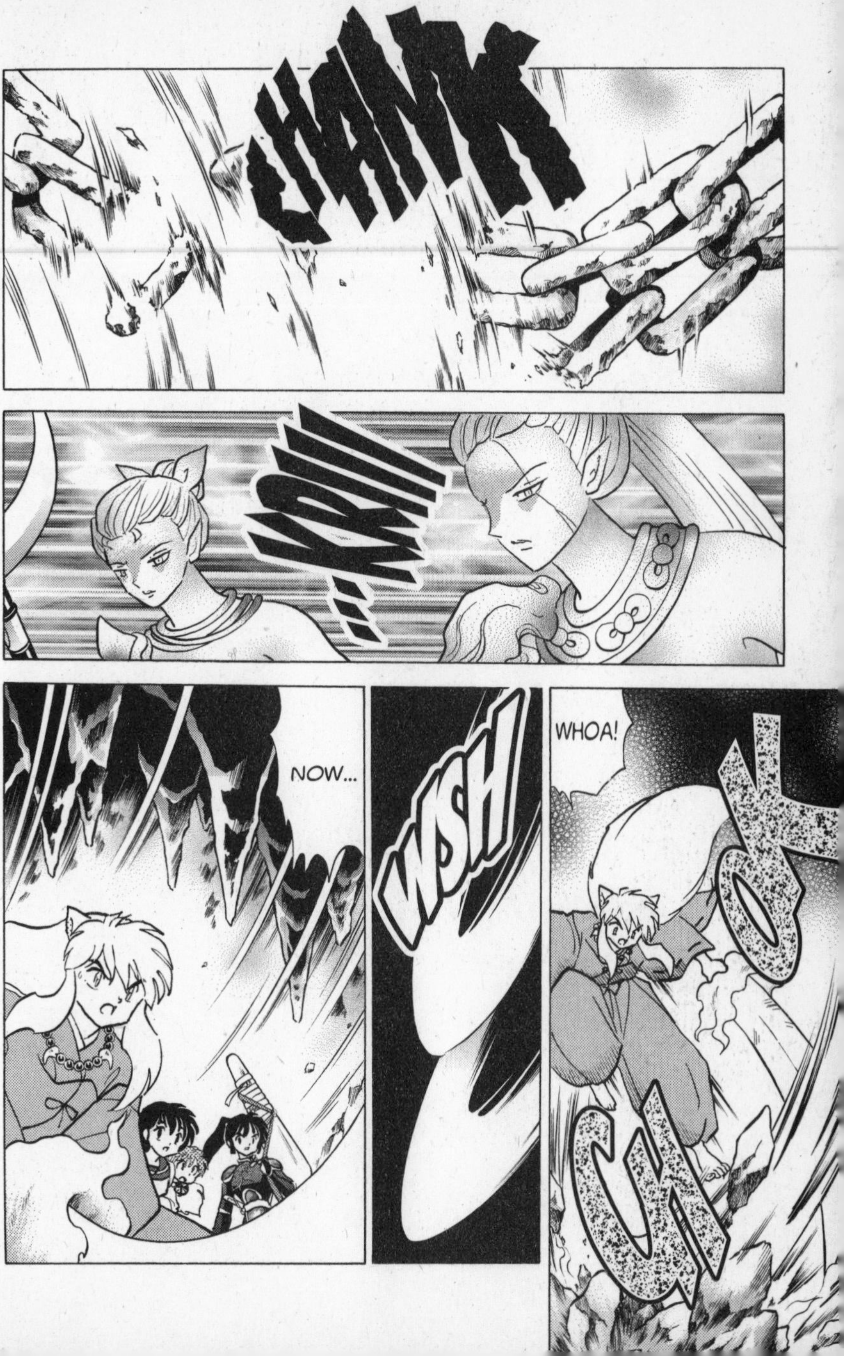
CHANK
NOW...
WSH
WHOA!

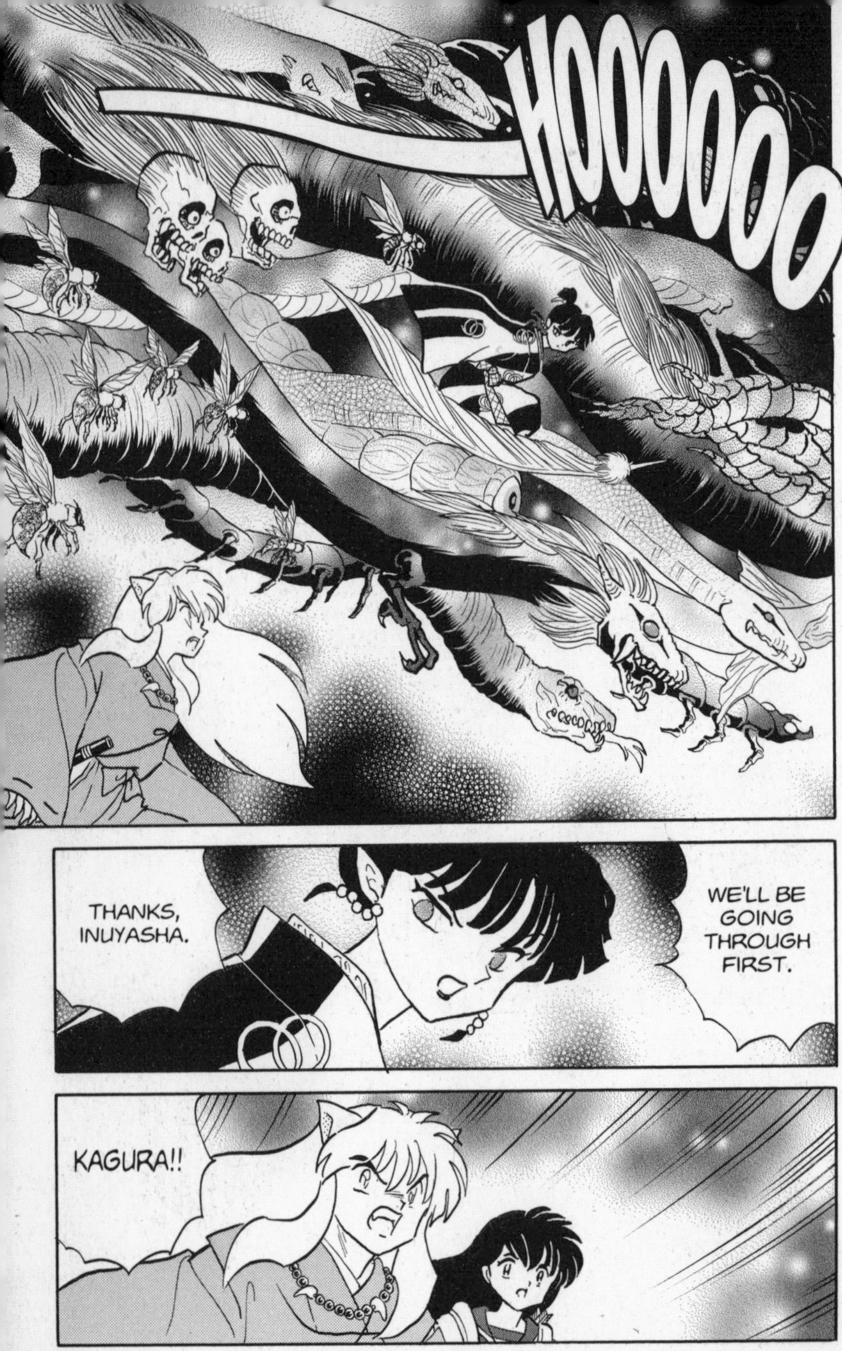
HOOOOOO
THANKS, INUYASHA.
WE'LL BE GOING THROUGH FIRST.
KAGURA!!

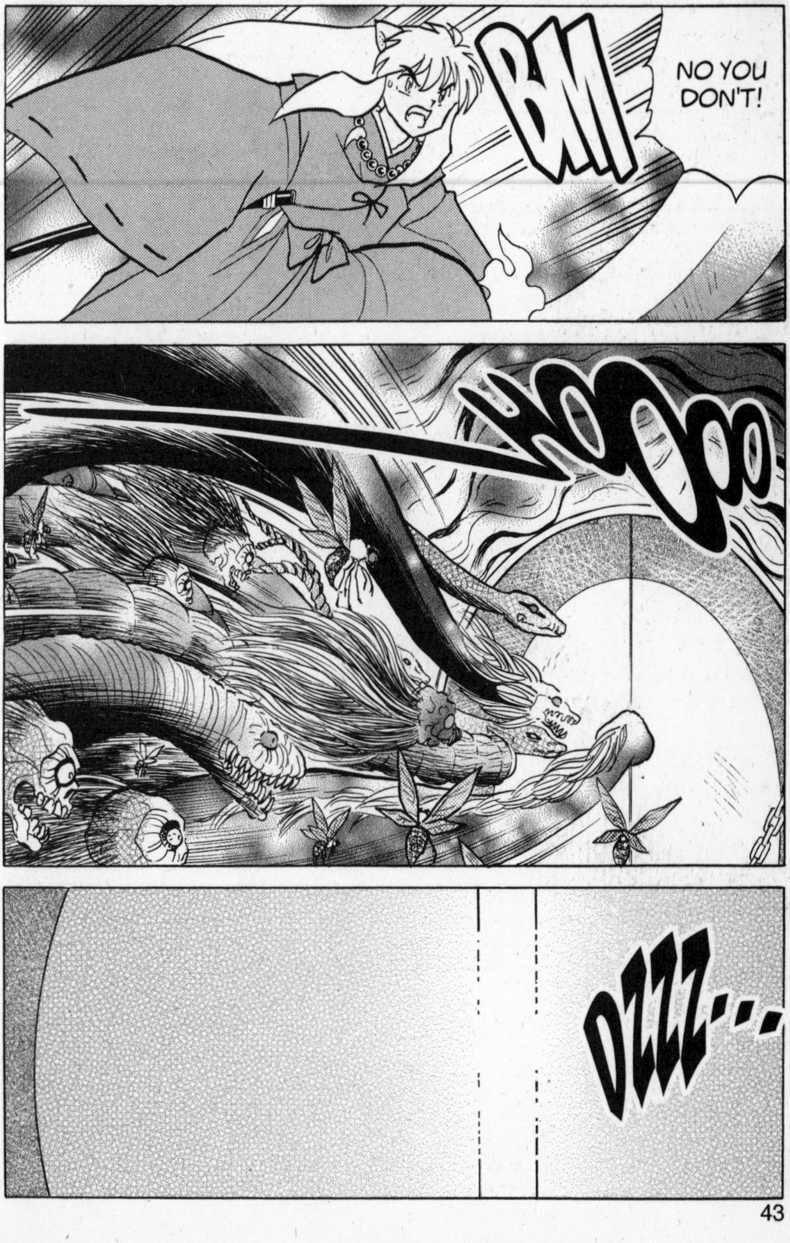
BM
NO YOU DON'T!
WOOOO
DZZZ...

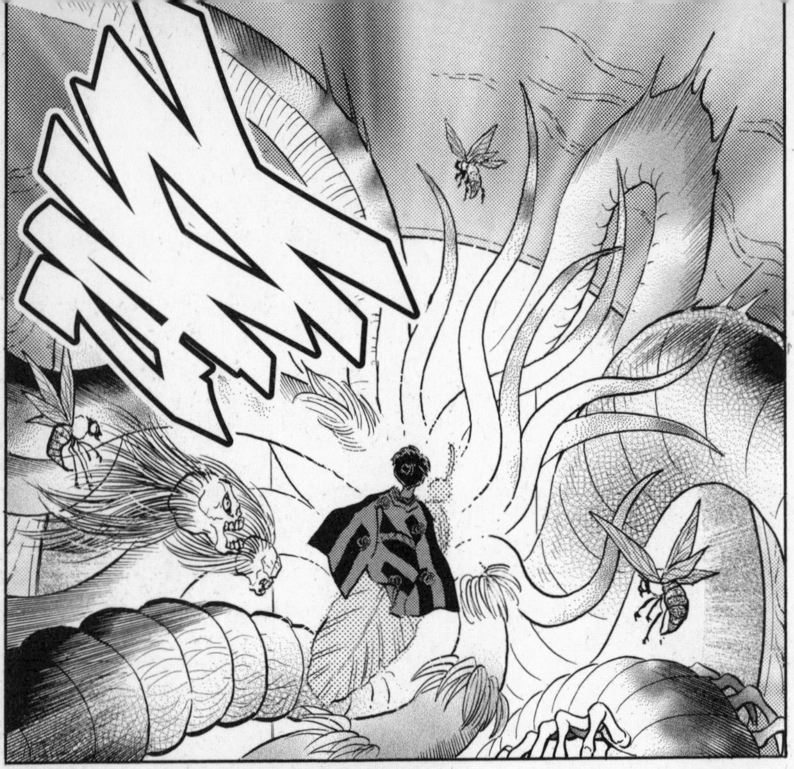

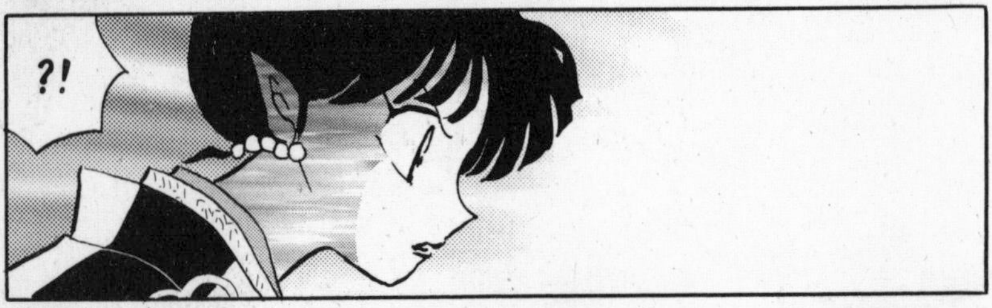
?!

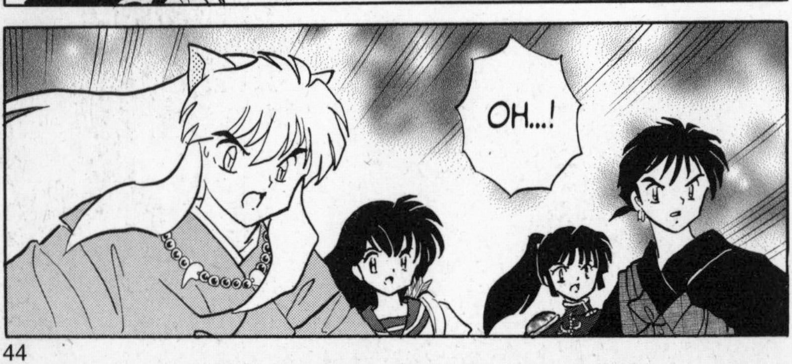
OH...!

SCROLL 3

BEYOND THE GATE

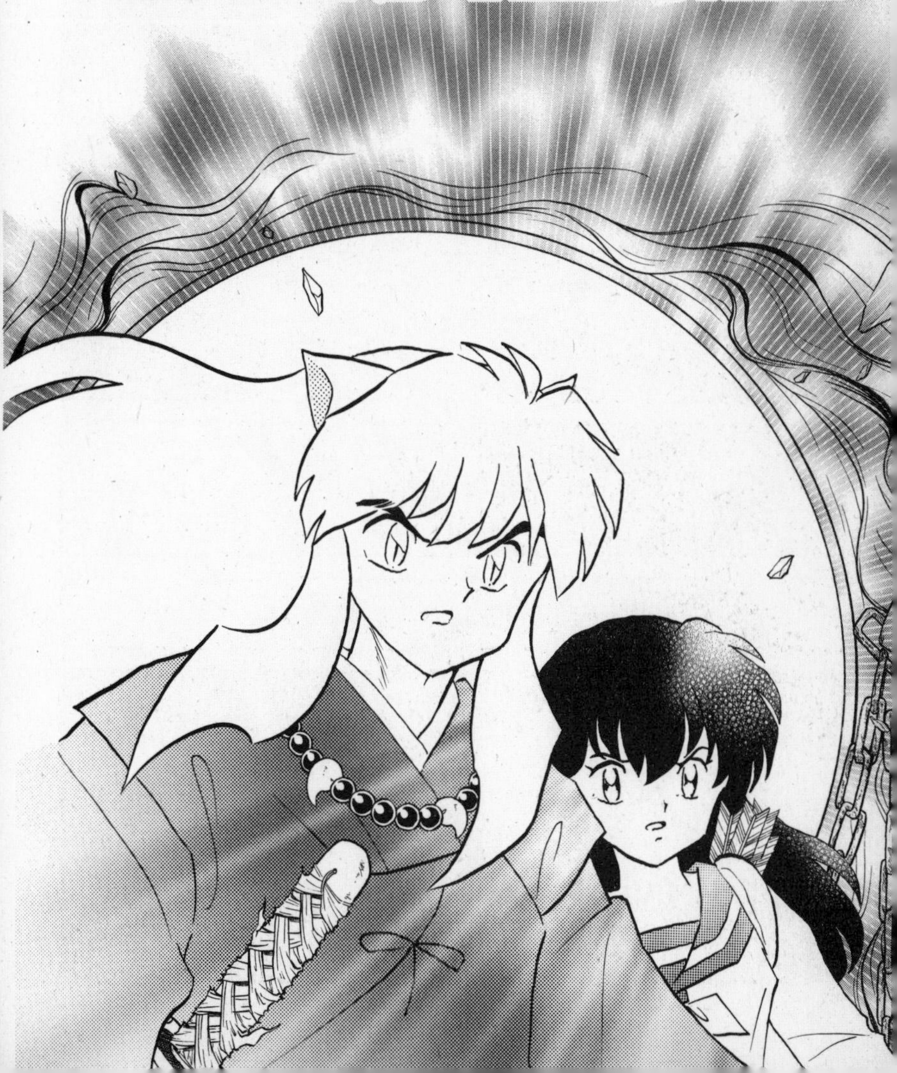

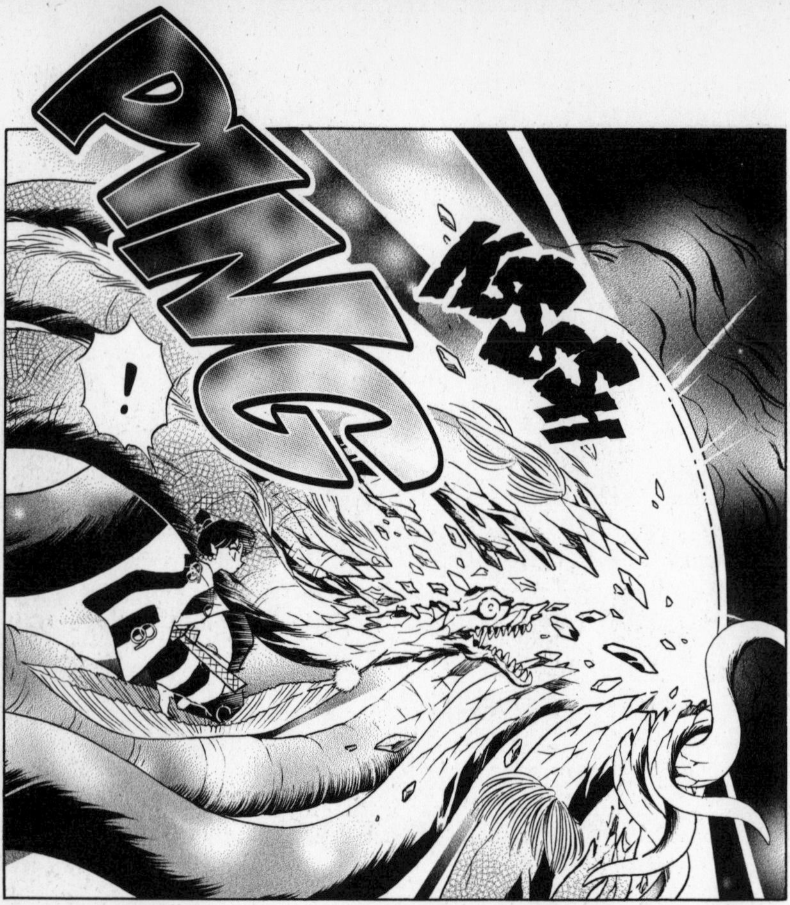
PING
KASH!
!

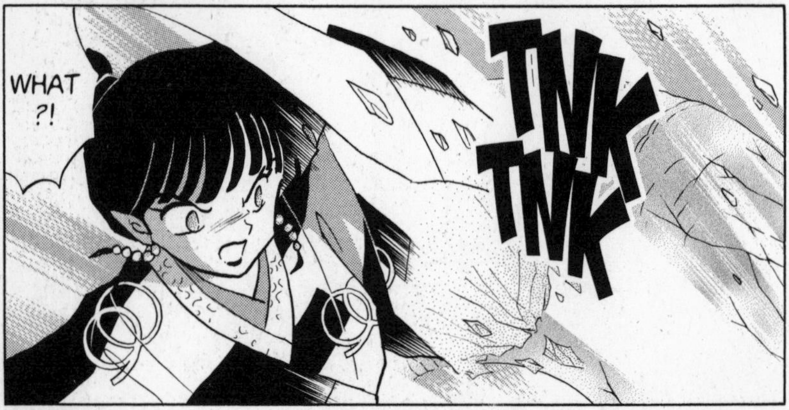
WHAT ?!
TINK TINK

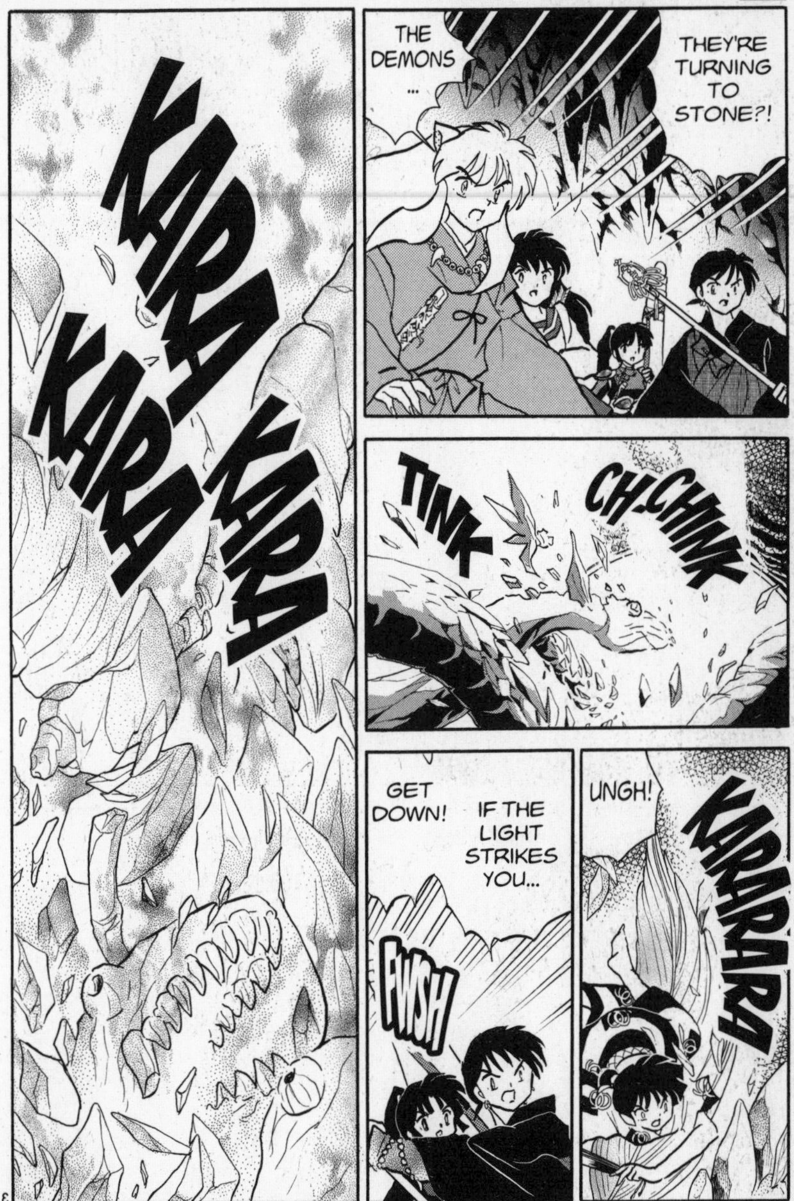
KARA KARA
KARA KARA!
THE DEMONS ...
THEY'RE TURNING TO STONE?!
TINK
CH-CHINK
GET DOWN!
IF THE LIGHT STRIKES YOU...
FWSH
UNGH!
KARARARA

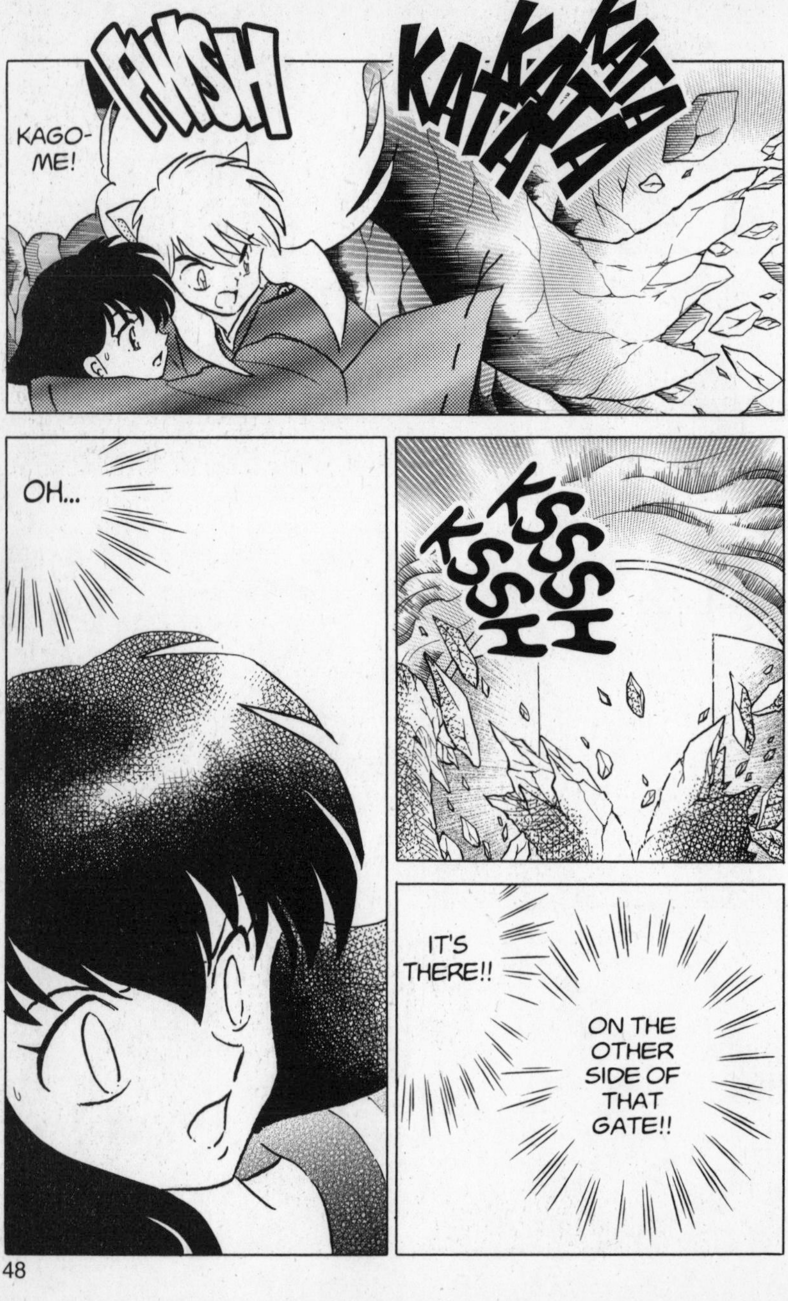
FWSH
KAGO-
ME!
KATA KATA KATA
OH...
KSSSH KSSSH
IT'S
THERE!!
ON THE
OTHER
SIDE OF
THAT
GATE!!

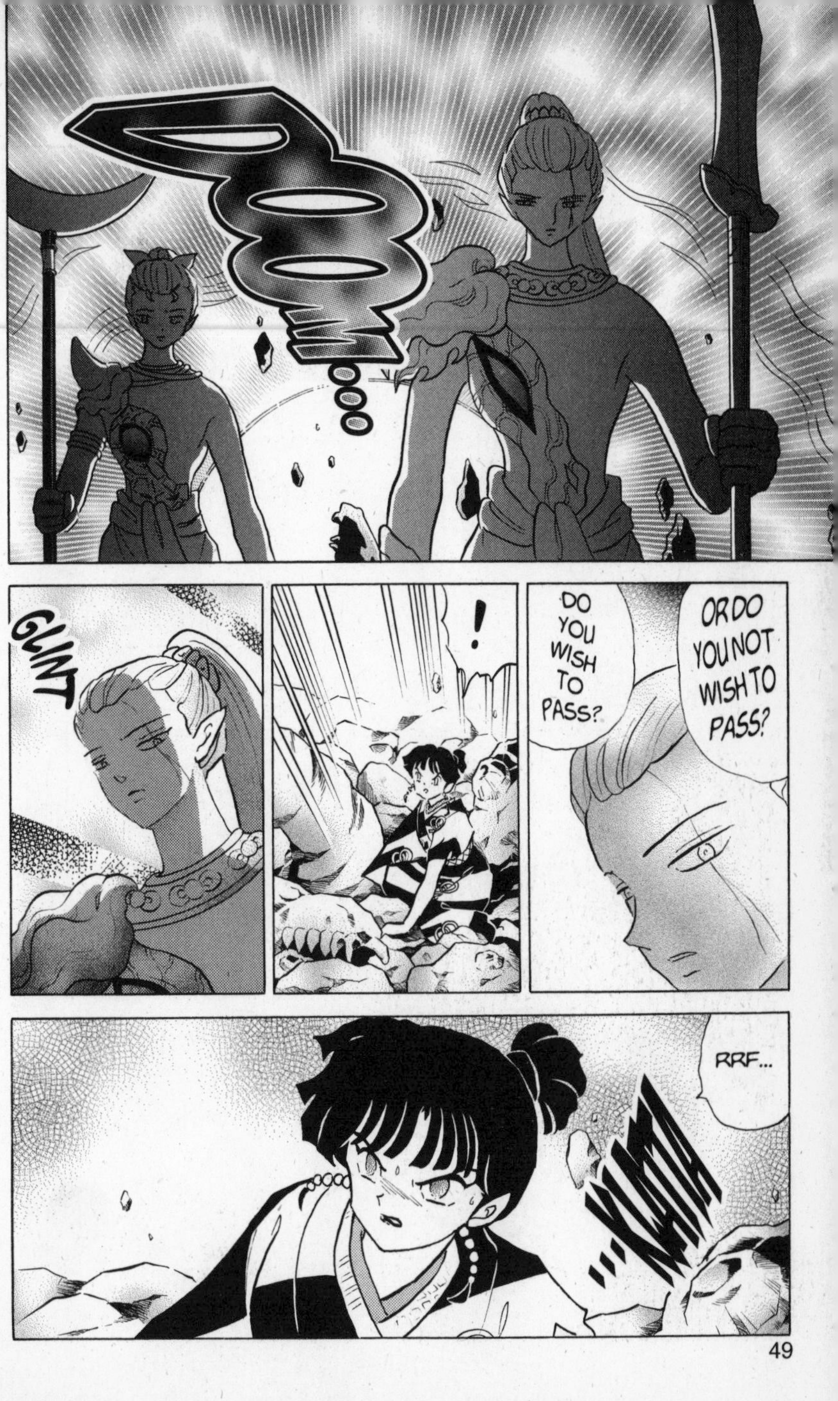
GLINT
!
DO YOU WISH TO PASS?
OR DO YOU NOT WISH TO PASS?
RRF...

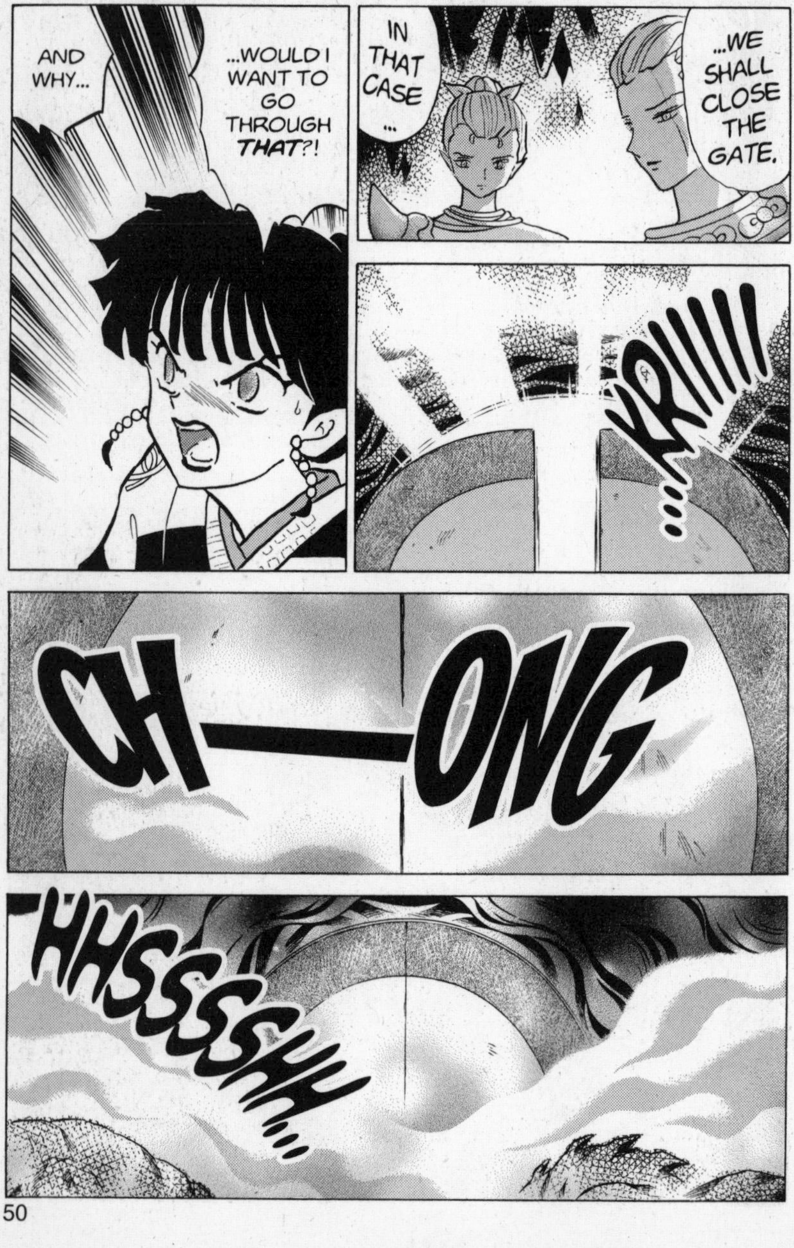

AND WHY...
...WOULD I WANT TO GO THROUGH *THAT*?!
IN THAT CASE ...
...WE SHALL CLOSE THE GATE.
KRIIII...
CH—ONG
HHSSSSH...

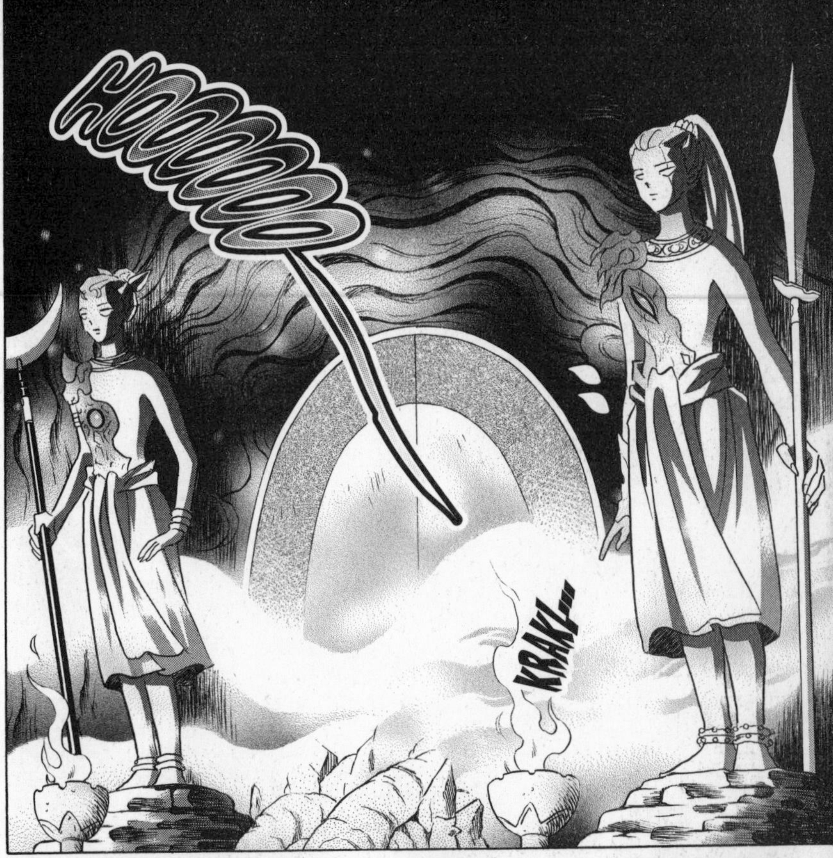
HOOOOOOO
KRAKI...
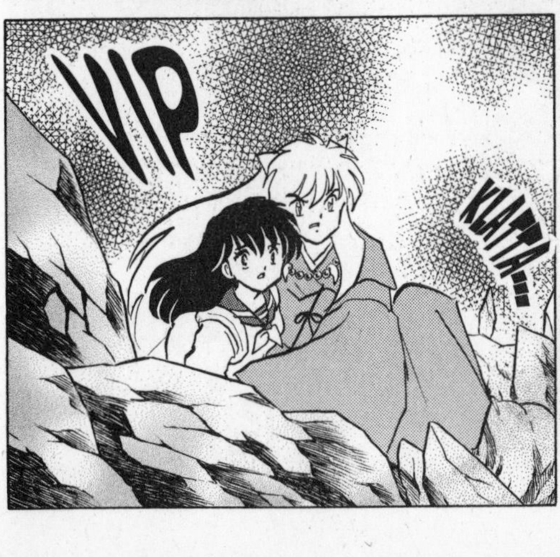
VIP
KLATTA...
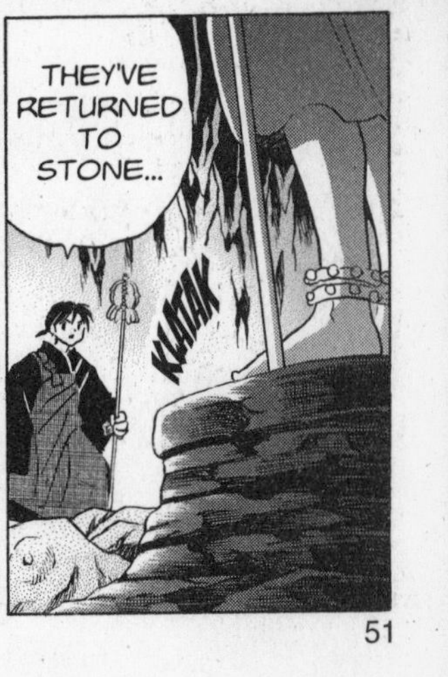
THEY'VE RETURNED TO STONE...
KLATAK

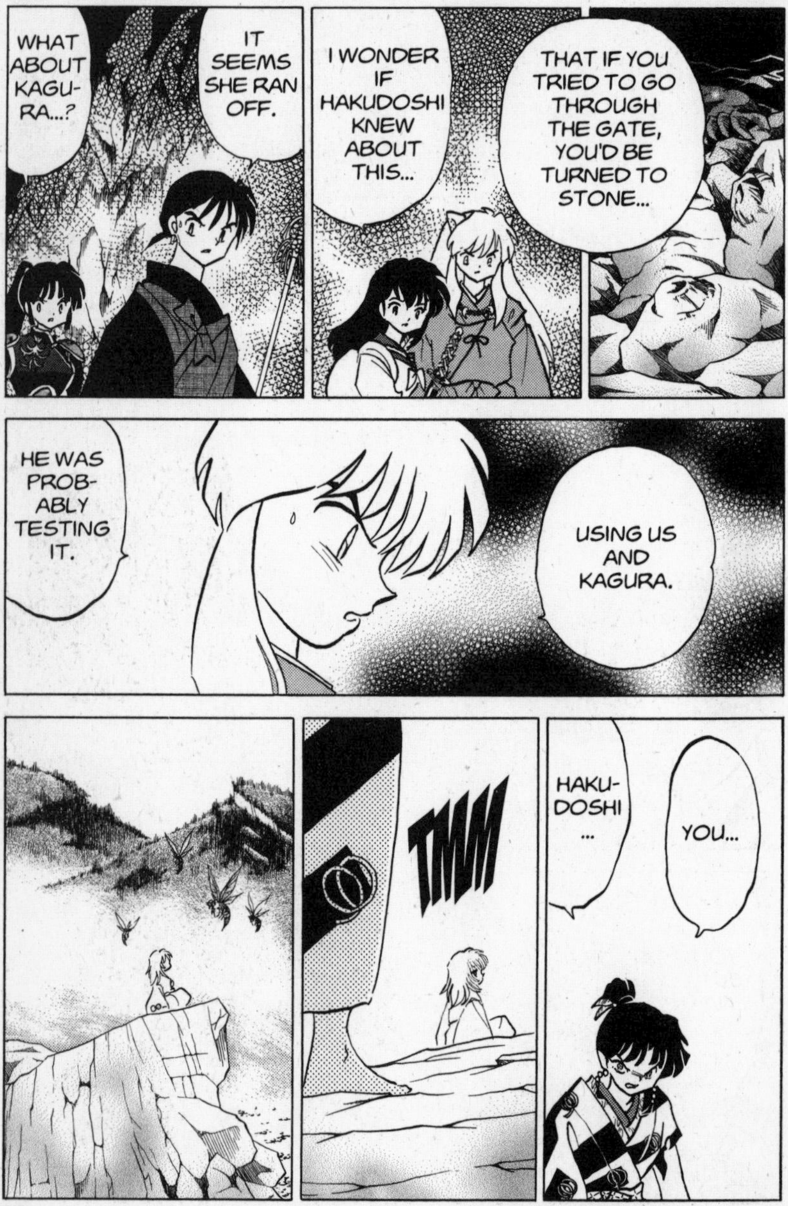
WHAT ABOUT KAGU-RA...?
IT SEEMS SHE RAN OFF.
I WONDER IF HAKUDOSHI KNEW ABOUT THIS...
THAT IF YOU TRIED TO GO THROUGH THE GATE, YOU'D BE TURNED TO STONE...
HE WAS PROB-ABLY TESTING IT.
USING US AND KAGURA.
TMM
HAKU-DOSHI ...
YOU...

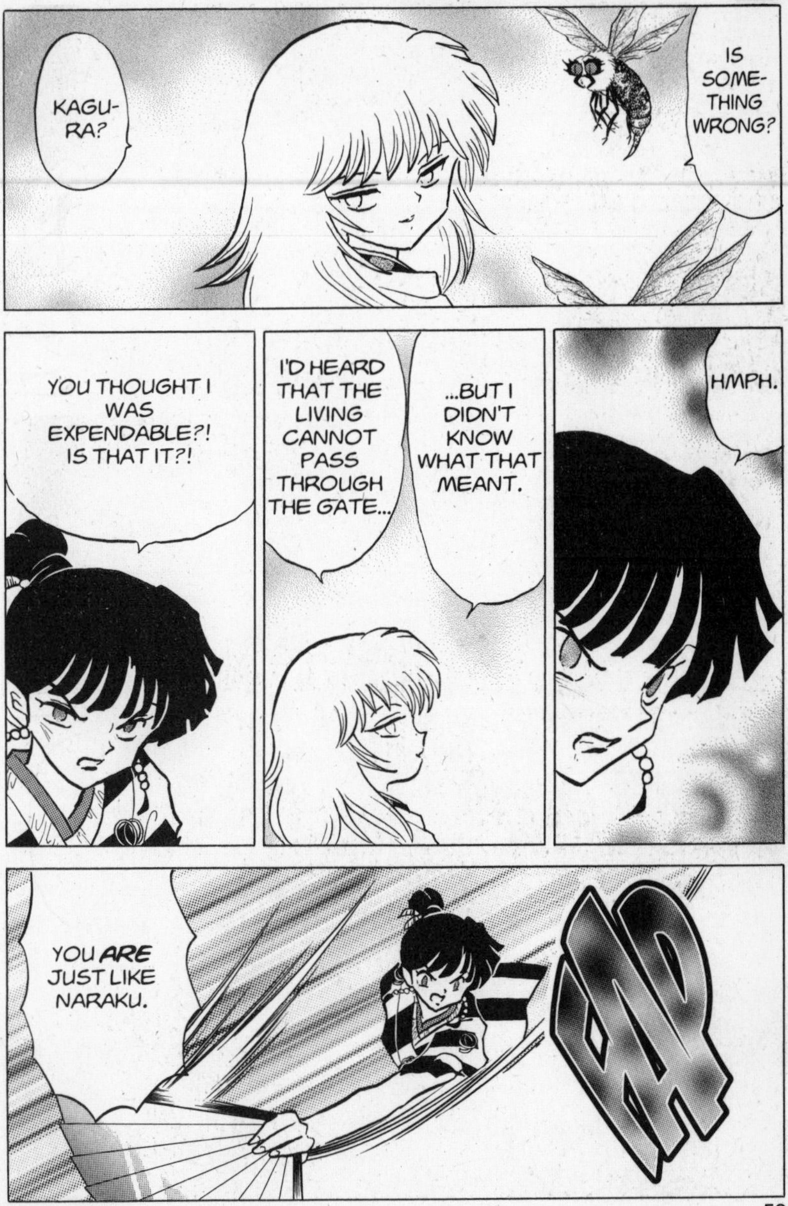
KAGU-RA?
IS SOME-THING WRONG?
YOU THOUGHT I WAS EXPENDABLE?! IS THAT IT?!
I'D HEARD THAT THE LIVING CANNOT PASS THROUGH THE GATE...
...BUT I DIDN'T KNOW WHAT THAT MEANT.
HMPH.
YOU **ARE** JUST LIKE NARAKU.
FAP

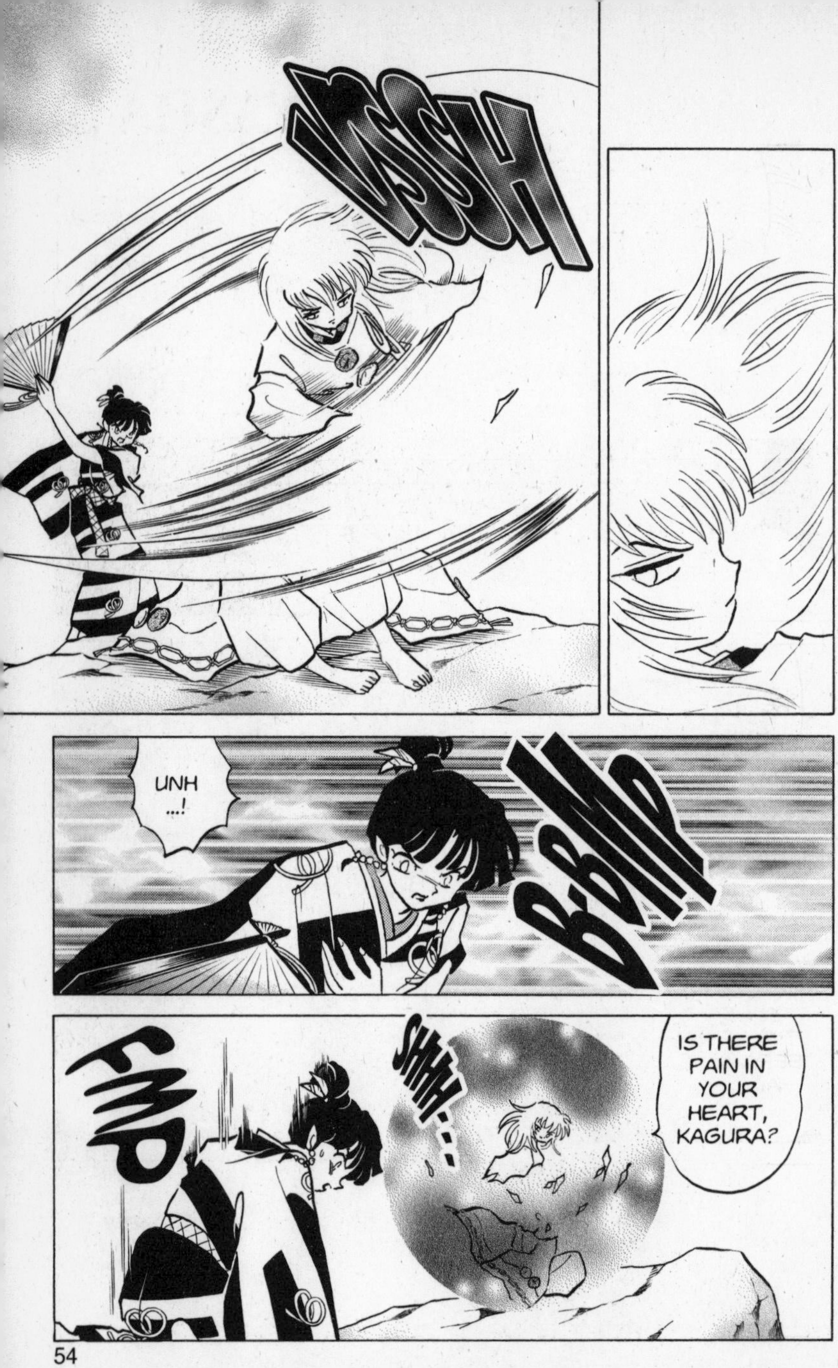
VSSH
UNH ...!
B-BMP
FMP
SHHH...
IS THERE PAIN IN YOUR HEART, KAGURA?

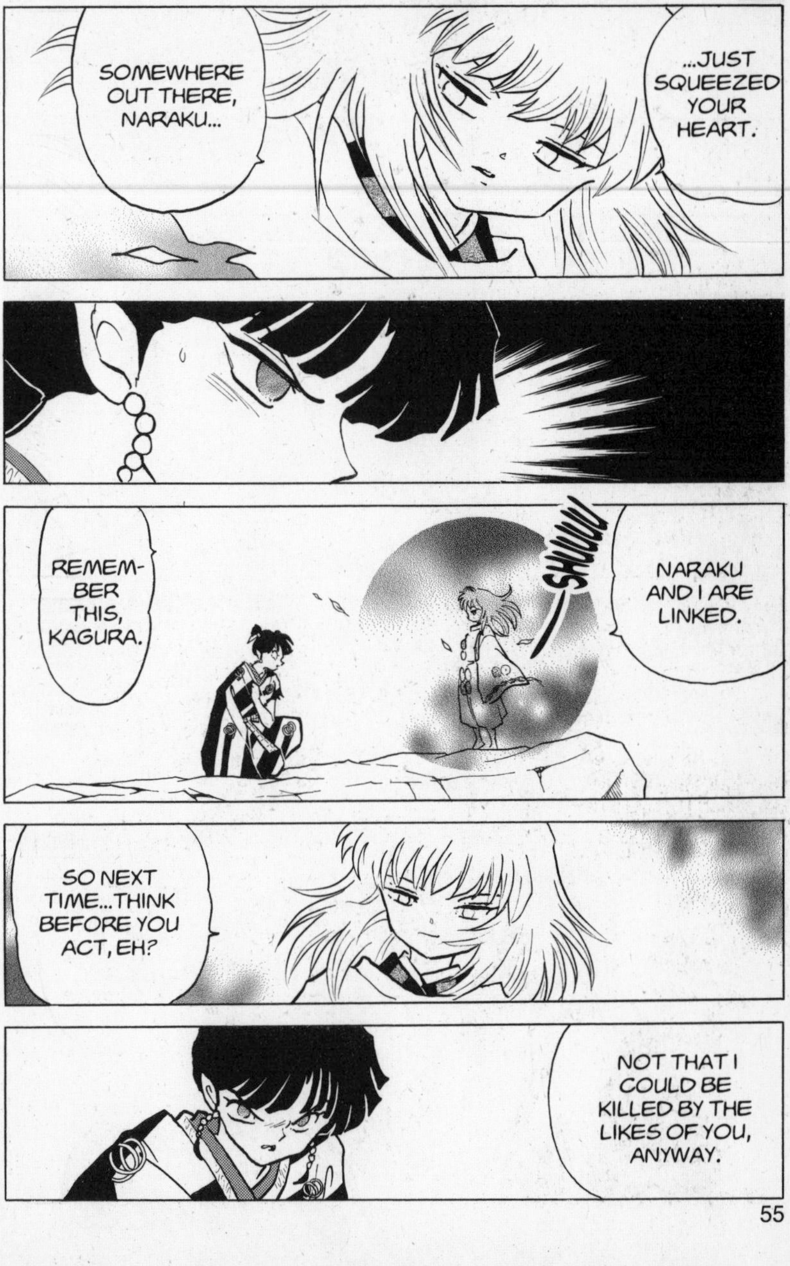
SOMEWHERE OUT THERE, NARAKU...
...JUST SQUEEZED YOUR HEART.
REMEM-BER THIS, KAGURA.
SHUUUU
NARAKU AND I ARE LINKED.
SO NEXT TIME...THINK BEFORE YOU ACT, EH?
NOT THAT I COULD BE KILLED BY THE LIKES OF YOU, ANYWAY.

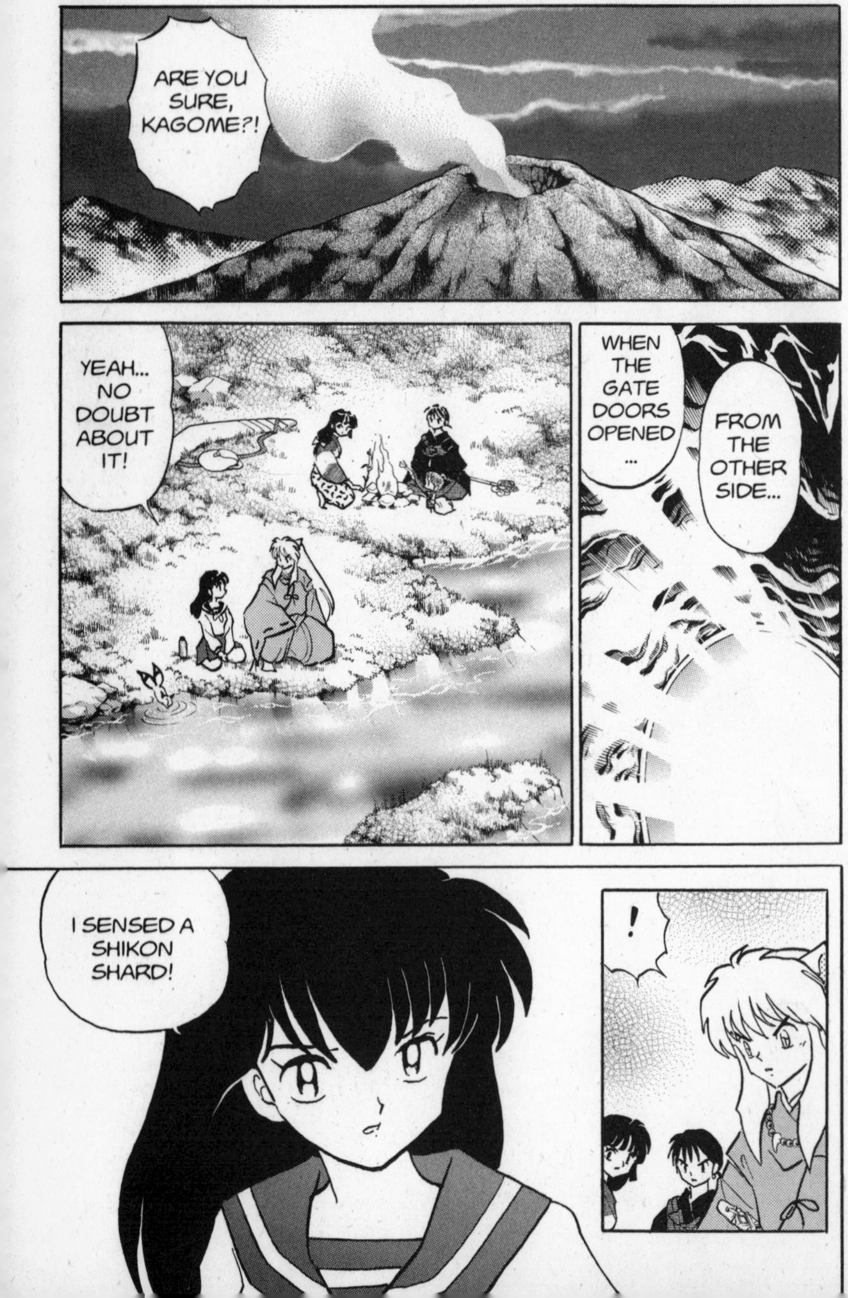

ARE YOU SURE, KAGOME?!
YEAH... NO DOUBT ABOUT IT!
WHEN THE GATE DOORS OPENED ...
FROM THE OTHER SIDE...
I SENSED A SHIKON SHARD!
!

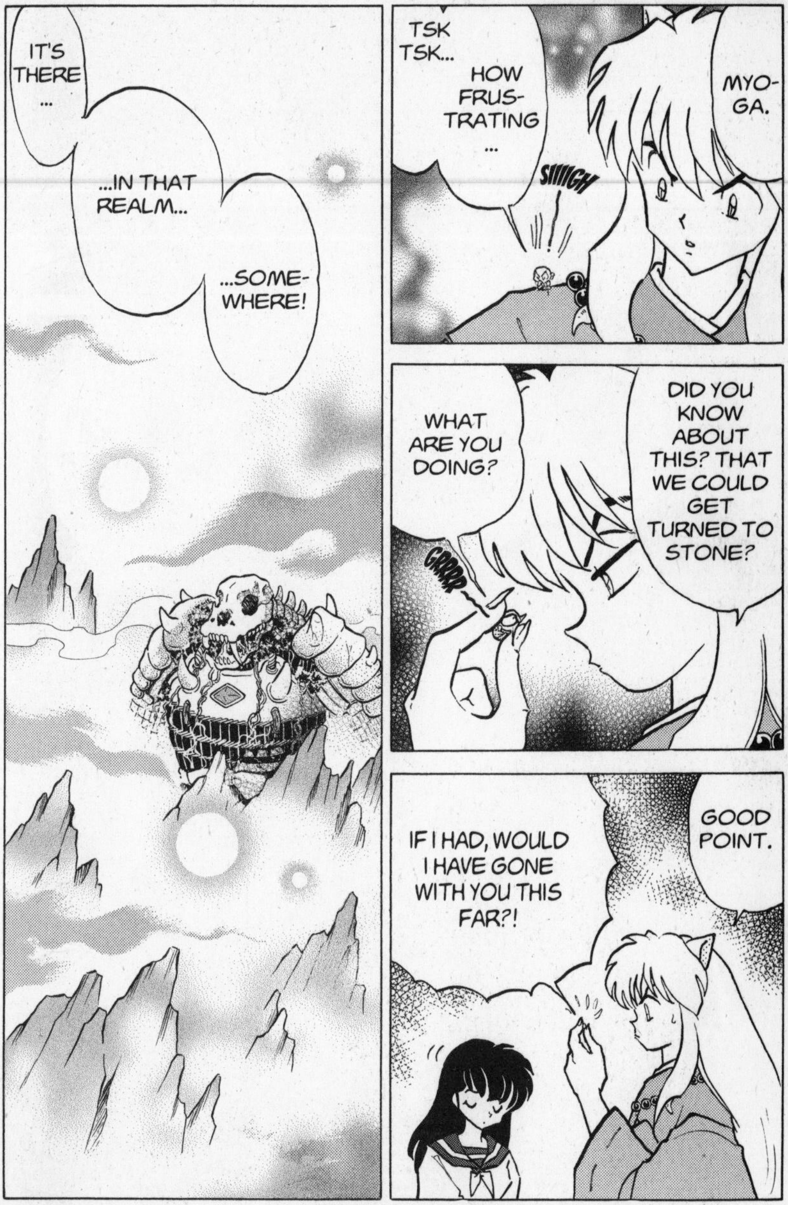
IT'S THERE ...
...IN THAT REALM...
...SOME-WHERE!
TSK TSK...
HOW FRUS-TRATING ...
SIIIGH
MYO-GA.
WHAT ARE YOU DOING?
GRRRR
DID YOU KNOW ABOUT THIS? THAT WE COULD GET TURNED TO STONE?
IF I HAD, WOULD I HAVE GONE WITH YOU THIS FAR?!
GOOD POINT.

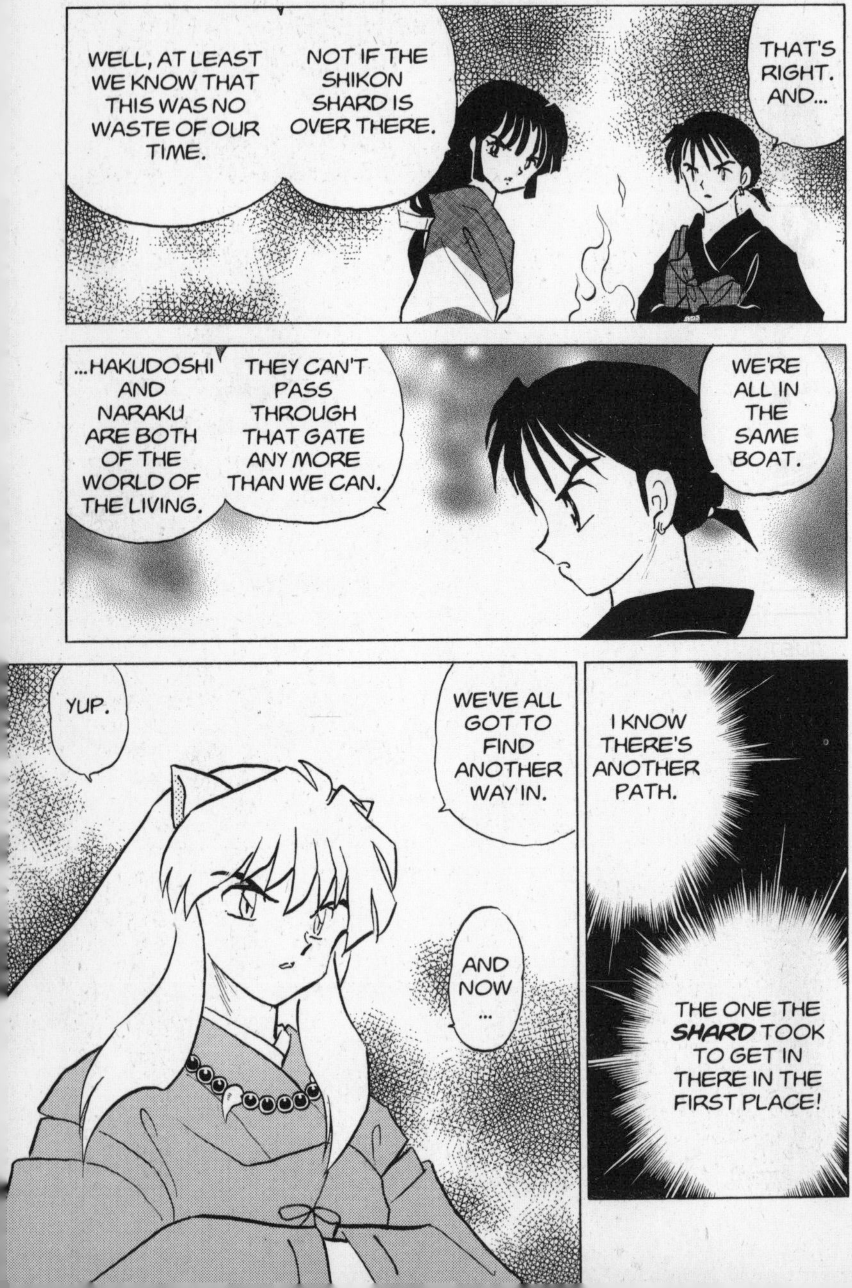
WELL, AT LEAST WE KNOW THAT THIS WAS NO WASTE OF OUR TIME.
NOT IF THE SHIKON SHARD IS OVER THERE.
THAT'S RIGHT. AND...
...HAKUDOSHI AND NARAKU ARE BOTH OF THE WORLD OF THE LIVING.
THEY CAN'T PASS THROUGH THAT GATE ANY MORE THAN WE CAN.
WE'RE ALL IN THE SAME BOAT.
YUP.
WE'VE ALL GOT TO FIND ANOTHER WAY IN.
AND NOW ...
I KNOW THERE'S ANOTHER PATH.
THE ONE THE SHARD TOOK TO GET IN THERE IN THE FIRST PLACE!

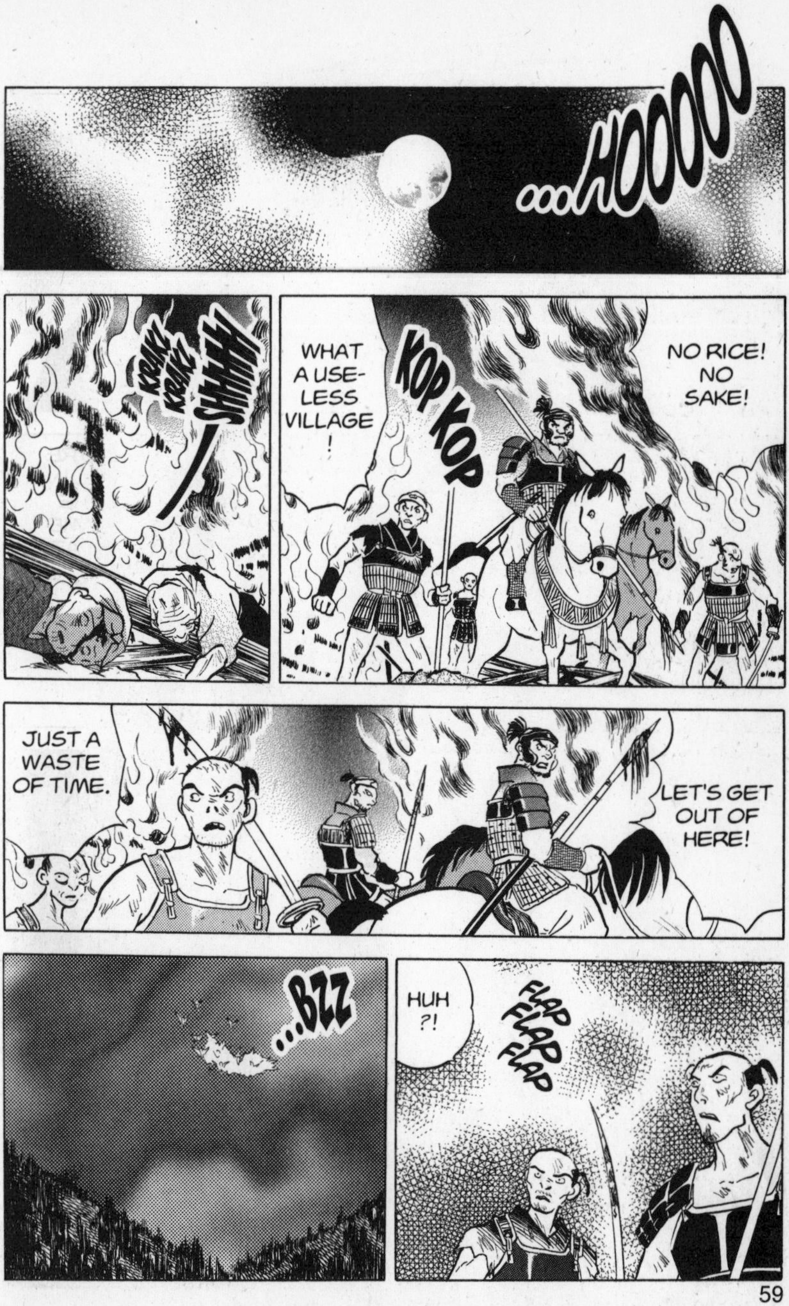
...HOOOOO
KRAK! KRAK!
SHHHHH
WHAT A USE-LESS VILLAGE!
KOP KOP
NO RICE! NO SAKE!
JUST A WASTE OF TIME.
LET'S GET OUT OF HERE!
...BZZ
HUH?!
FLAP FLAP FLAP

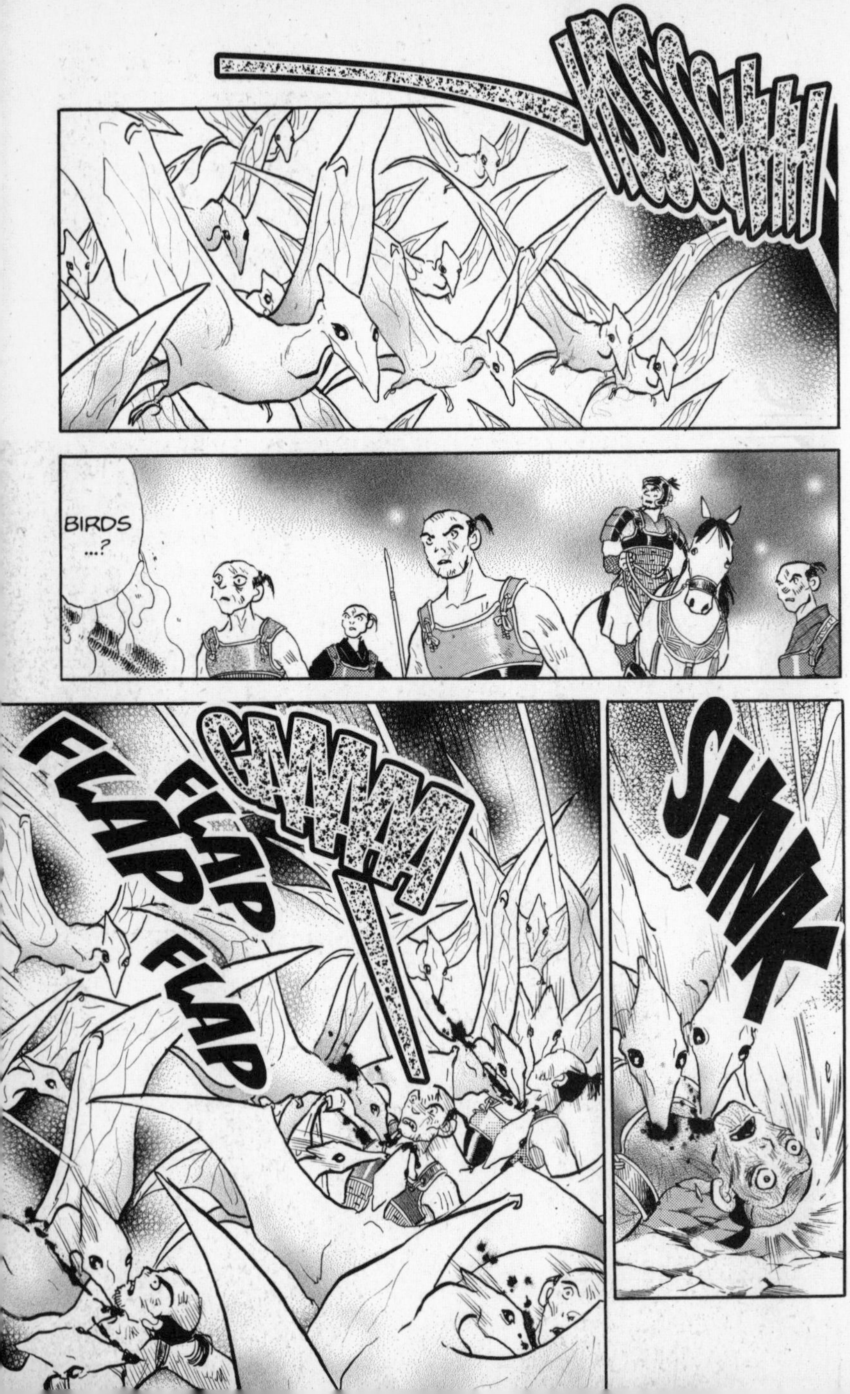
WSSSHHH
BIRDS ...?
FLAP FLAP FLAP
GWAAA!
SHNK

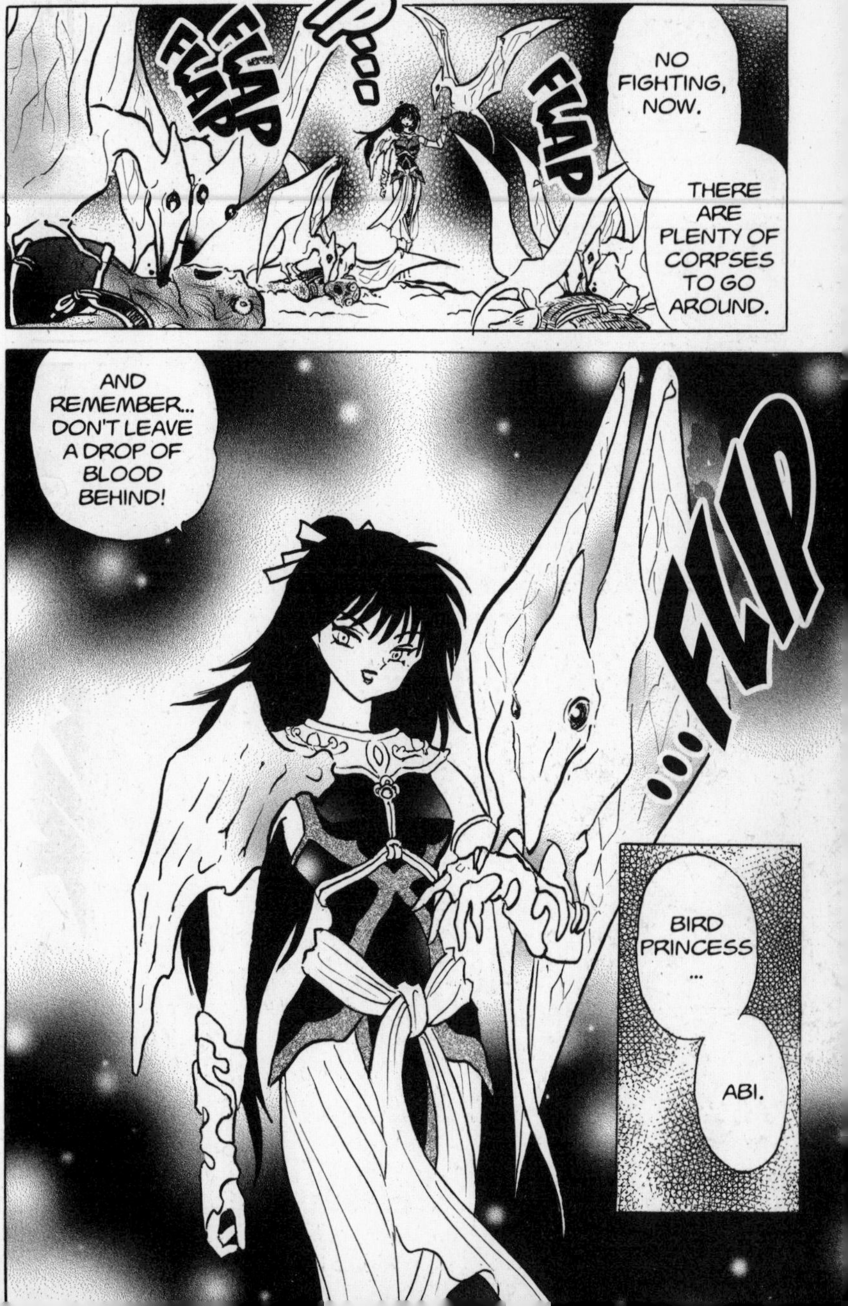
FLAP FLAP
FLAP
NO FIGHTING, NOW.
THERE ARE PLENTY OF CORPSES TO GO AROUND.
AND REMEMBER... DON'T LEAVE A DROP OF BLOOD BEHIND!
...FLIP
BIRD PRINCESS ...
ABI.

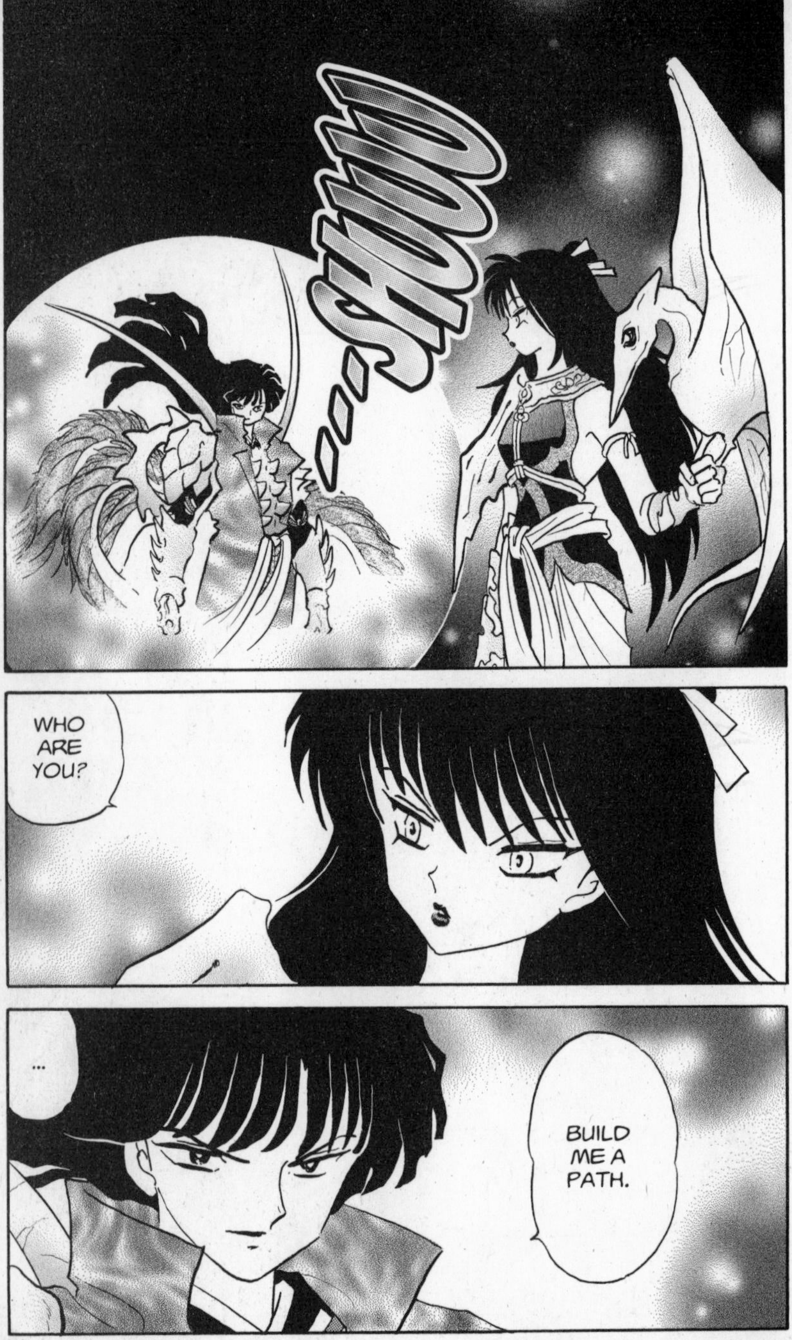
...SHOOOO
WHO ARE YOU?
BUILD ME A PATH.
...

SCROLL 4
PRINCESS ABI

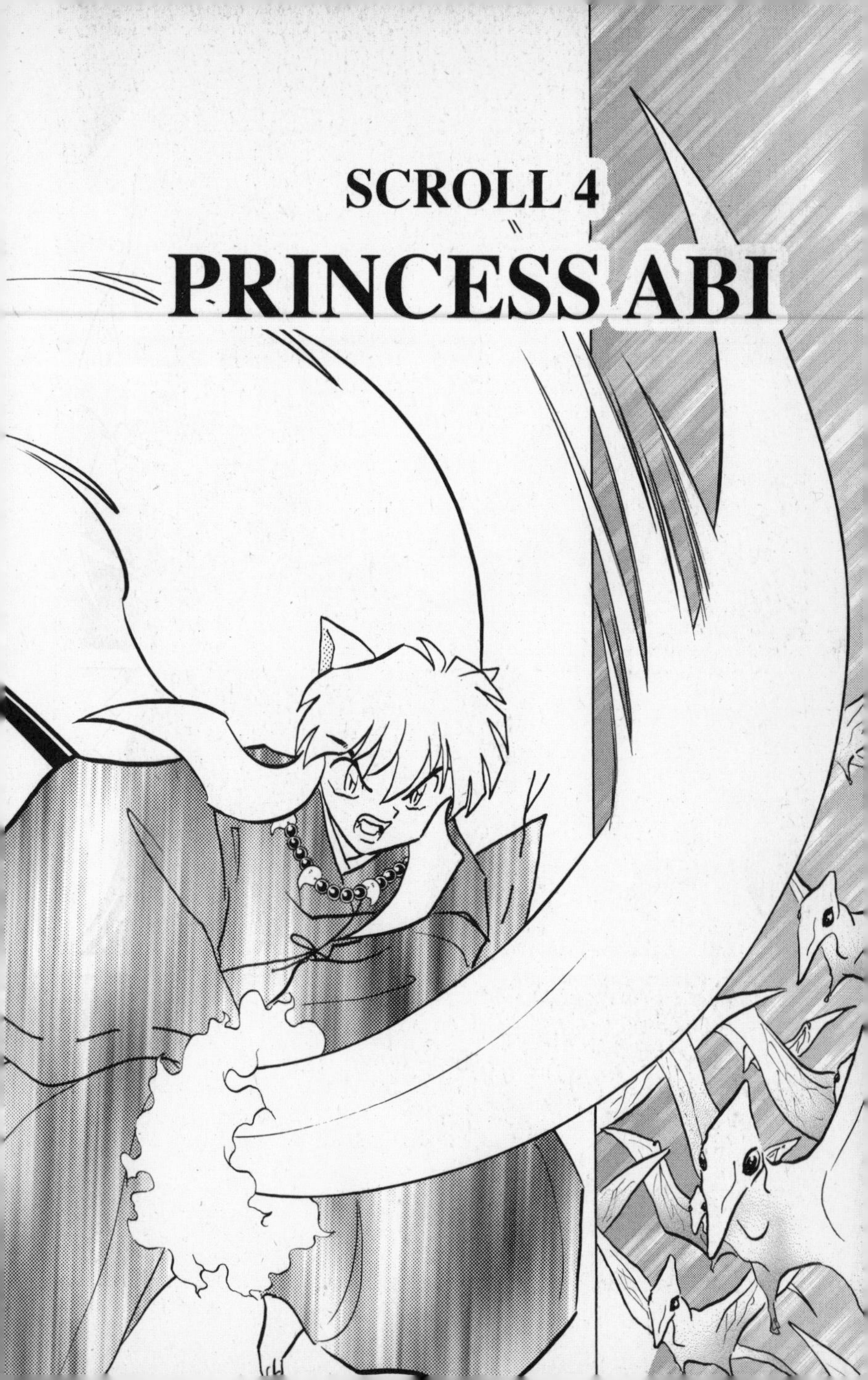

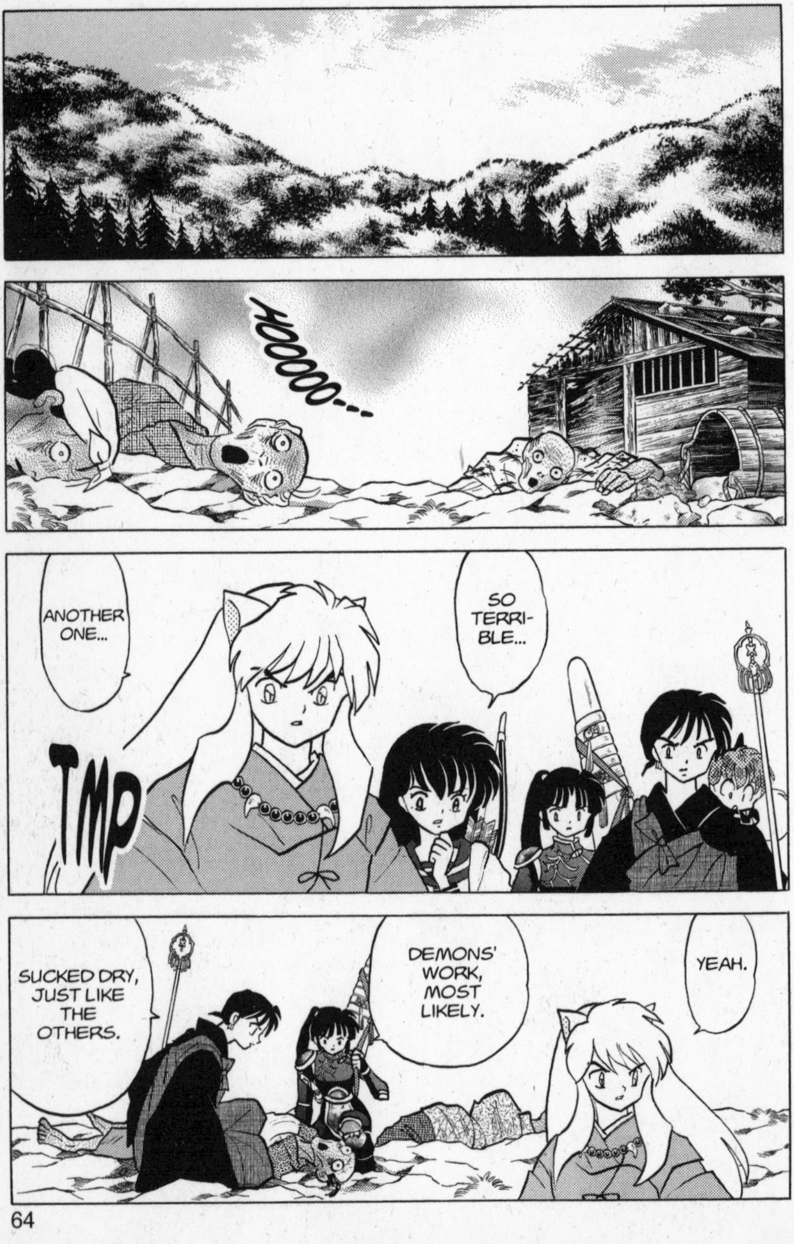
HOOOOOO-...
ANOTHER ONE...
TMP
SO TERRIBLE...
SUCKED DRY, JUST LIKE THE OTHERS.
DEMONS' WORK, MOST LIKELY.
YEAH.

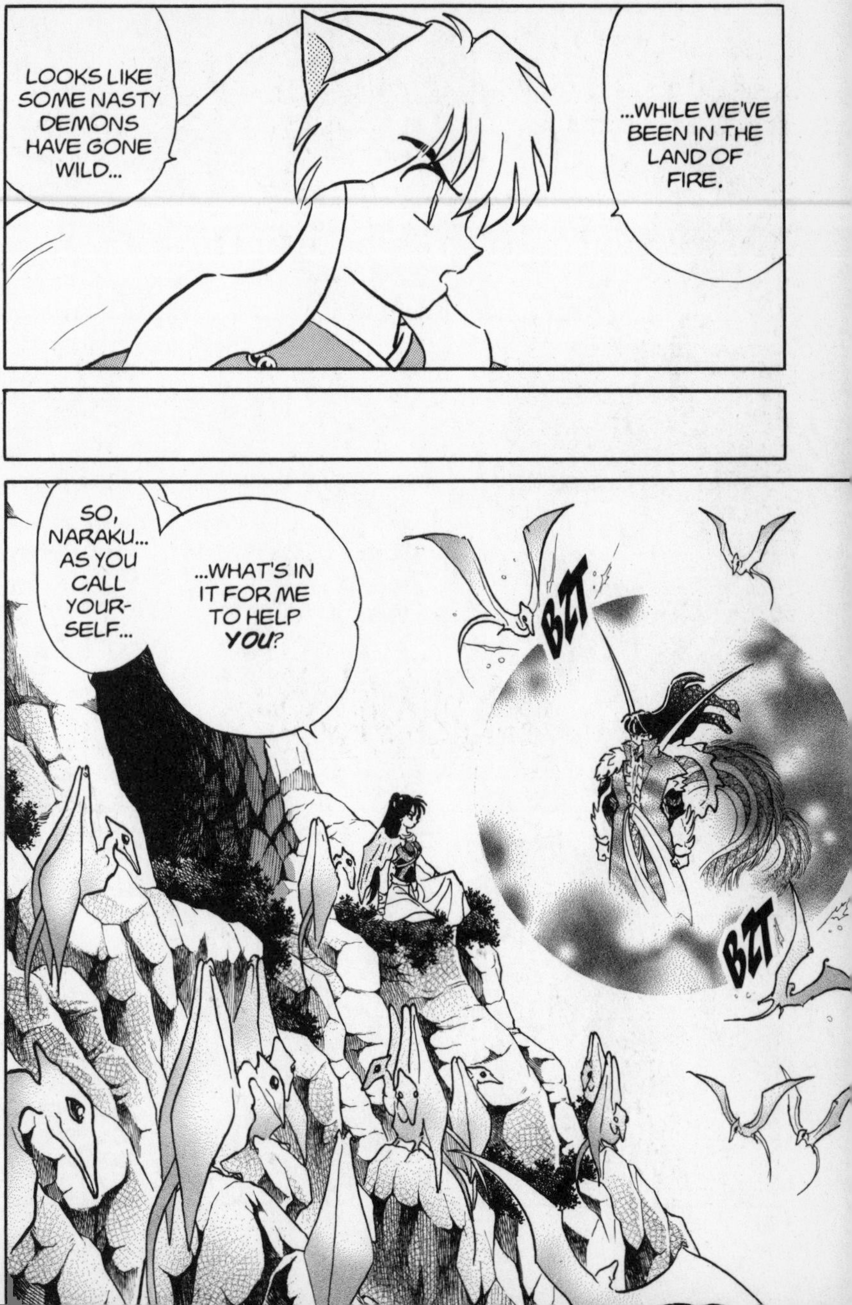
LOOKS LIKE SOME NASTY DEMONS HAVE GONE WILD...
...WHILE WE'VE BEEN IN THE LAND OF FIRE.
SO, NARAKU... AS YOU CALL YOURSELF...
...WHAT'S IN IT FOR ME TO HELP *YOU*?
BZT
BZT

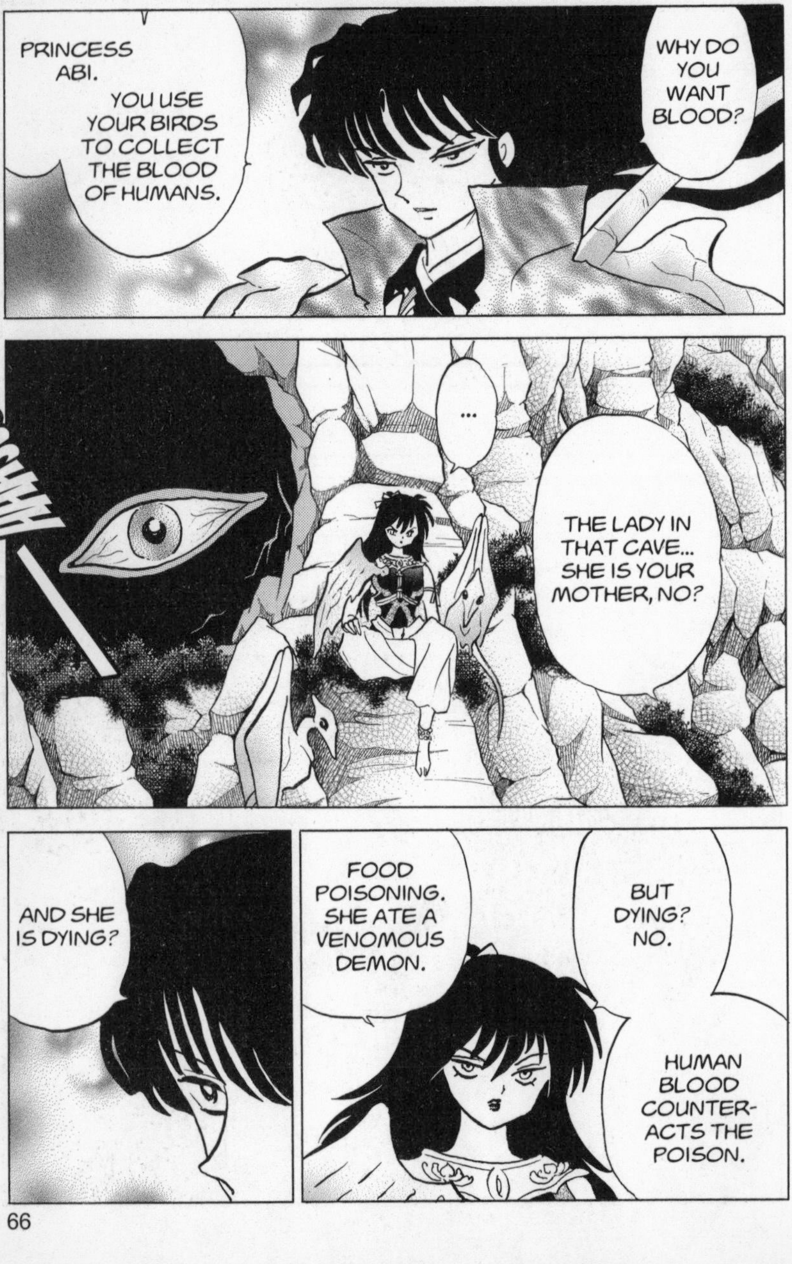

PRINCESS ABI.
YOU USE YOUR BIRDS TO COLLECT THE BLOOD OF HUMANS.
WHY DO YOU WANT BLOOD?
SSHHHH
...
THE LADY IN THAT CAVE... SHE IS YOUR MOTHER, NO?
AND SHE IS DYING?
FOOD POISONING. SHE ATE A VENOMOUS DEMON.
BUT DYING? NO.
HUMAN BLOOD COUNTER-ACTS THE POISON.

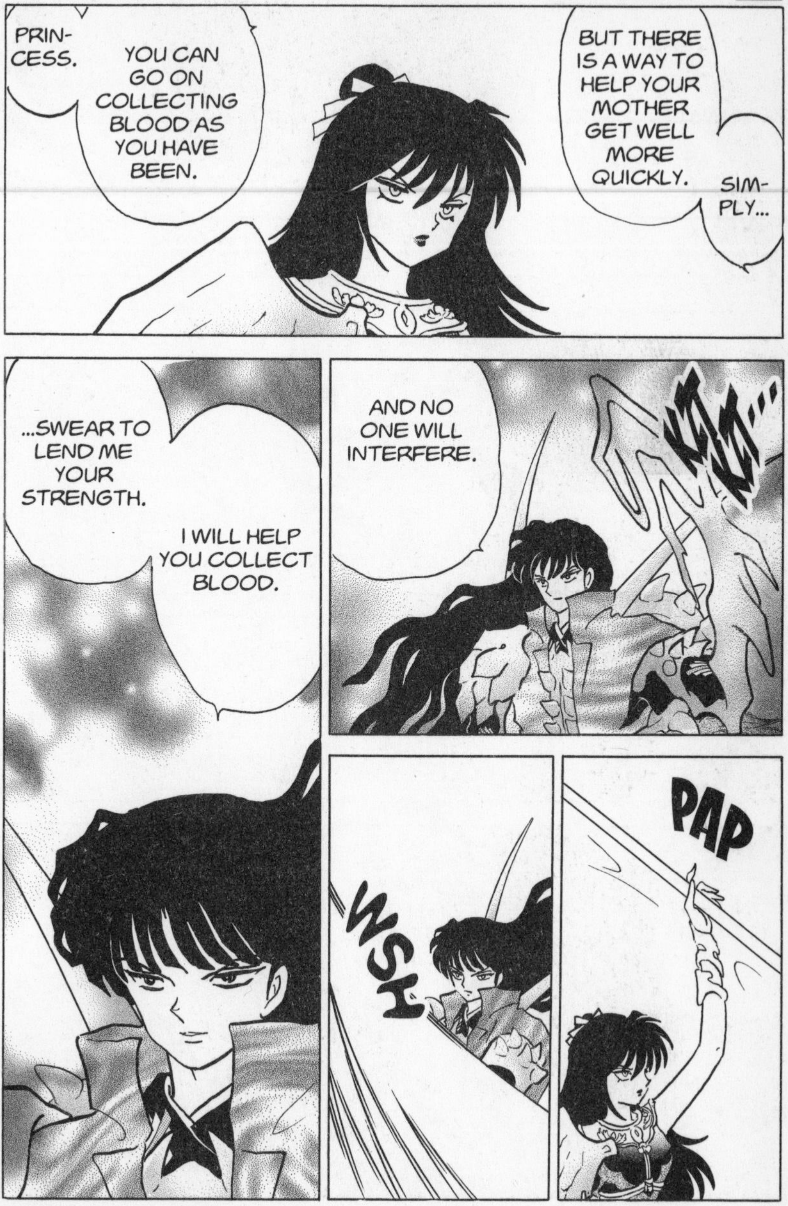
PRIN-CESS.
YOU CAN GO ON COLLECTING BLOOD AS YOU HAVE BEEN.
BUT THERE IS A WAY TO HELP YOUR MOTHER GET WELL MORE QUICKLY.
SIM-PLY...
...SWEAR TO LEND ME YOUR STRENGTH.
I WILL HELP YOU COLLECT BLOOD.
AND NO ONE WILL INTERFERE.
WSH
PAP

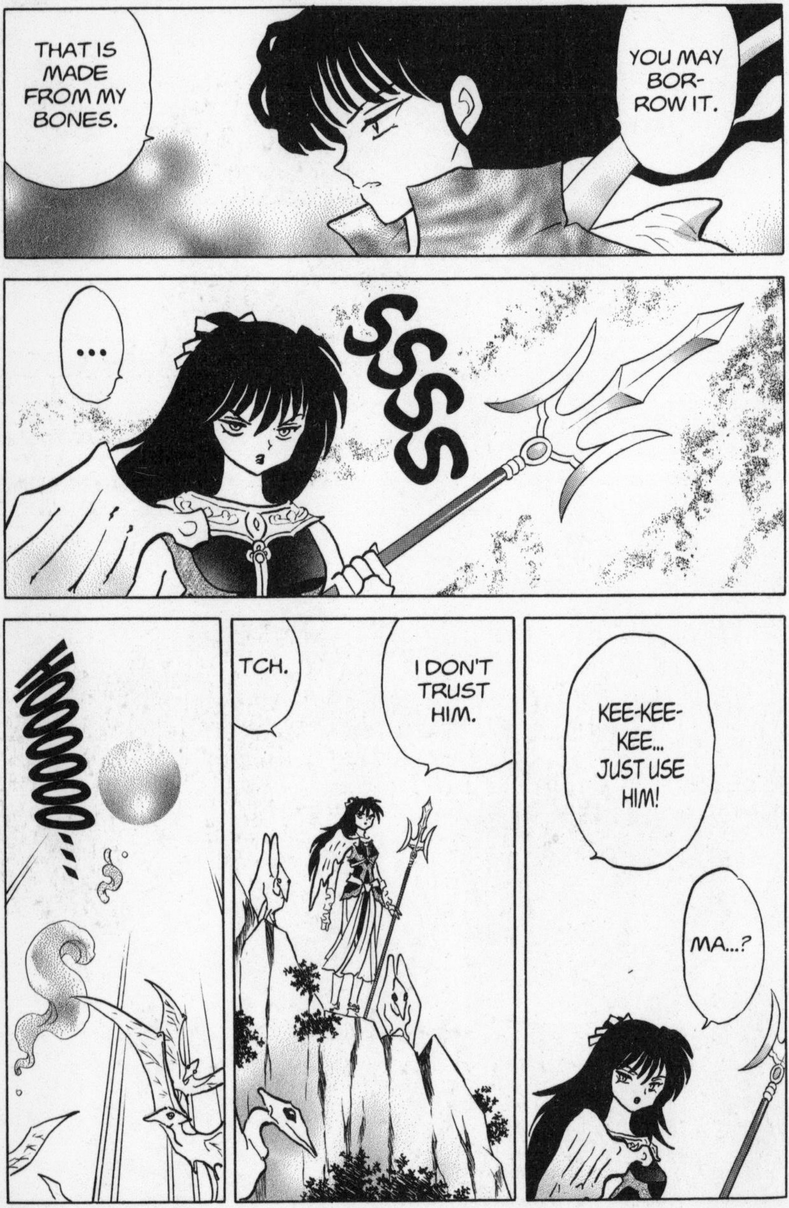
THAT IS MADE FROM MY BONES.
YOU MAY BOR-ROW IT.
...
SSSS
HOOOOOO...
TCH.
I DON'T TRUST HIM.
KEE-KEE-KEE... JUST USE HIM!
MA...?

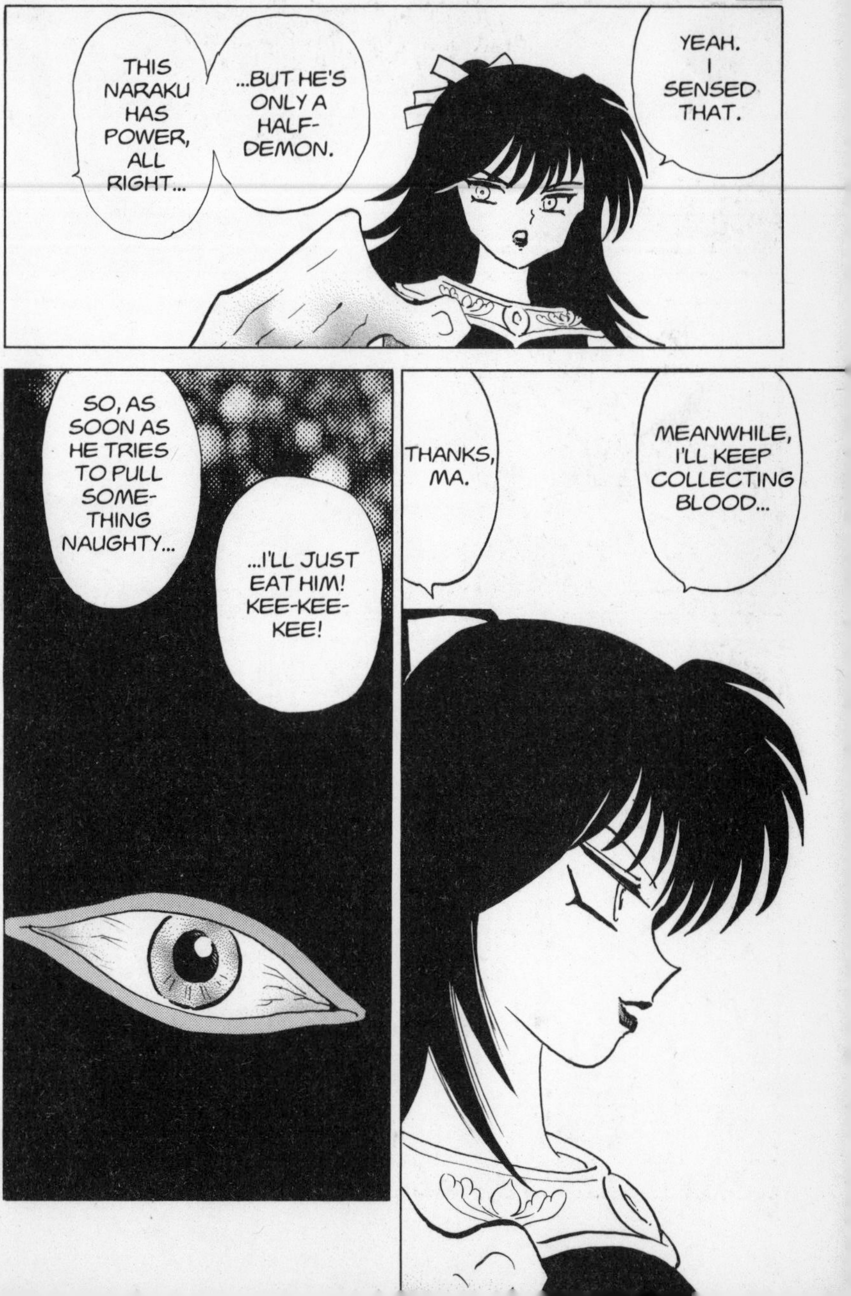
THIS NARAKU HAS POWER, ALL RIGHT...
...BUT HE'S ONLY A HALF-DEMON.
YEAH. I SENSED THAT.
SO, AS SOON AS HE TRIES TO PULL SOME-THING NAUGHTY...
...I'LL JUST EAT HIM! KEE-KEE-KEE!
THANKS, MA.
MEANWHILE, I'LL KEEP COLLECTING BLOOD...

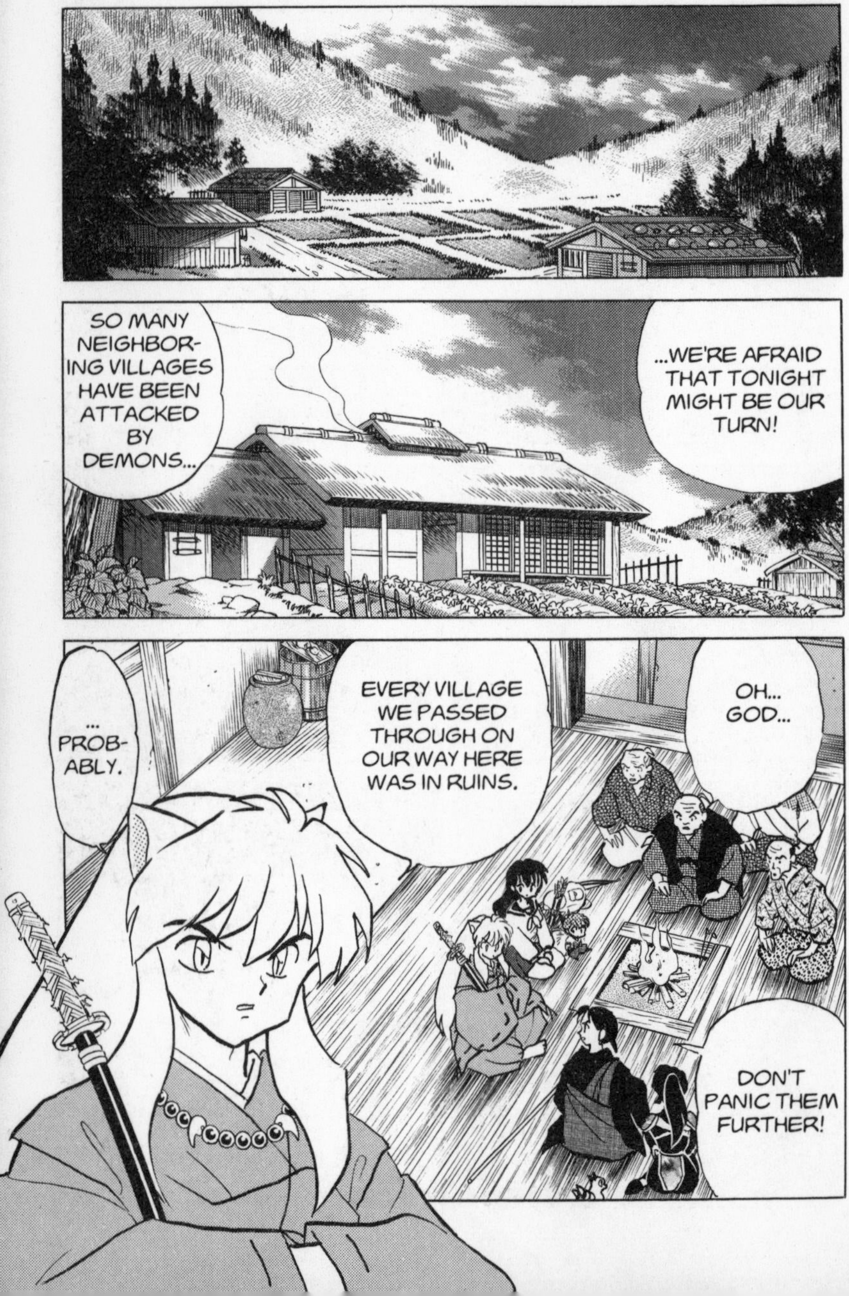
SO MANY NEIGHBORING VILLAGES HAVE BEEN ATTACKED BY DEMONS...
...WE'RE AFRAID THAT TONIGHT MIGHT BE OUR TURN!
...PROBABLY.
EVERY VILLAGE WE PASSED THROUGH ON OUR WAY HERE WAS IN RUINS.
OH... GOD...
DON'T PANIC THEM FURTHER!

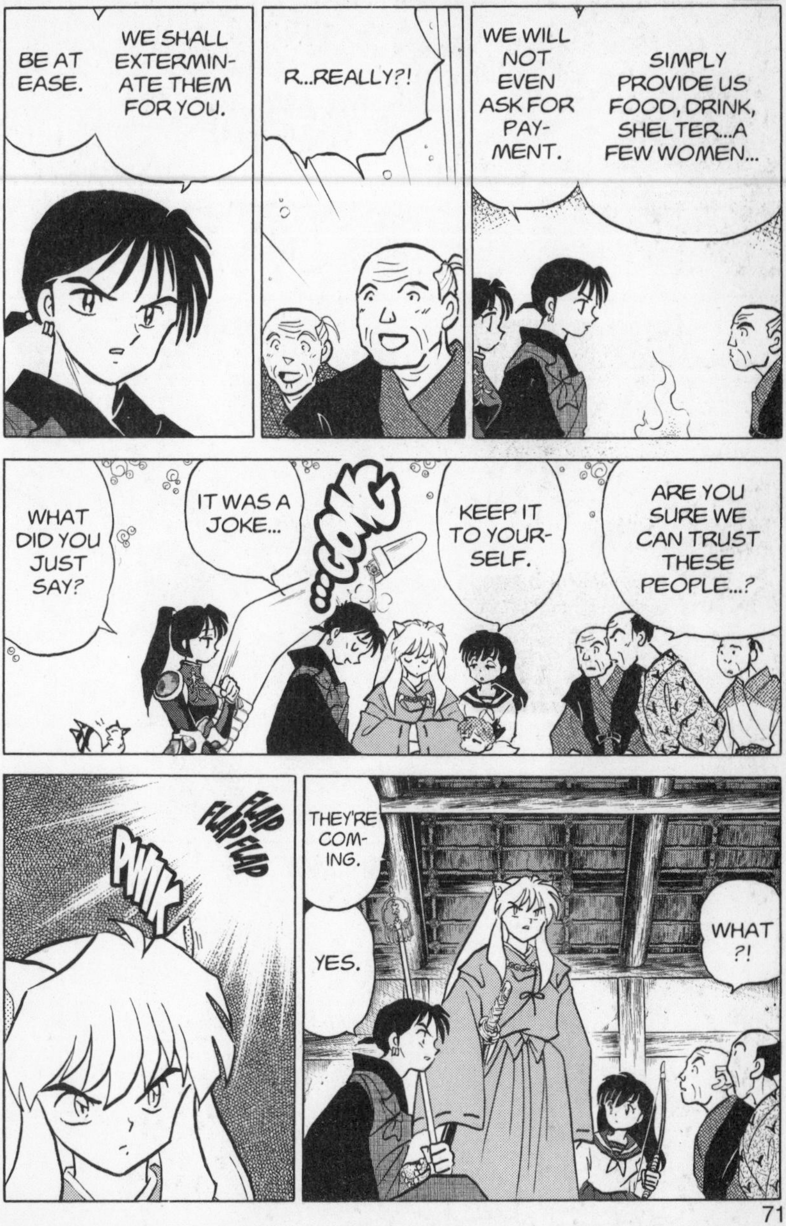
BE AT EASE.
WE SHALL EXTERMINATE THEM FOR YOU.
R...REALLY?!
WE WILL NOT EVEN ASK FOR PAYMENT.
SIMPLY PROVIDE US FOOD, DRINK, SHELTER...A FEW WOMEN...
WHAT DID YOU JUST SAY?
IT WAS A JOKE...
...GONG
KEEP IT TO YOURSELF.
ARE YOU SURE WE CAN TRUST THESE PEOPLE...?
PWIK
FLAP FLAP FLAP
THEY'RE COMING.
YES.
WHAT?!

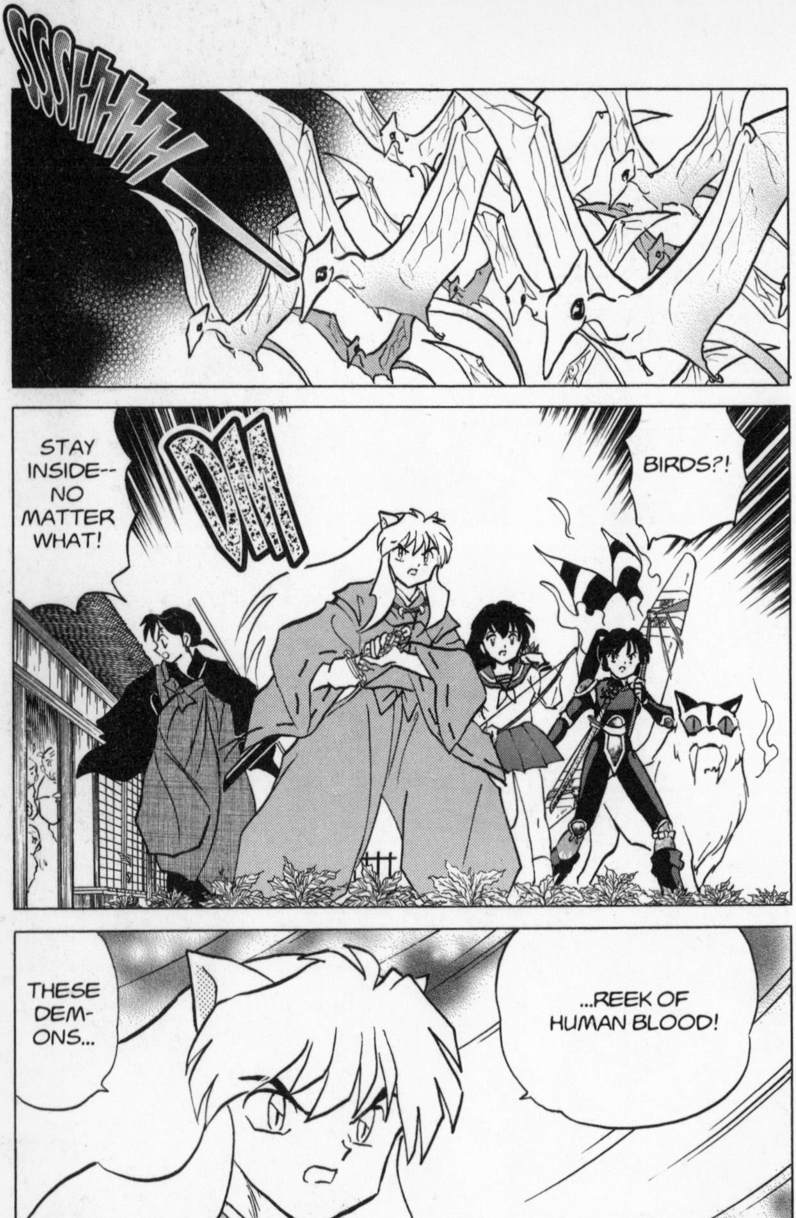
SSSHHHH!
STAY INSIDE--NO MATTER WHAT!
DM
BIRDS?!
THESE DEM-ONS...
...REEK OF HUMAN BLOOD!

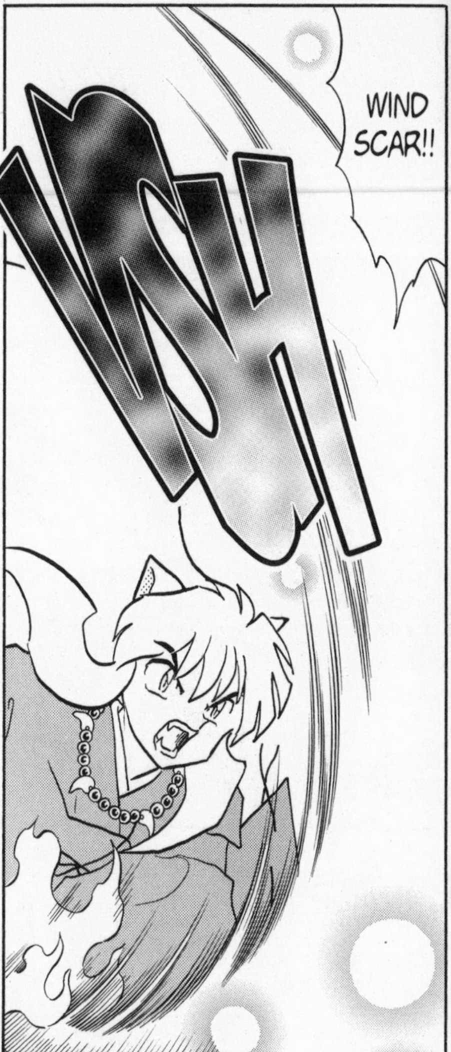
WIND
SCAR!!
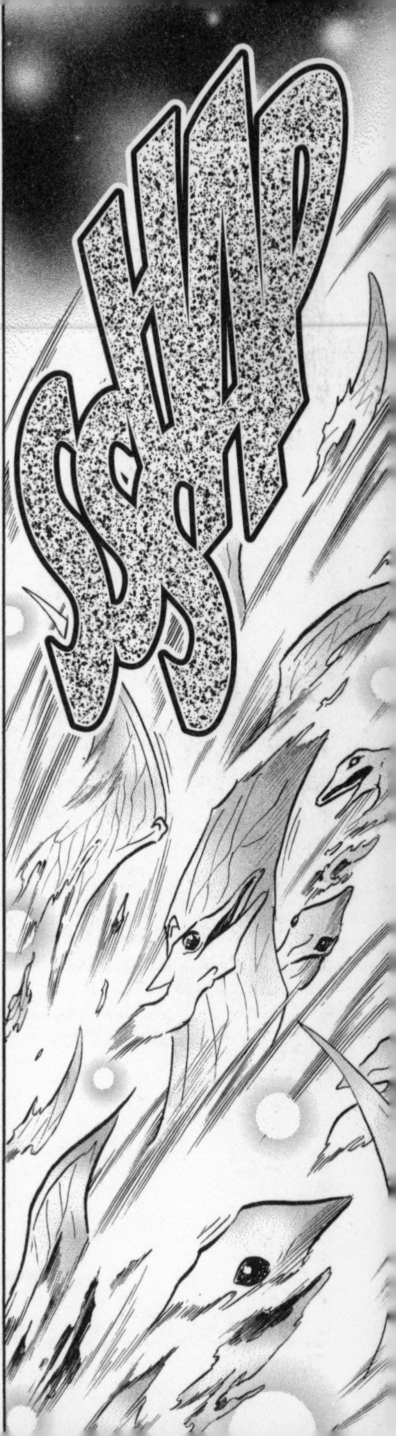

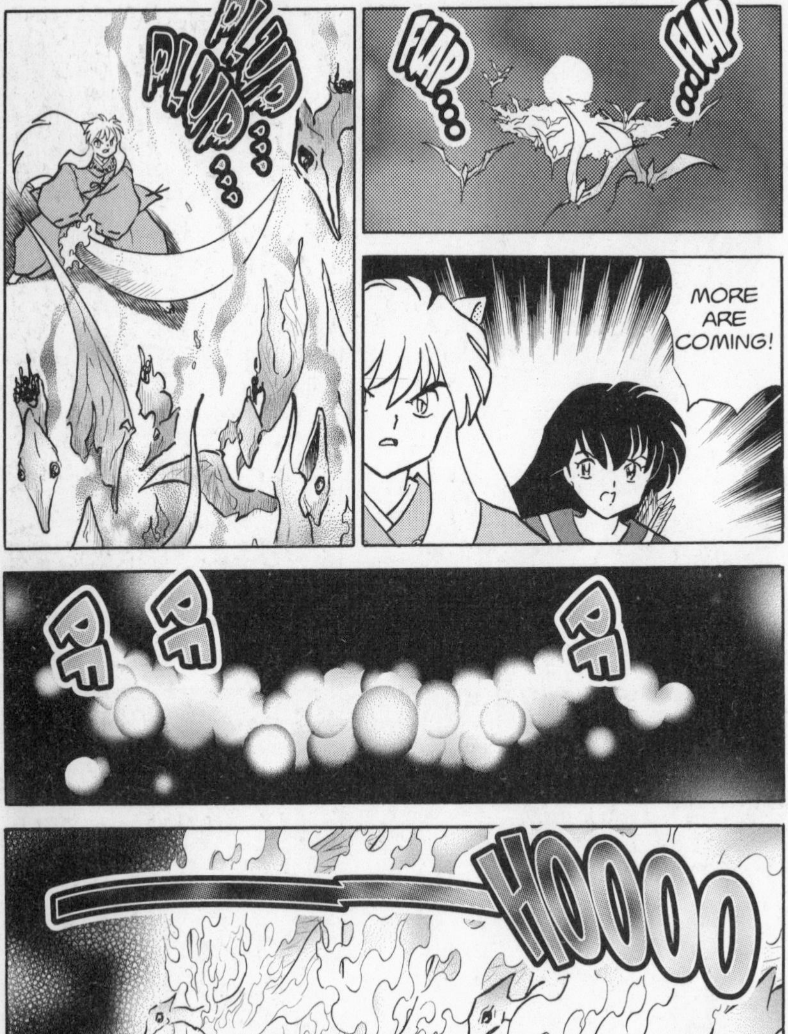
PLUD PLUD...
FLAP...
...FLAP
MORE ARE COMING!
PF
PF
PF
HOOOO

TH...
THEY'RE
ON
FIRE!

FP

FP

FIRE!!

KRAKL
KRAKL

KRAKL

HISS

SSS

WAAA!

RGH!

VSH

SHAP

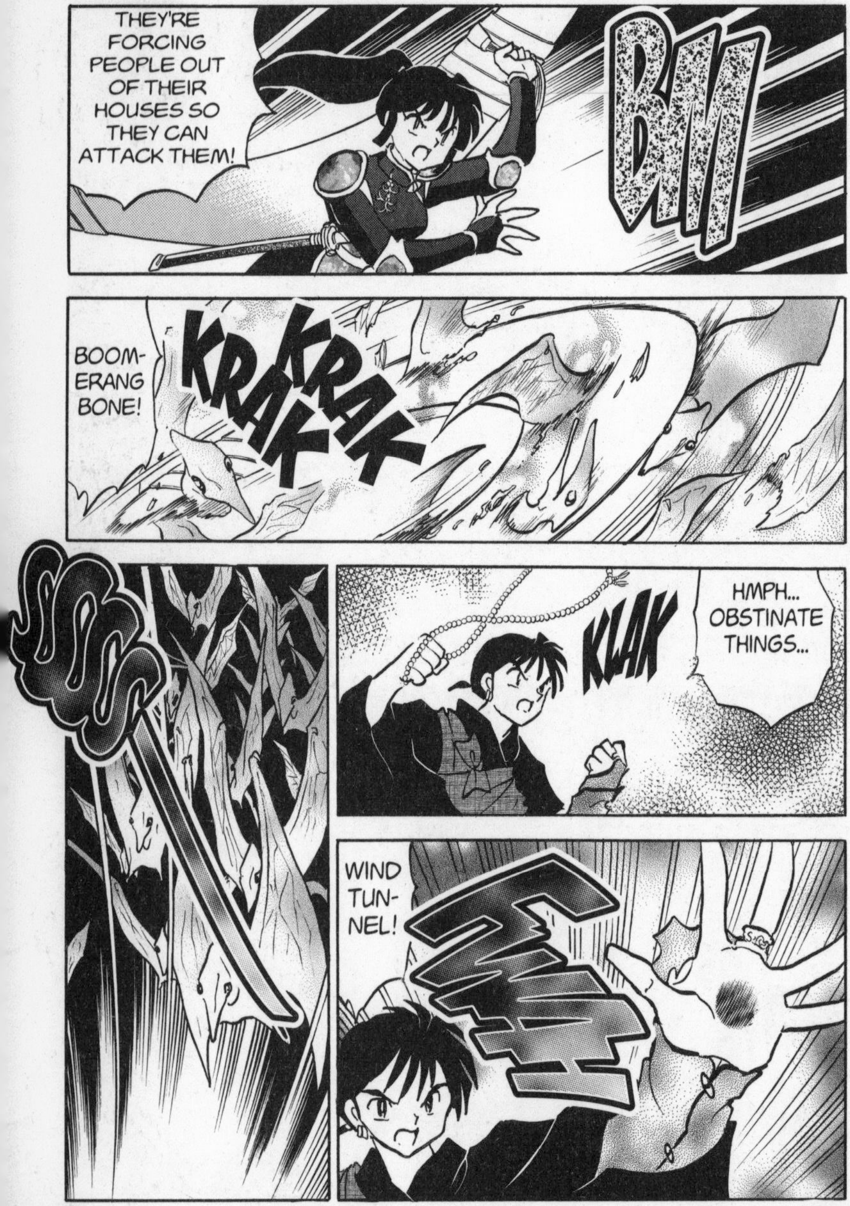
THEY'RE FORCING PEOPLE OUT OF THEIR HOUSES SO THEY CAN ATTACK THEM!
BM
BOOM-ERANG BONE!
KRAK KRAK
KLAK
HMPH... OBSTINATE THINGS...
WIND TUN-NEL!

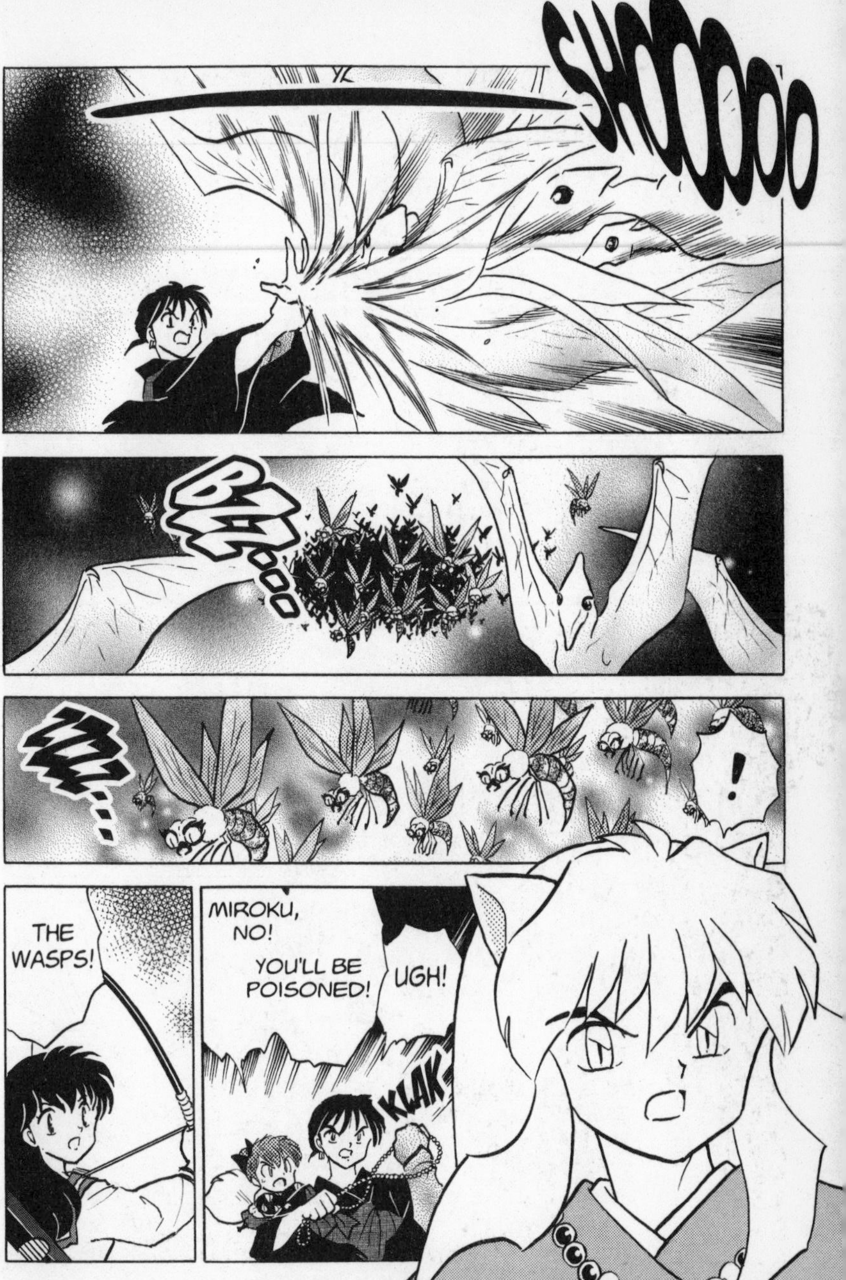
SHOOOOO
BZZOOOO
ZZZ...
!
THE WASPS!
MIROKU, NO!
YOU'LL BE POISONED!
UGH!
KLAK

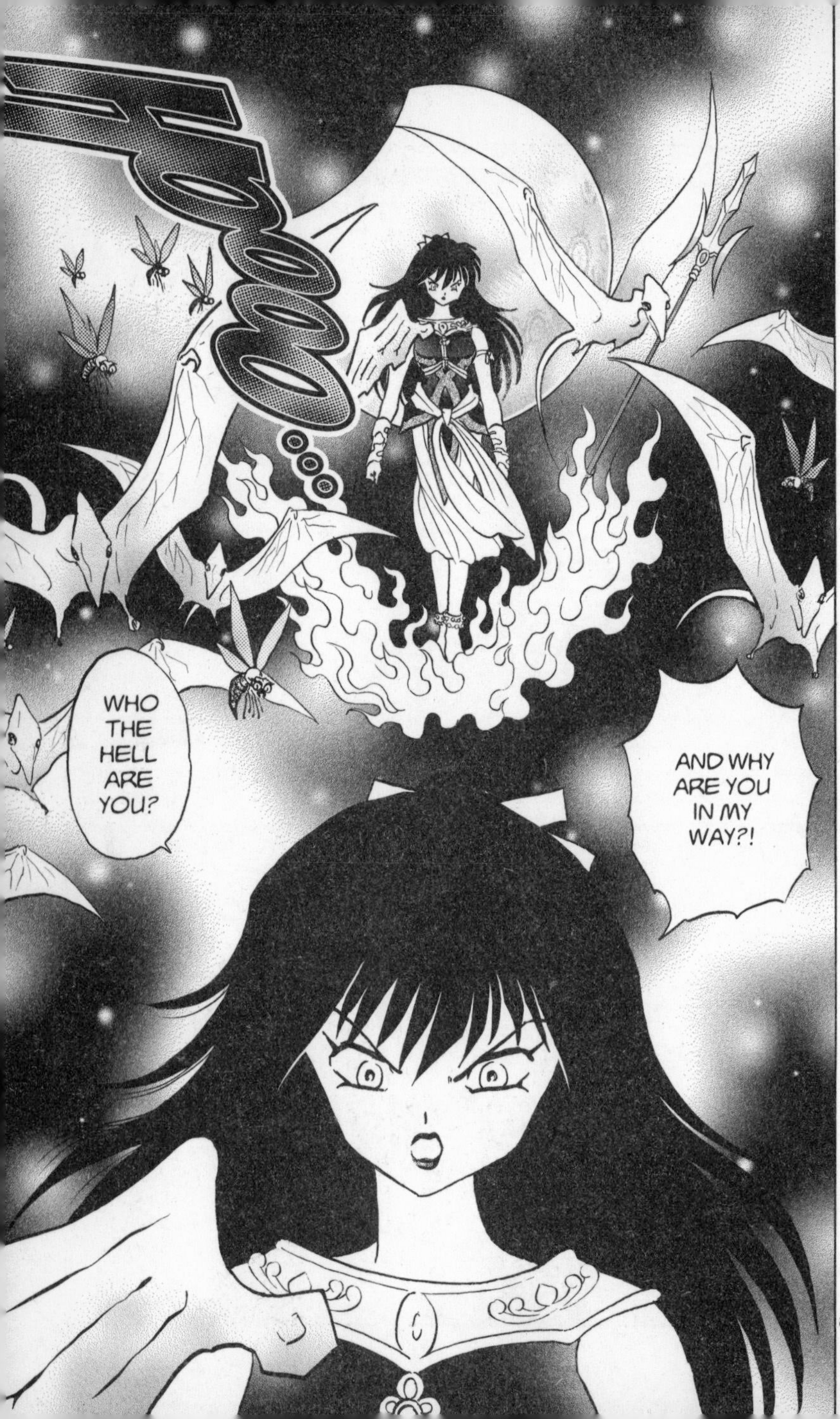
HOOOO.....
WHO THE HELL ARE YOU?
AND WHY ARE YOU IN MY WAY?!

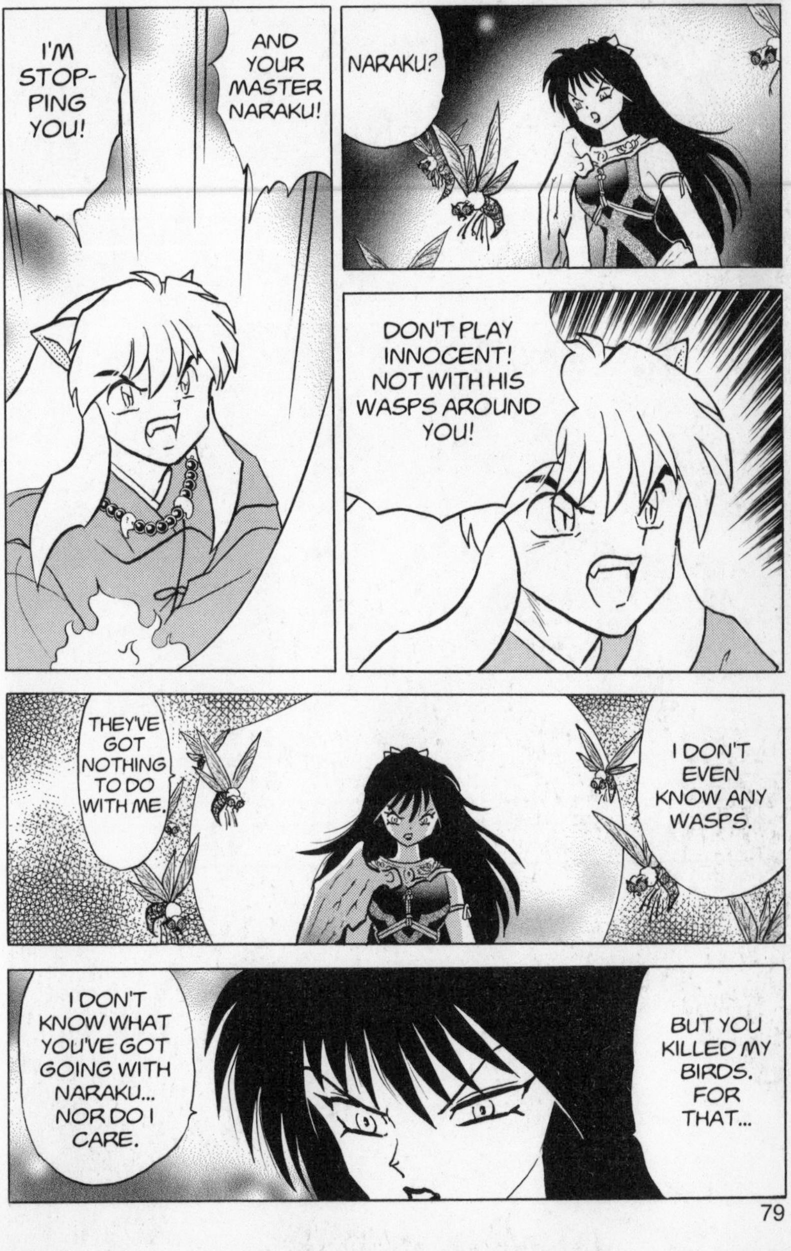
I'M STOP-PING YOU!
AND YOUR MASTER NARAKU!
NARAKU?
DON'T PLAY INNOCENT! NOT WITH HIS WASPS AROUND YOU!
THEY'VE GOT NOTHING TO DO WITH ME.
I DON'T EVEN KNOW ANY WASPS.
I DON'T KNOW WHAT YOU'VE GOT GOING WITH NARAKU... NOR DO I CARE.
BUT YOU KILLED MY BIRDS. FOR THAT...

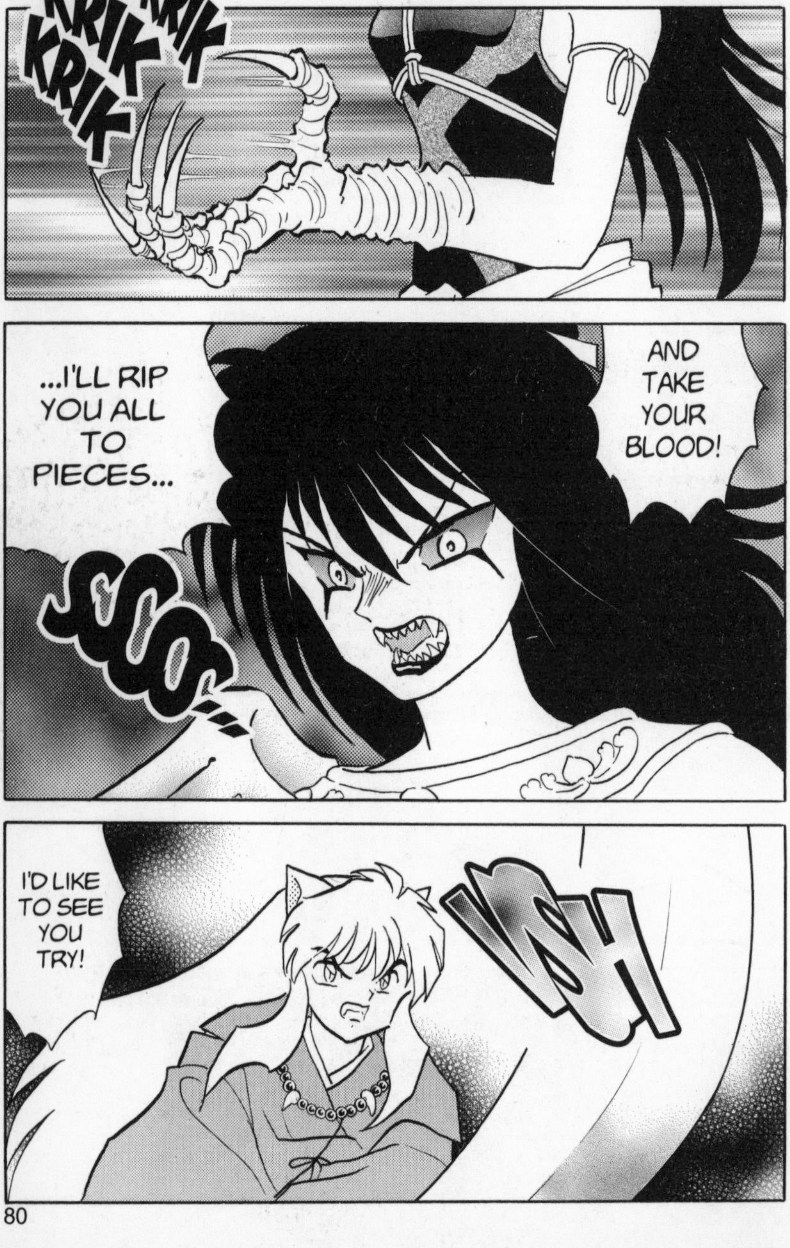
KRIK
KRIK
KRIK
...I'LL RIP YOU ALL TO PIECES...
AND TAKE YOUR BLOOD!
SSSS...
I'D LIKE TO SEE YOU TRY!
VSH

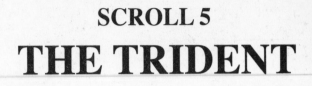

SCROLL 5

THE TRIDENT

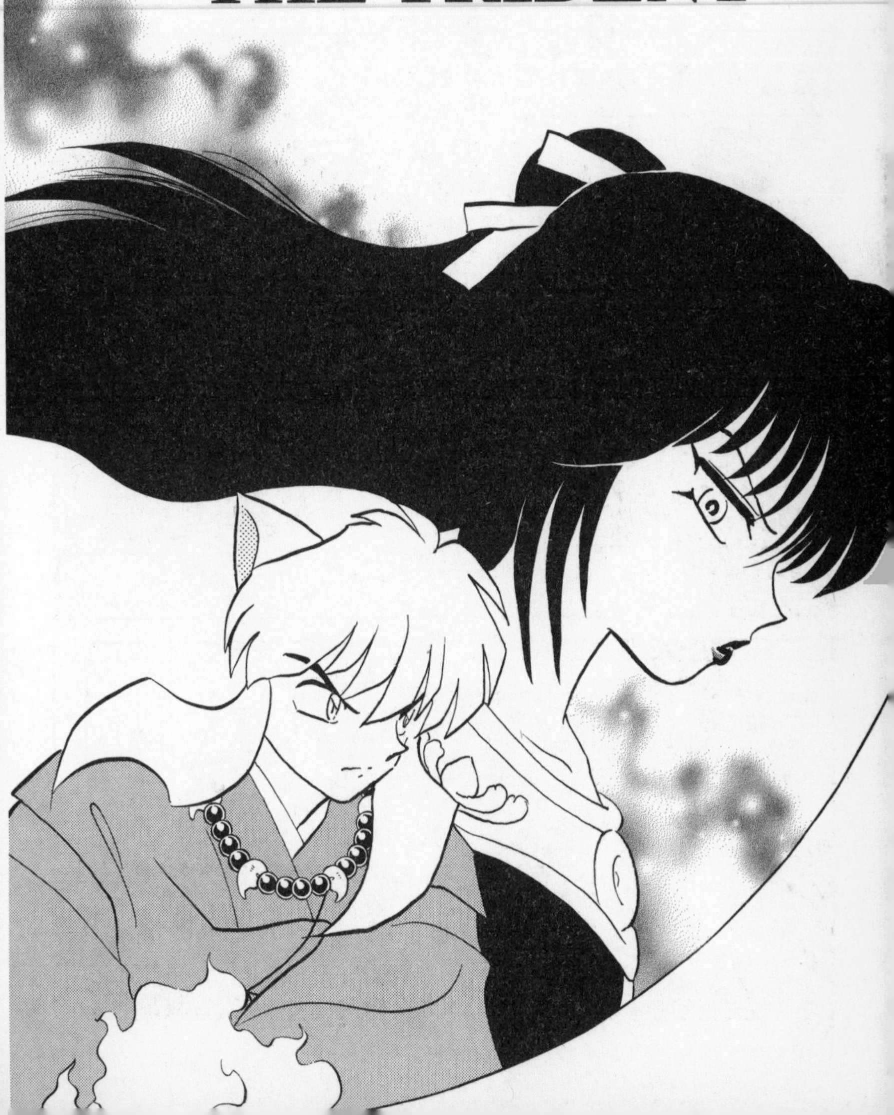

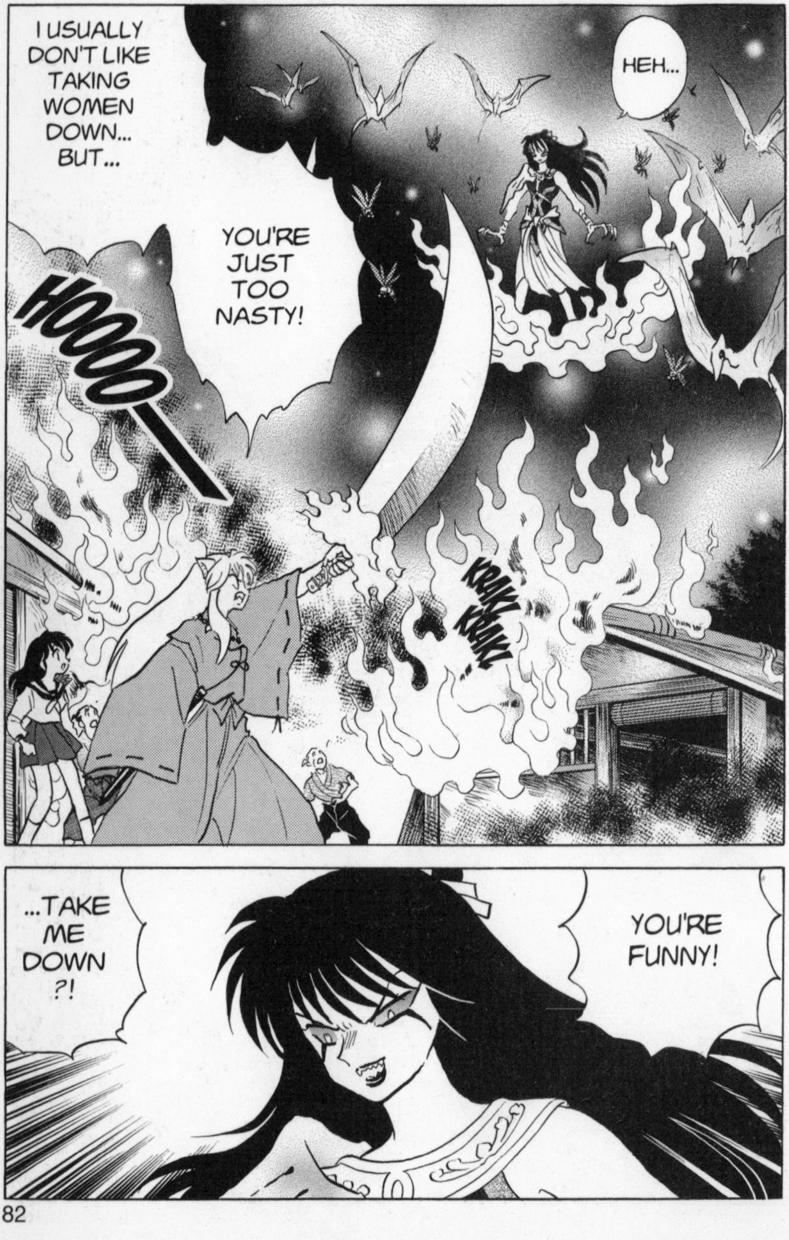

I USUALLY DON'T LIKE TAKING WOMEN DOWN... BUT...
HEH...
YOU'RE JUST TOO NASTY!
HOOOO
KRAK! KRAK!
...TAKE ME DOWN ?!
YOU'RE FUNNY!

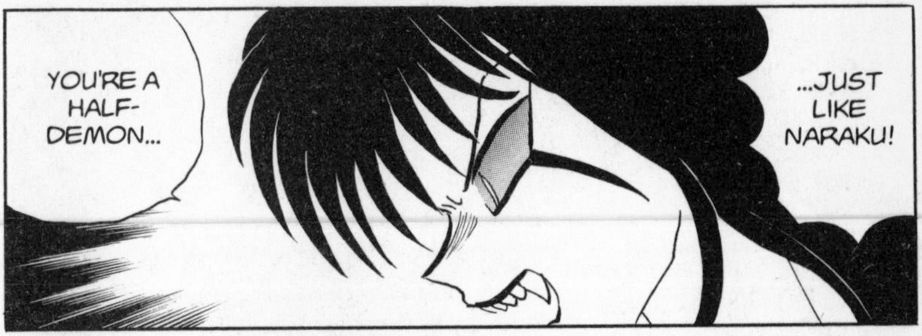
YOU'RE A HALF-DEMON...
...JUST LIKE NARAKU!

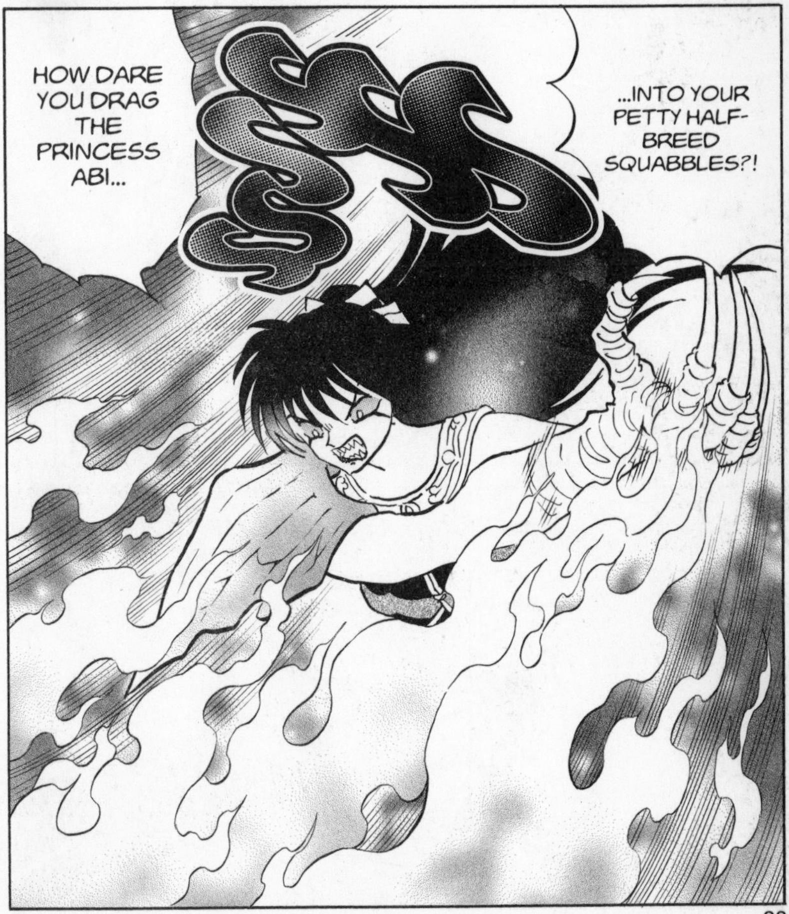
HOW DARE YOU DRAG THE PRINCESS ABI...
...INTO YOUR PETTY HALF-BREED SQUABBLES?!

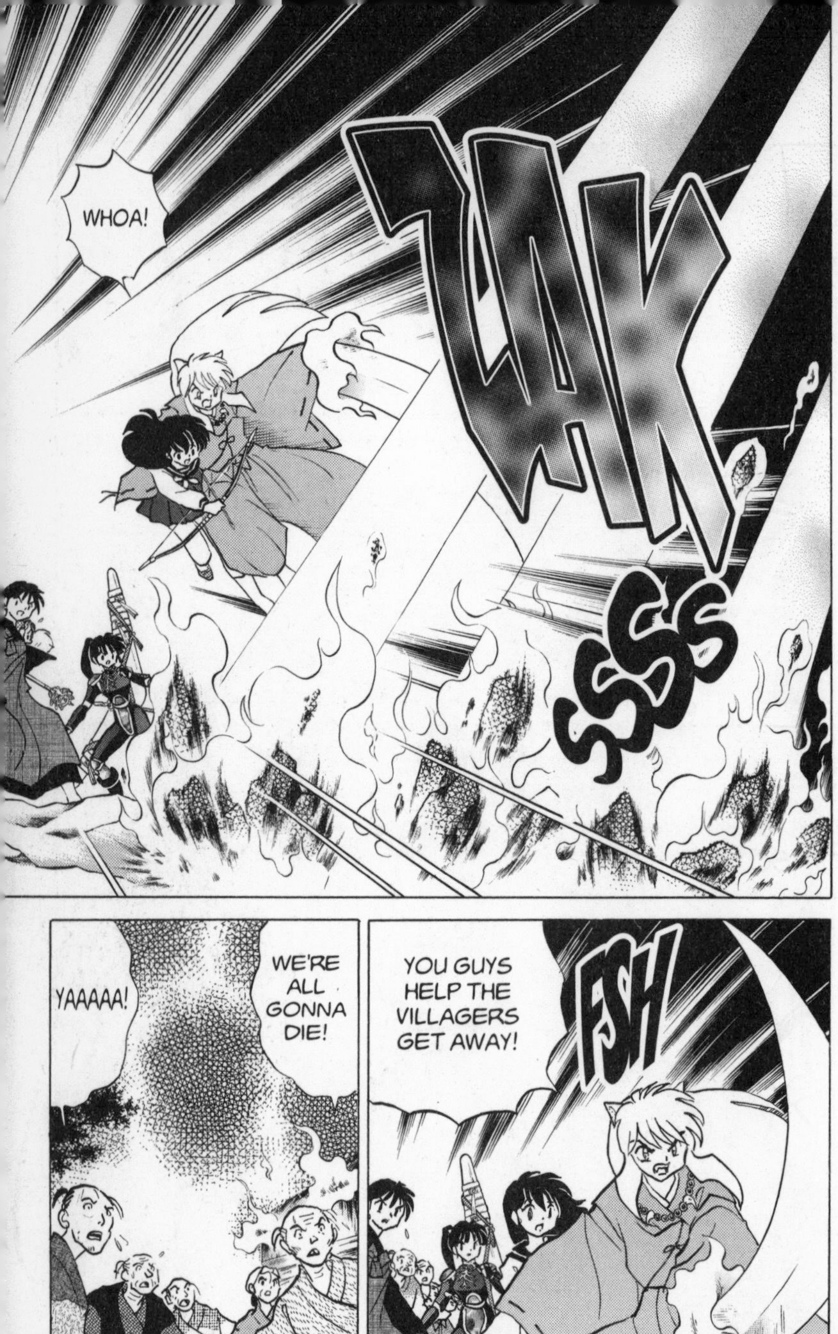
WHOA!
ZAK
SSSS
YAAAAA!
WE'RE ALL GONNA DIE!
YOU GUYS HELP THE VILLAGERS GET AWAY!
FSH

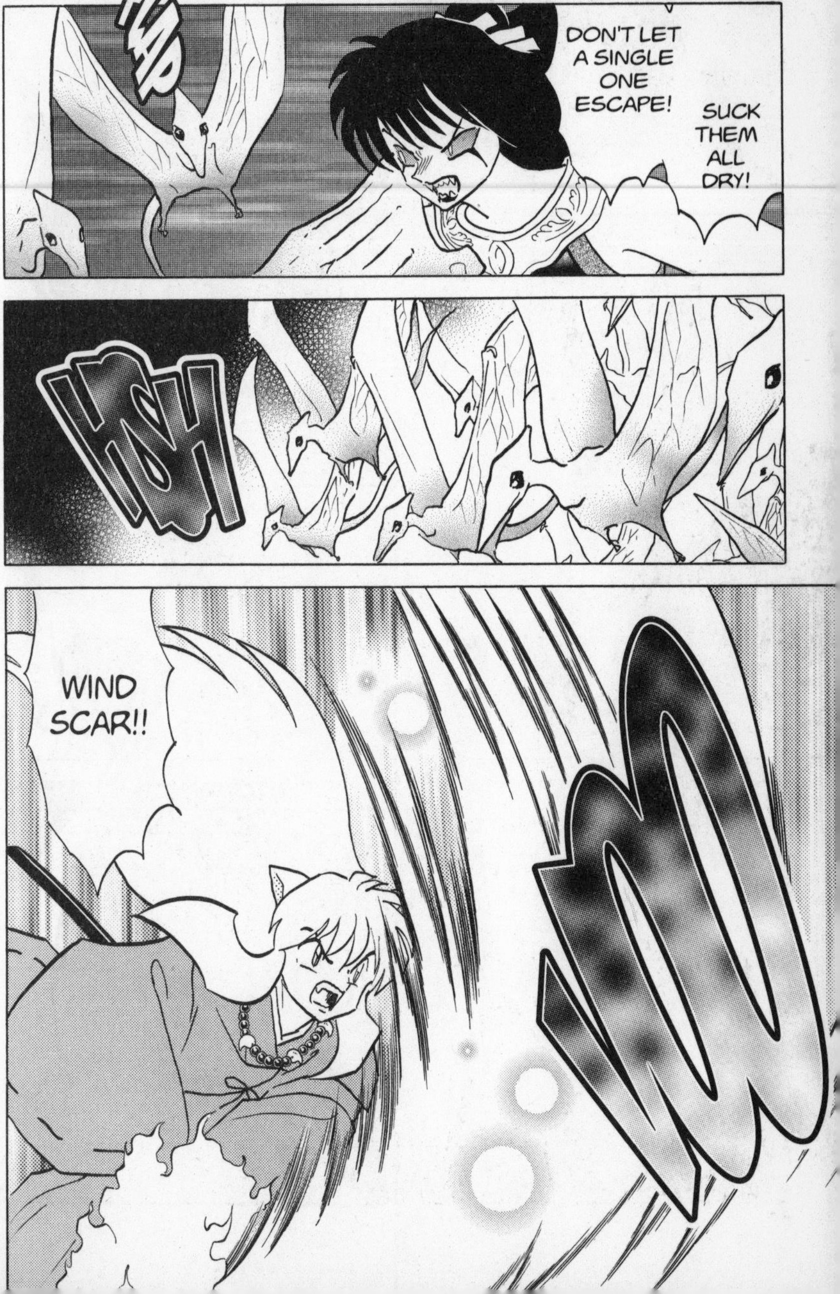
FLAP
DON'T LET A SINGLE ONE ESCAPE!
SUCK THEM ALL DRY!
WIND SCAR!!

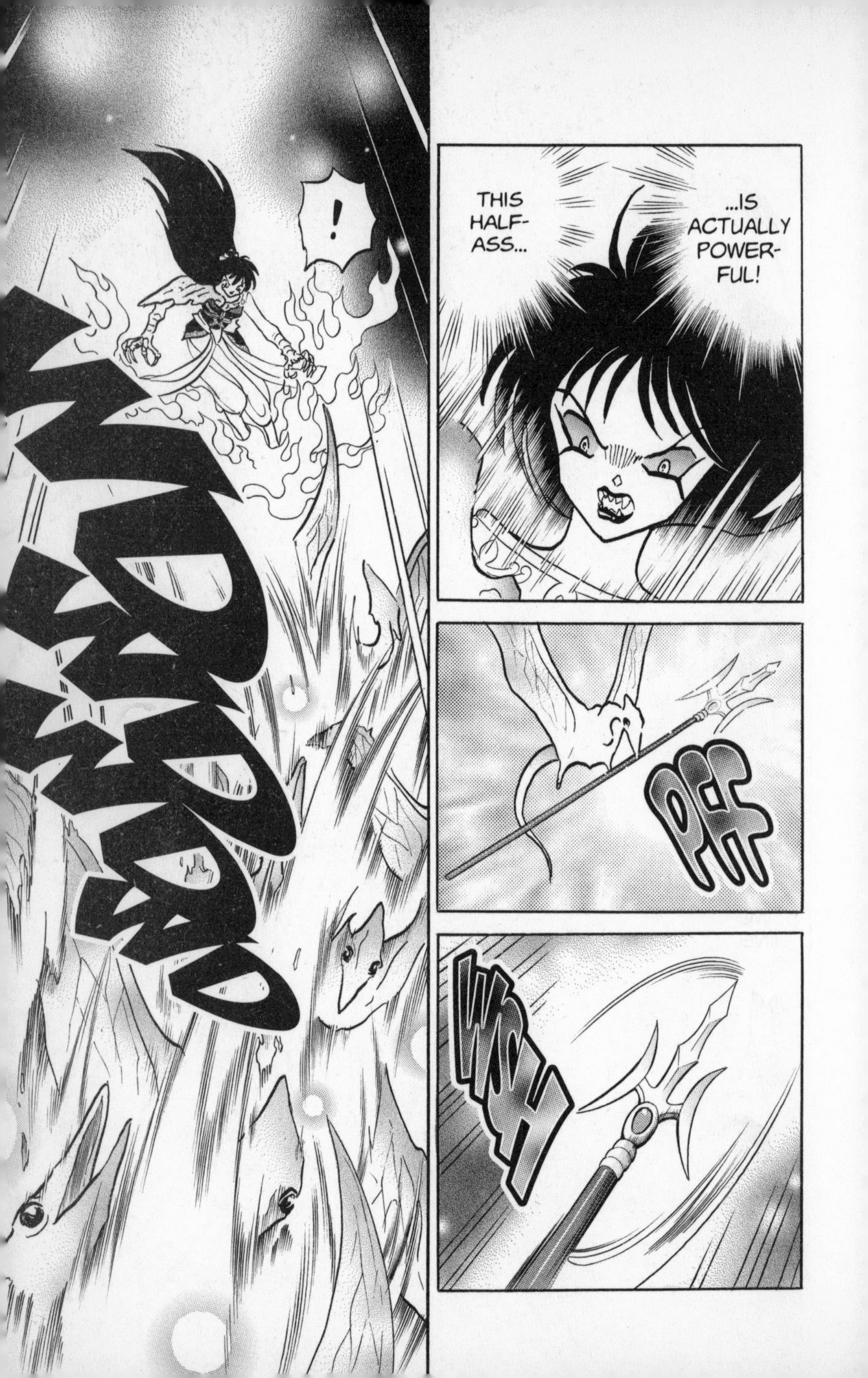
!
THIS HALF-ASS...
...IS ACTUALLY POWER-FUL!
WSH

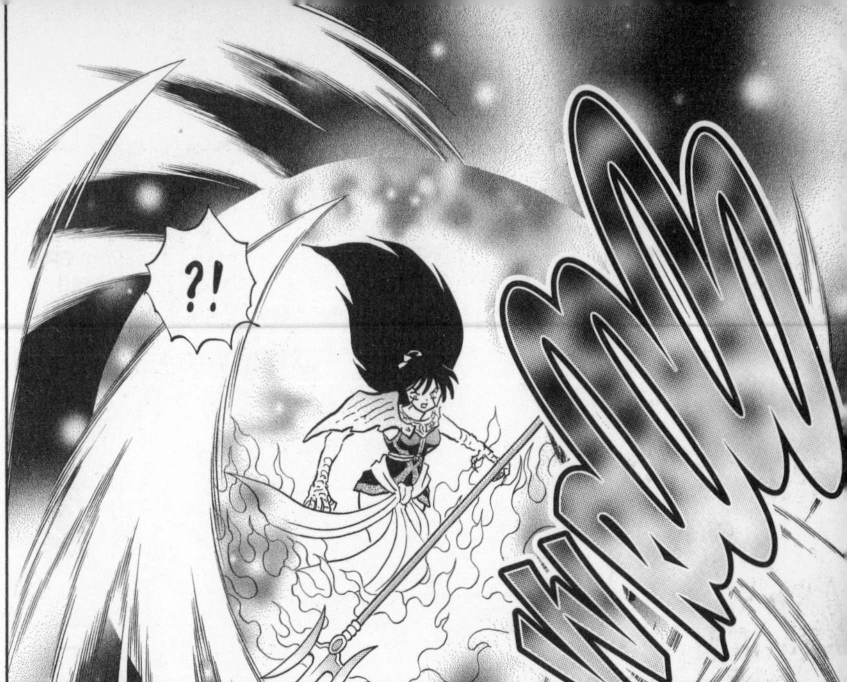
?!

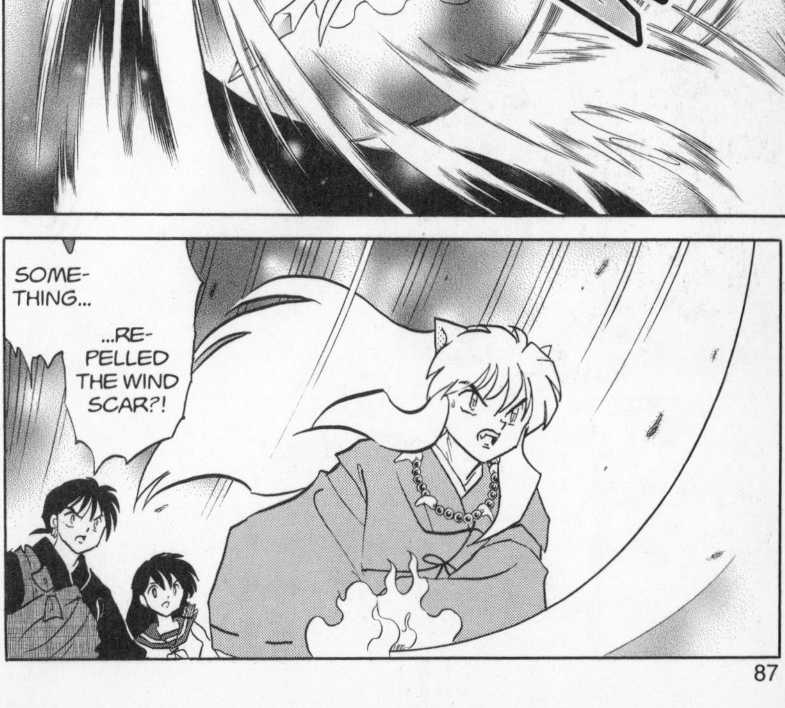
SOME-THING...
...RE-PELLED THE WIND SCAR?!

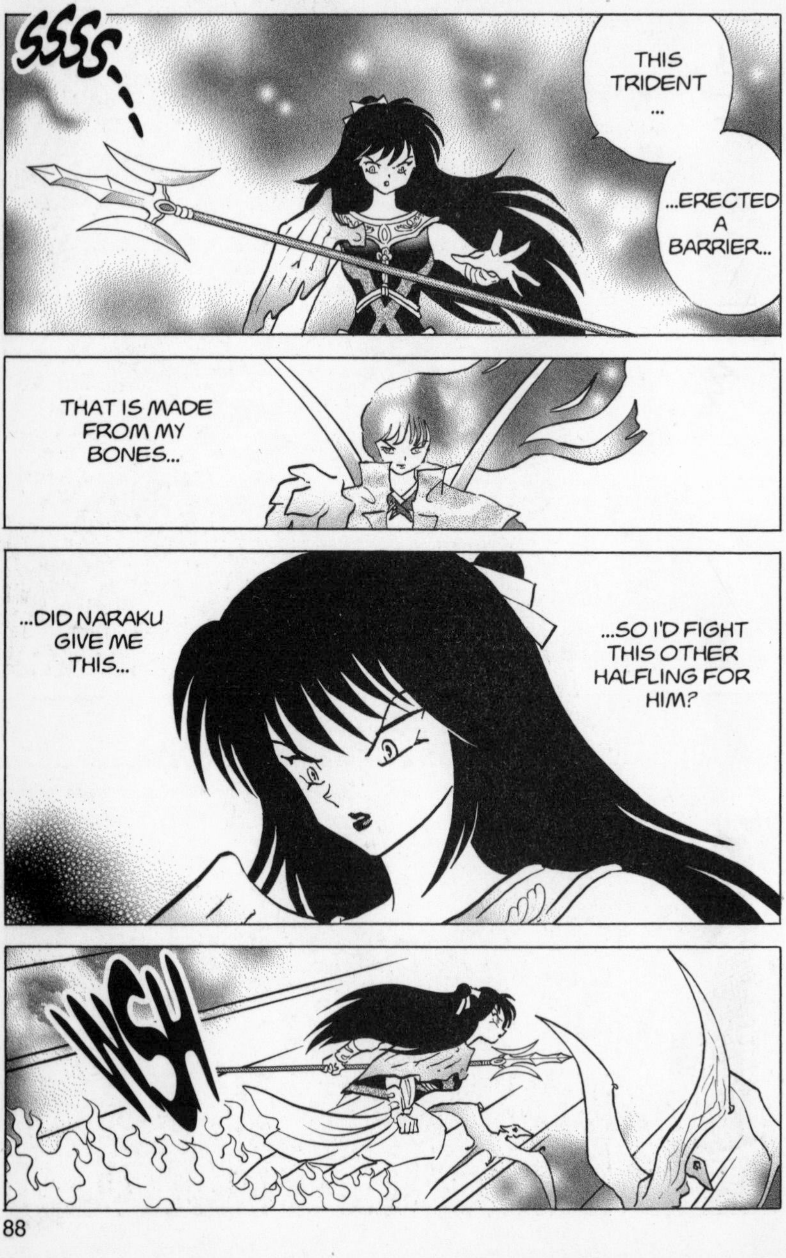
SSSS...
THIS TRIDENT ...
...ERECTED A BARRIER...
THAT IS MADE FROM MY BONES...
...DID NARAKU GIVE ME THIS...
...SO I'D FIGHT THIS OTHER HALFLING FOR HIM?
WSH

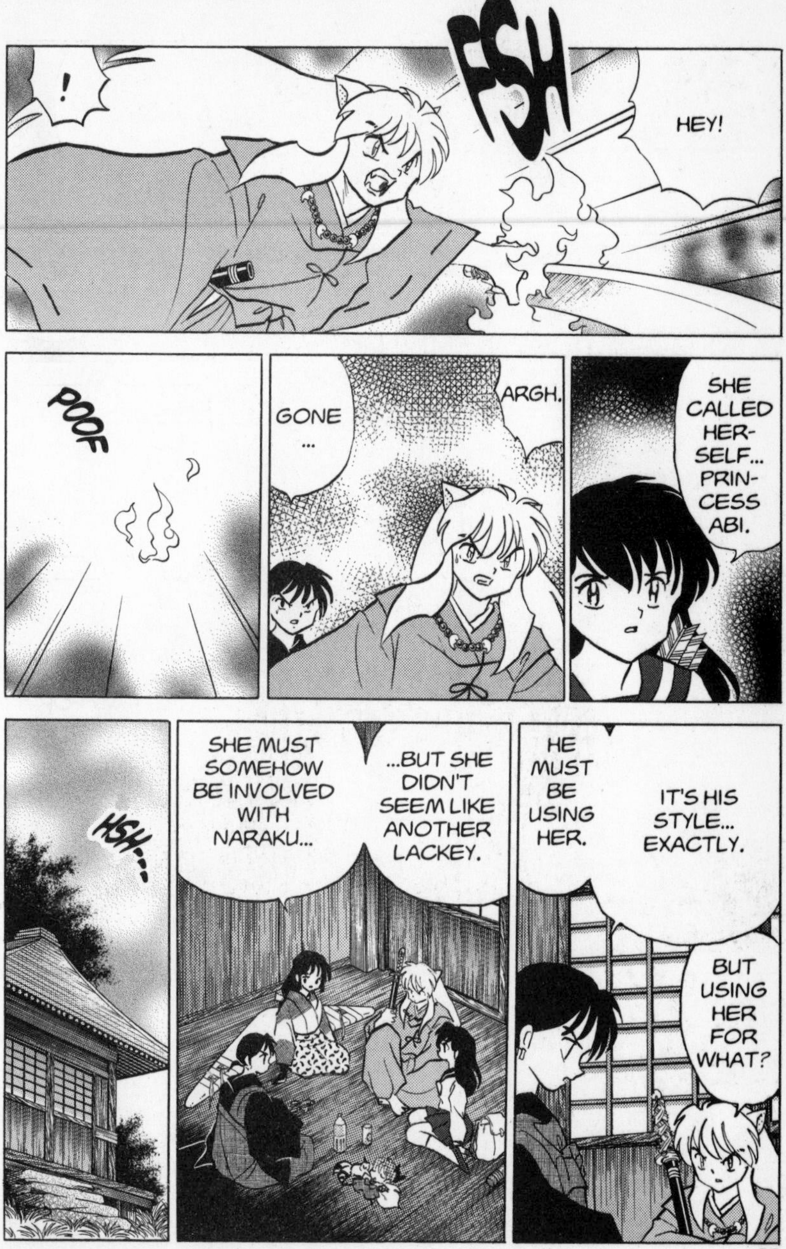
!
FSH
HEY!
POOF
GONE...
ARGH.
SHE CALLED HER-SELF... PRIN-CESS ABI.
HSH...
SHE MUST SOMEHOW BE INVOLVED WITH NARAKU...
...BUT SHE DIDN'T SEEM LIKE ANOTHER LACKEY.
HE MUST BE USING HER.
IT'S HIS STYLE... EXACTLY.
BUT USING HER FOR WHAT?

HE WANTS A DEMON RUNNING AROUND...

...HAVING HER BIRDS SUCK THE BLOOD OF HUMANS?

HOW CAN HE PROFIT FROM THAT?

NARAKU IS AS DETERMINED AS WE ARE TO GET THAT SHIKON SHARD...

...WHICH MEANS REACHING THE BORDERLAND BETWEEN THIS WORLD AND THE NEXT.

SO COLLECTING HUMAN BLOOD...

...HAS SOMETHING TO WITH THE BORDERLAND...?

IT'S THE ONLY THING THAT MAKES SENSE.

BUT HOW COULD THEY BE CONNECTED ...?

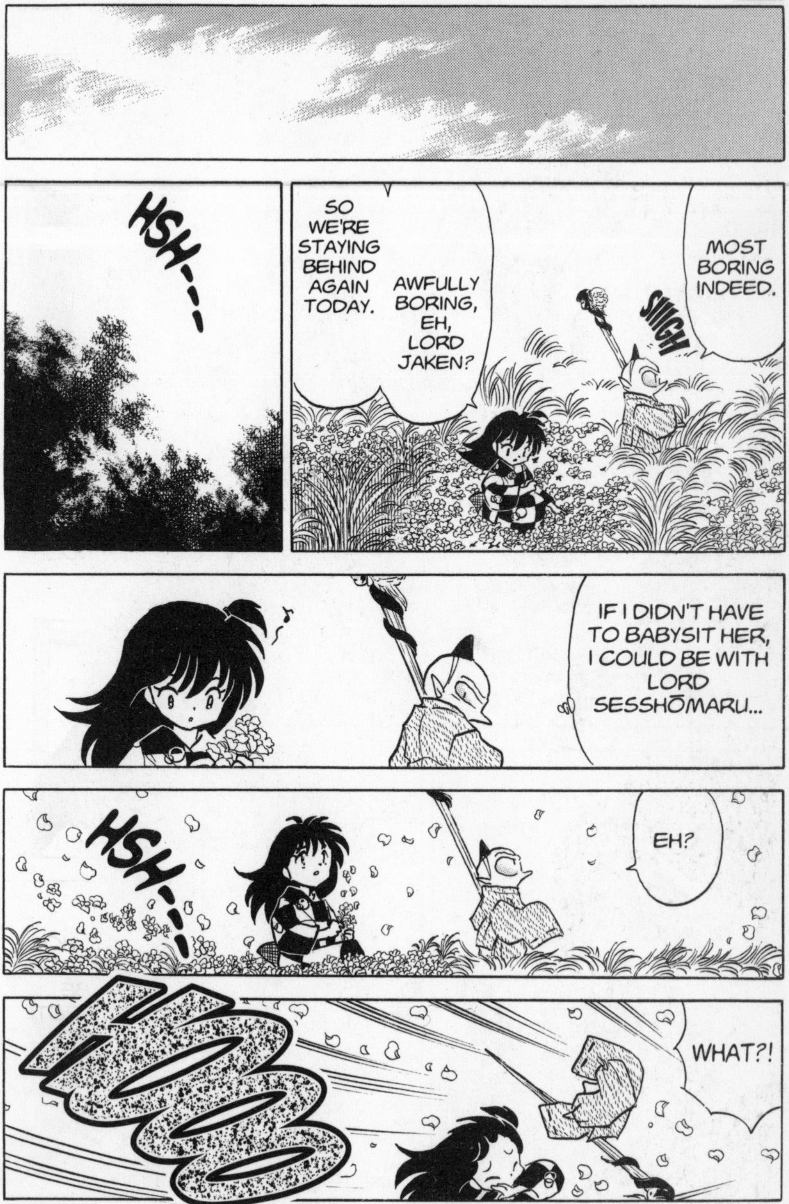
HSH-...
SO WE'RE STAYING BEHIND AGAIN TODAY.
AWFULLY BORING, EH, LORD JAKEN?
SIIGH
MOST BORING INDEED.
IF I DIDN'T HAVE TO BABYSIT HER, I COULD BE WITH LORD SESSHŌMARU...
HSH-...
EH?
WHAT?!

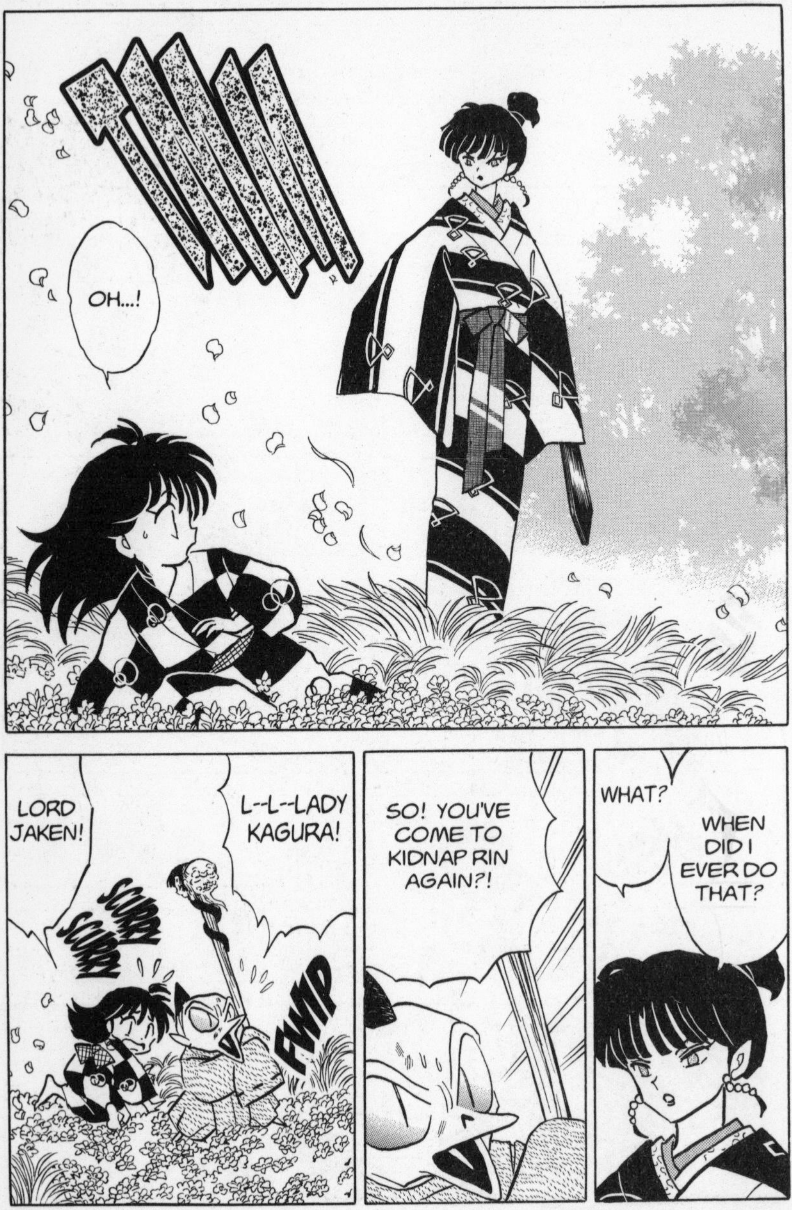
OH...!
LORD JAKEN!
L--L--LADY KAGURA!
SCURRY SCURRY
FWIP
SO! YOU'VE COME TO KIDNAP RIN AGAIN?!
WHAT?
WHEN DID I EVER DO THAT?

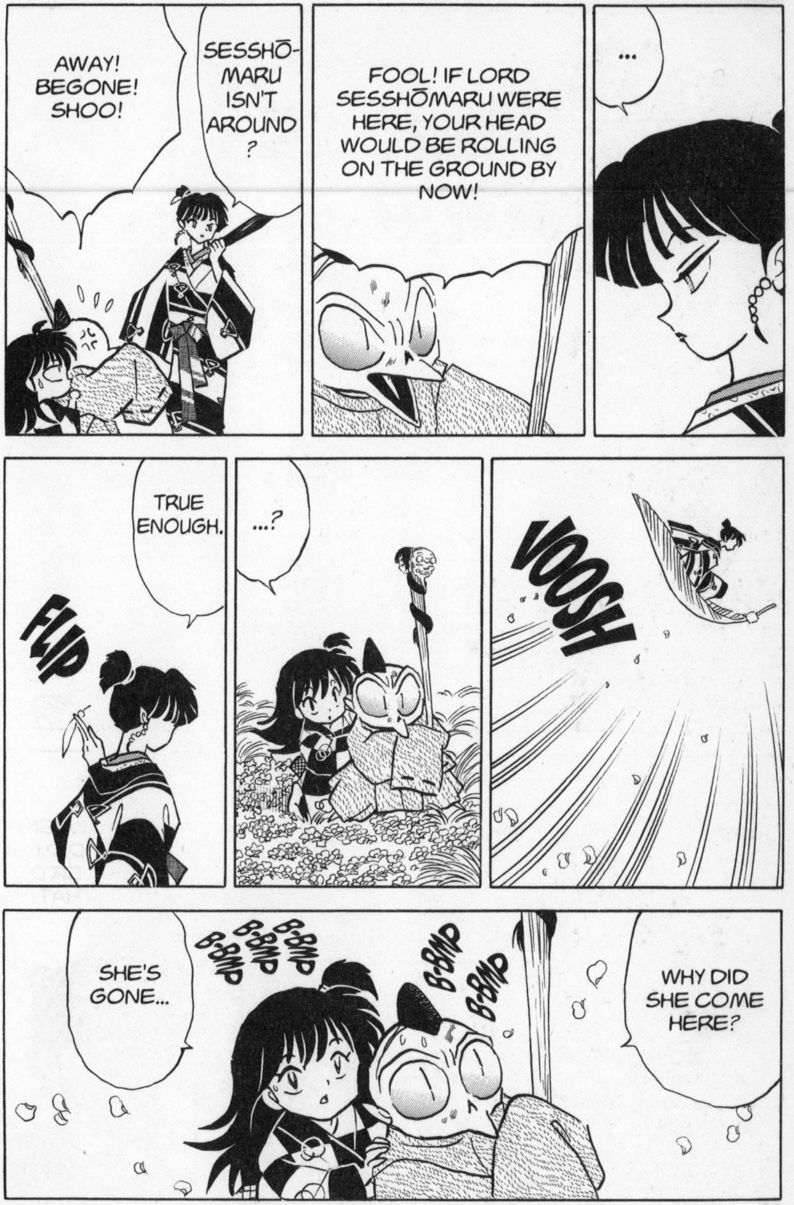
AWAY! BEGONE! SHOO!
SESSHŌ-MARU ISN'T AROUND?
FOOL! IF LORD SESSHŌMARU WERE HERE, YOUR HEAD WOULD BE ROLLING ON THE GROUND BY NOW!
...
TRUE ENOUGH.
FLIP
...?
VOOSH
SHE'S GONE...
B-BMP B-BMP B-BMP
B-BMP B-BMP
WHY DID SHE COME HERE?

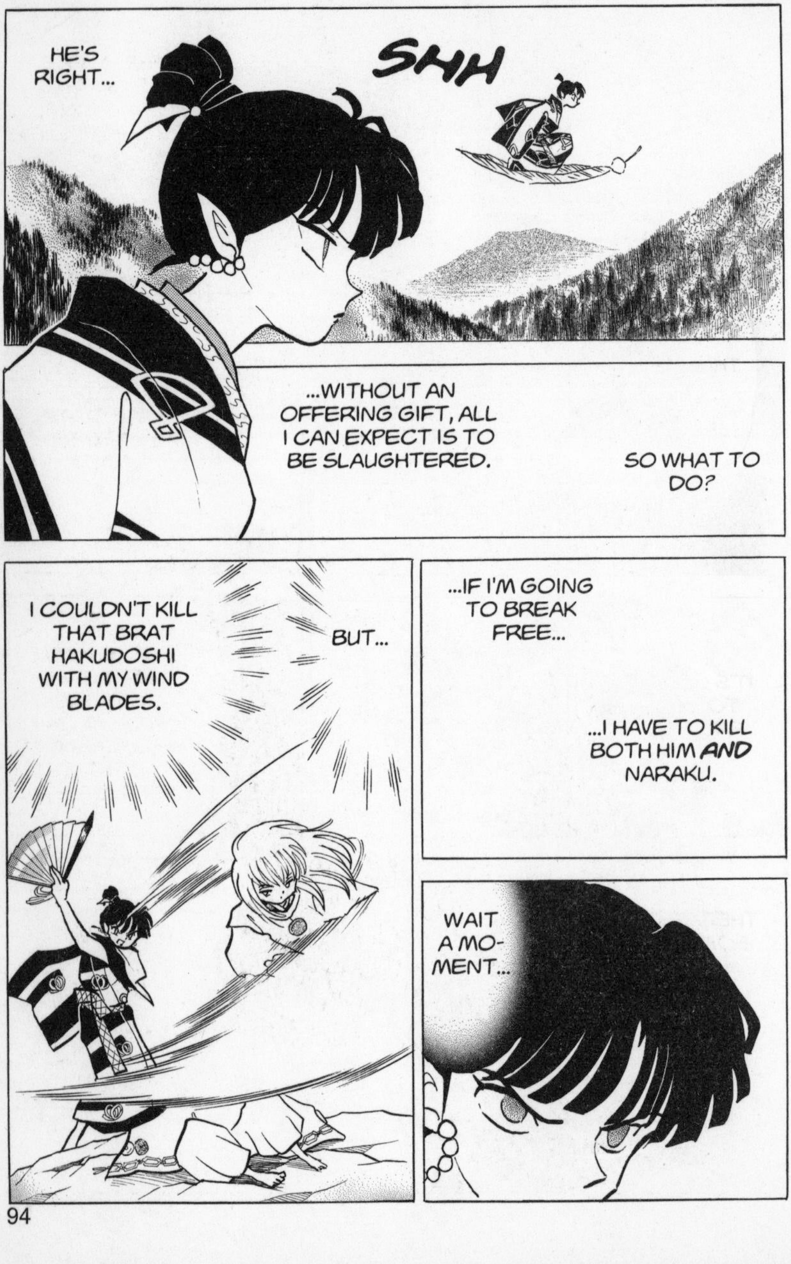
HE'S RIGHT...
SHH
...WITHOUT AN OFFERING GIFT, ALL I CAN EXPECT IS TO BE SLAUGHTERED.
SO WHAT TO DO?
I COULDN'T KILL THAT BRAT HAKUDOSHI WITH MY WIND BLADES.
BUT...
...IF I'M GOING TO BREAK FREE...
...I HAVE TO KILL BOTH HIM AND NARAKU.
WAIT A MO-MENT...

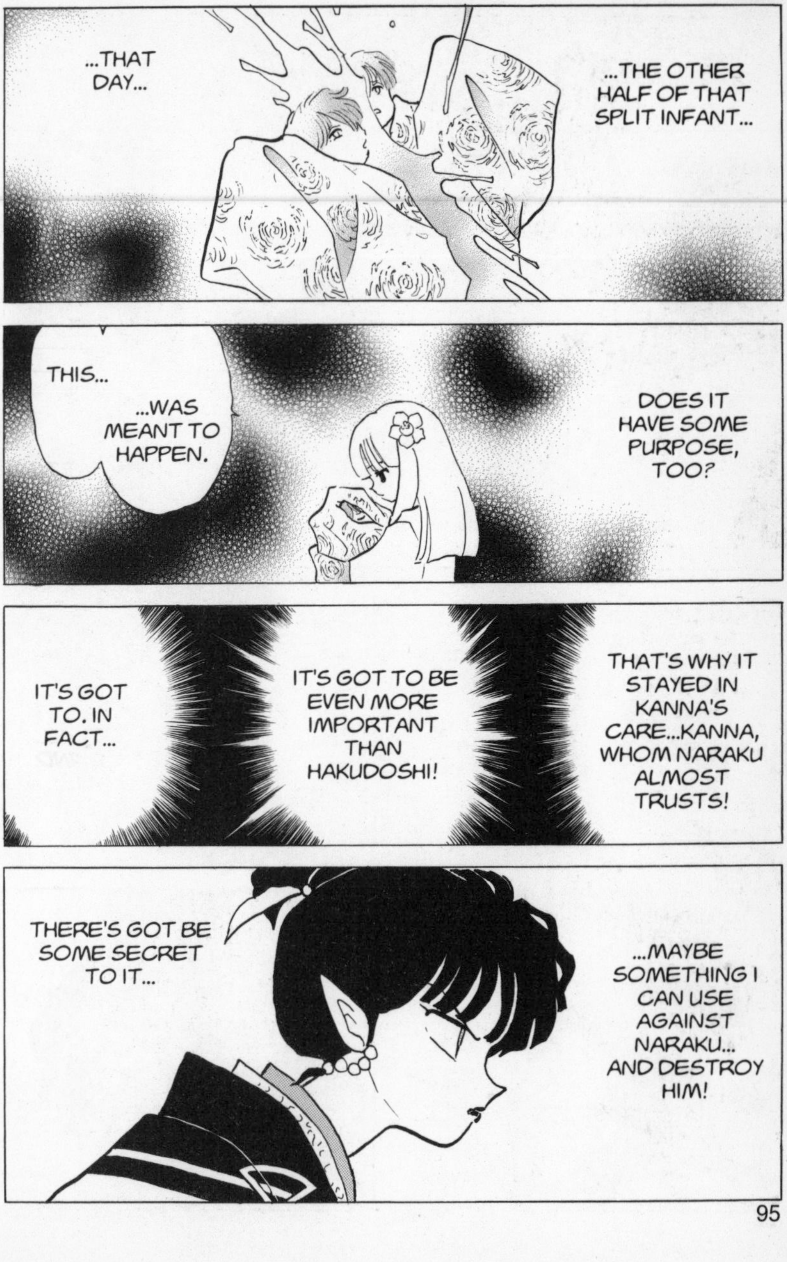
...THAT DAY...
...THE OTHER HALF OF THAT SPLIT INFANT...
THIS...
...WAS MEANT TO HAPPEN.
DOES IT HAVE SOME PURPOSE, TOO?
IT'S GOT TO. IN FACT...
IT'S GOT TO BE EVEN MORE IMPORTANT THAN HAKUDOSHI!
THAT'S WHY IT STAYED IN KANNA'S CARE...KANNA, WHOM NARAKU ALMOST TRUSTS!
THERE'S GOT BE SOME SECRET TO IT...
...MAYBE SOMETHING I CAN USE AGAINST NARAKU... AND DESTROY HIM!

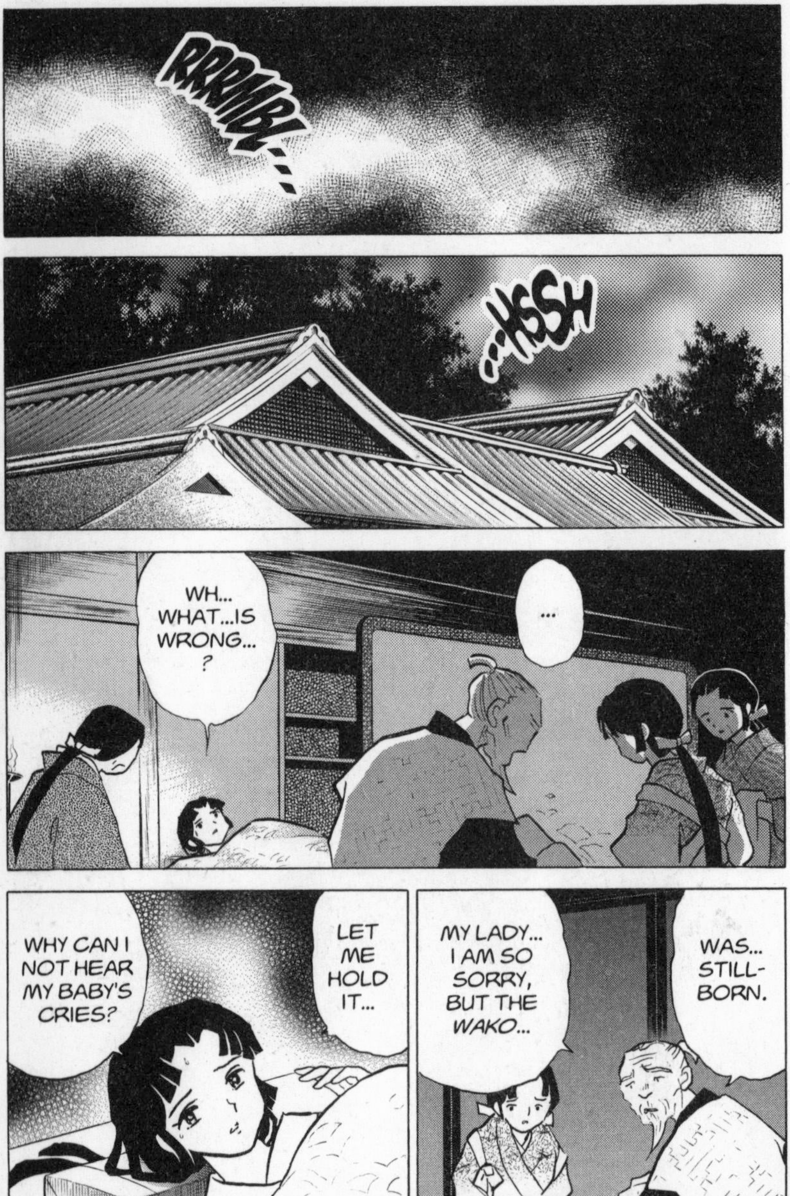
RRRMBL...
...HSSH
WH... WHAT...IS WRONG... ?
...
WHY CAN I NOT HEAR MY BABY'S CRIES?
LET ME HOLD IT...
MY LADY... I AM SO SORRY, BUT THE WAKO...
WAS... STILL-BORN.

*WAKO: THE MALE CHILD OF A NOBLEMAN OR LADY.

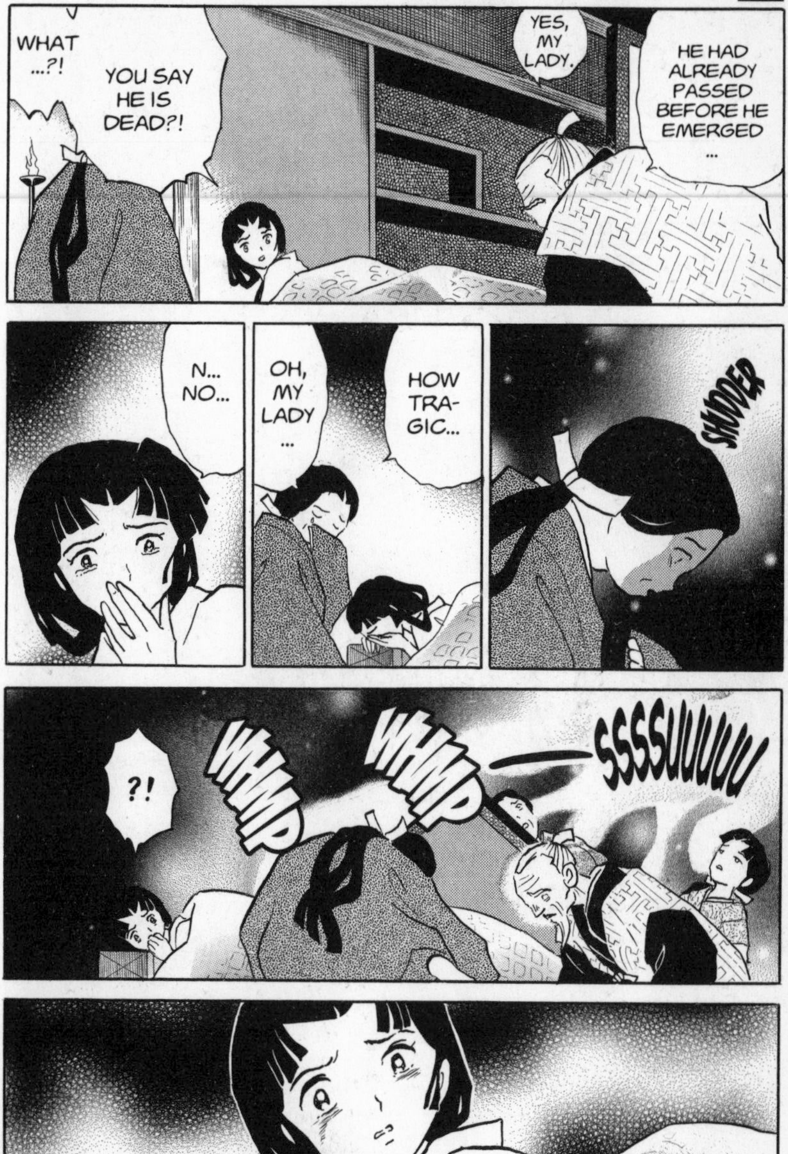
WHAT ...?!
YOU SAY HE IS DEAD?!
YES, MY LADY.
HE HAD ALREADY PASSED BEFORE HE EMERGED ...
N... NO...
OH, MY LADY ...
HOW TRA-GIC...
SHUDDER
?!
WHMP
WHMP
SSSUUUUUU

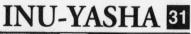

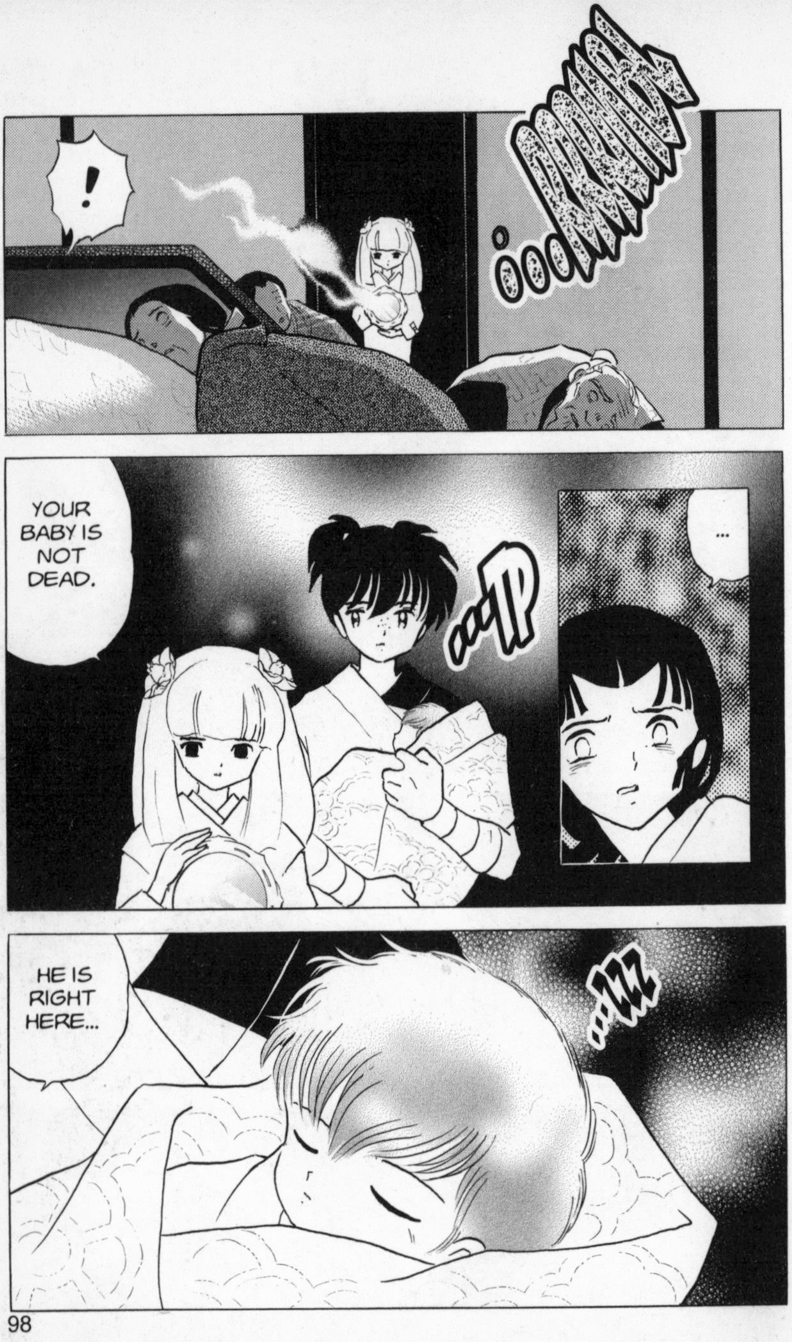
!
YOUR BABY IS NOT DEAD.
...
HE IS RIGHT HERE...

SCROLL 6

THE VILLAGE OF THE HOLY WOMAN

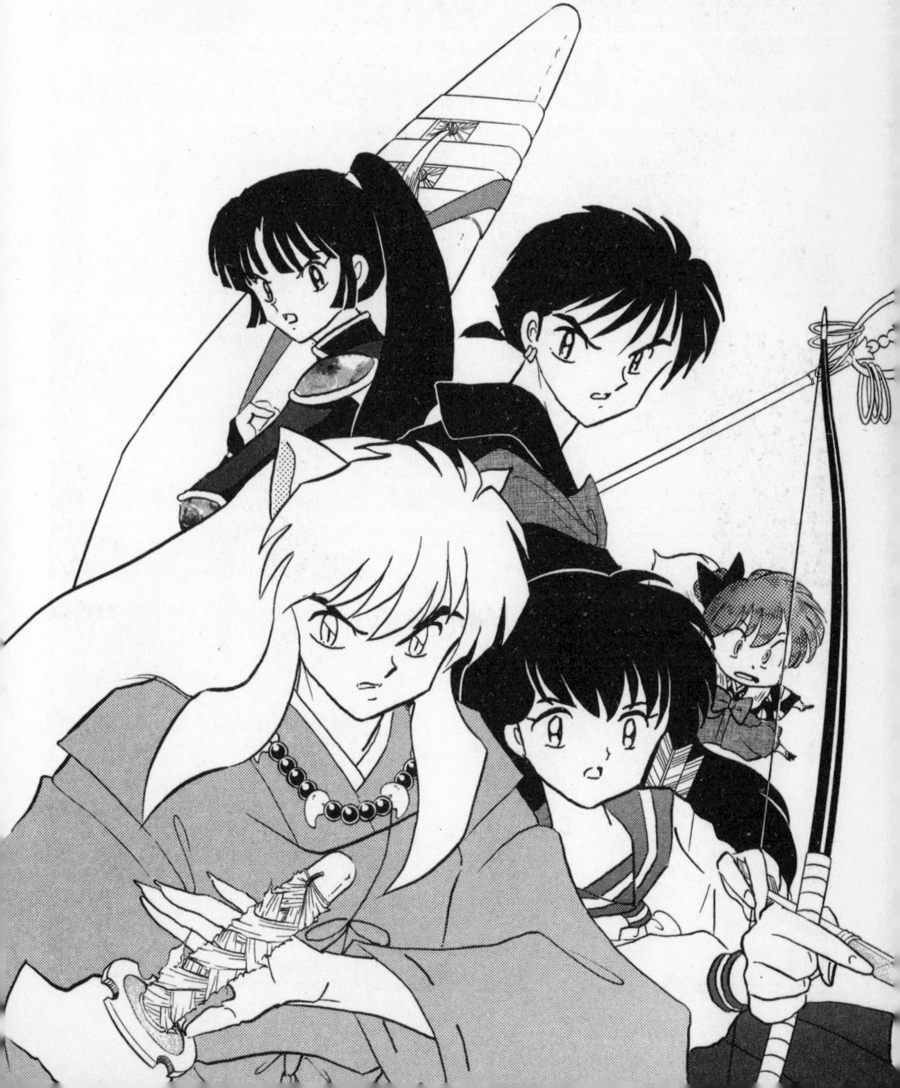

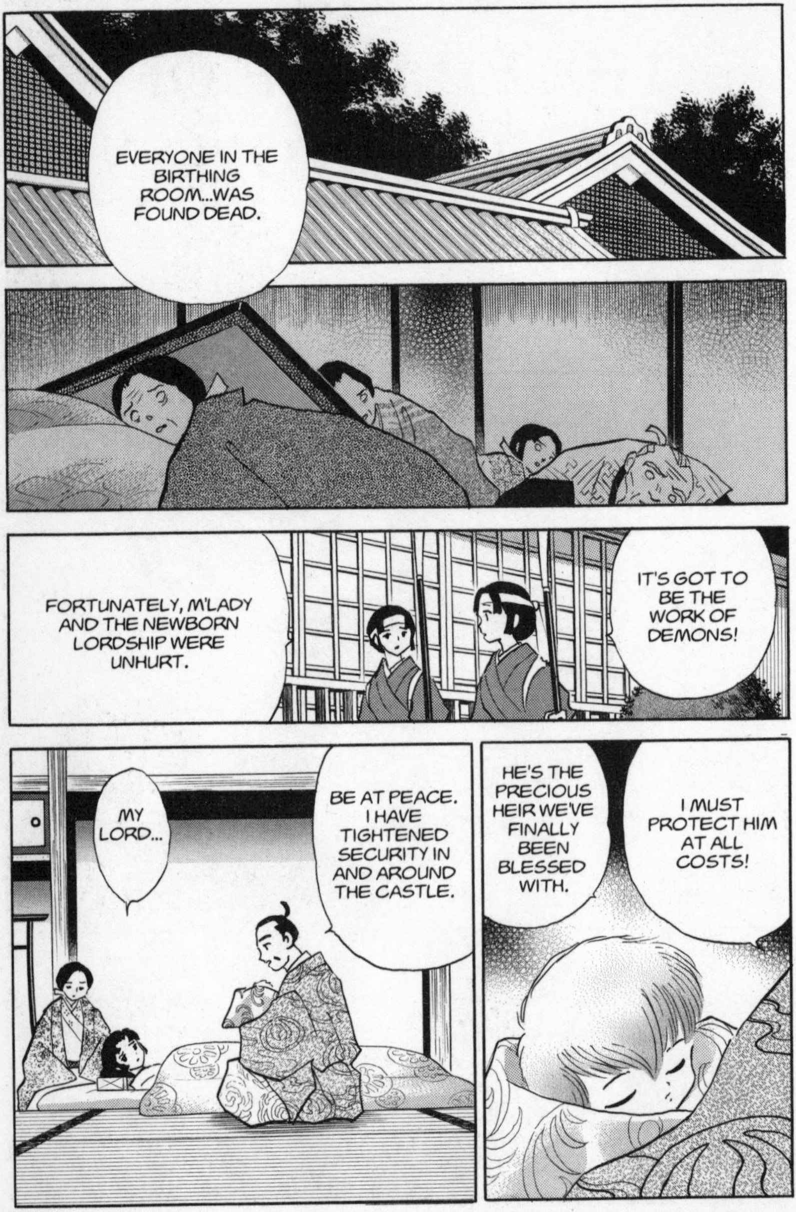
EVERYONE IN THE BIRTHING ROOM...WAS FOUND DEAD.
FORTUNATELY, M'LADY AND THE NEWBORN LORDSHIP WERE UNHURT.
IT'S GOT TO BE THE WORK OF DEMONS!
MY LORD...
BE AT PEACE. I HAVE TIGHTENED SECURITY IN AND AROUND THE CASTLE.
HE'S THE PRECIOUS HEIR WE'VE FINALLY BEEN BLESSED WITH.
I MUST PROTECT HIM AT ALL COSTS!

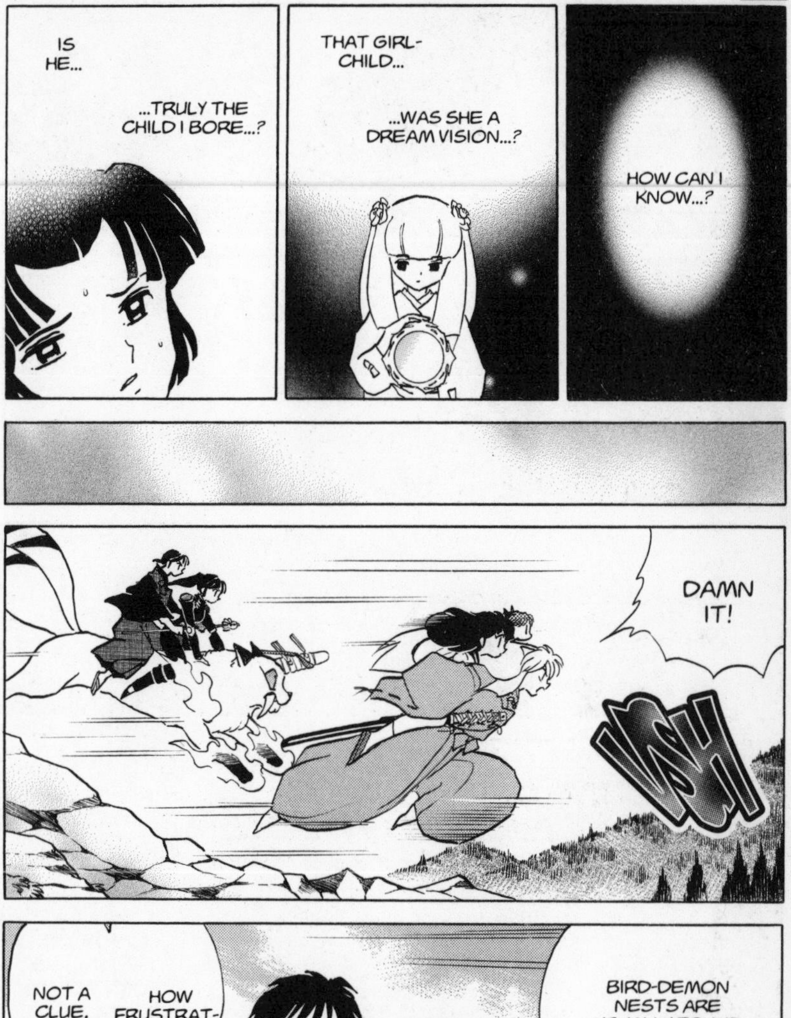
IS HE...
...TRULY THE CHILD I BORE...?
THAT GIRL-CHILD...
...WAS SHE A DREAM VISION...?
HOW CAN I KNOW...?
DAMN IT!
VSH
NOT A CLUE.
HOW FRUSTRAT-ING.
BIRD-DEMON NESTS ARE USUALLY FOUND HIGH ON CRAGGY PEAKS, BUT...

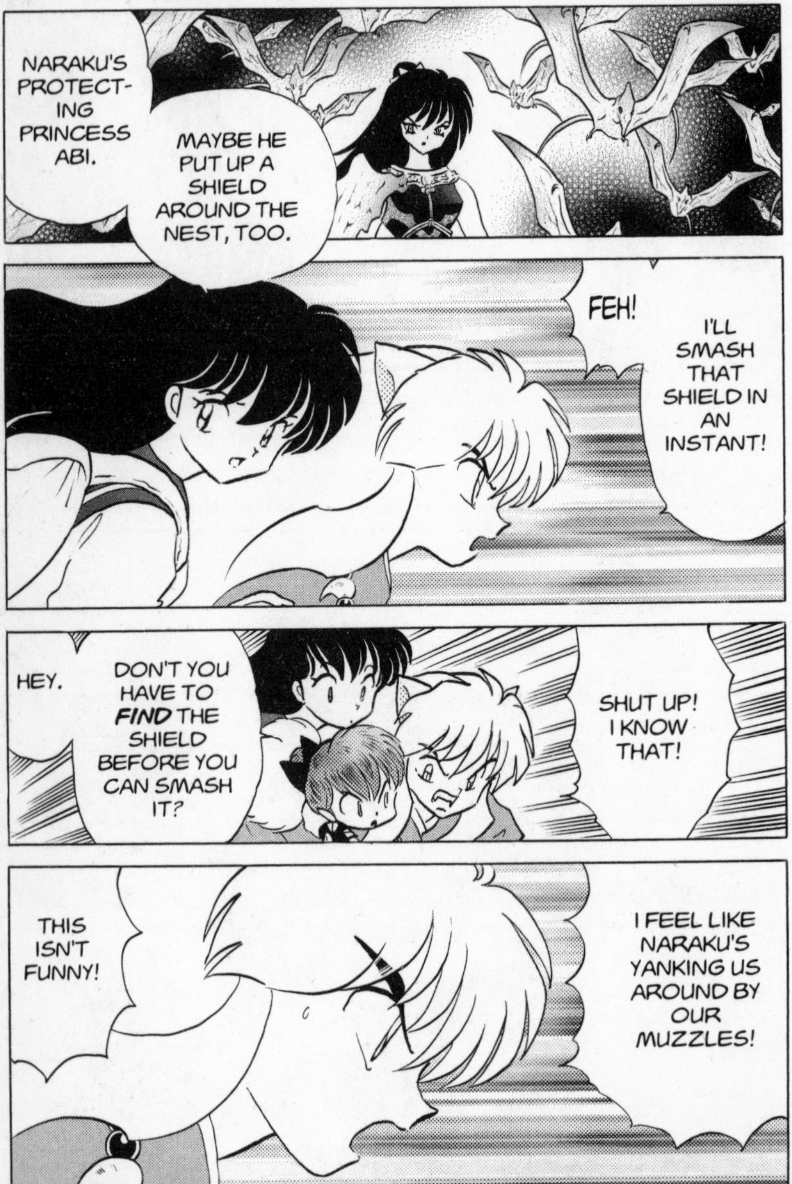
NARAKU'S PROTECT-ING PRINCESS ABI.
MAYBE HE PUT UP A SHIELD AROUND THE NEST, TOO.
FEH!
I'LL SMASH THAT SHIELD IN AN INSTANT!
HEY.
DON'T YOU HAVE TO ***FIND*** THE SHIELD BEFORE YOU CAN SMASH IT?
SHUT UP! I KNOW THAT!
THIS ISN'T FUNNY!
I FEEL LIKE NARAKU'S YANKING US AROUND BY OUR MUZZLES!

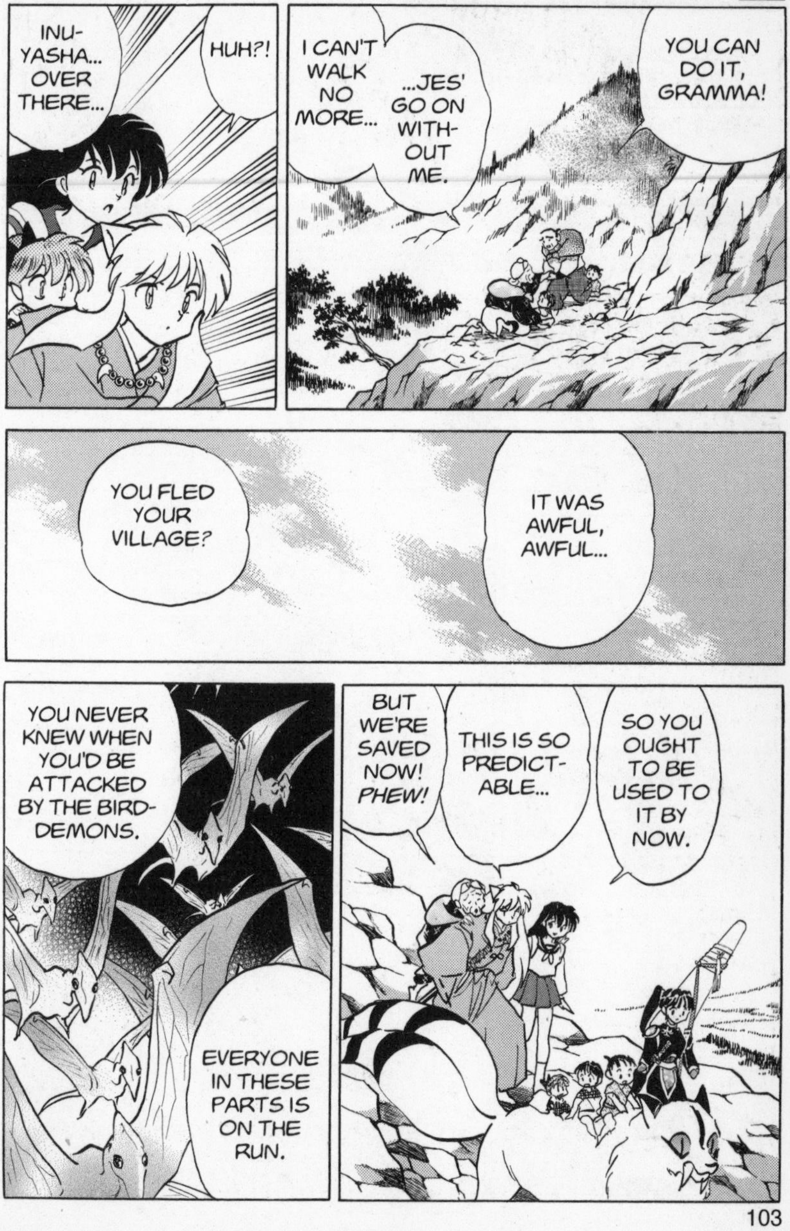
INU-YASHA... OVER THERE...
HUH?!
I CAN'T WALK NO MORE...
...JES' GO ON WITHOUT ME.
YOU CAN DO IT, GRAMMA!
YOU FLED YOUR VILLAGE?
IT WAS AWFUL, AWFUL...
YOU NEVER KNEW WHEN YOU'D BE ATTACKED BY THE BIRD-DEMONS.
EVERYONE IN THESE PARTS IS ON THE RUN.
BUT WE'RE SAVED NOW! *PHEW!*
THIS IS SO PREDICTABLE...
SO YOU OUGHT TO BE USED TO IT BY NOW.

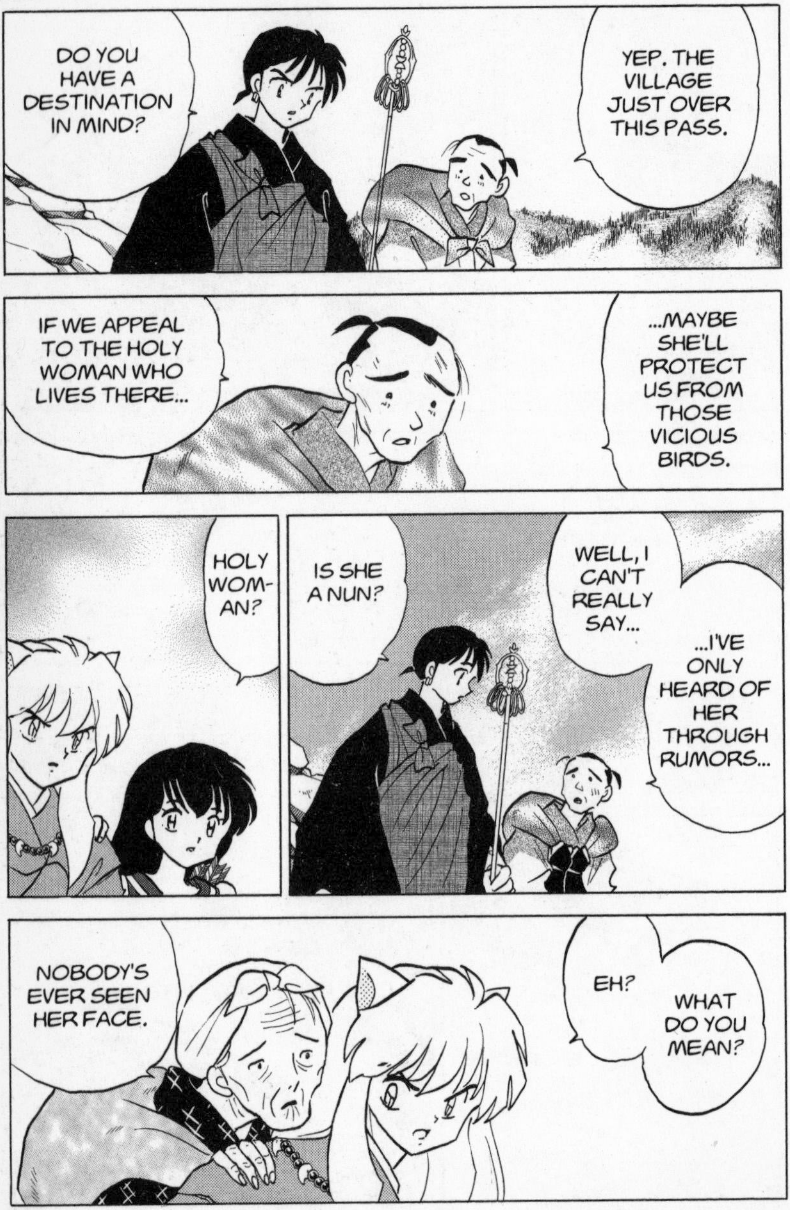
DO YOU HAVE A DESTINATION IN MIND?
YEP. THE VILLAGE JUST OVER THIS PASS.
IF WE APPEAL TO THE HOLY WOMAN WHO LIVES THERE...
...MAYBE SHE'LL PROTECT US FROM THOSE VICIOUS BIRDS.
HOLY WOM-AN?
IS SHE A NUN?
WELL, I CAN'T REALLY SAY...
...I'VE ONLY HEARD OF HER THROUGH RUMORS...
NOBODY'S EVER SEEN HER FACE.
EH?
WHAT DO YOU MEAN?

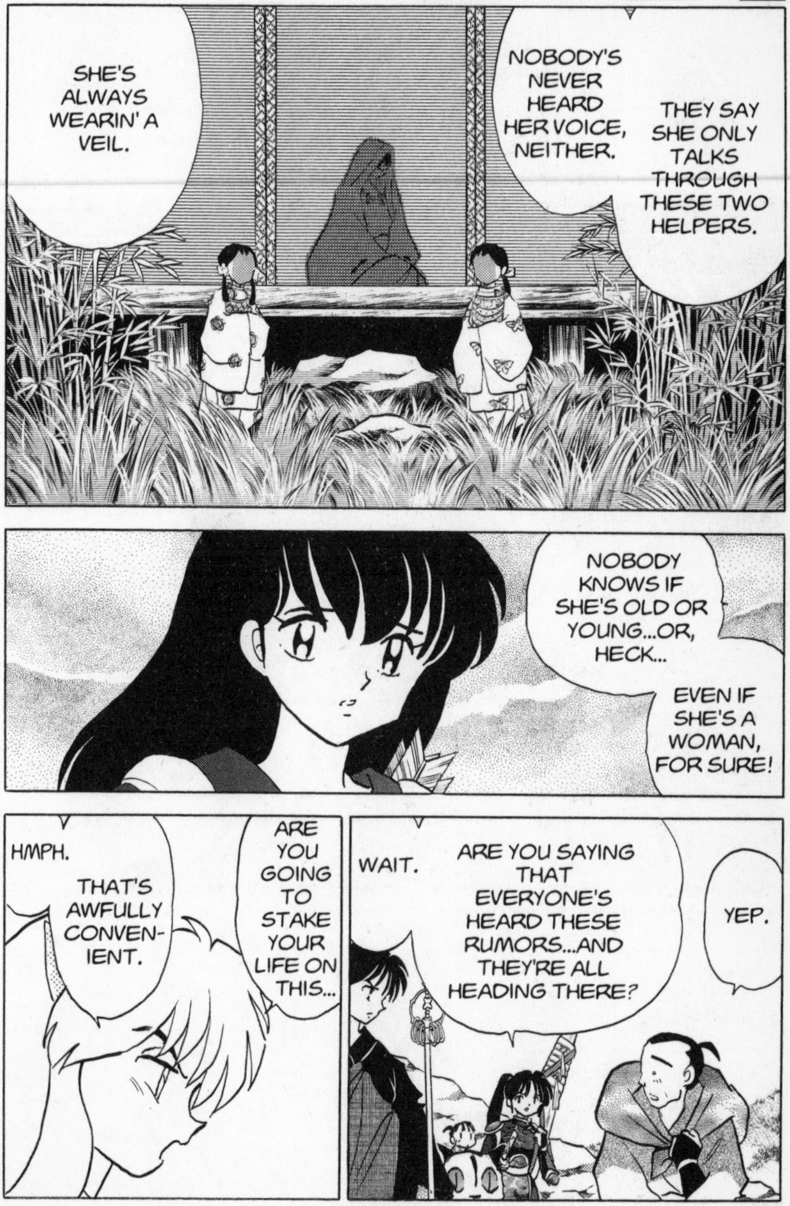
SHE'S ALWAYS WEARIN' A VEIL.
NOBODY'S NEVER HEARD HER VOICE, NEITHER.
THEY SAY SHE ONLY TALKS THROUGH THESE TWO HELPERS.
NOBODY KNOWS IF SHE'S OLD OR YOUNG...OR, HECK...
EVEN IF SHE'S A WOMAN, FOR SURE!
HMPH.
THAT'S AWFULLY CONVEN-IENT.
ARE YOU GOING TO STAKE YOUR LIFE ON THIS...
WAIT.
ARE YOU SAYING THAT EVERYONE'S HEARD THESE RUMORS...AND THEY'RE ALL HEADING THERE?
YEP.

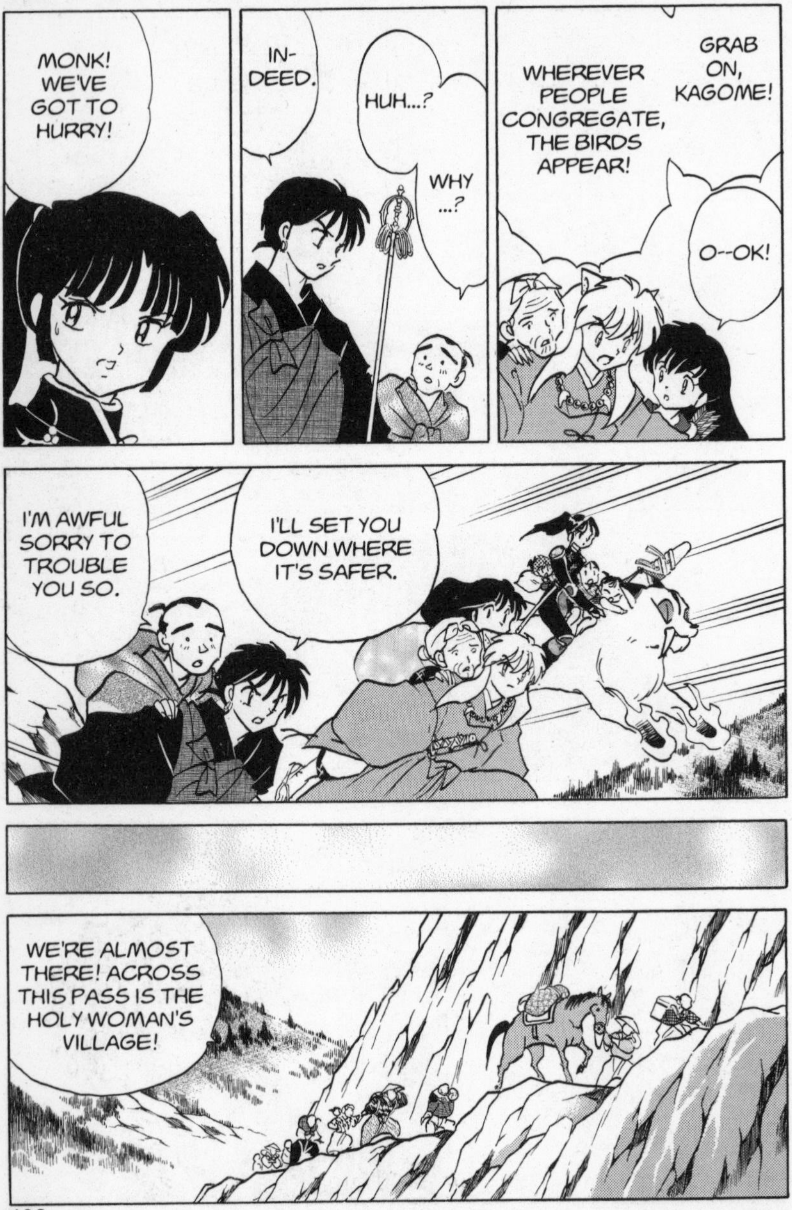
MONK! WE'VE GOT TO HURRY!
IN-DEED.
HUH...?
WHY ...?
WHEREVER PEOPLE CONGREGATE, THE BIRDS APPEAR!
GRAB ON, KAGOME!
O--OK!
I'M AWFUL SORRY TO TROUBLE YOU SO.
I'LL SET YOU DOWN WHERE IT'S SAFER.
WE'RE ALMOST THERE! ACROSS THIS PASS IS THE HOLY WOMAN'S VILLAGE!

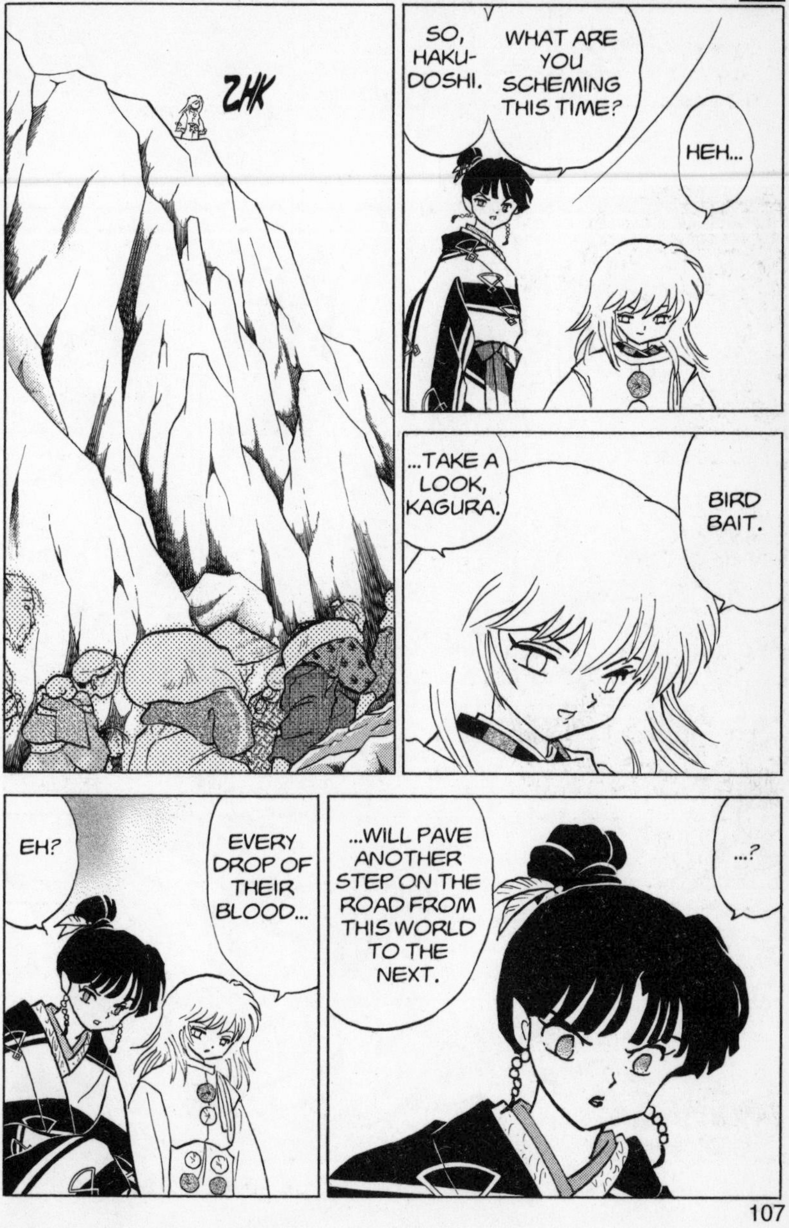
ZHK
SO, HAKU-DOSHI.
WHAT ARE YOU SCHEMING THIS TIME?
HEH...
...TAKE A LOOK, KAGURA.
BIRD BAIT.
EH?
EVERY DROP OF THEIR BLOOD...
...WILL PAVE ANOTHER STEP ON THE ROAD FROM THIS WORLD TO THE NEXT.
...?

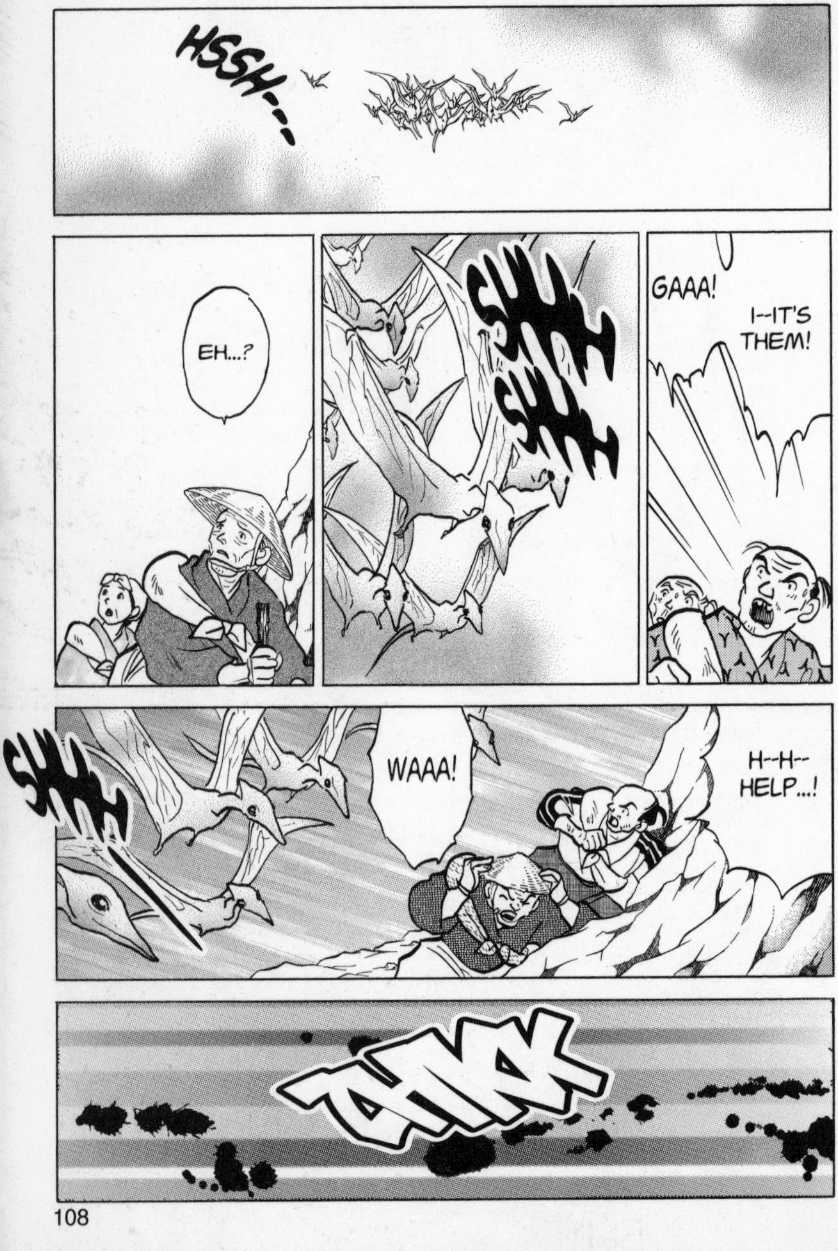
HSSH...
EH...?
SHH
SHH
GAAA!
I--IT'S THEM!
SHH
WAAA!
H--H-- HELP...!

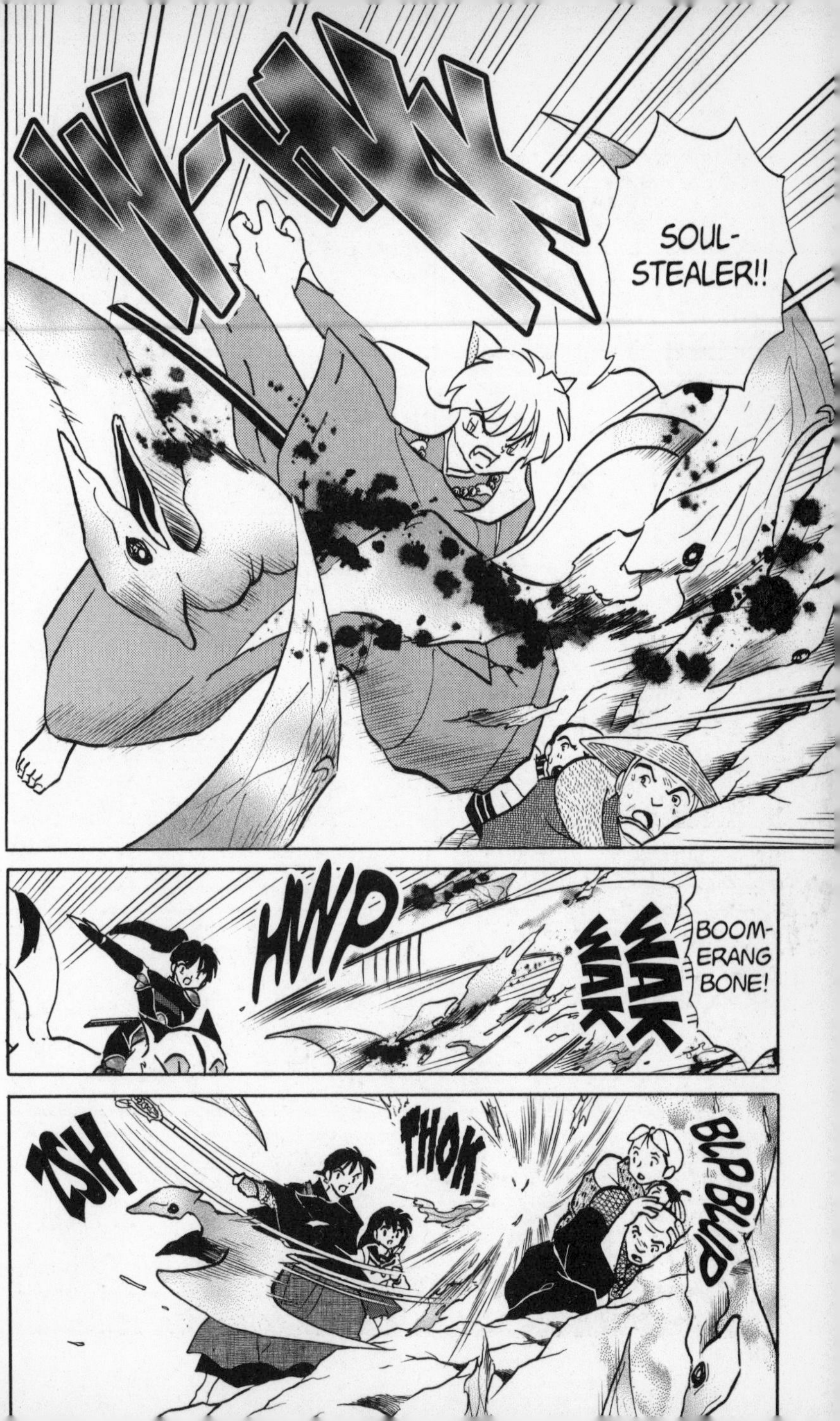
WHAM
SOUL-
STEALER!!
HWP
WAK WAK
BOOM-
ERANG
BONE!
TSH
THOK
BLUP BLUP

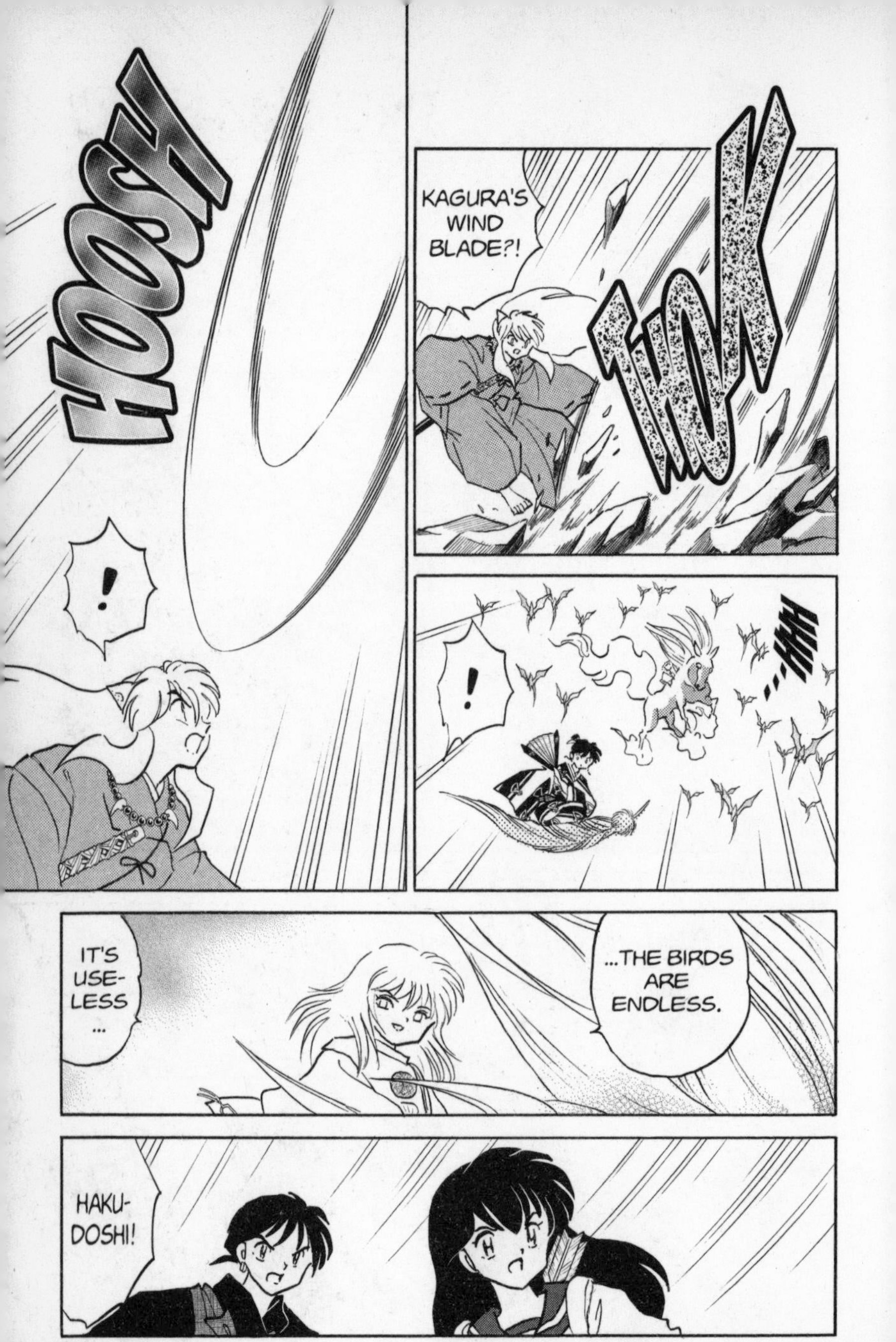
WHOOSH
!
KAGURA'S WIND BLADE?!
THOCK
!
...HHH
IT'S USELESS...
...THE BIRDS ARE ENDLESS.
HAKU-DOSHI!

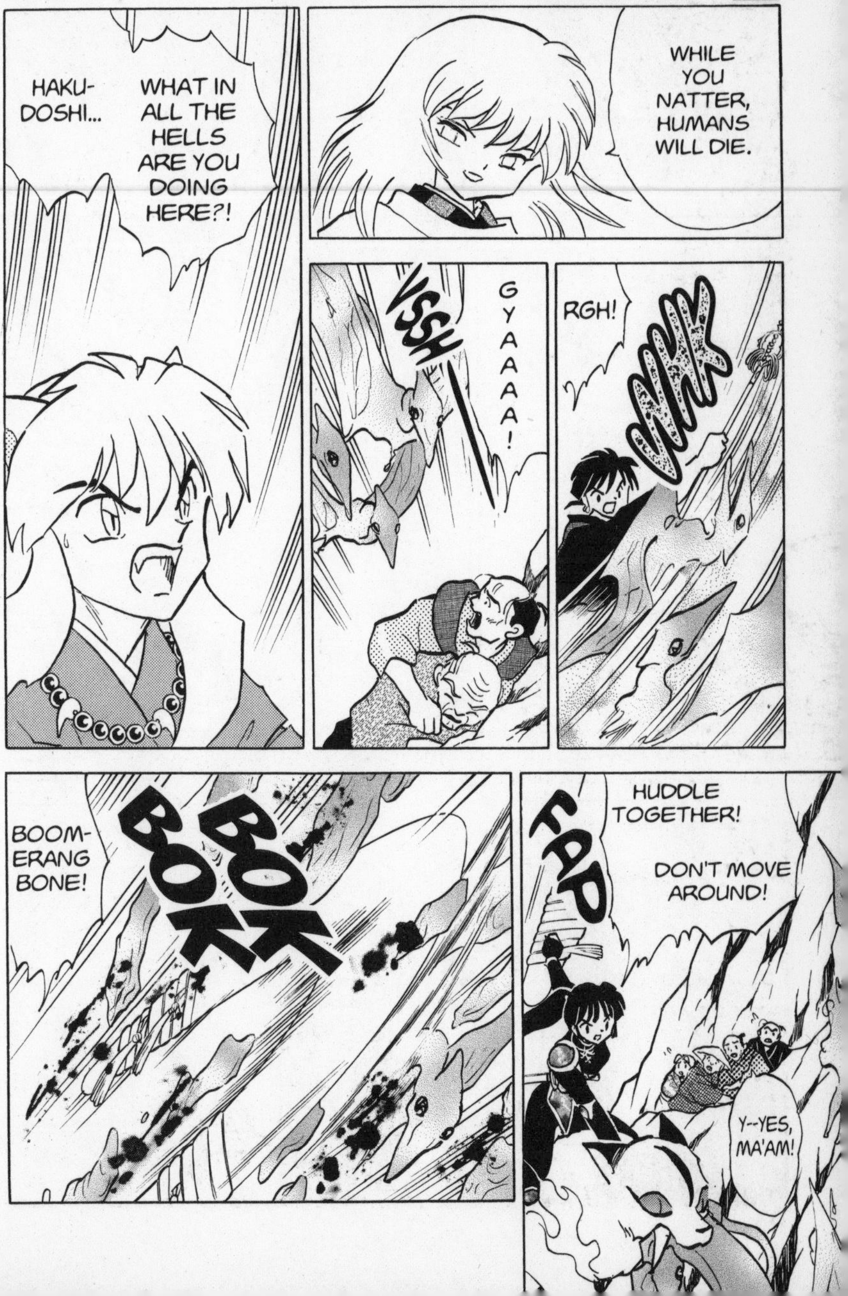
WHILE YOU NATTER, HUMANS WILL DIE.
HAKU-DOSHI...
WHAT IN ALL THE HELLS ARE YOU DOING HERE?!
RGH!
WHAK
GYAAAAA!
VSSH
HUDDLE TOGETHER!
DON'T MOVE AROUND!
FAP
Y--YES, MA'AM!
BOOM-ERANG BONE!
BOKK

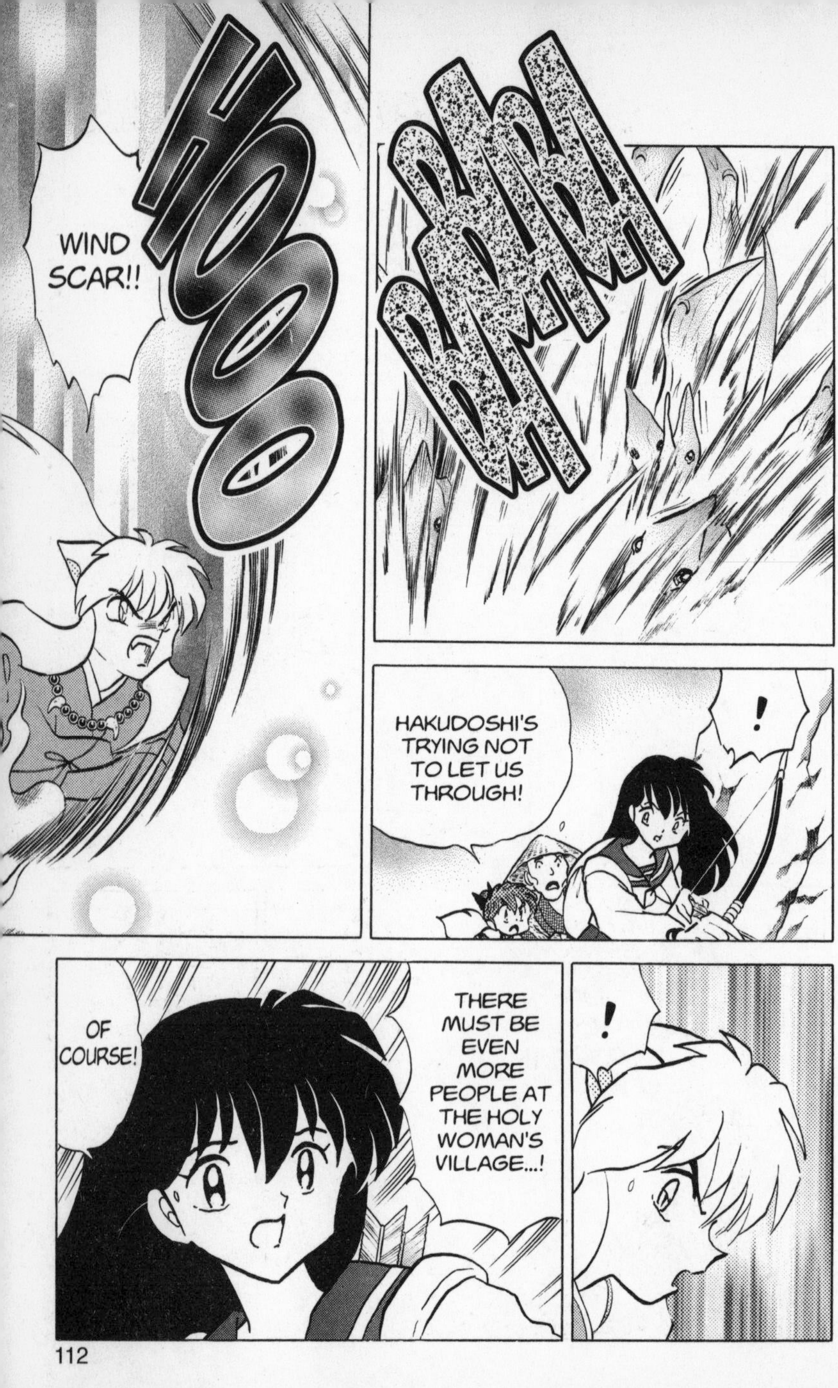
WIND SCAR!!
HOOOO
BAM BAM BAM
HAKUDOSHI'S TRYING NOT TO LET US THROUGH!
!
OF COURSE!
THERE MUST BE EVEN MORE PEOPLE AT THE HOLY WOMAN'S VILLAGE...!
!

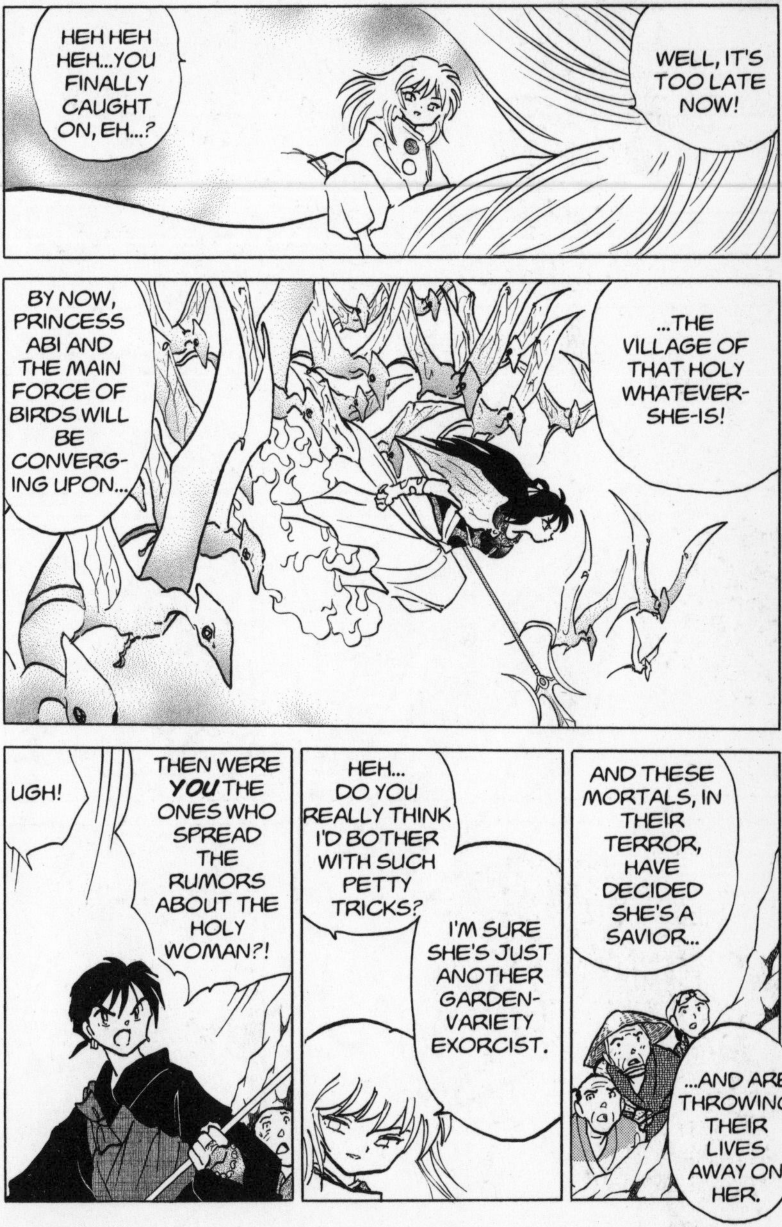
HEH HEH HEH...YOU FINALLY CAUGHT ON, EH...?
WELL, IT'S TOO LATE NOW!
BY NOW, PRINCESS ABI AND THE MAIN FORCE OF BIRDS WILL BE CONVERG-ING UPON...
...THE VILLAGE OF THAT HOLY WHATEVER-SHE-IS!
UGH!
THEN WERE *YOU* THE ONES WHO SPREAD THE RUMORS ABOUT THE HOLY WOMAN?!
HEH... DO YOU REALLY THINK I'D BOTHER WITH SUCH PETTY TRICKS?
I'M SURE SHE'S JUST ANOTHER GARDEN-VARIETY EXORCIST.
AND THESE MORTALS, IN THEIR TERROR, HAVE DECIDED SHE'S A SAVIOR...
...AND ARE THROWING THEIR LIVES AWAY ON HER.

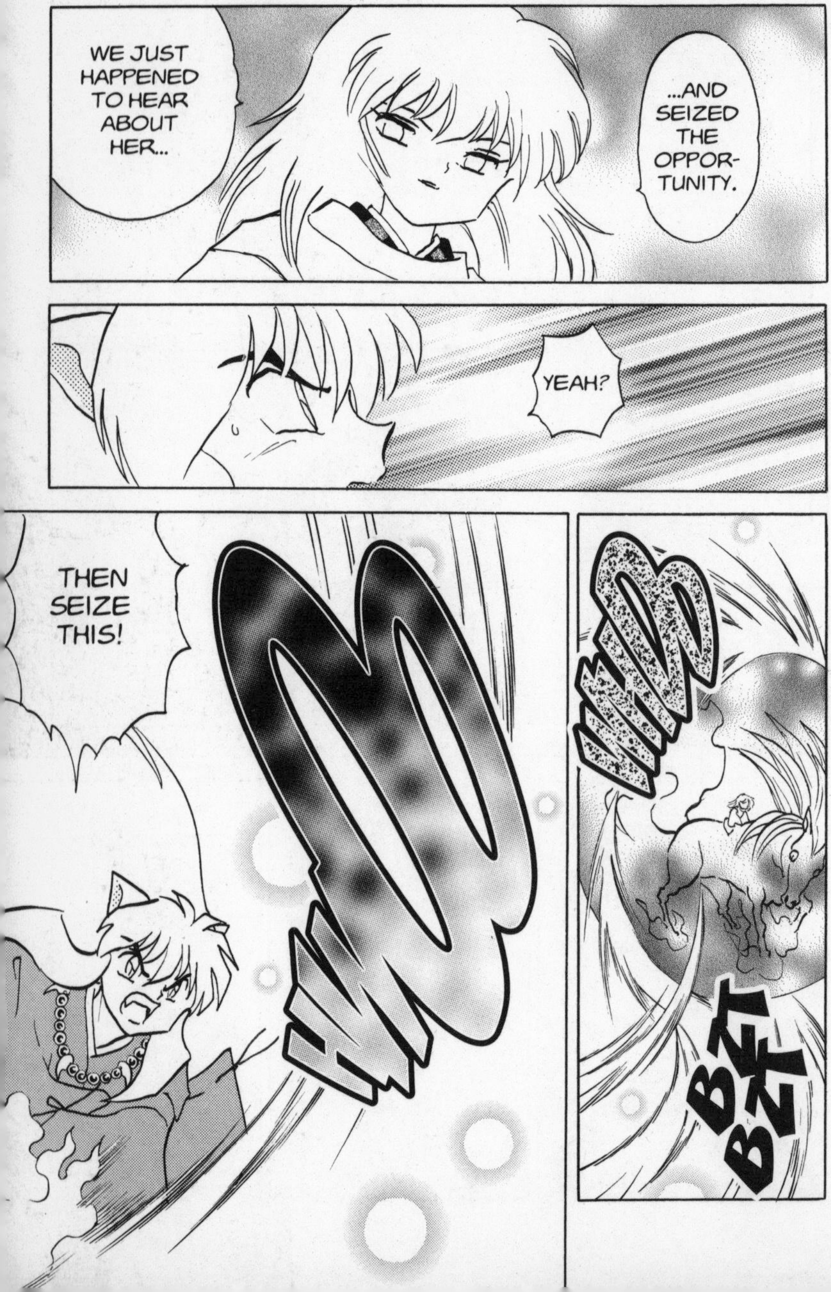
WE JUST HAPPENED TO HEAR ABOUT HER...
...AND SEIZED THE OPPOR-TUNITY.
YEAH?
THEN SEIZE THIS!
BZT BZT

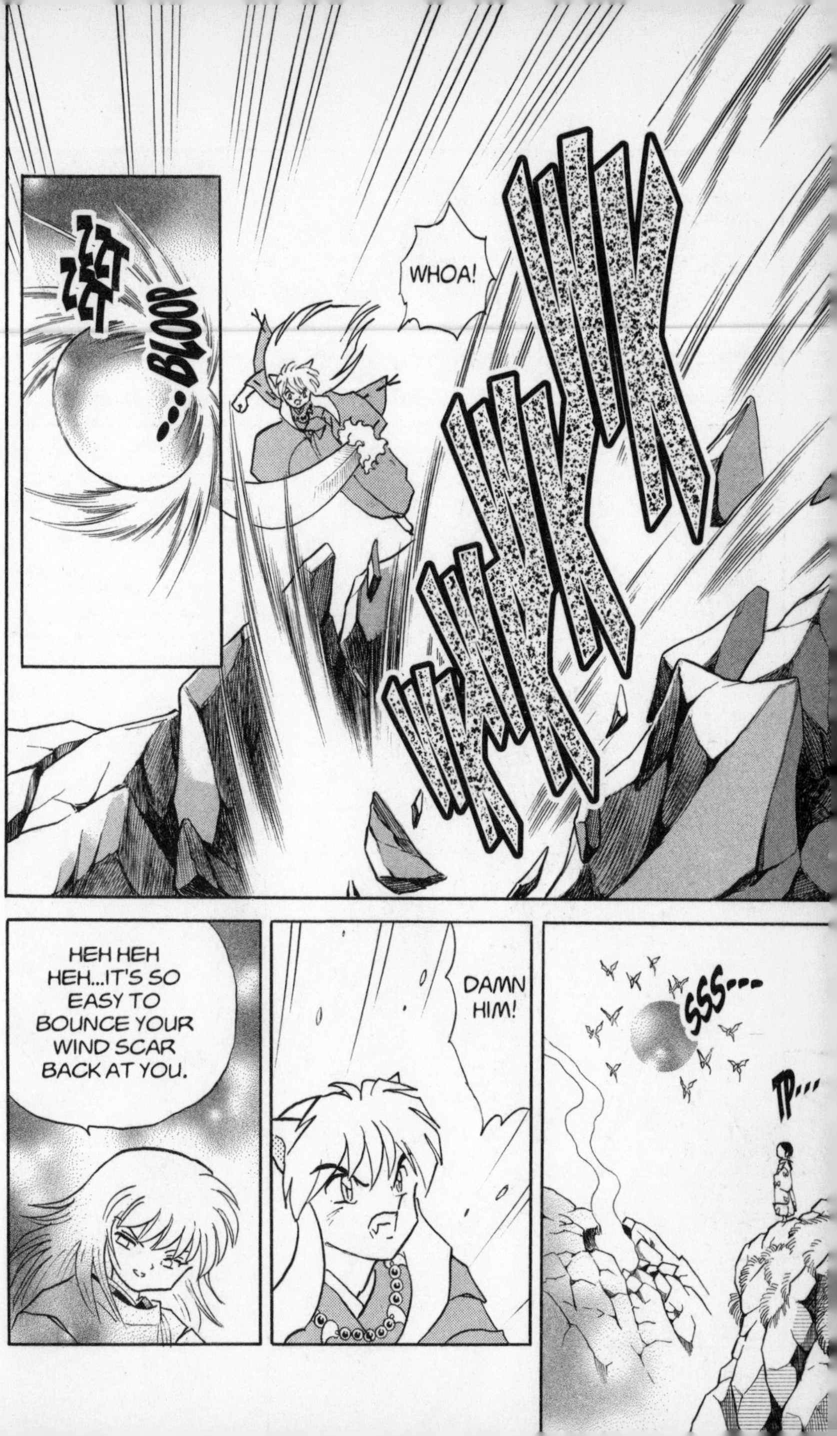
ZZZT ZZZT
...BLOOP
WHOA!
HEH HEH HEH...IT'S SO EASY TO BOUNCE YOUR WIND SCAR BACK AT YOU.
DAMN HIM!
SSS...
TP...

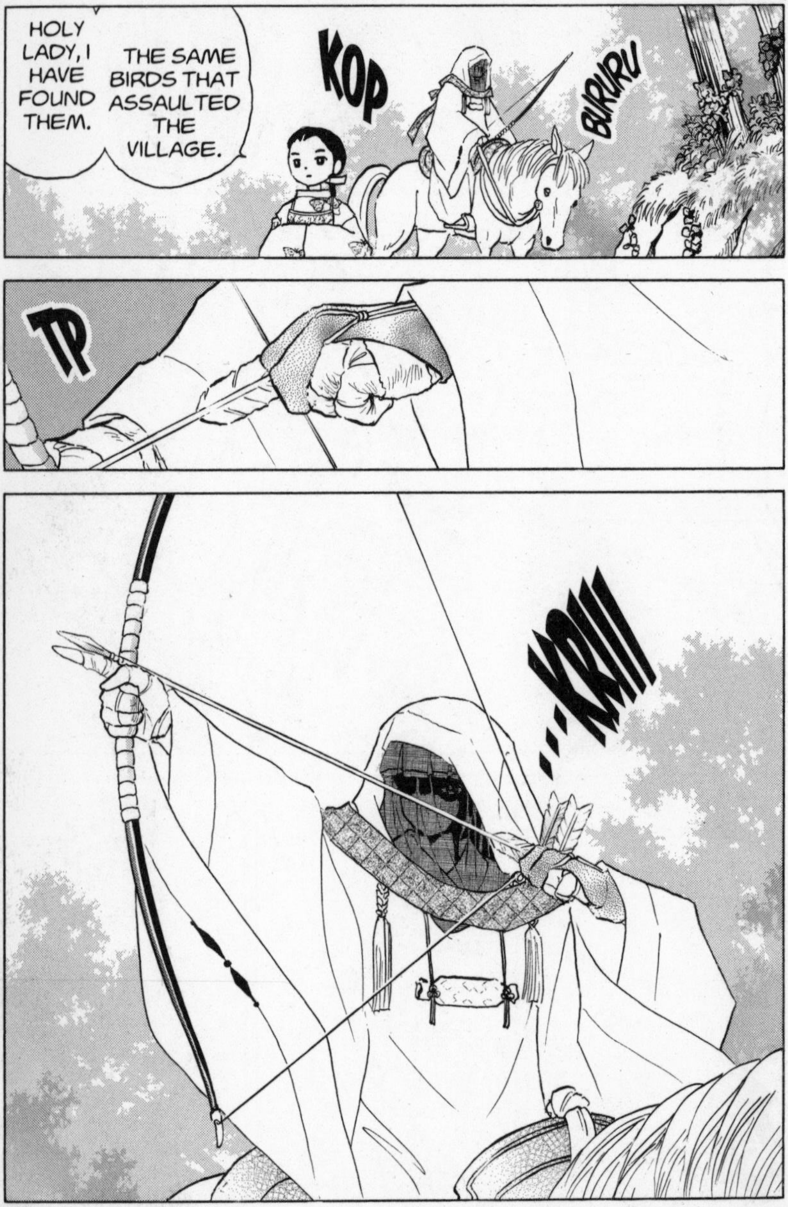
HOLY LADY, I HAVE FOUND THEM.
THE SAME BIRDS THAT ASSAULTED THE VILLAGE.
KOP
BURURU
TP
...KRIII

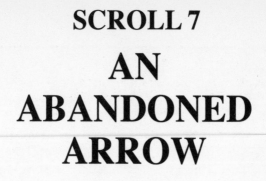

SCROLL 7

AN ABANDONED ARROW

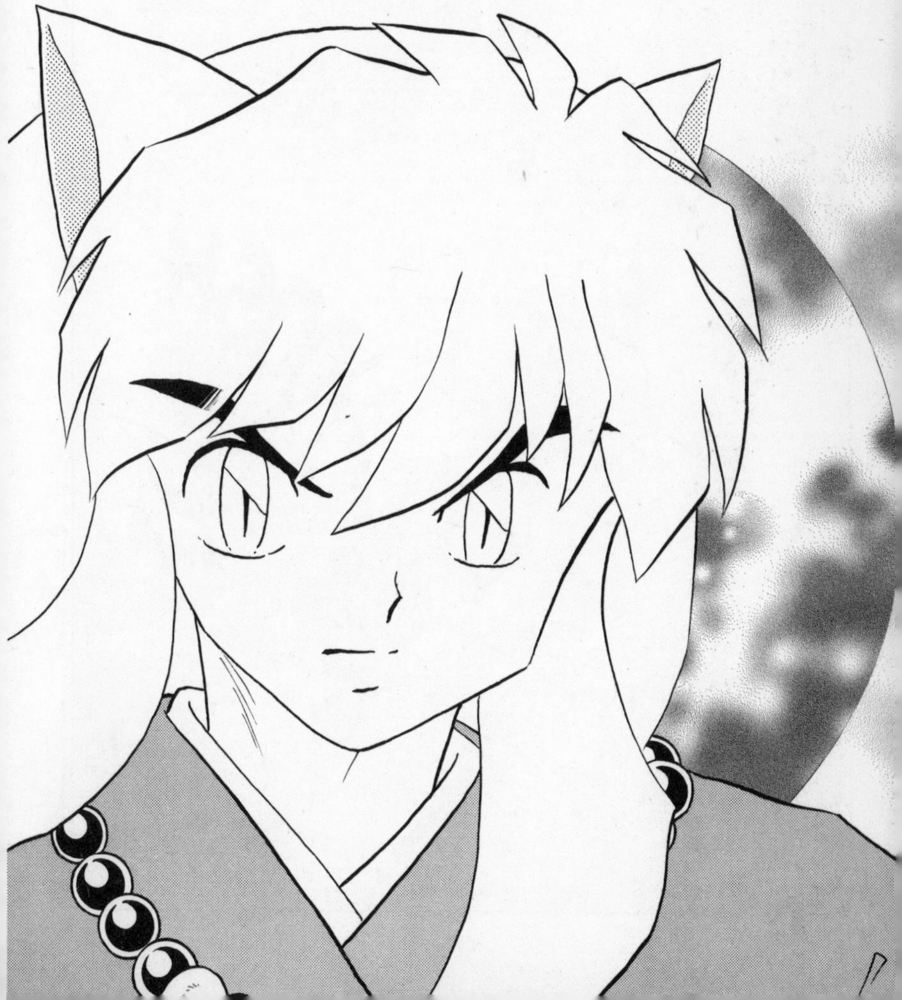

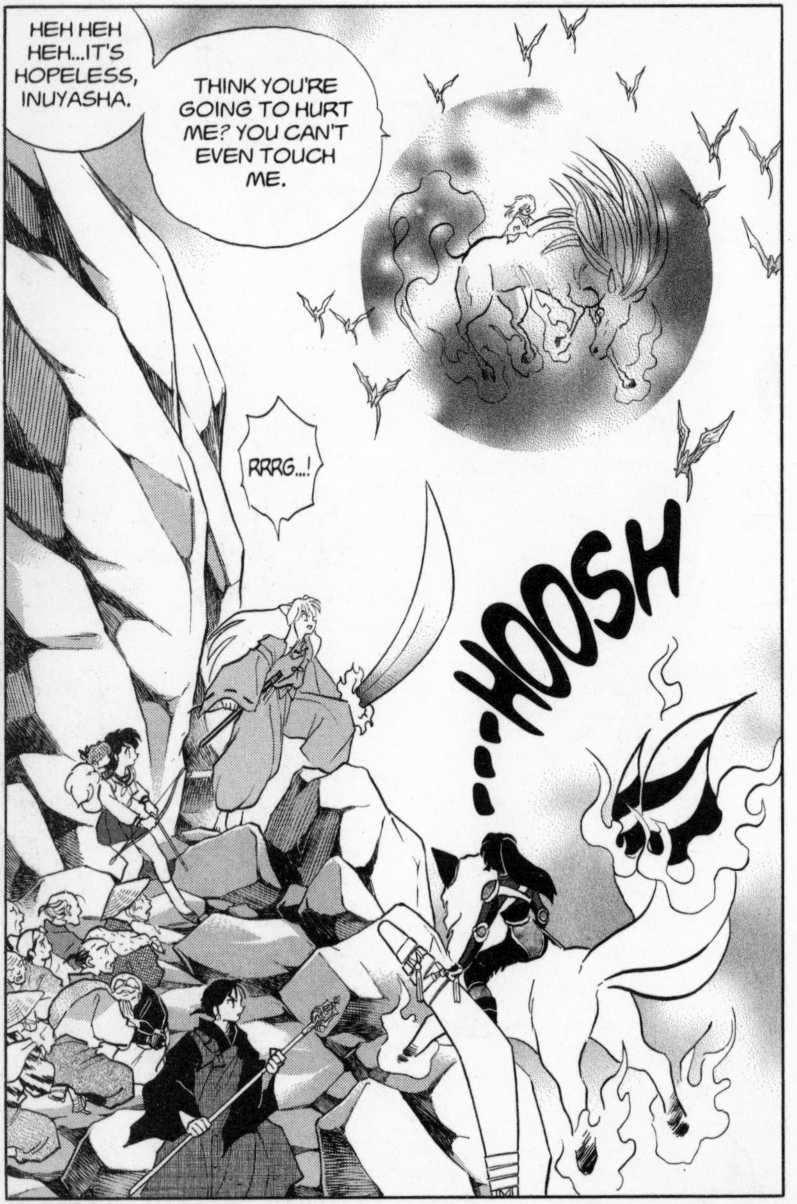
HEH HEH HEH...IT'S HOPELESS, INUYASHA.
THINK YOU'RE GOING TO HURT ME? YOU CAN'T EVEN TOUCH ME.
RRRG...!
...HOOSH

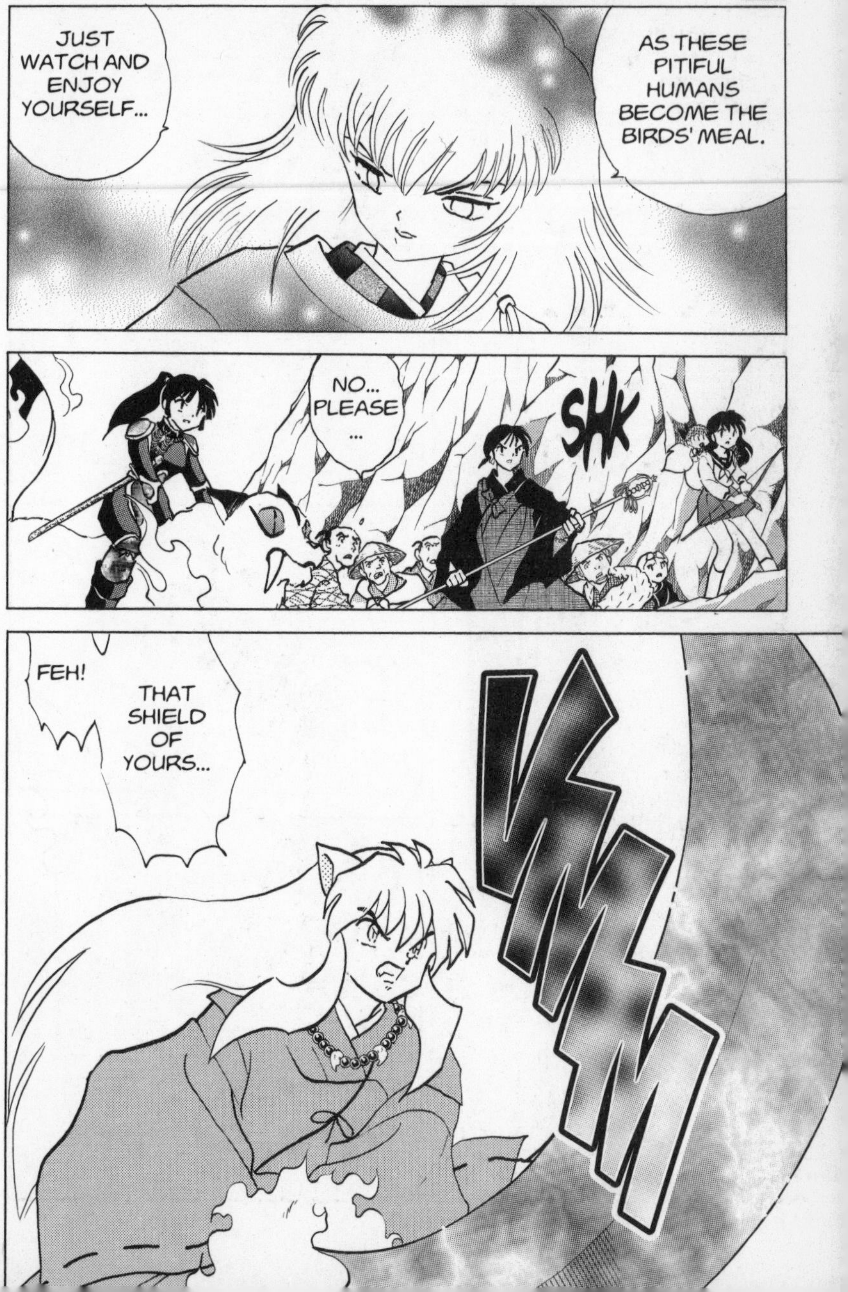
JUST WATCH AND ENJOY YOURSELF...
AS THESE PITIFUL HUMANS BECOME THE BIRDS' MEAL.
NO... PLEASE ...
SHK
FEH!
THAT SHIELD OF YOURS...
VMMM

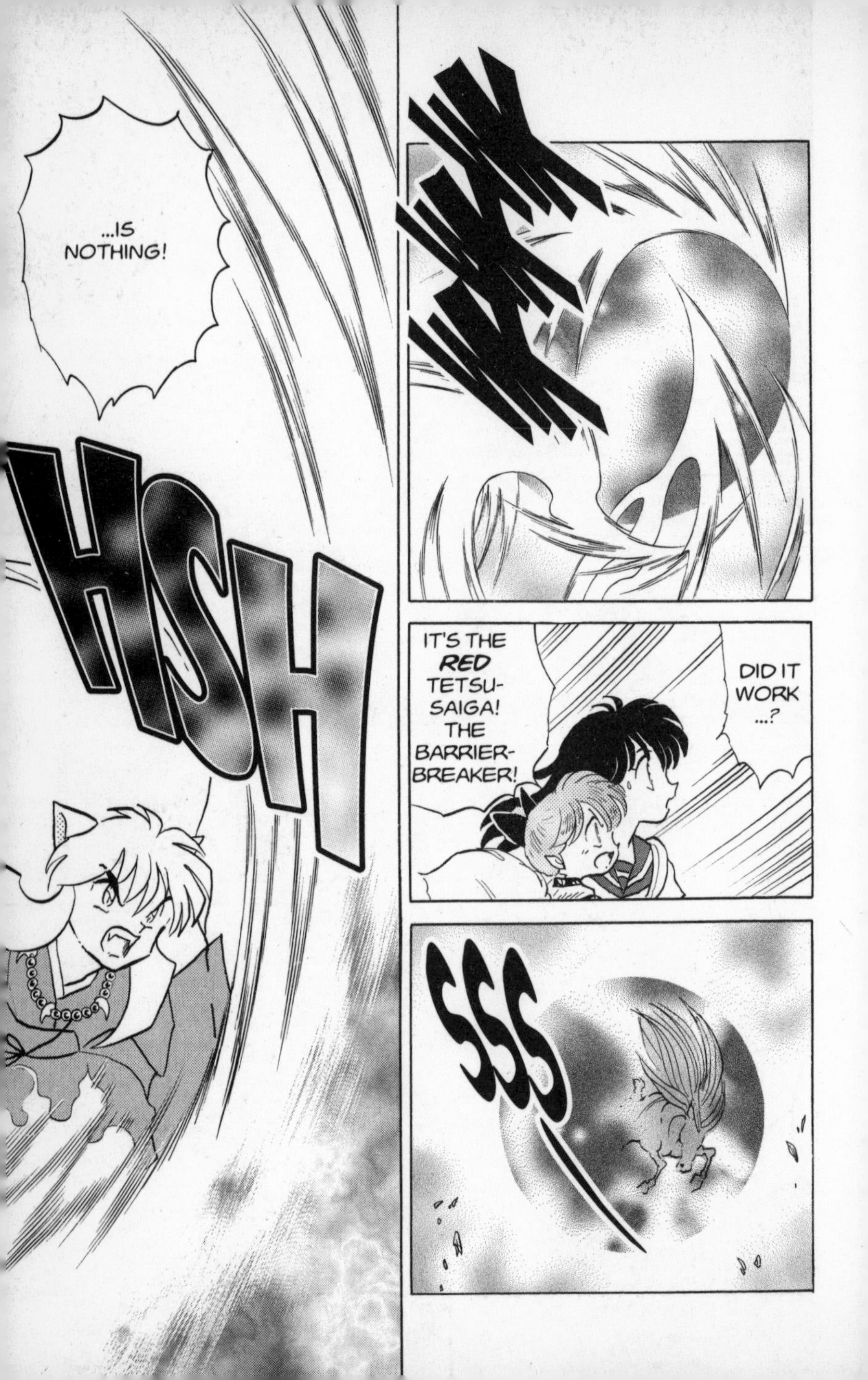
...IS NOTHING!
HISH
IT'S THE RED TETSU-SAIGA! THE BARRIER-BREAKER!
DID IT WORK ...?
SSS

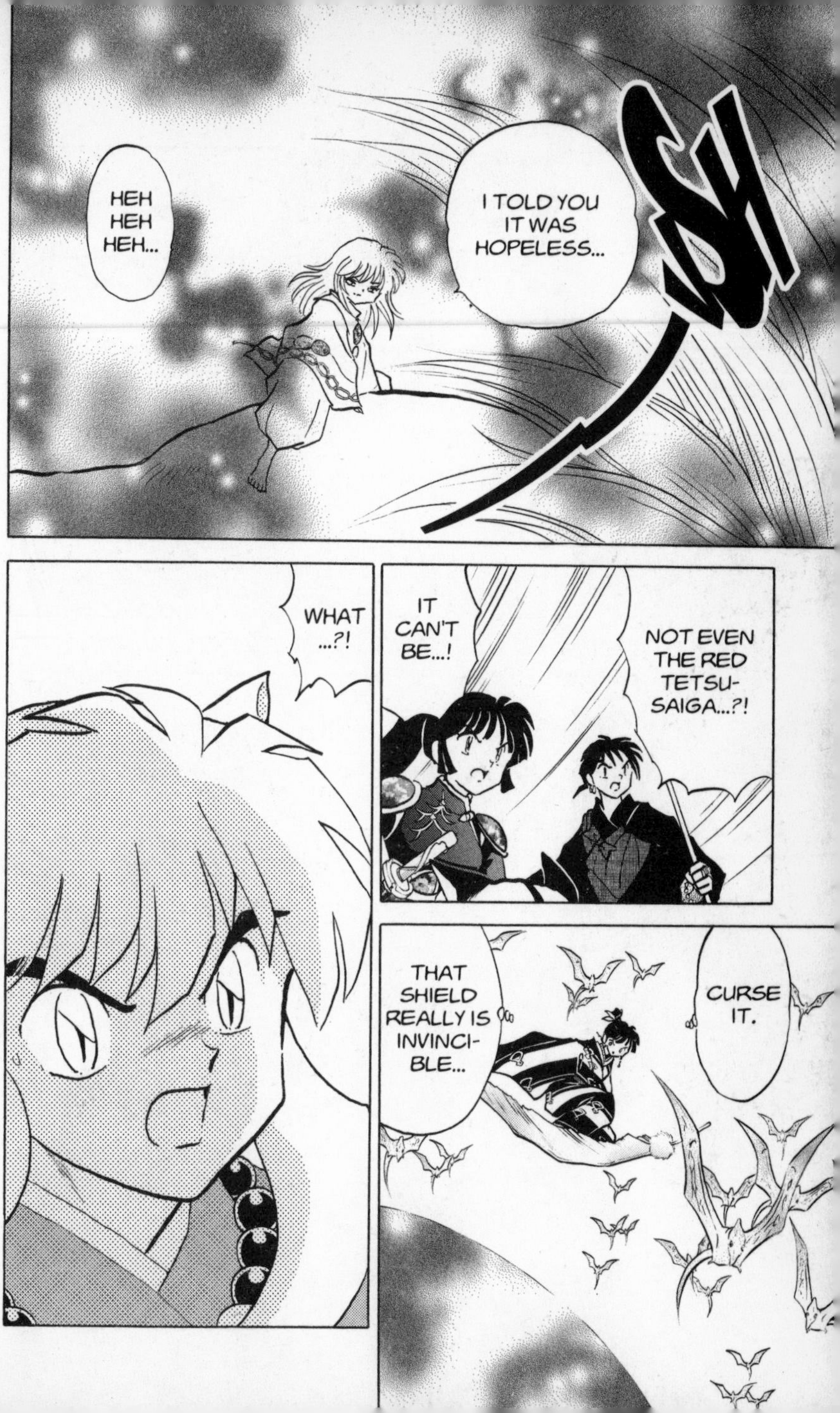
HEH HEH HEH...
I TOLD YOU IT WAS HOPELESS...
WHAT ...?!
IT CAN'T BE...!
NOT EVEN THE RED TETSU-SAIGA...?!
THAT SHIELD REALLY IS INVINCI-BLE...
CURSE IT.

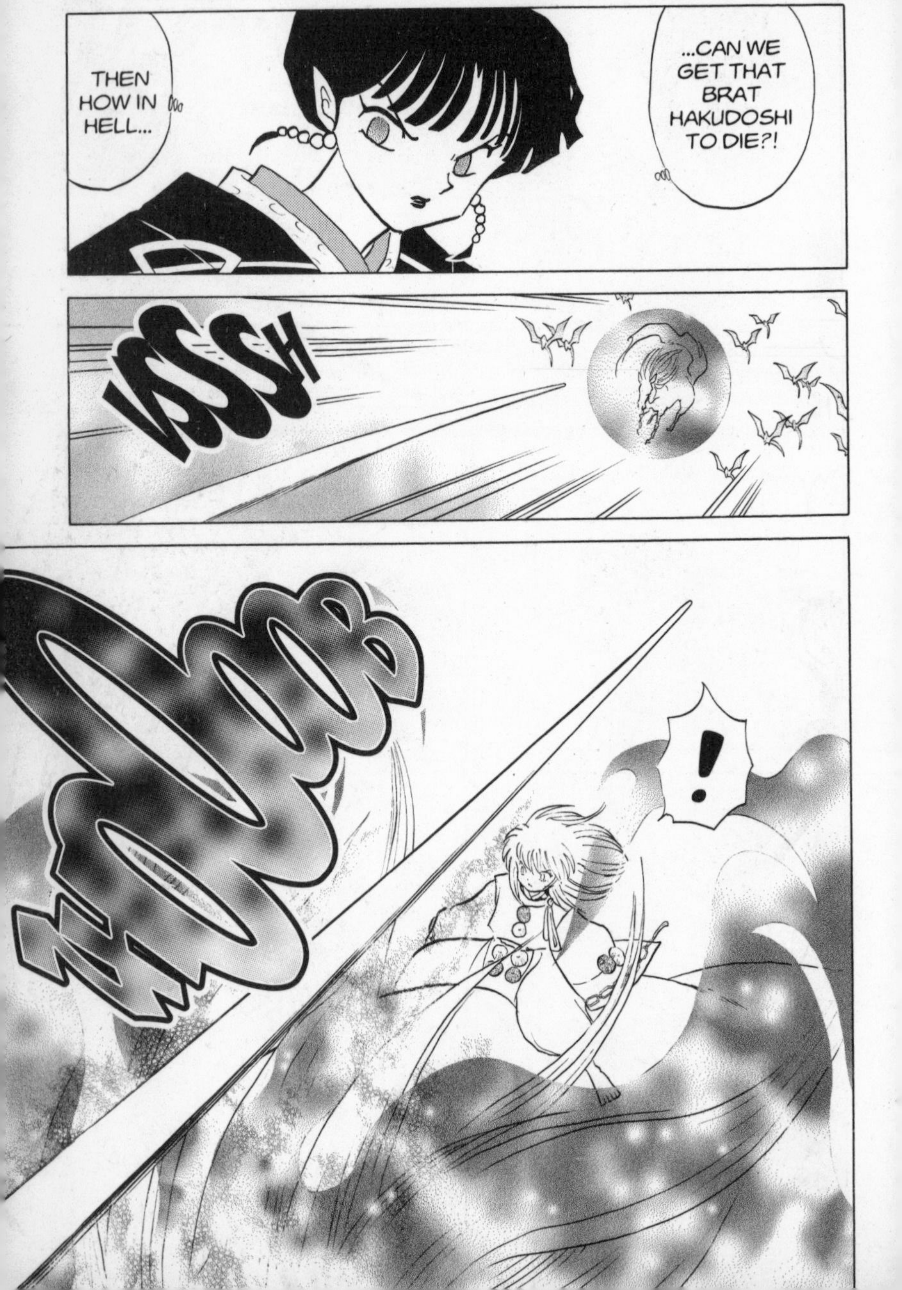
THEN HOW IN HELL...
...CAN WE GET THAT BRAT HAKUDOSHI TO DIE?!
VOSSH
WHOOB
!

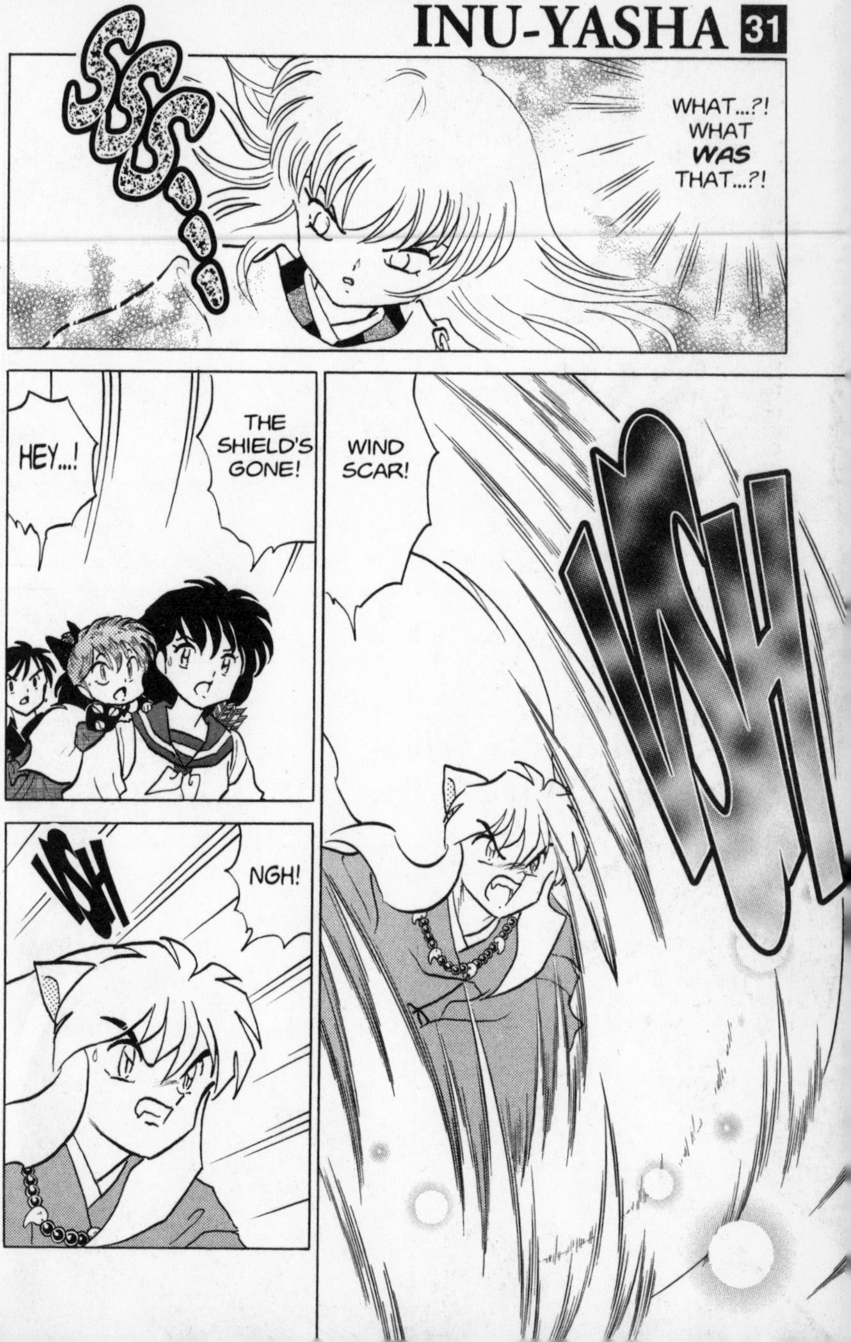
SSSS...
WHAT...?!
WHAT WAS
THAT...?!
HEY...!
THE SHIELD'S GONE!
VSH
NGH!
WIND SCAR!
VSH

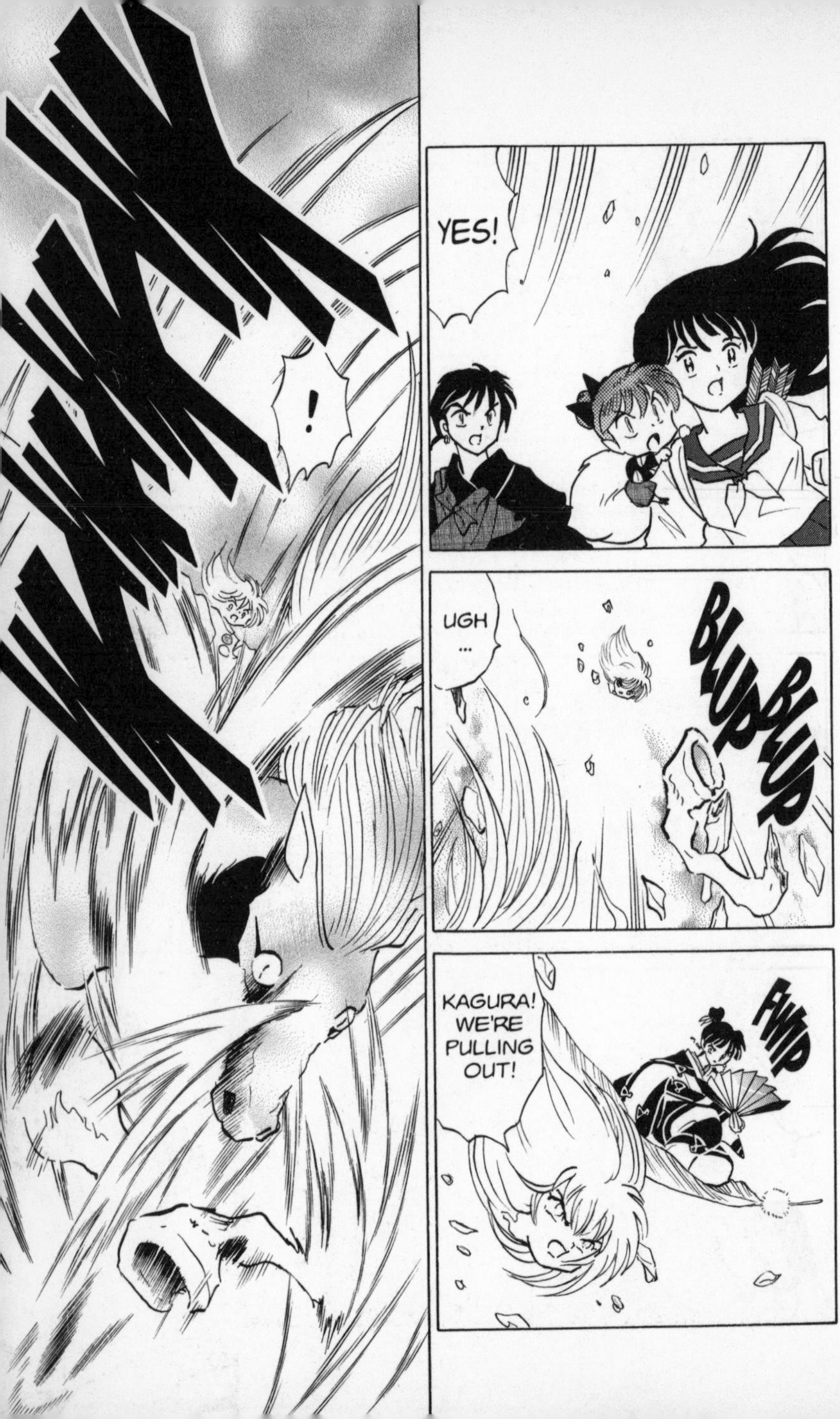
!
YES!
UGH ...
BLUP BLUP
KAGURA! WE'RE PULLING OUT!
FWIP

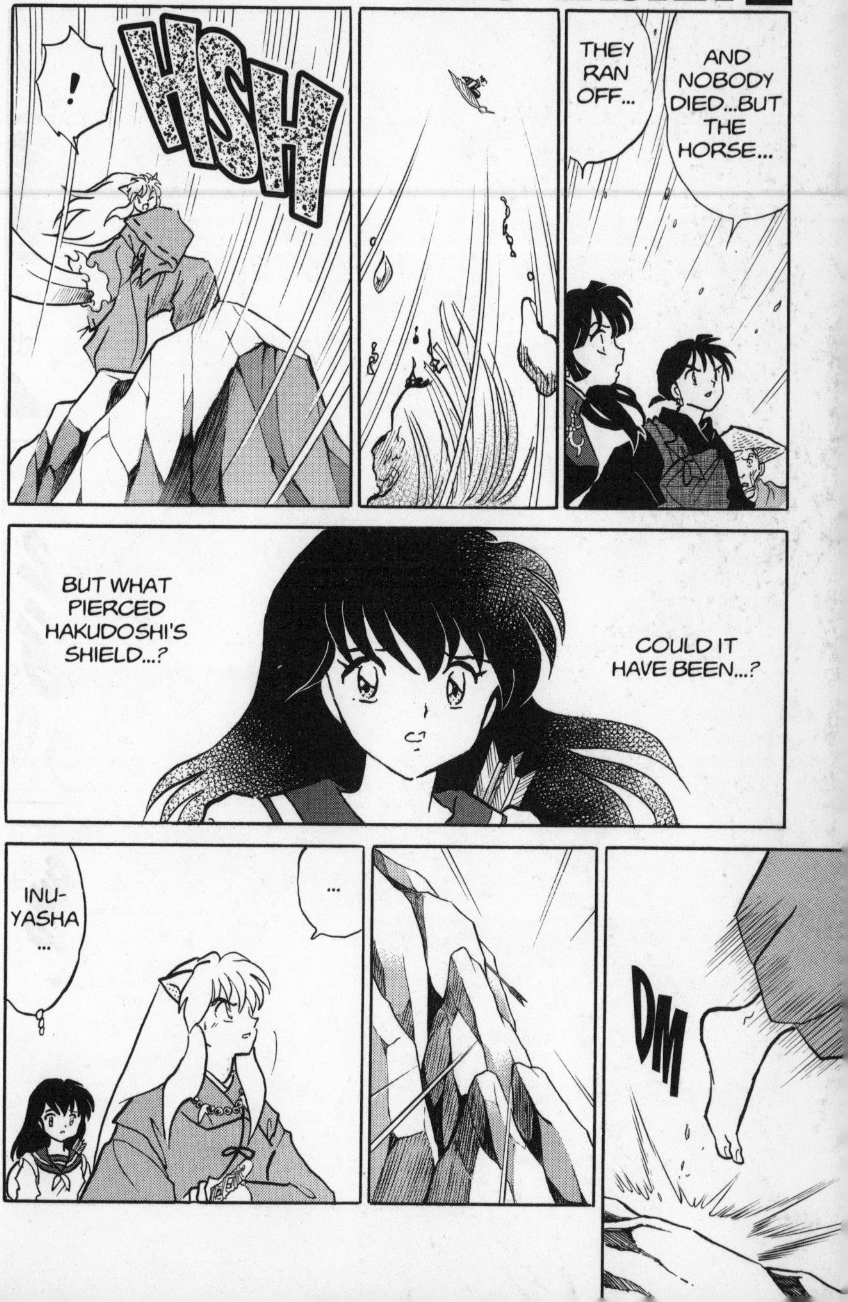
!
HSH
THEY RAN OFF...
AND NOBODY DIED...BUT THE HORSE...
BUT WHAT PIERCED HAKUDOSHI'S SHIELD...?
COULD IT HAVE BEEN...?
INU-YASHA ...
...
DM

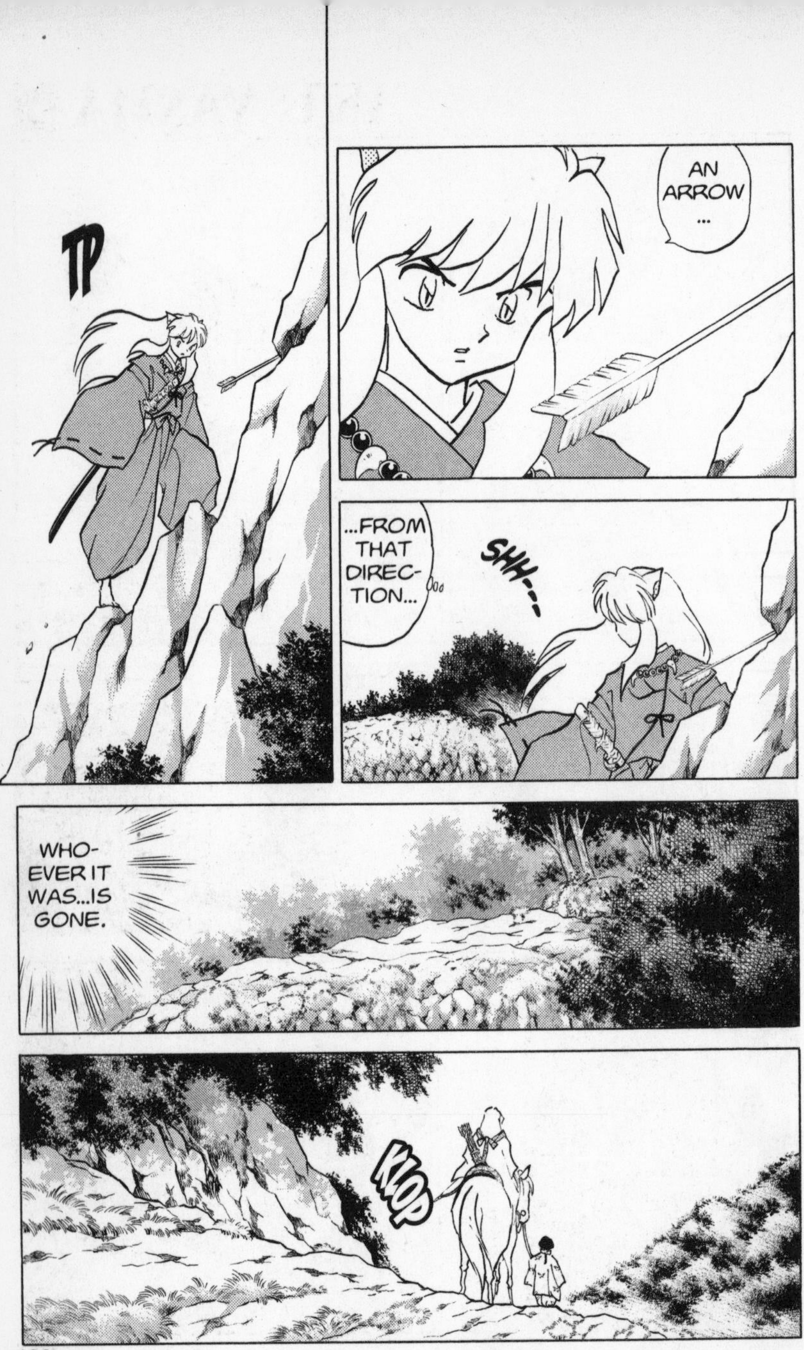
TP
AN ARROW ...
...FROM THAT DIREC-TION...
SHH...
WHO-EVER IT WAS...IS GONE.
KLOP

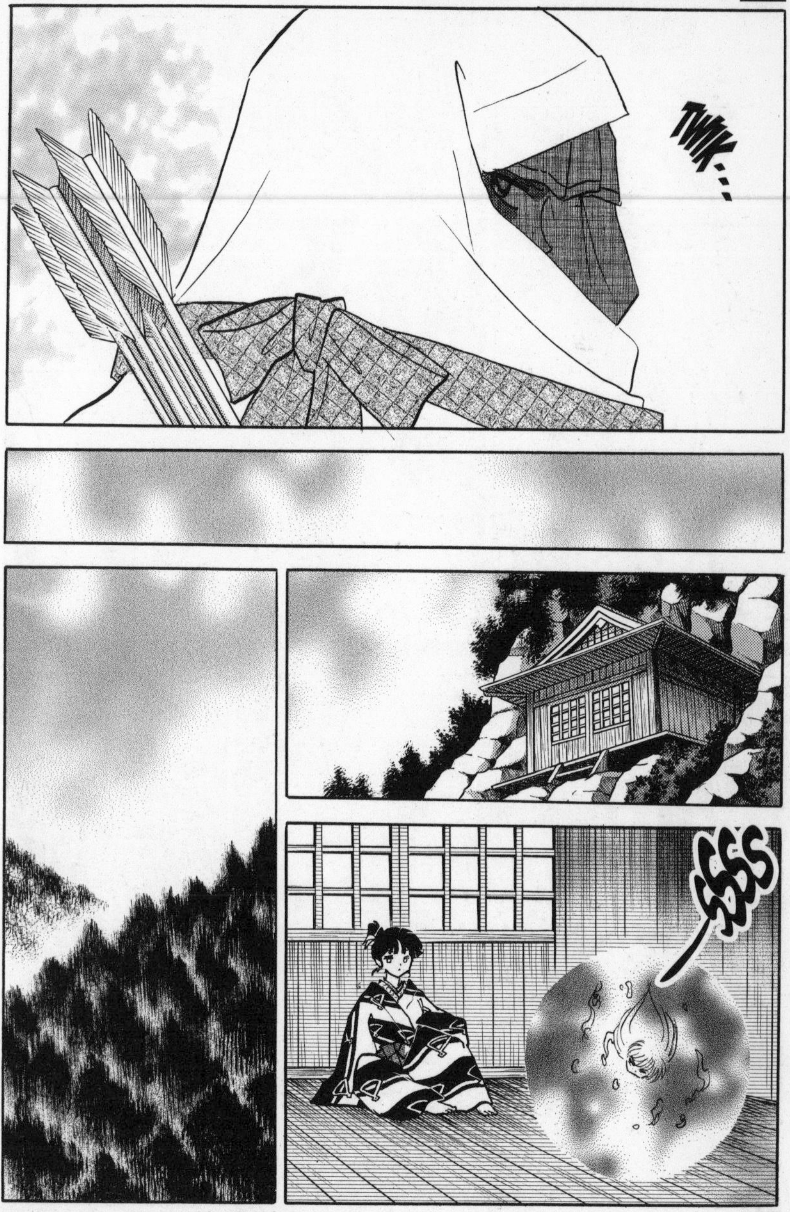
TWIK...
SSSS

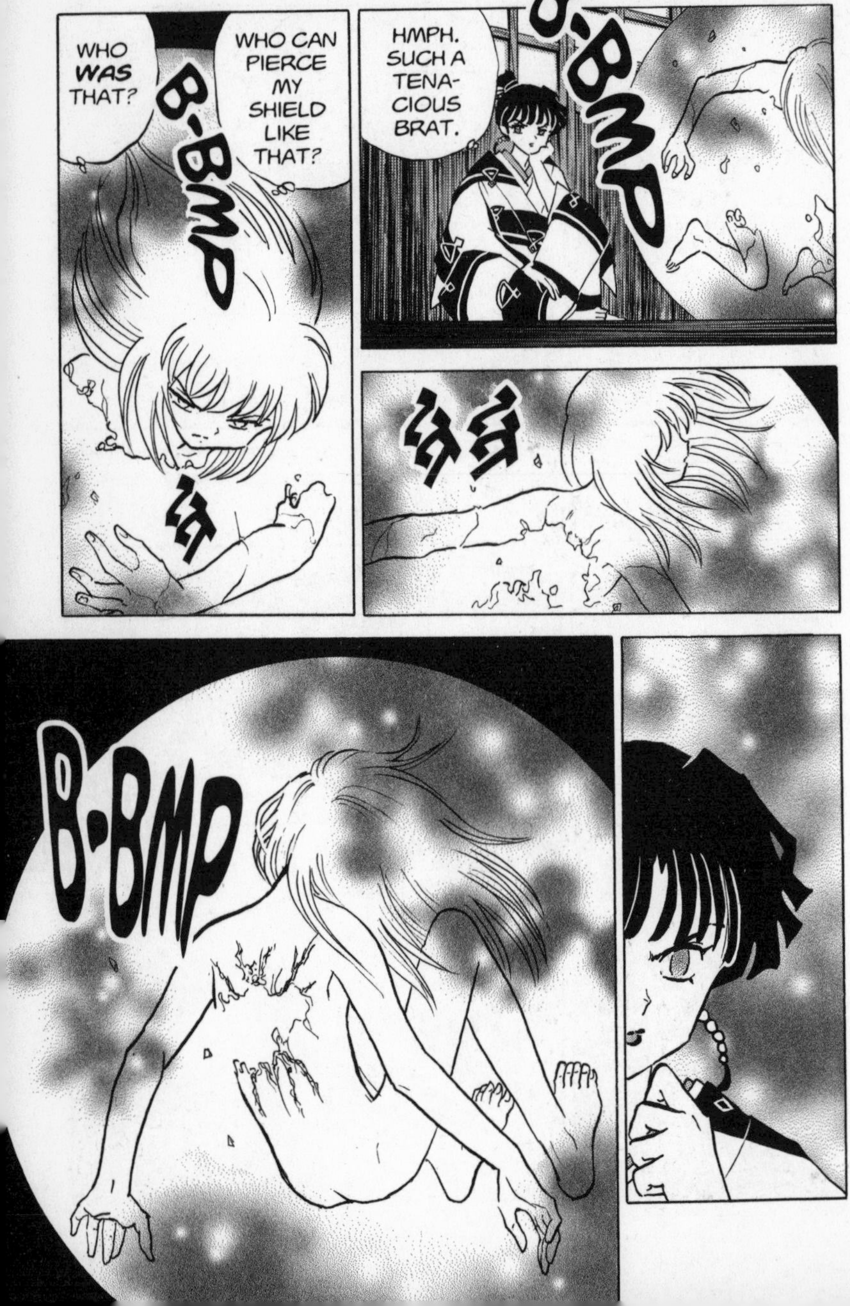
WHO WAS THAT?
WHO CAN PIERCE MY SHIELD LIKE THAT?
B-BMP
HMPH. SUCH A TENA-CIOUS BRAT.
B-BMP
B-BMP

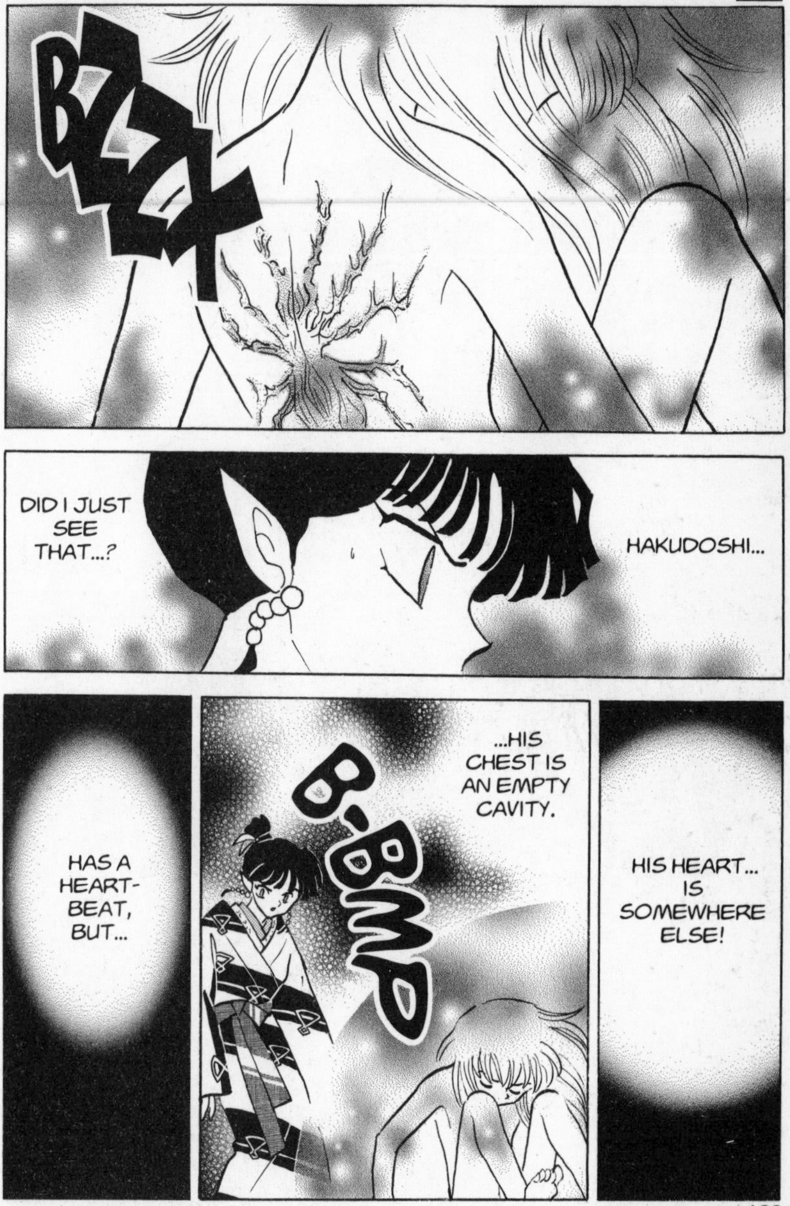
BZZT
DID I JUST SEE THAT...?
HAKUDOSHI...
HAS A HEART-BEAT, BUT...
...HIS CHEST IS AN EMPTY CAVITY.
B-BMP
HIS HEART... IS SOMEWHERE ELSE!

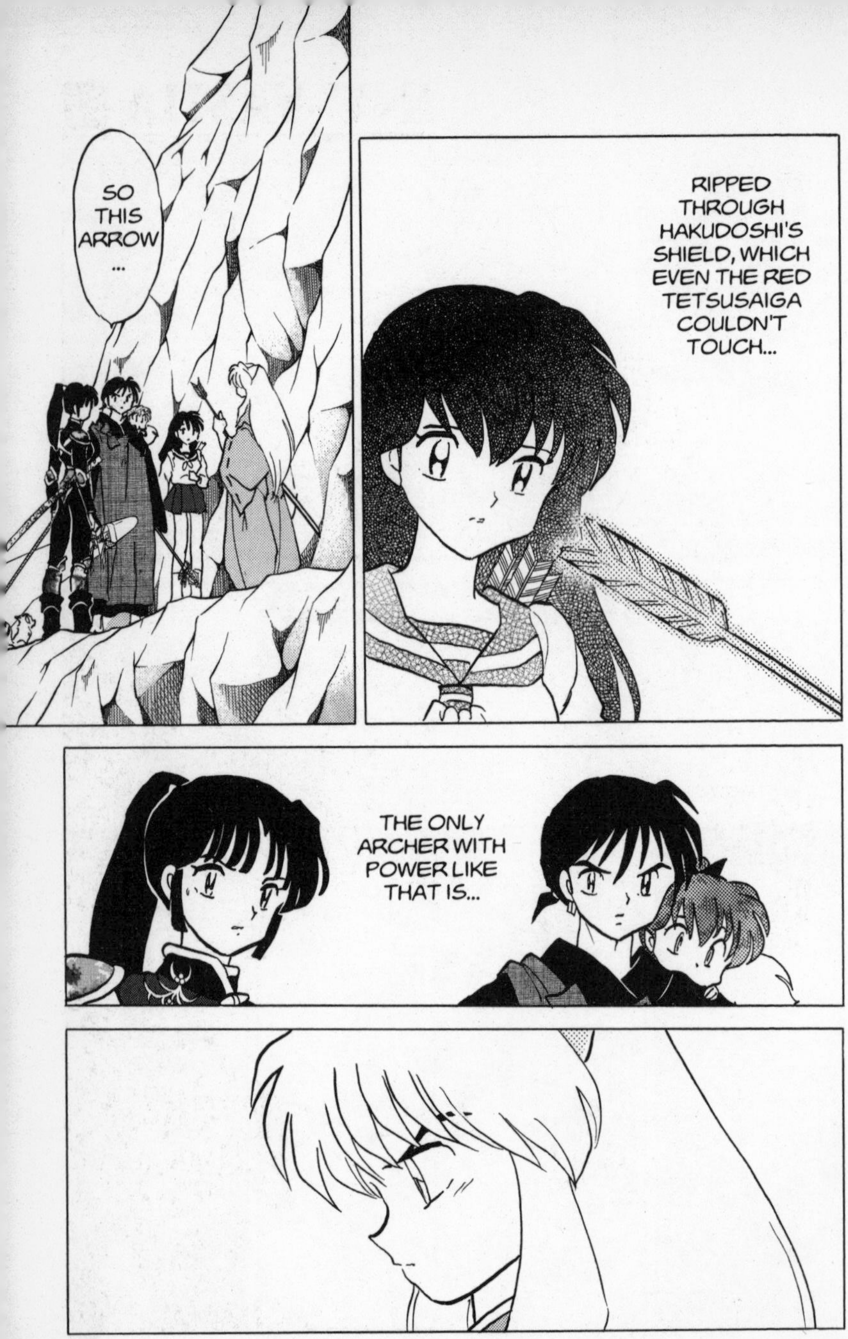
SO THIS ARROW ...
RIPPED THROUGH HAKUDOSHI'S SHIELD, WHICH EVEN THE RED TETSUSAIGA COULDN'T TOUCH...
THE ONLY ARCHER WITH POWER LIKE THAT IS...

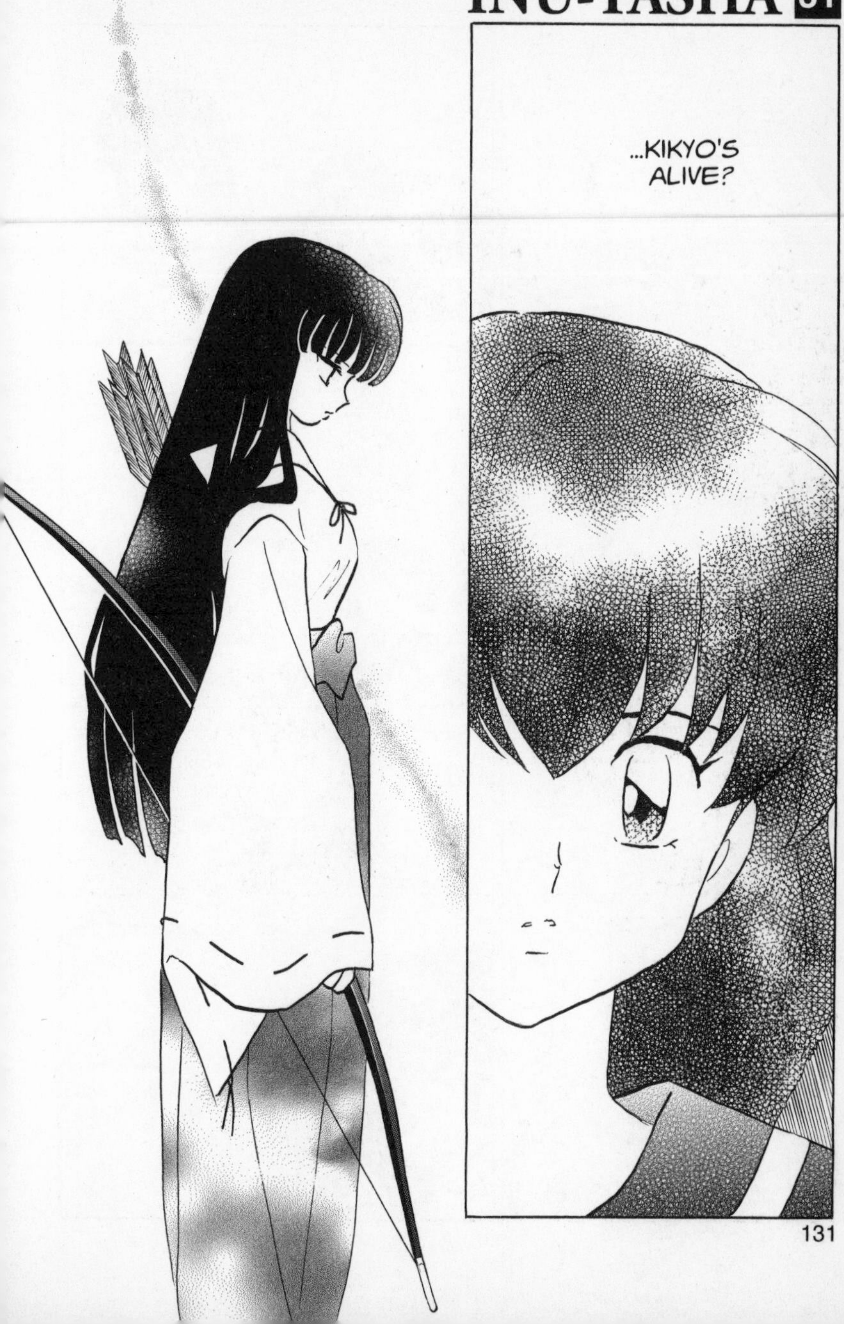
...KIKYO'S
ALIVE?

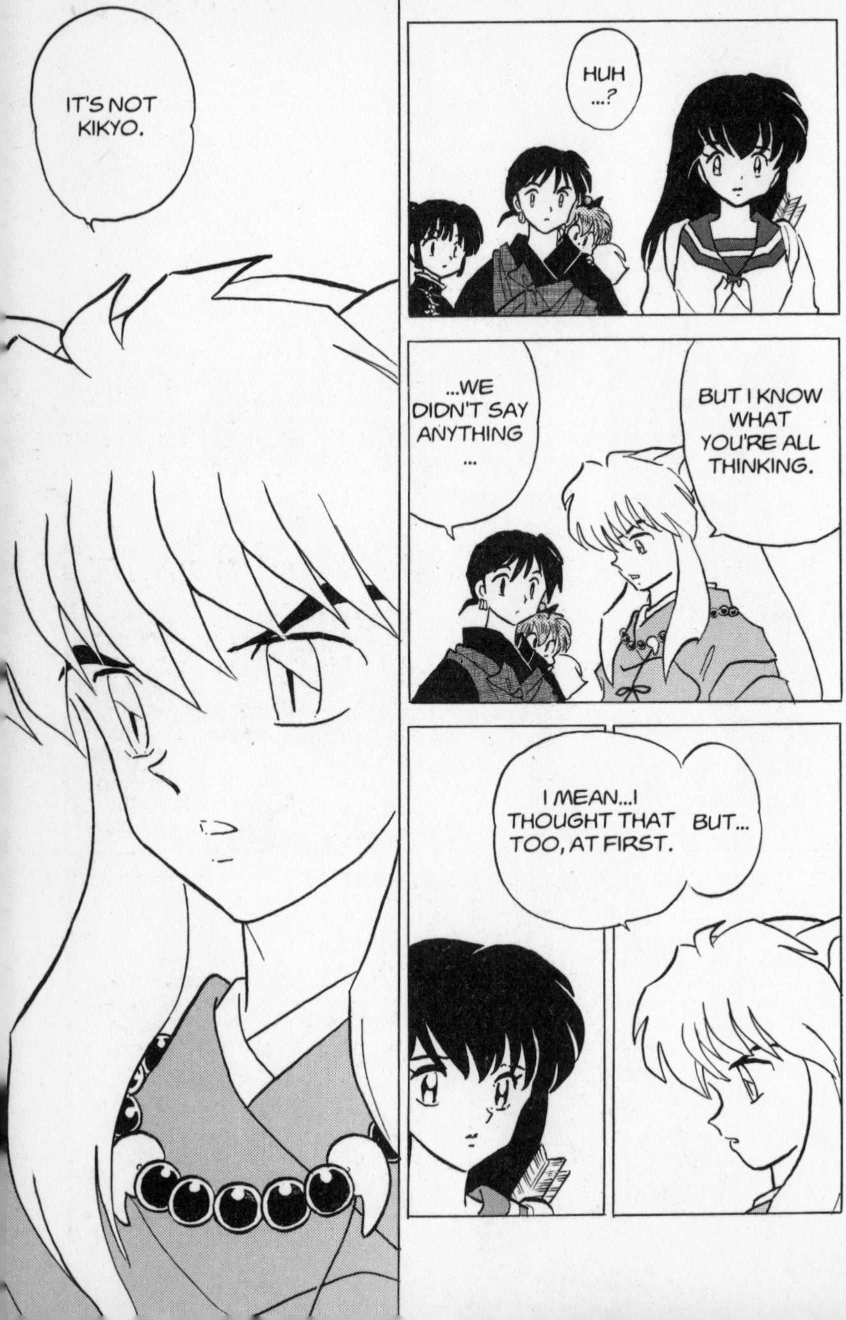
IT'S NOT KIKYO.
HUH ...?
...WE DIDN'T SAY ANYTHING ...
BUT I KNOW WHAT YOU'RE ALL THINKING.
I MEAN...I THOUGHT THAT TOO, AT FIRST.
BUT...

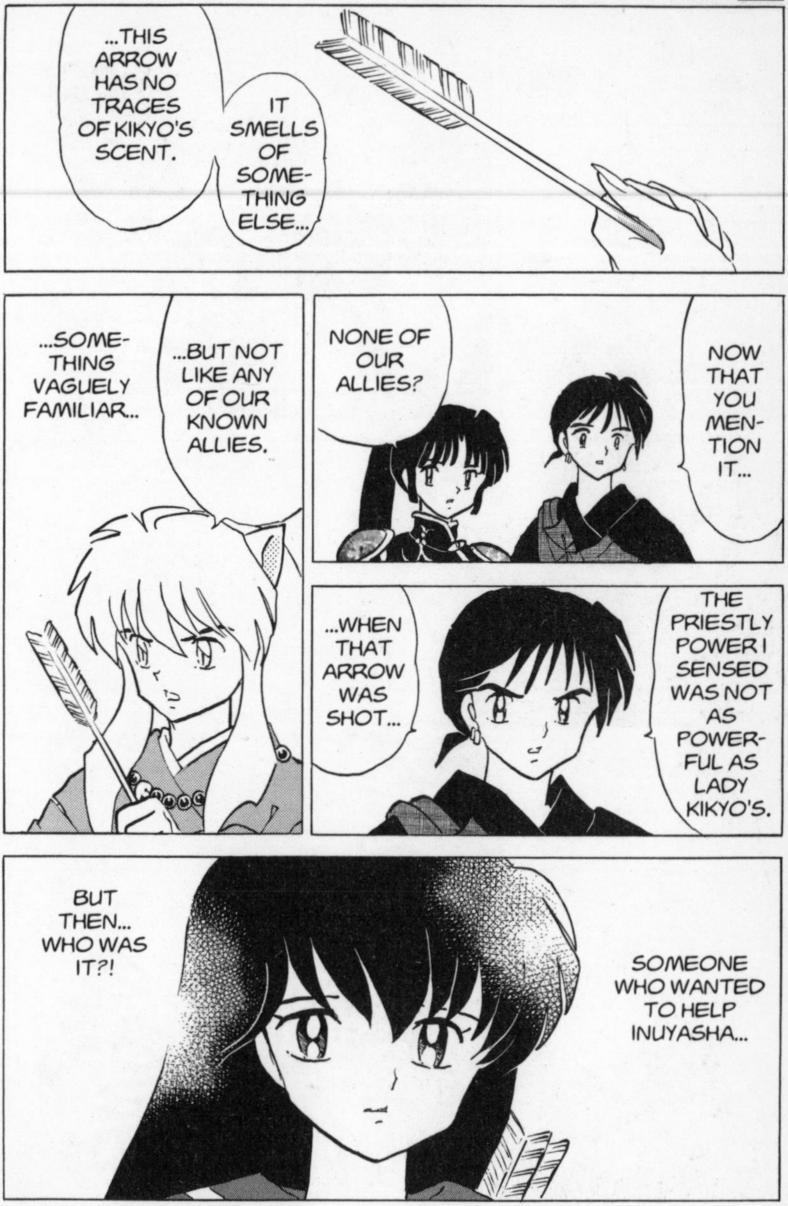
...THIS ARROW HAS NO TRACES OF KIKYO'S SCENT.
IT SMELLS OF SOME-THING ELSE...
...SOME-THING VAGUELY FAMILIAR...
...BUT NOT LIKE ANY OF OUR KNOWN ALLIES.
NONE OF OUR ALLIES?
NOW THAT YOU MEN-TION IT...
...WHEN THAT ARROW WAS SHOT...
THE PRIESTLY POWER I SENSED WAS NOT AS POWER-FUL AS LADY KIKYO'S.
BUT THEN... WHO WAS IT?!
SOMEONE WHO WANTED TO HELP INUYASHA...

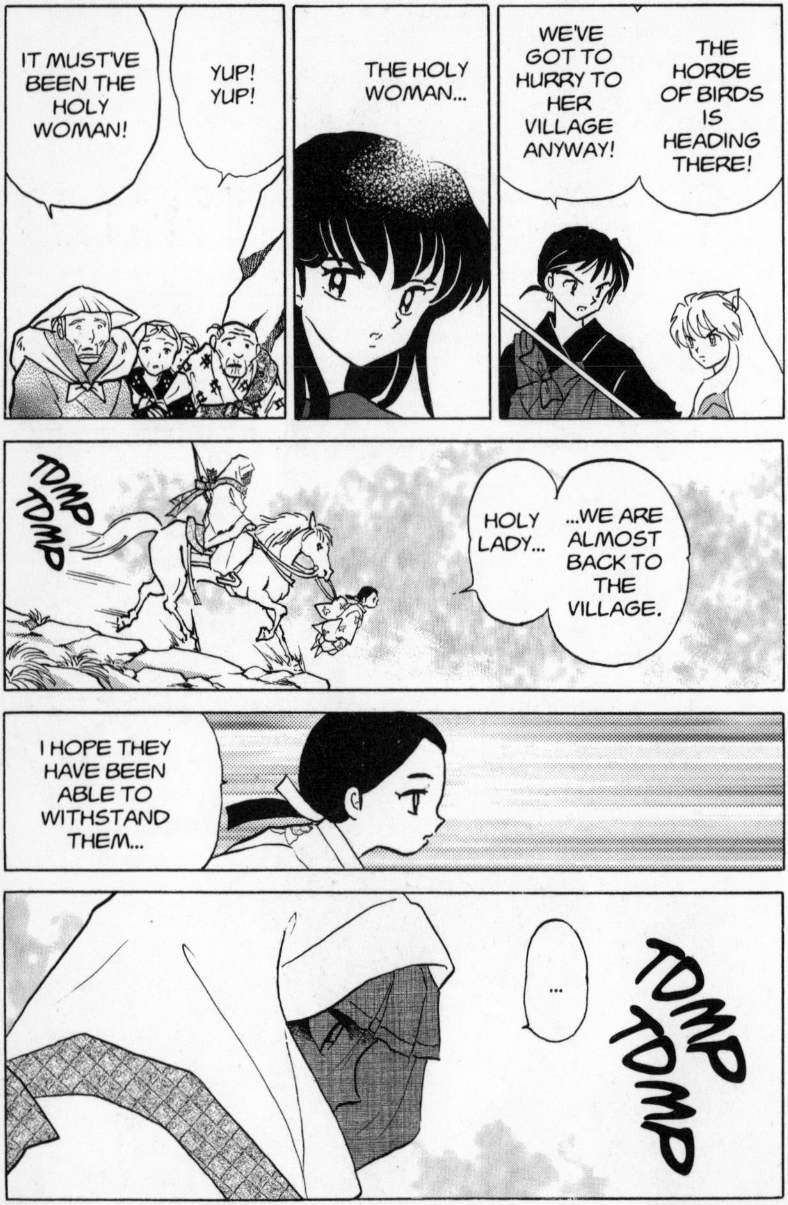

IT MUST'VE BEEN THE HOLY WOMAN!
YUP! YUP!
THE HOLY WOMAN...
WE'VE GOT TO HURRY TO HER VILLAGE ANYWAY!
THE HORDE OF BIRDS IS HEADING THERE!
TOMP TOMP
HOLY LADY...
...WE ARE ALMOST BACK TO THE VILLAGE.
I HOPE THEY HAVE BEEN ABLE TO WITHSTAND THEM...
...
TOMP TOMP

SCROLL 8

THE VILLAGE SHIELD

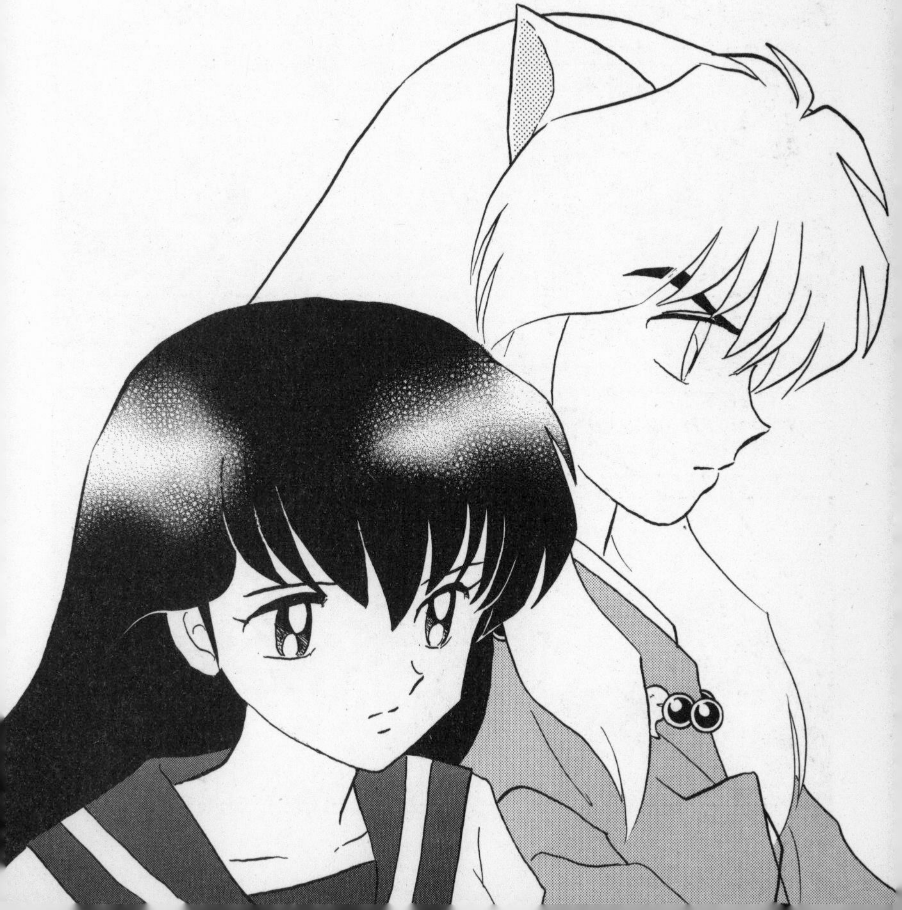

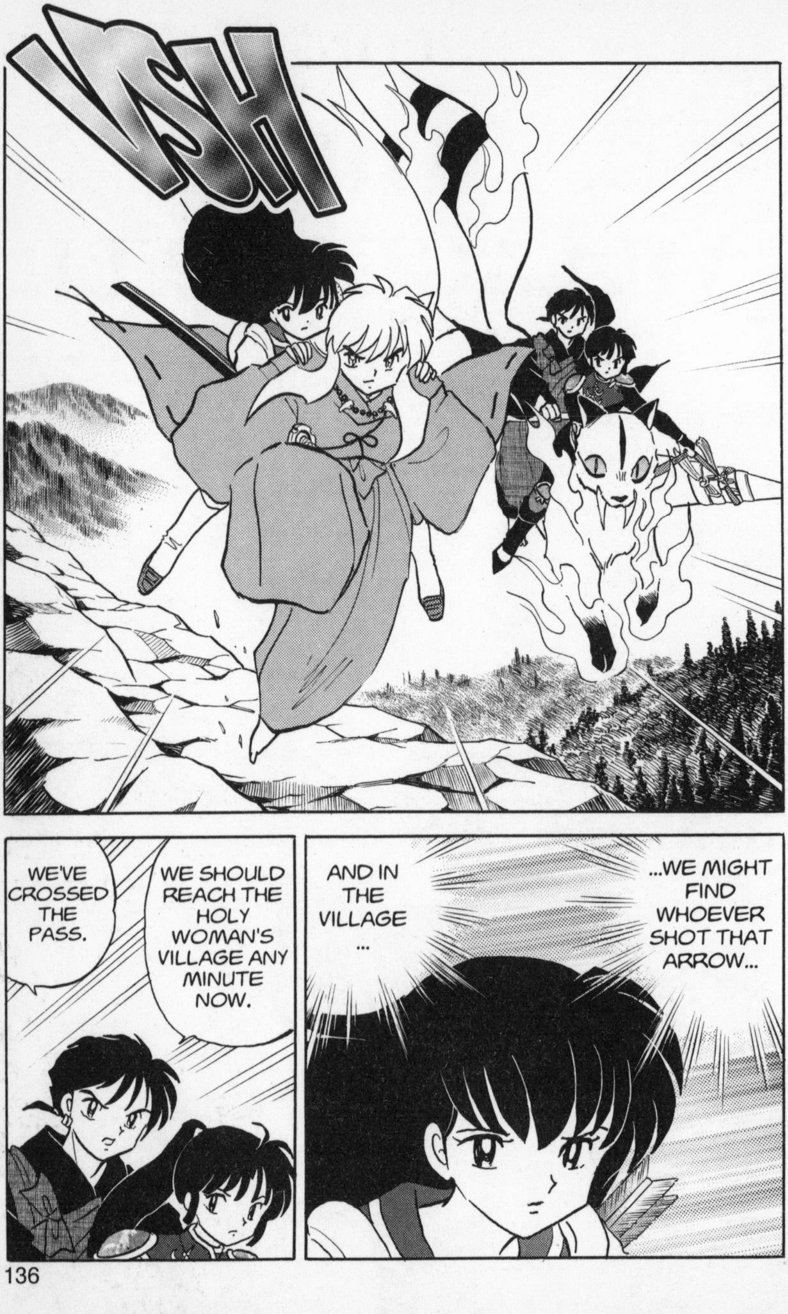
VSSH
WE'VE CROSSED THE PASS.
WE SHOULD REACH THE HOLY WOMAN'S VILLAGE ANY MINUTE NOW.
AND IN THE VILLAGE ...
...WE MIGHT FIND WHOEVER SHOT THAT ARROW...

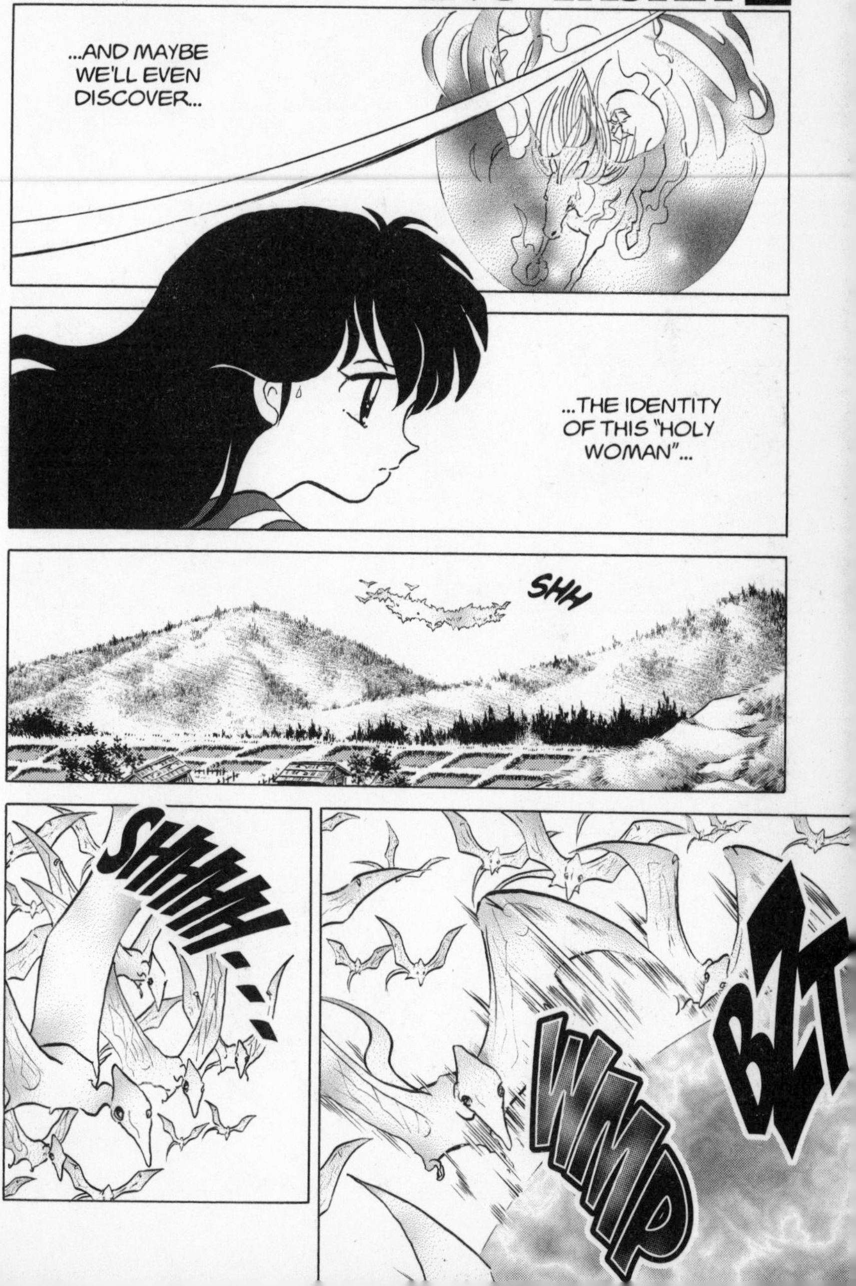
...AND MAYBE WE'LL EVEN DISCOVER...
...THE IDENTITY OF THIS "HOLY WOMAN"...
SHH
SHHHH...
WMP
BZT

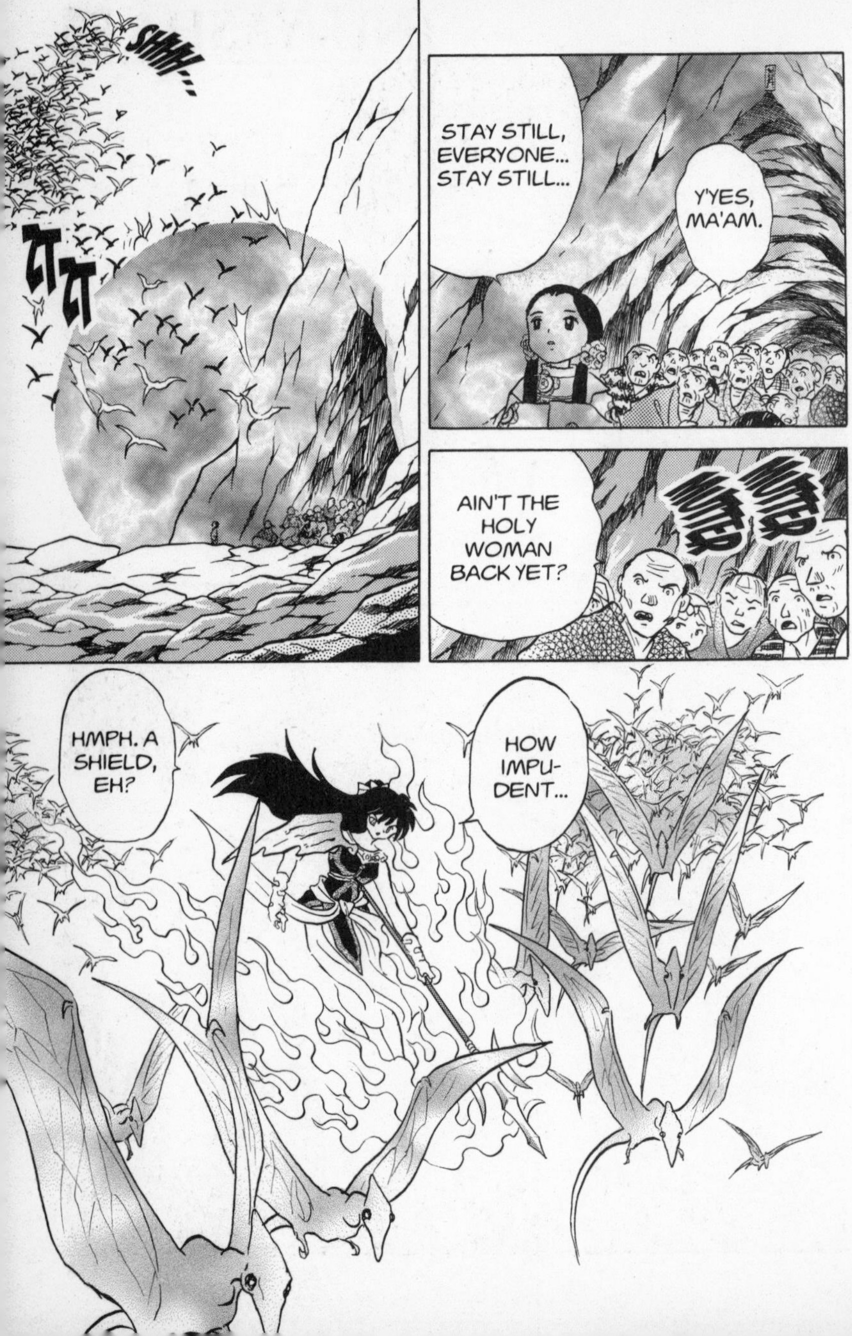
SHHH...
STAY STILL, EVERYONE... STAY STILL...
Y'YES, MA'AM.
AIN'T THE HOLY WOMAN BACK YET?
HMPH. A SHIELD, EH?
HOW IMPU-DENT...

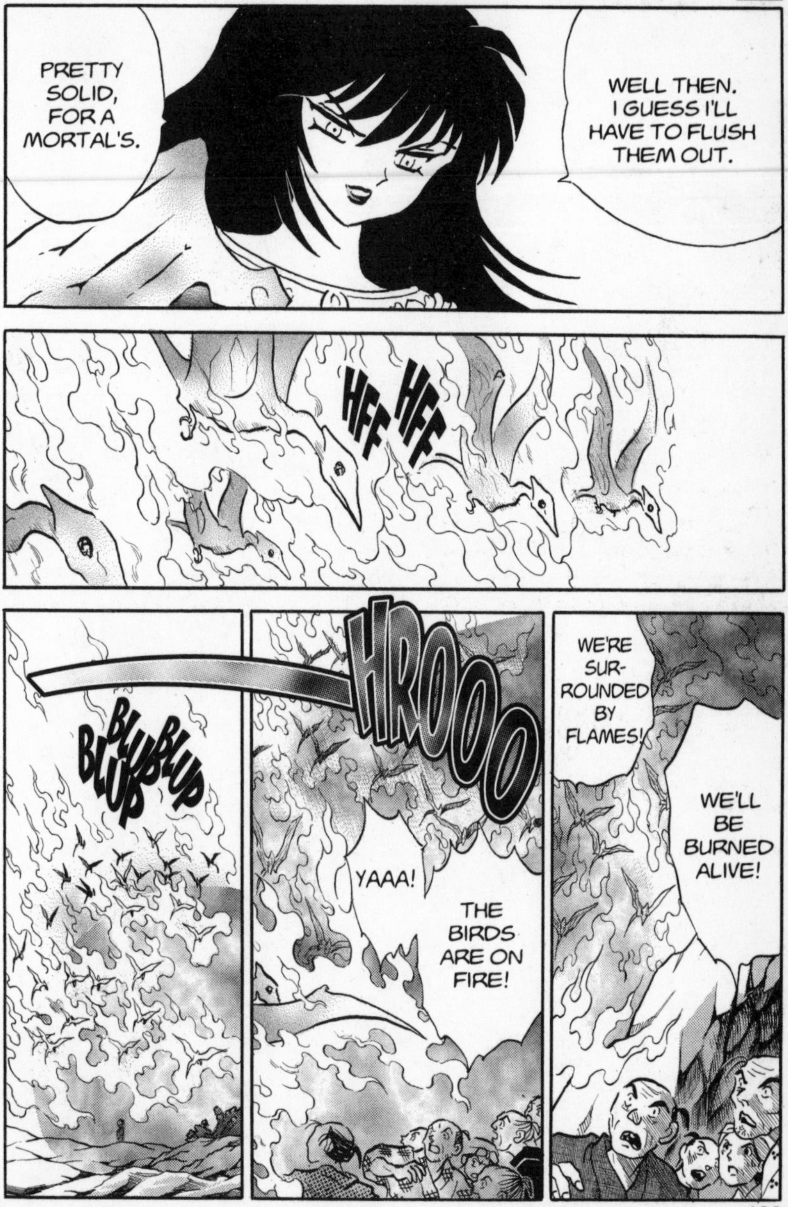
PRETTY SOLID, FOR A MORTAL'S.
WELL THEN. I GUESS I'LL HAVE TO FLUSH THEM OUT.
HFF HFF
BLUB BLUP BLUB BLUP
HROOOO
YAAA!
THE BIRDS ARE ON FIRE!
WE'RE SURROUNDED BY FLAMES!
WE'LL BE BURNED ALIVE!

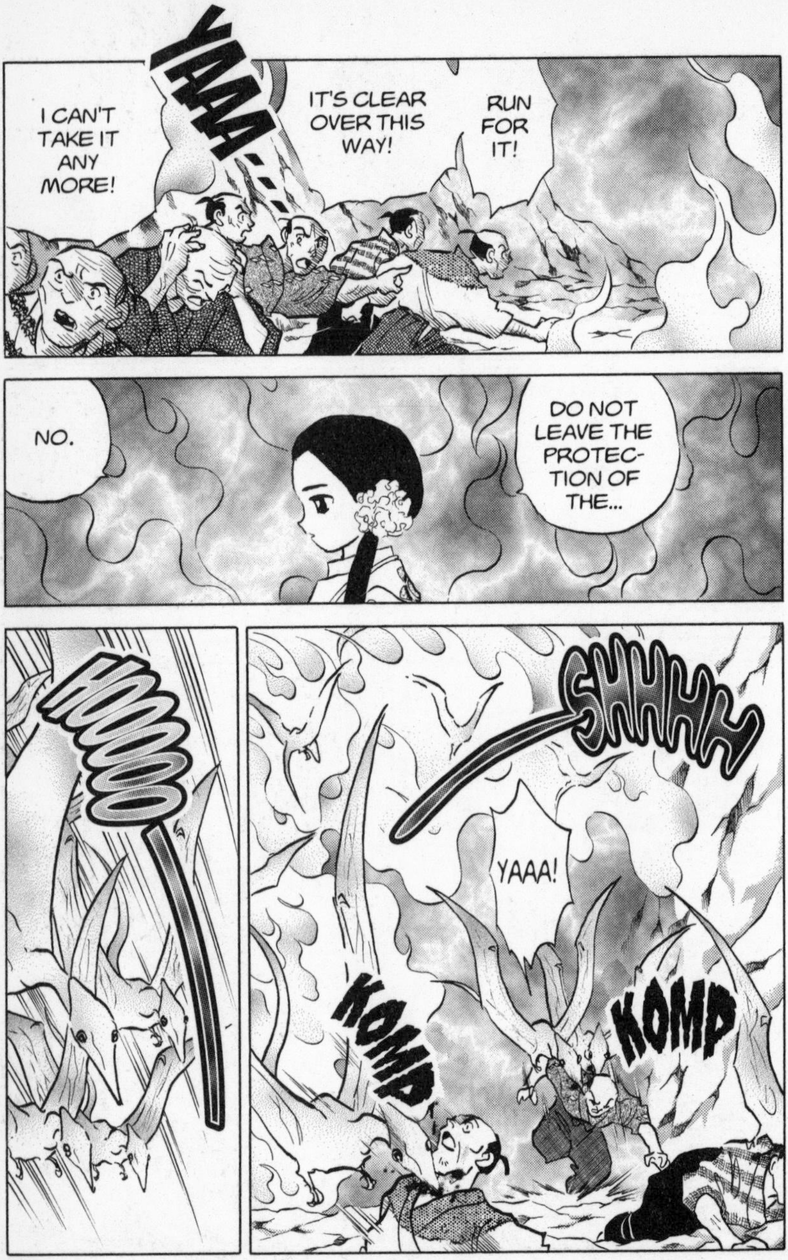

I CAN'T TAKE IT ANY MORE!
YAAAA...
IT'S CLEAR OVER THIS WAY!
RUN FOR IT!
NO.
DO NOT LEAVE THE PROTECTION OF THE...
HOOOOO
SHHHH
YAAA!
KOMP
KOMP

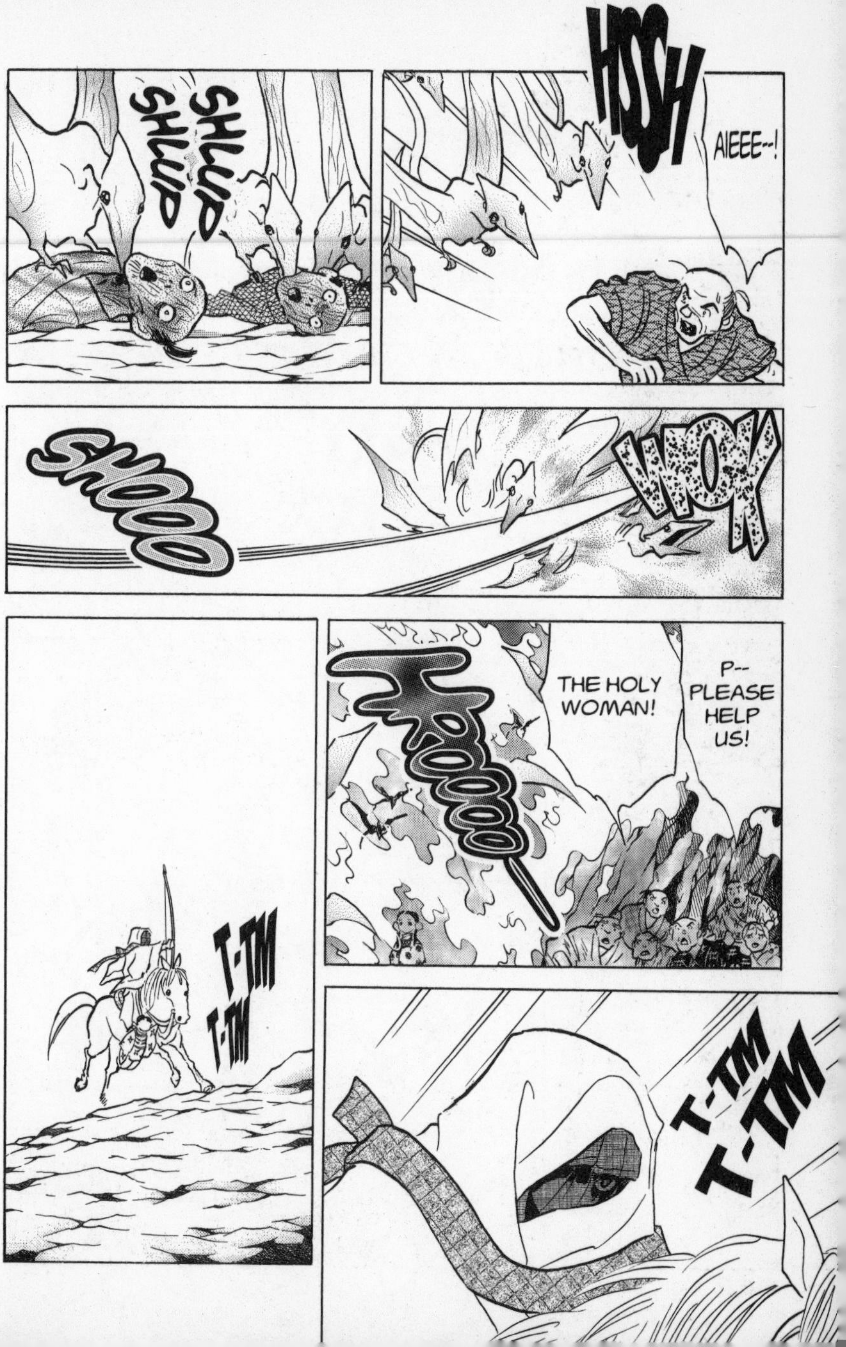
SHLUP SHLUP
HISSH
AIEEE--!
SHOOO
WOK
HOOOOOO
THE HOLY WOMAN!
P-- PLEASE HELP US!
T-TM T-TM
T-TM T-TM

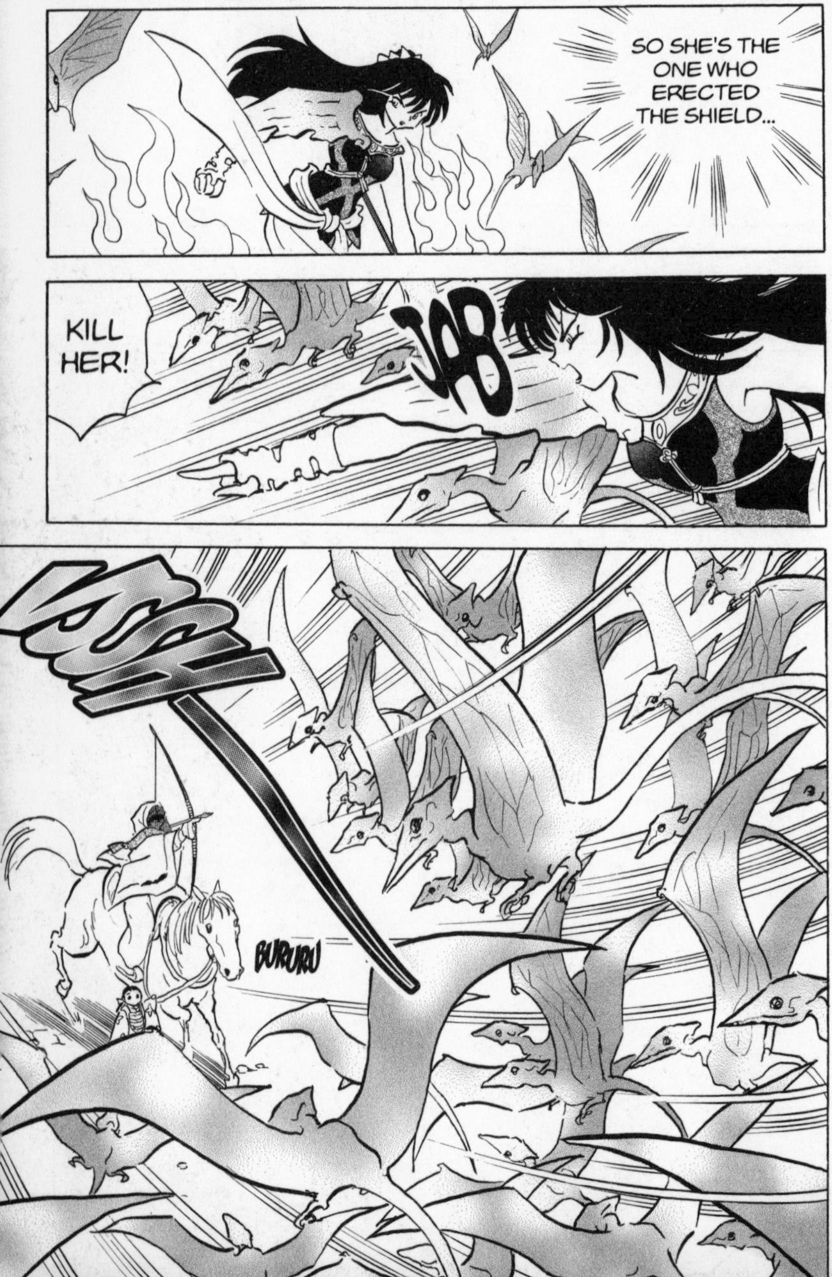
SO SHE'S THE ONE WHO ERECTED THE SHIELD...
KILL HER!
JAB
VOSH
BURURU

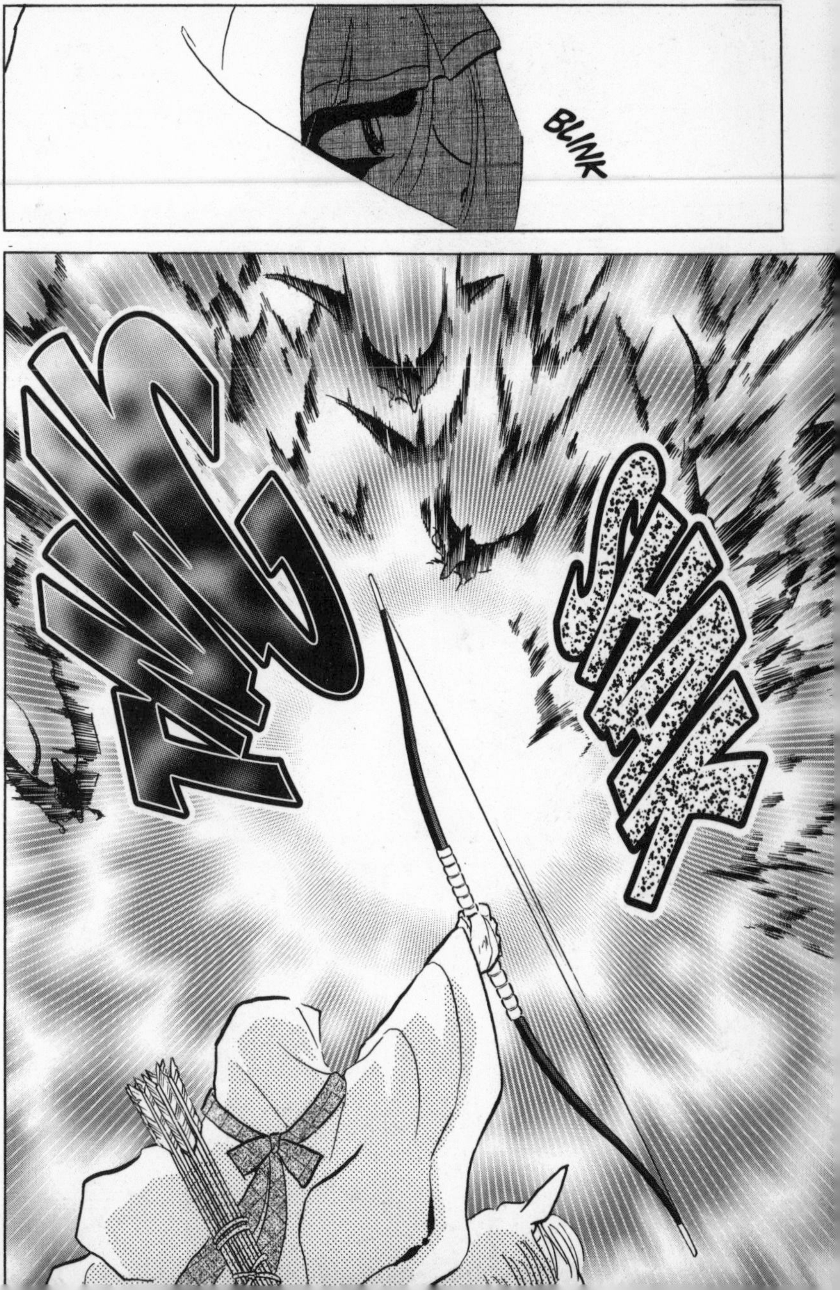
BLINK
SHWA
SHNK

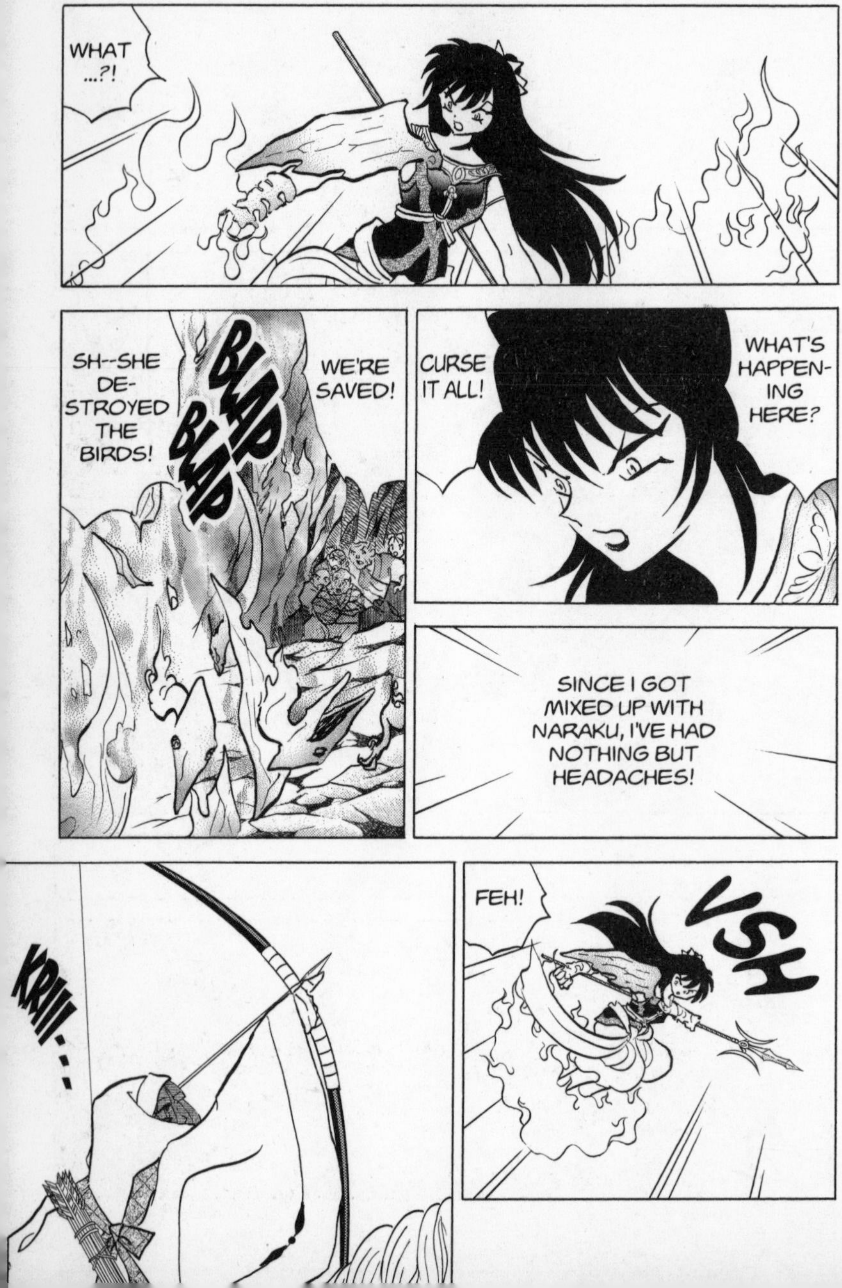
WHAT ...?!
SH--SHE DE-STROYED THE BIRDS!
BLAP BLAP
WE'RE SAVED!
CURSE IT ALL!
WHAT'S HAPPEN-ING HERE?
SINCE I GOT MIXED UP WITH NARAKU, I'VE HAD NOTHING BUT HEADACHES!
KRIII...
FEH!
VSH

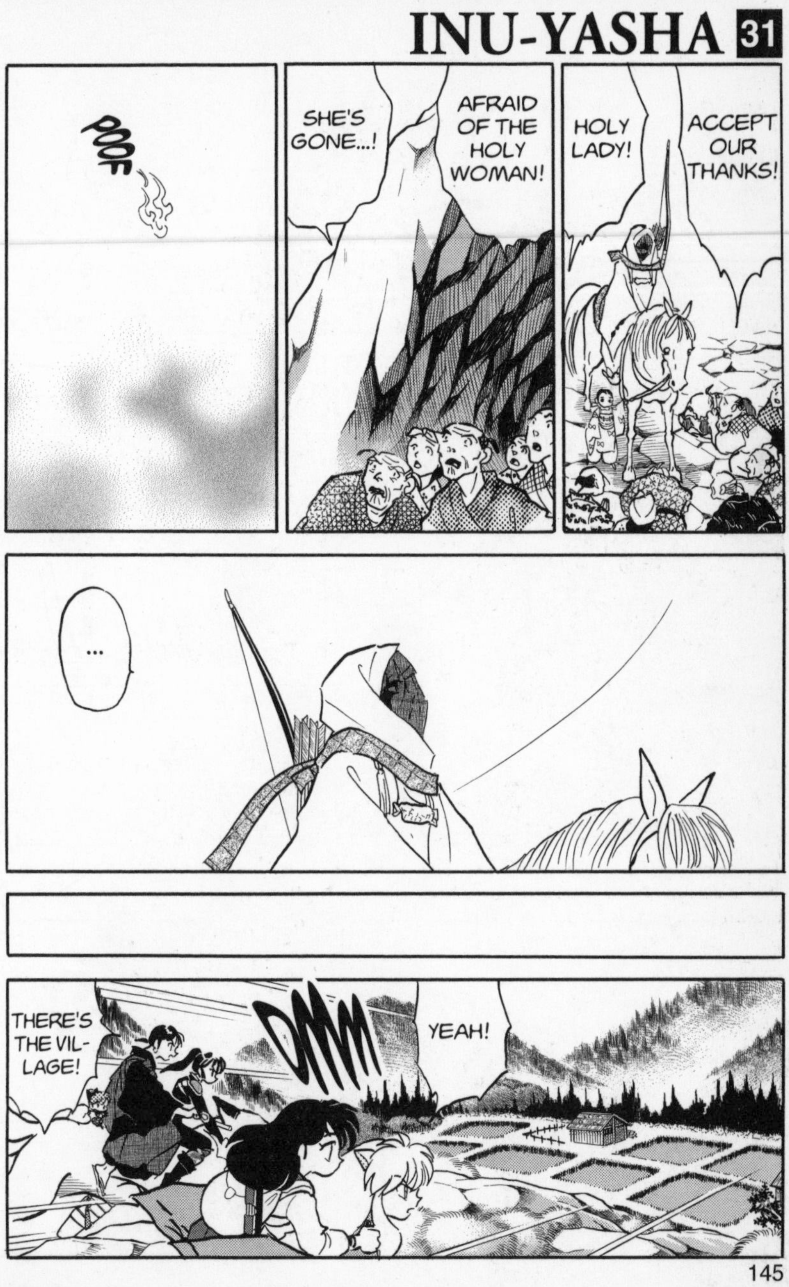
POOF
SHE'S GONE...!
AFRAID OF THE HOLY WOMAN!
HOLY LADY!
ACCEPT OUR THANKS!
...
THERE'S THE VIL-LAGE!
DMM
YEAH!

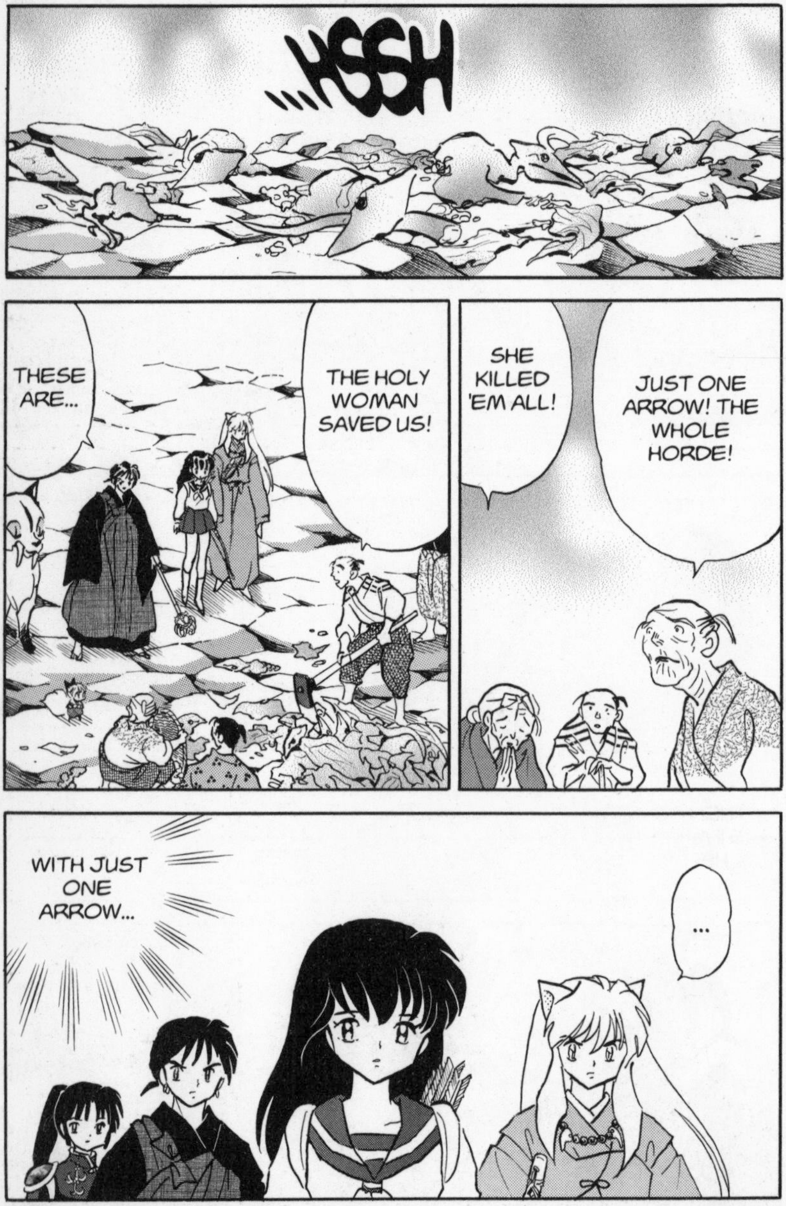
...HSSH
THESE ARE...
THE HOLY WOMAN SAVED US!
SHE KILLED 'EM ALL!
JUST ONE ARROW! THE WHOLE HORDE!
WITH JUST ONE ARROW...
...

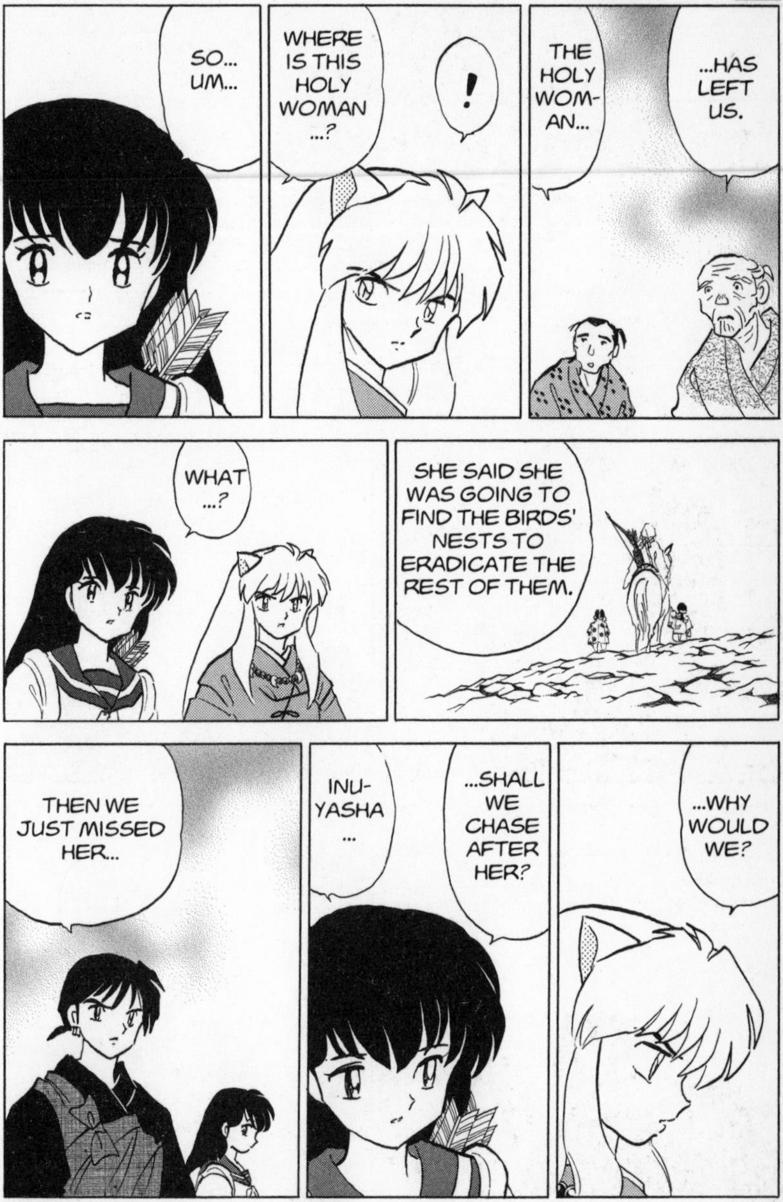
SO... UM...
WHERE IS THIS HOLY WOMAN ...?
!
THE HOLY WOM-AN...
...HAS LEFT US.
WHAT ...?
SHE SAID SHE WAS GOING TO FIND THE BIRDS' NESTS TO ERADICATE THE REST OF THEM.
THEN WE JUST MISSED HER...
INU-YASHA ...
...SHALL WE CHASE AFTER HER?
...WHY WOULD WE?

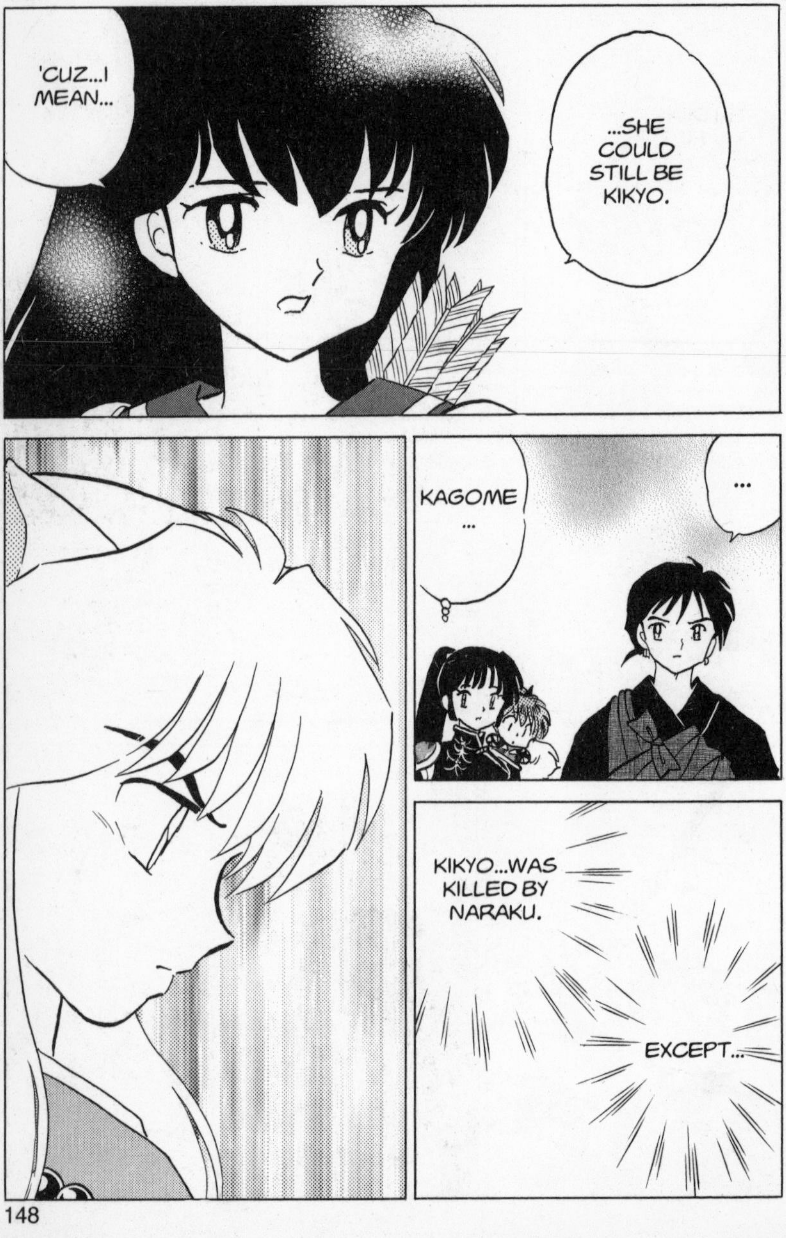
'CUZ...I MEAN...
...SHE COULD STILL BE KIKYO.
KAGOME ...
...
KIKYO...WAS KILLED BY NARAKU.
EXCEPT...

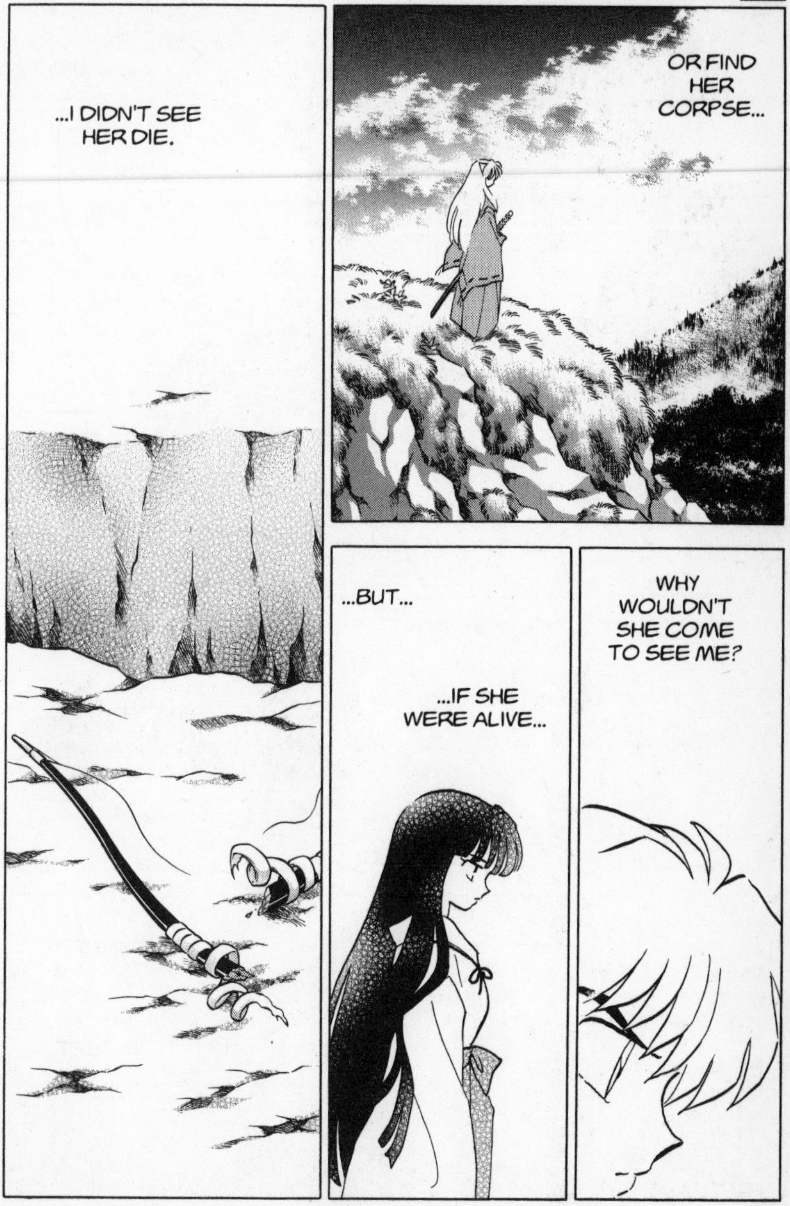
...I DIDN'T SEE HER DIE.
OR FIND HER CORPSE...
...BUT...
...IF SHE WERE ALIVE...
WHY WOULDN'T SHE COME TO SEE ME?

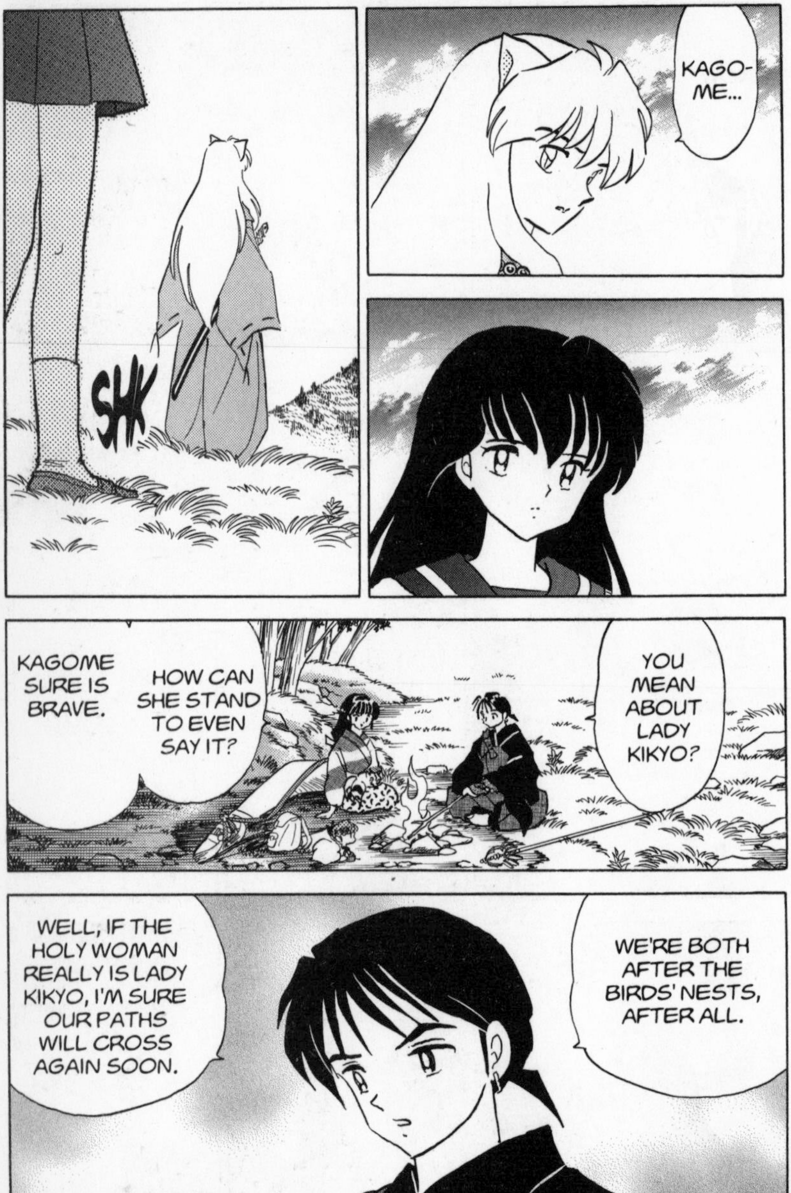
SHK
KAGO-ME...
KAGOME SURE IS BRAVE.
HOW CAN SHE STAND TO EVEN SAY IT?
YOU MEAN ABOUT LADY KIKYO?
WELL, IF THE HOLY WOMAN REALLY IS LADY KIKYO, I'M SURE OUR PATHS WILL CROSS AGAIN SOON.
WE'RE BOTH AFTER THE BIRDS' NESTS, AFTER ALL.

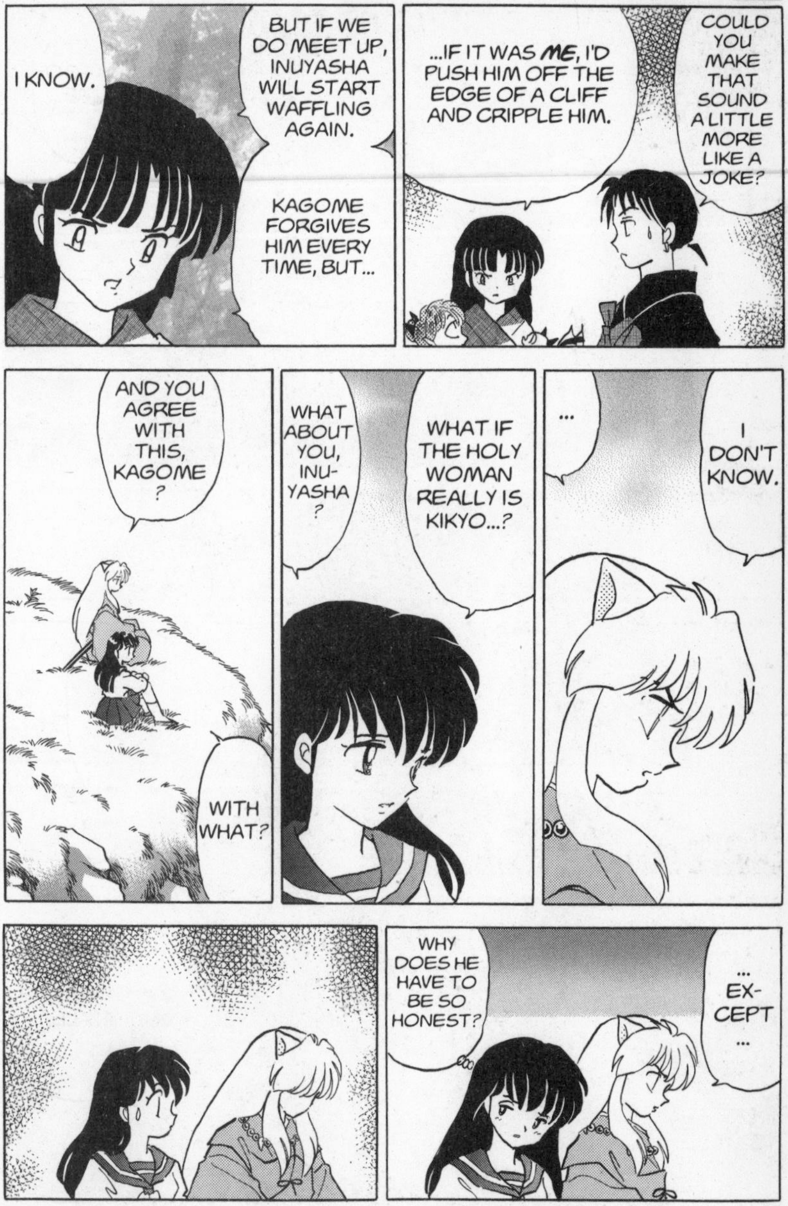
I KNOW.
BUT IF WE DO MEET UP, INUYASHA WILL START WAFFLING AGAIN.
KAGOME FORGIVES HIM EVERY TIME, BUT...
...IF IT WAS ME, I'D PUSH HIM OFF THE EDGE OF A CLIFF AND CRIPPLE HIM.
COULD YOU MAKE THAT SOUND A LITTLE MORE LIKE A JOKE?
AND YOU AGREE WITH THIS, KAGOME?
WITH WHAT?
WHAT ABOUT YOU, INU-YASHA?
WHAT IF THE HOLY WOMAN REALLY IS KIKYO...?
...
I DON'T KNOW.
WHY DOES HE HAVE TO BE SO HONEST?
...EX-CEPT...

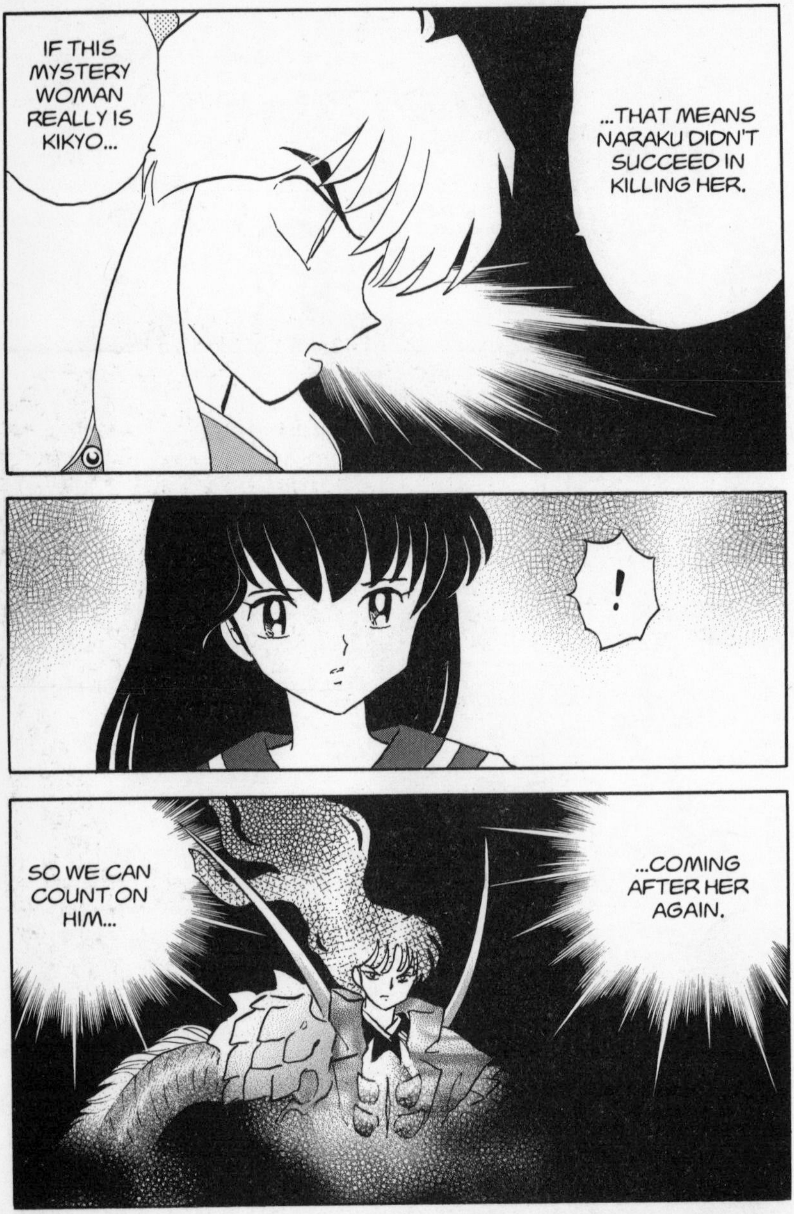
IF THIS MYSTERY WOMAN REALLY IS KIKYO...
...THAT MEANS NARAKU DIDN'T SUCCEED IN KILLING HER.
!
SO WE CAN COUNT ON HIM...
...COMING AFTER HER AGAIN.

SCROLL 9

THE FORBIDDEN MOUNTAIN

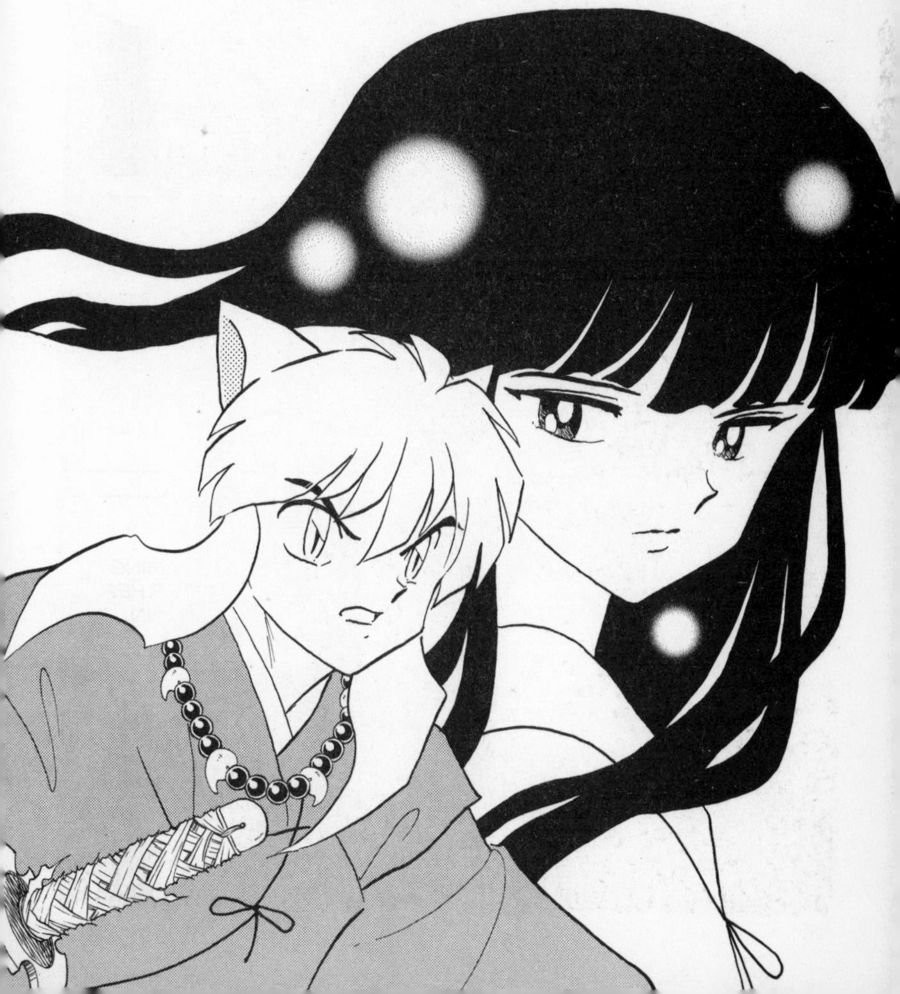

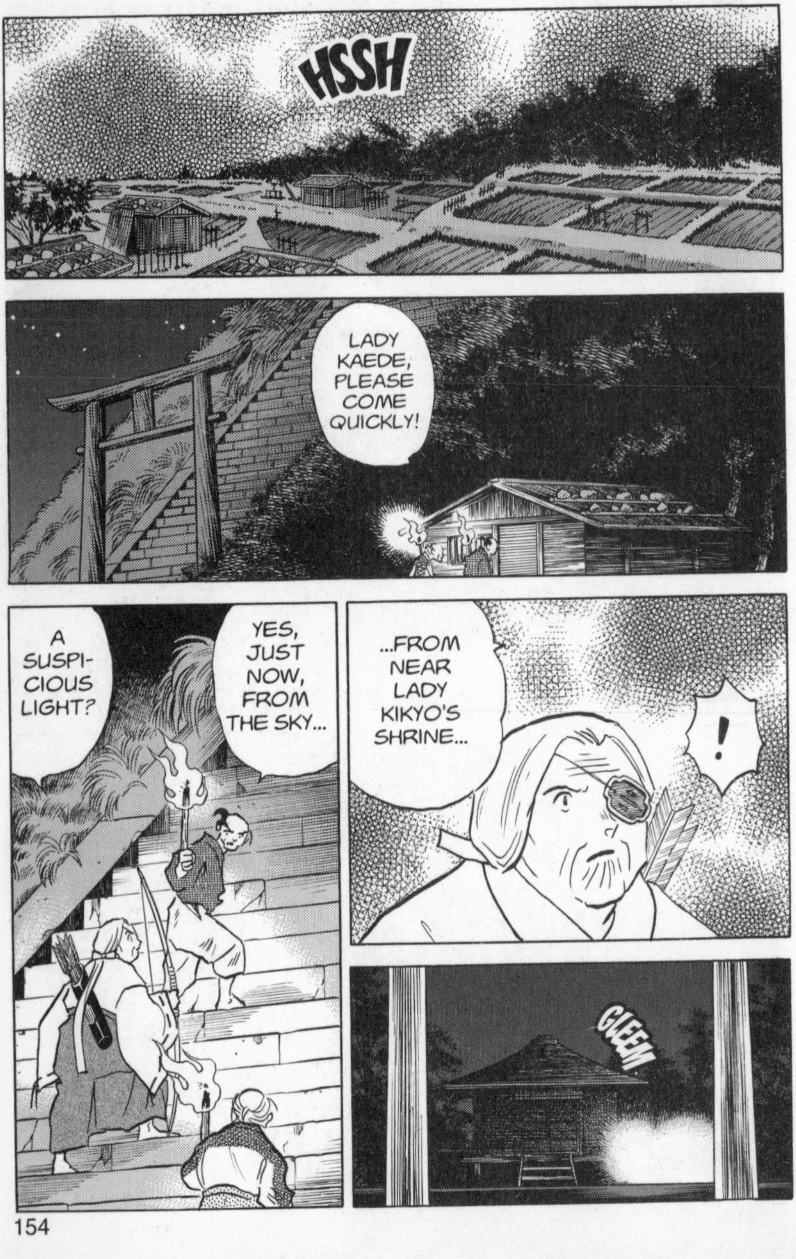
HSSH
LADY KAEDE, PLEASE COME QUICKLY!
A SUSPI-CIOUS LIGHT?
YES, JUST NOW, FROM THE SKY...
...FROM NEAR LADY KIKYO'S SHRINE...
!
GLEEM

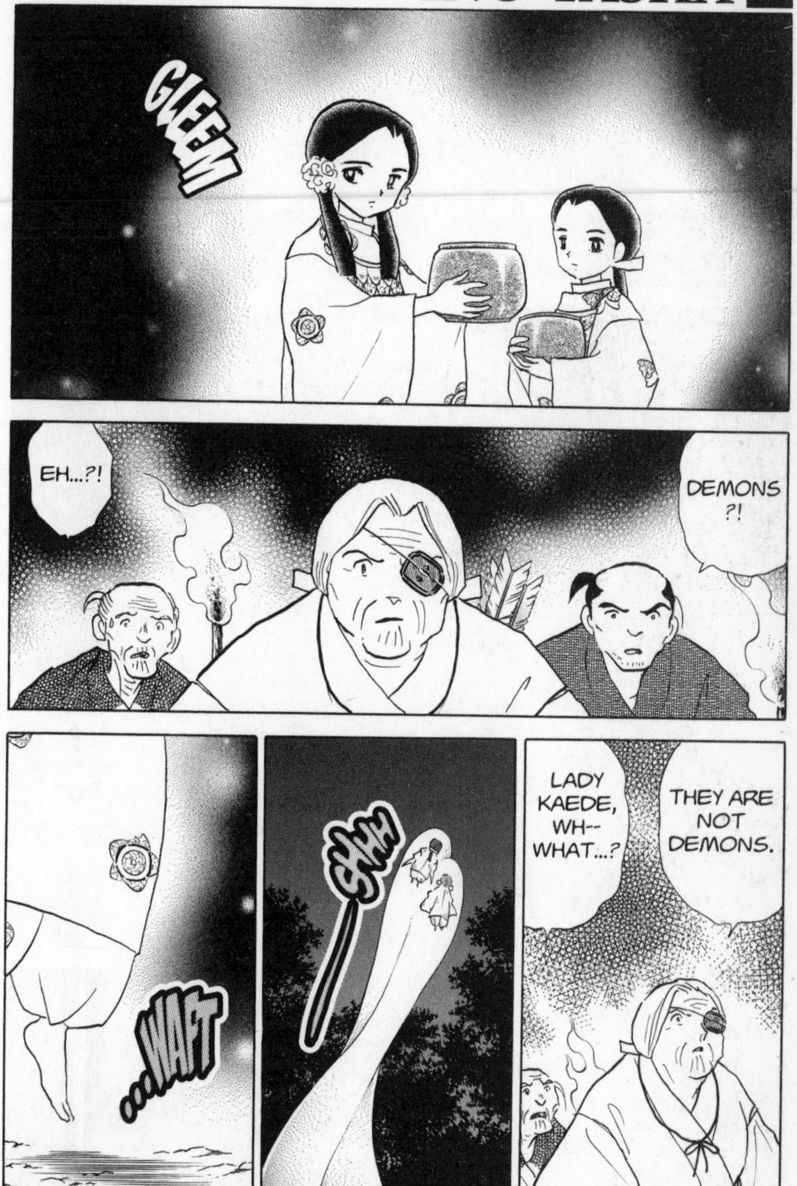
GLEEM
EH...?!
DEMONS ?!
...WAFT
SHAH
LADY KAEDE, WH-- WHAT...?
THEY ARE NOT DEMONS.

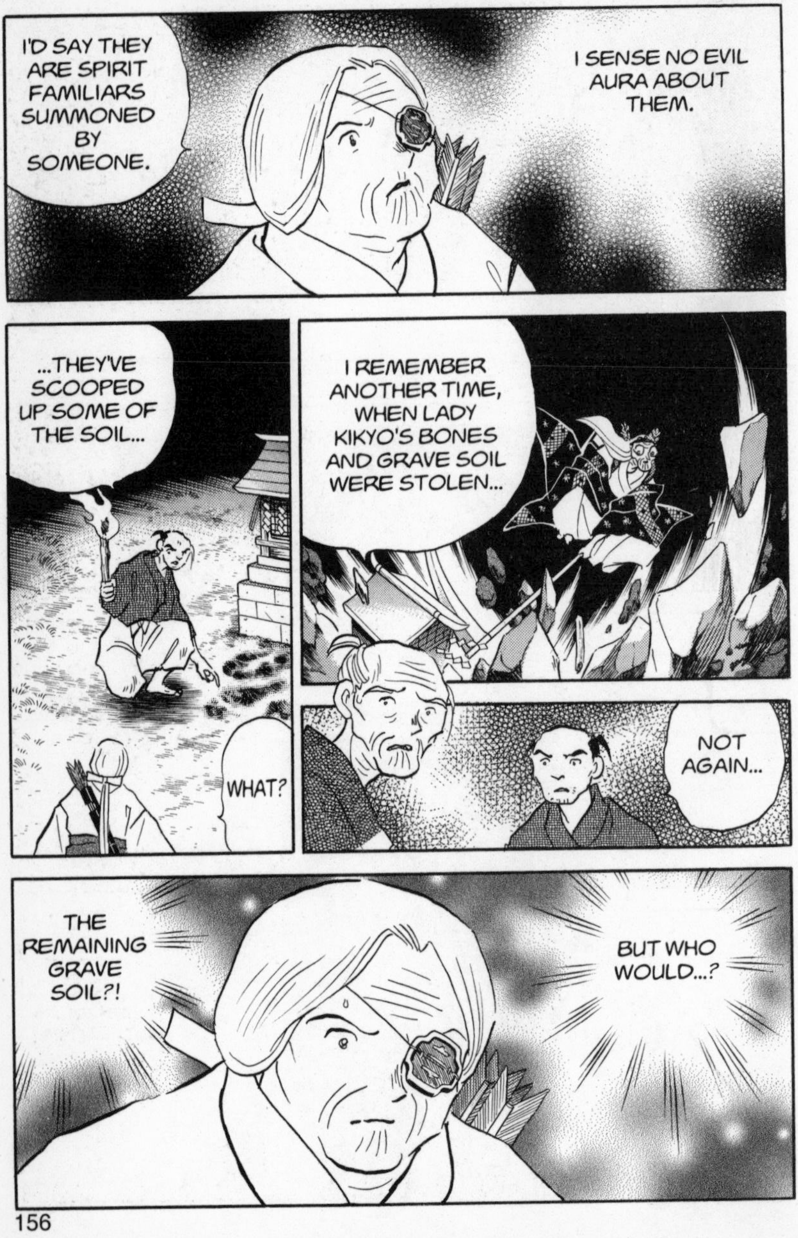
I'D SAY THEY ARE SPIRIT FAMILIARS SUMMONED BY SOMEONE.
I SENSE NO EVIL AURA ABOUT THEM.
...THEY'VE SCOOPED UP SOME OF THE SOIL...
WHAT?
I REMEMBER ANOTHER TIME, WHEN LADY KIKYO'S BONES AND GRAVE SOIL WERE STOLEN...
NOT AGAIN...
THE REMAINING GRAVE SOIL?!
BUT WHO WOULD...?

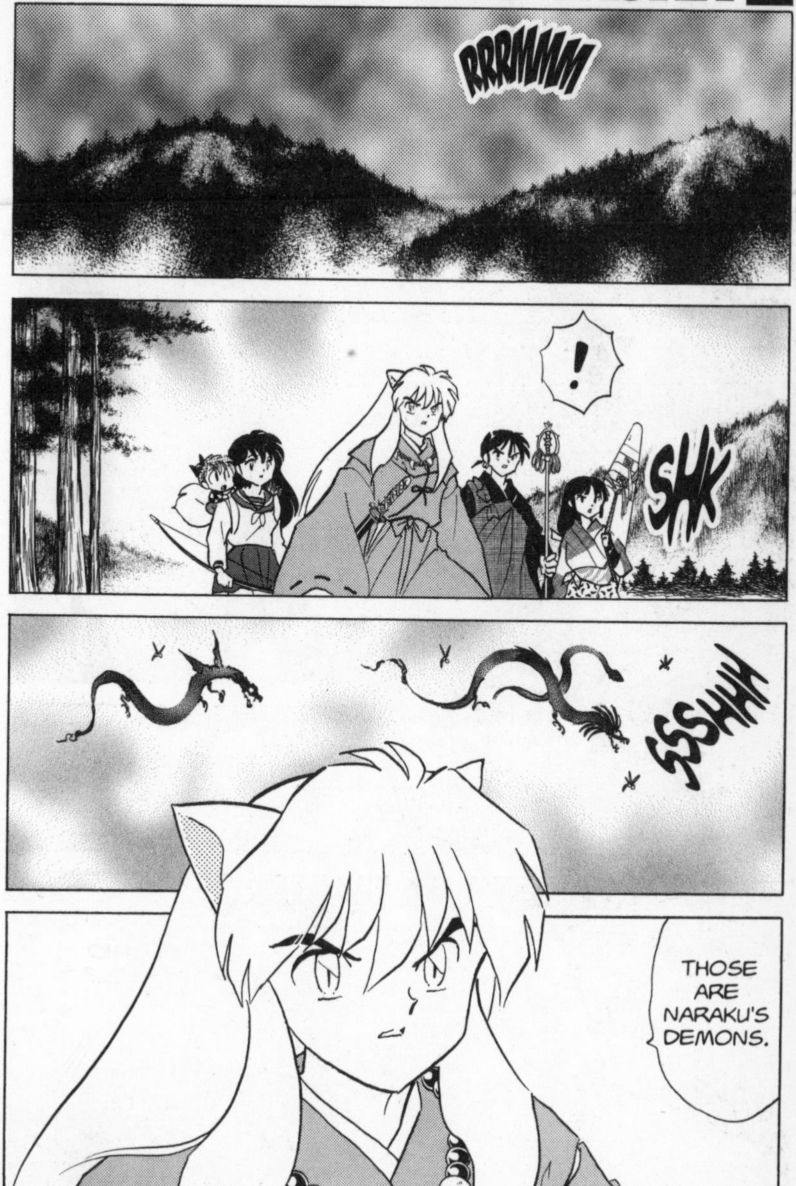
RRRMMM
!
SHK
SSSHHH
THOSE ARE NARAKU'S DEMONS.

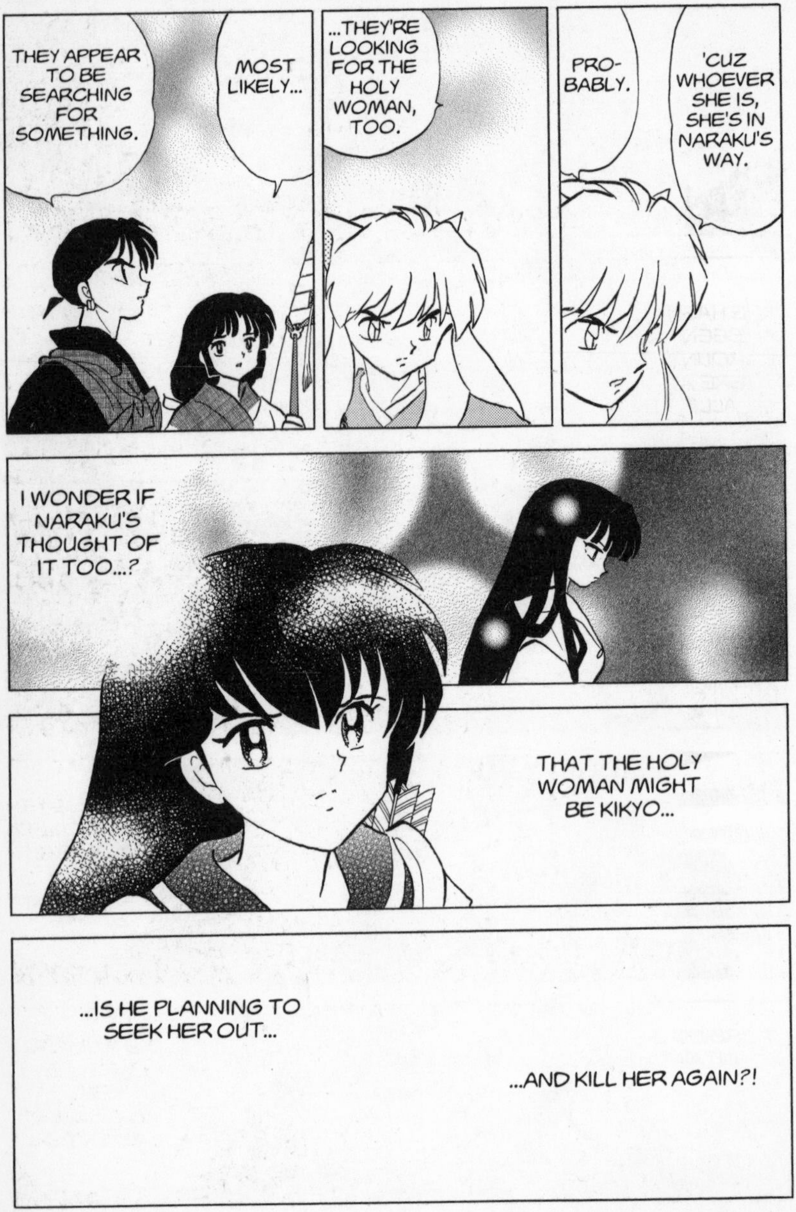
THEY APPEAR TO BE SEARCHING FOR SOMETHING.
MOST LIKELY...
...THEY'RE LOOKING FOR THE HOLY WOMAN, TOO.
PRO-BABLY.
'CUZ WHOEVER SHE IS, SHE'S IN NARAKU'S WAY.
I WONDER IF NARAKU'S THOUGHT OF IT TOO...?
THAT THE HOLY WOMAN MIGHT BE KIKYO...
...IS HE PLANNING TO SEEK HER OUT...
...AND KILL HER AGAIN?!

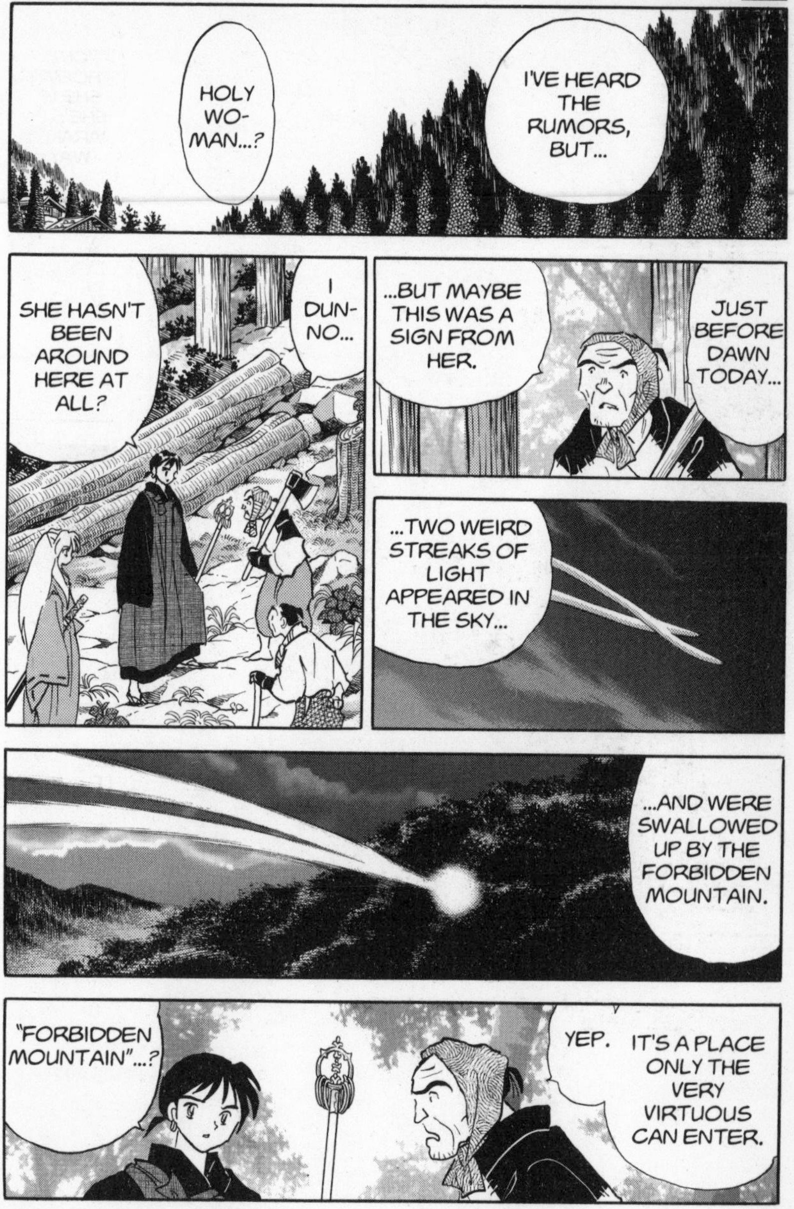
HOLY WO-MAN...?
I'VE HEARD THE RUMORS, BUT...
SHE HASN'T BEEN AROUND HERE AT ALL?
I DUN-NO...
...BUT MAYBE THIS WAS A SIGN FROM HER.
JUST BEFORE DAWN TODAY...
...TWO WEIRD STREAKS OF LIGHT APPEARED IN THE SKY...
...AND WERE SWALLOWED UP BY THE FORBIDDEN MOUNTAIN.
"FORBIDDEN MOUNTAIN"...?
YEP.
IT'S A PLACE ONLY THE VERY VIRTUOUS CAN ENTER.

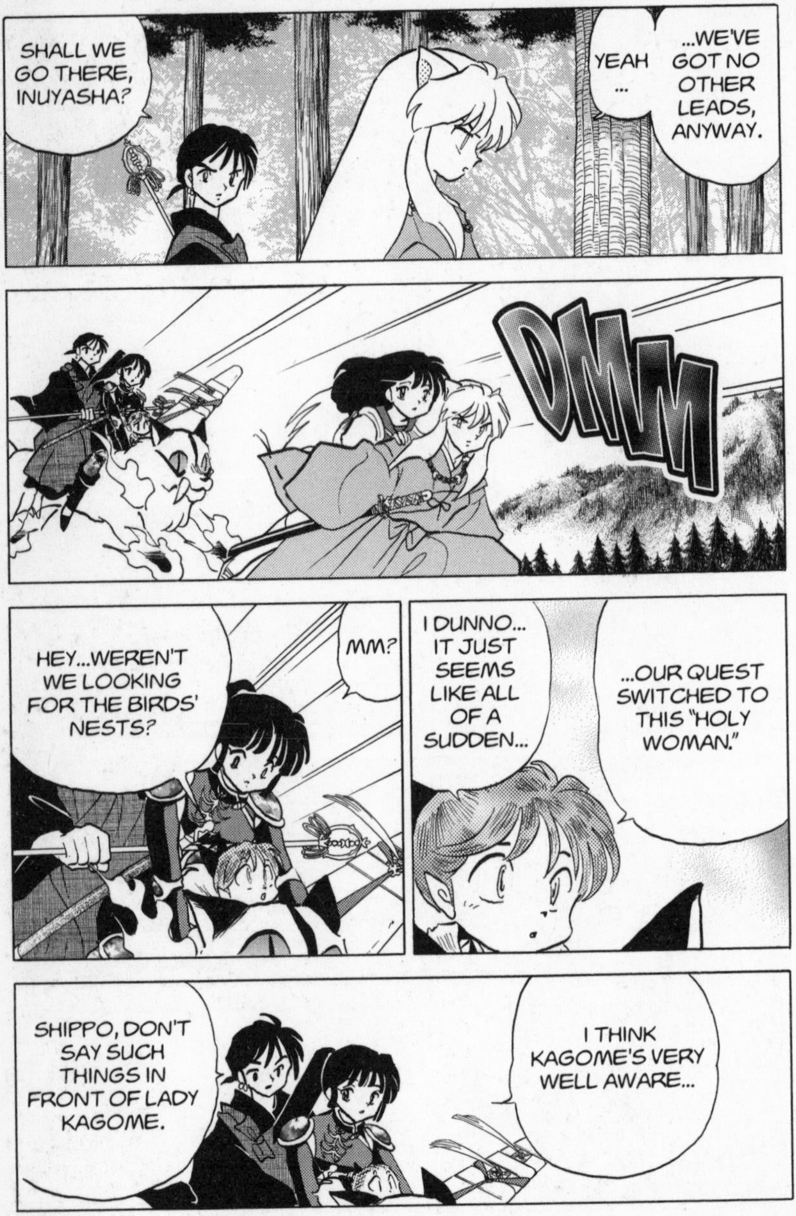
SHALL WE GO THERE, INUYASHA?
YEAH ...
...WE'VE GOT NO OTHER LEADS, ANYWAY.
DMMM
HEY...WEREN'T WE LOOKING FOR THE BIRDS' NESTS?
MM?
I DUNNO... IT JUST SEEMS LIKE ALL OF A SUDDEN...
...OUR QUEST SWITCHED TO THIS "HOLY WOMAN."
SHIPPO, DON'T SAY SUCH THINGS IN FRONT OF LADY KAGOME.
I THINK KAGOME'S VERY WELL AWARE...

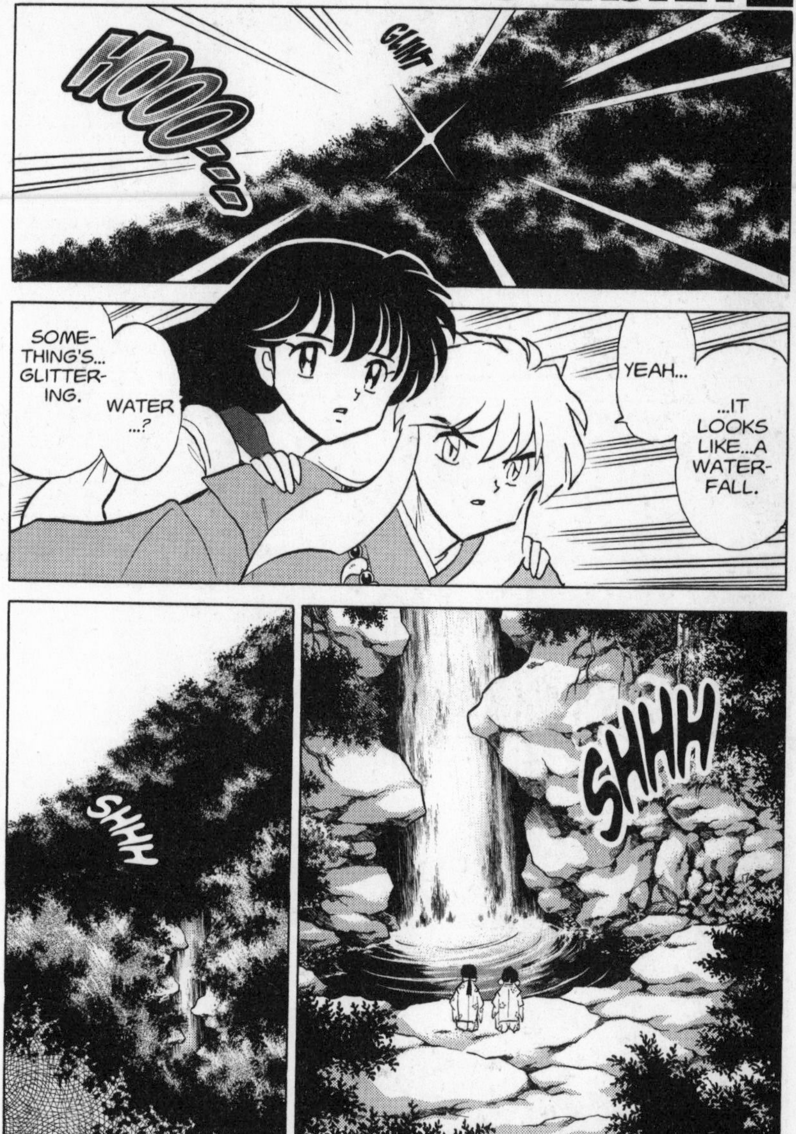
HOOO...
GLINT
SOME-THING'S... GLITTER-ING.
WATER ...?
YEAH...
...IT LOOKS LIKE...A WATER-FALL.
SHHH
SHHH

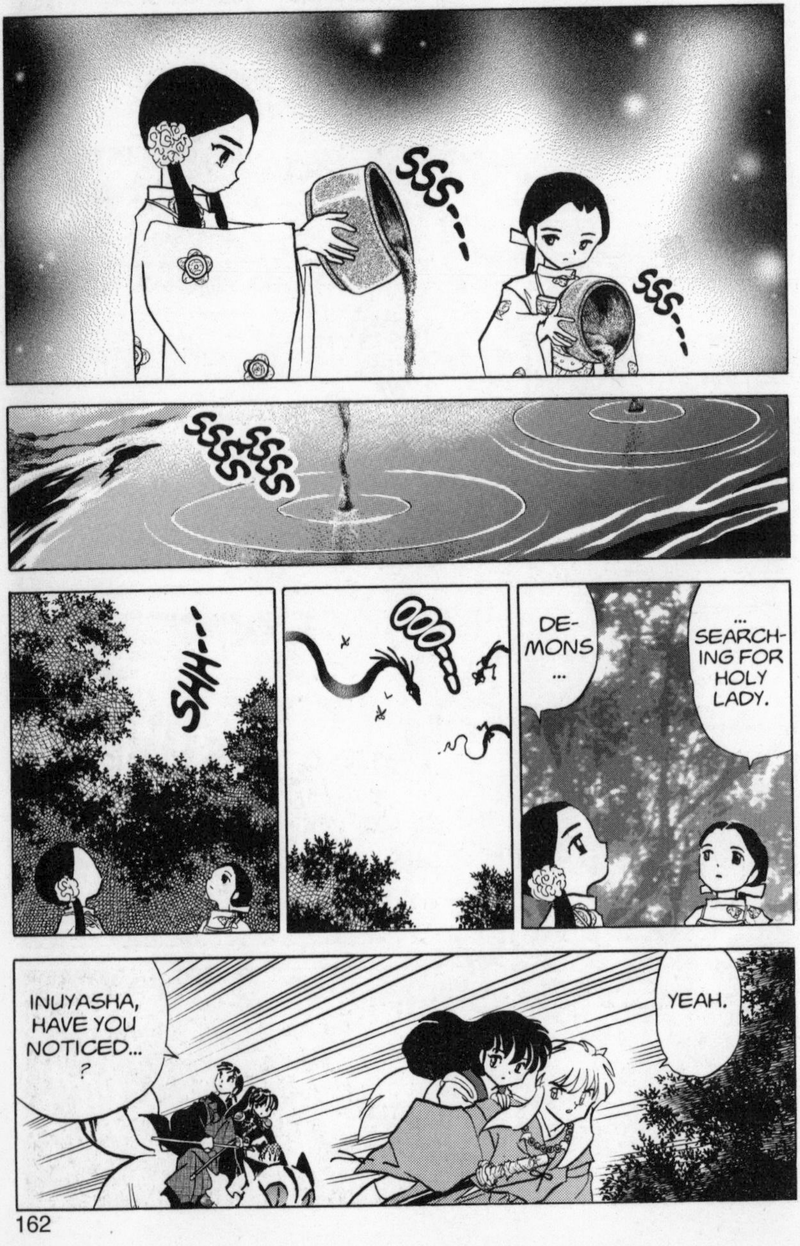
SSS...
SSS...
SSSSSS
SHH...
OOO
DE-MONS...
...SEARCH-ING FOR HOLY LADY.
INUYASHA, HAVE YOU NOTICED...?
YEAH.

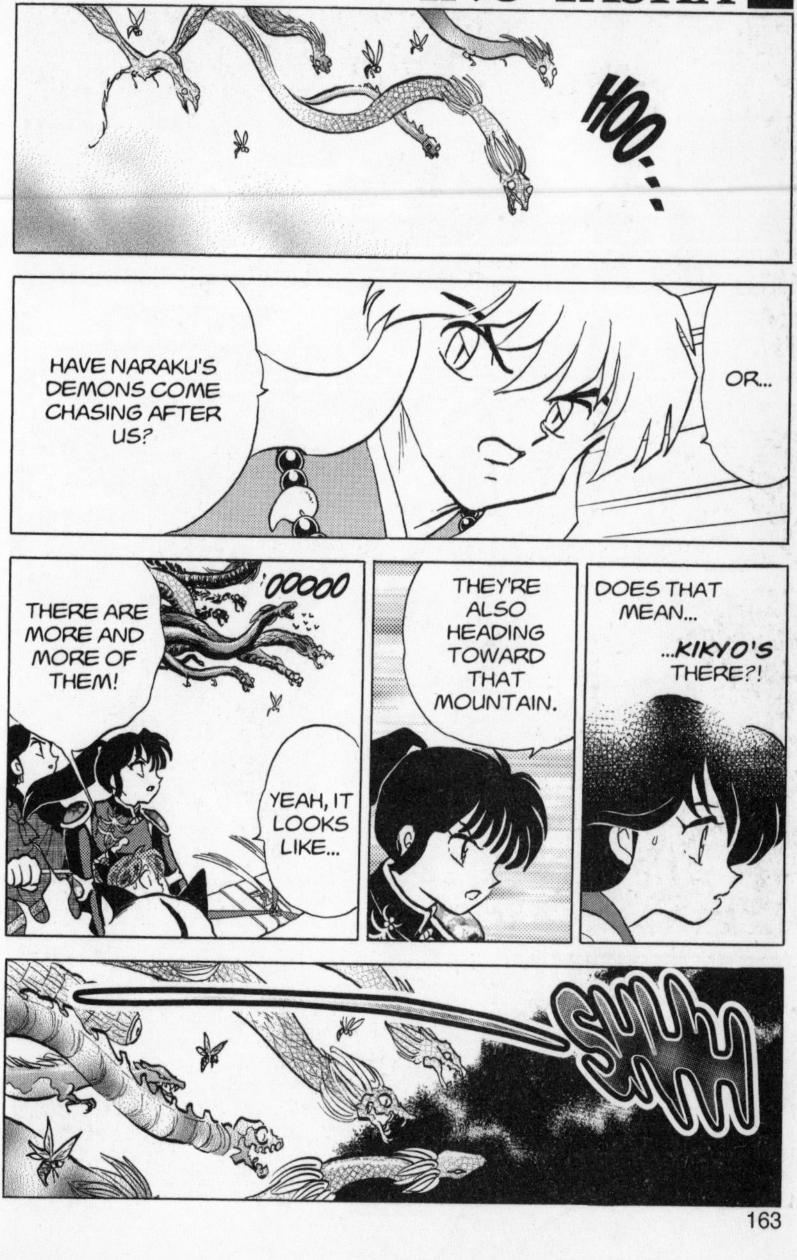
HOO...
HAVE NARAKU'S DEMONS COME CHASING AFTER US?
OR...
THERE ARE MORE AND MORE OF THEM!
OOOOO
YEAH, IT LOOKS LIKE...
THEY'RE ALSO HEADING TOWARD THAT MOUNTAIN.
DOES THAT MEAN...
...*KIKYO'S* THERE?!
SHHH

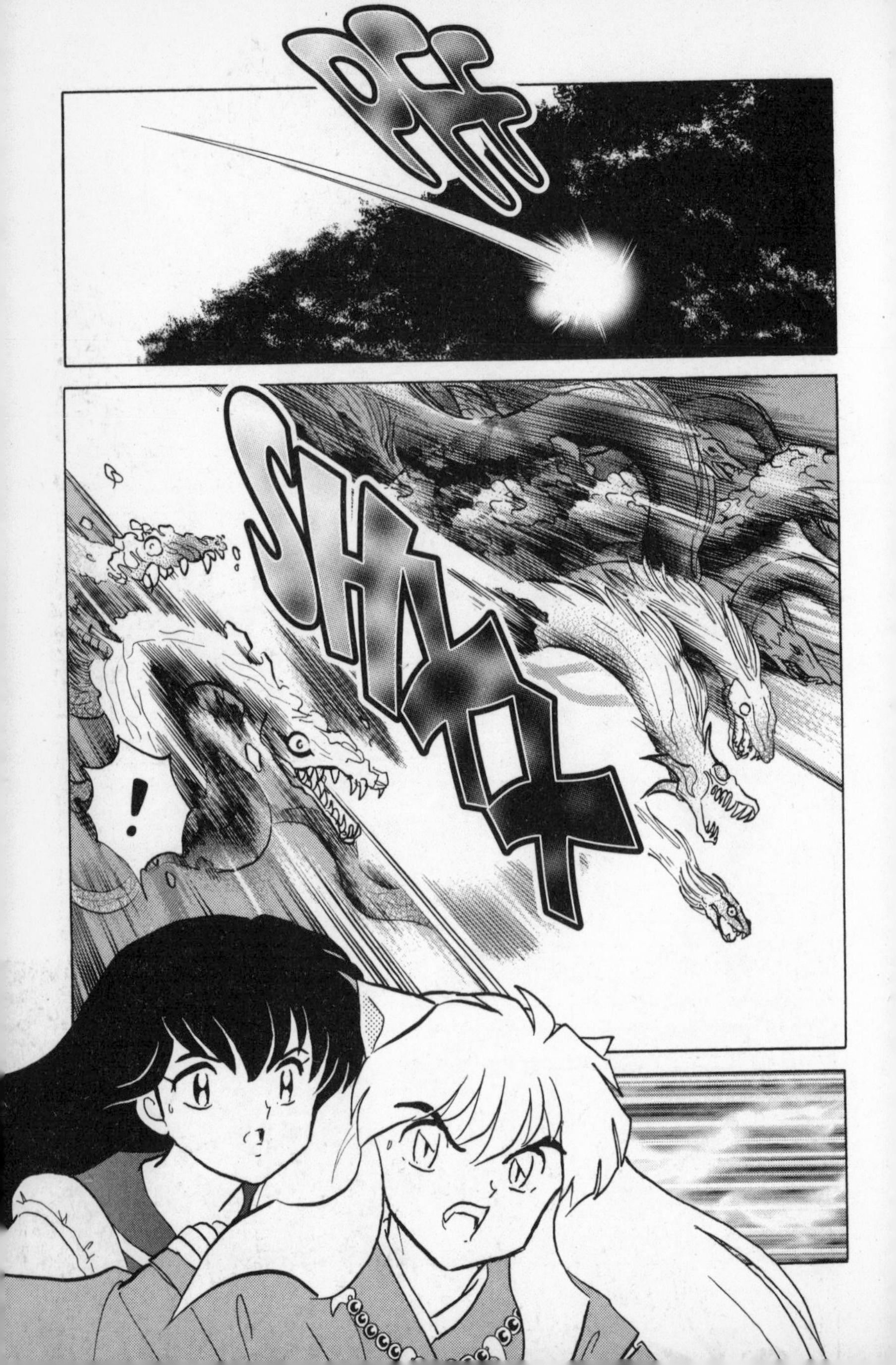
!

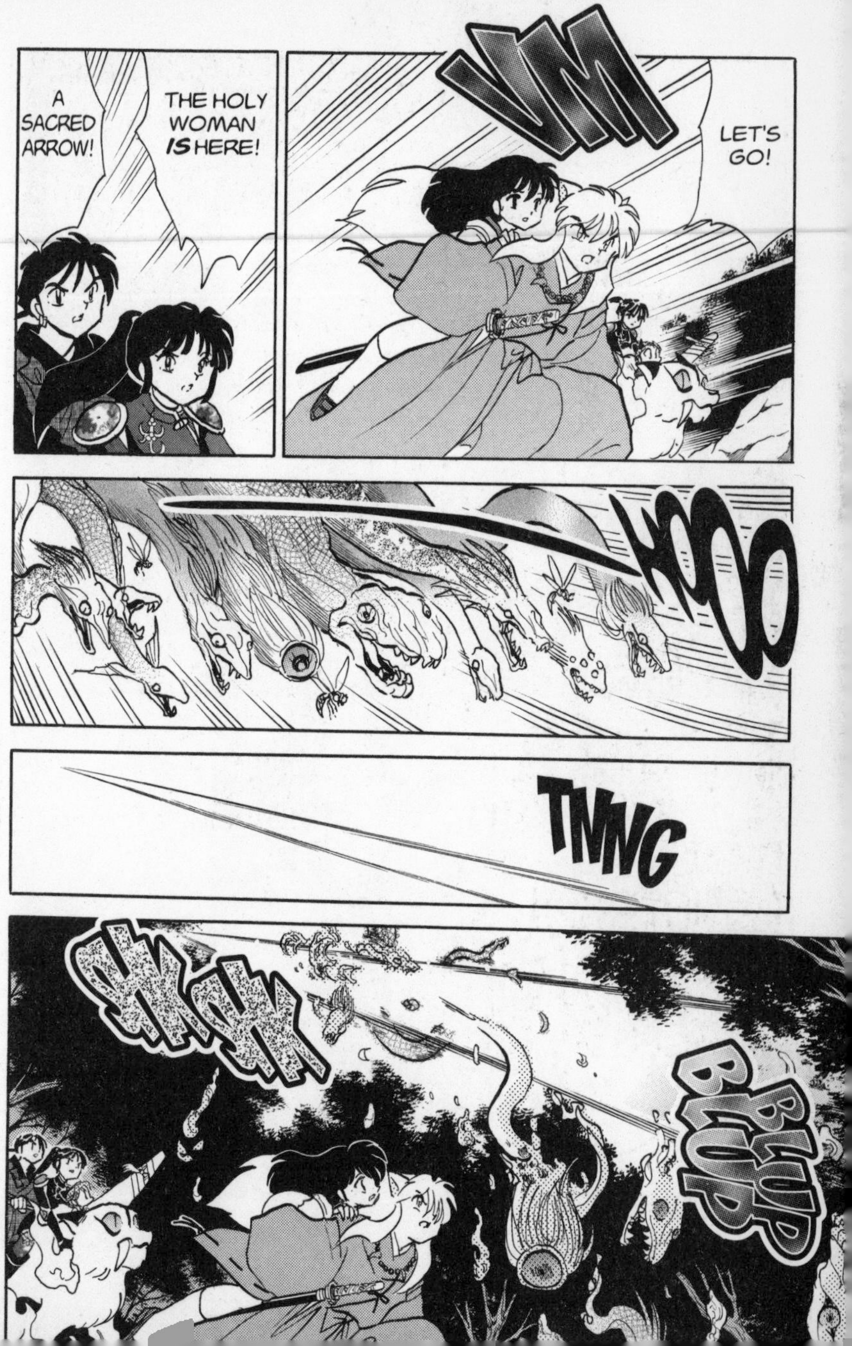
A SACRED ARROW!
THE HOLY WOMAN *IS* HERE!
VM
LET'S GO!
WHOOSH
TINNG
SHASHK
BLUP BLUP

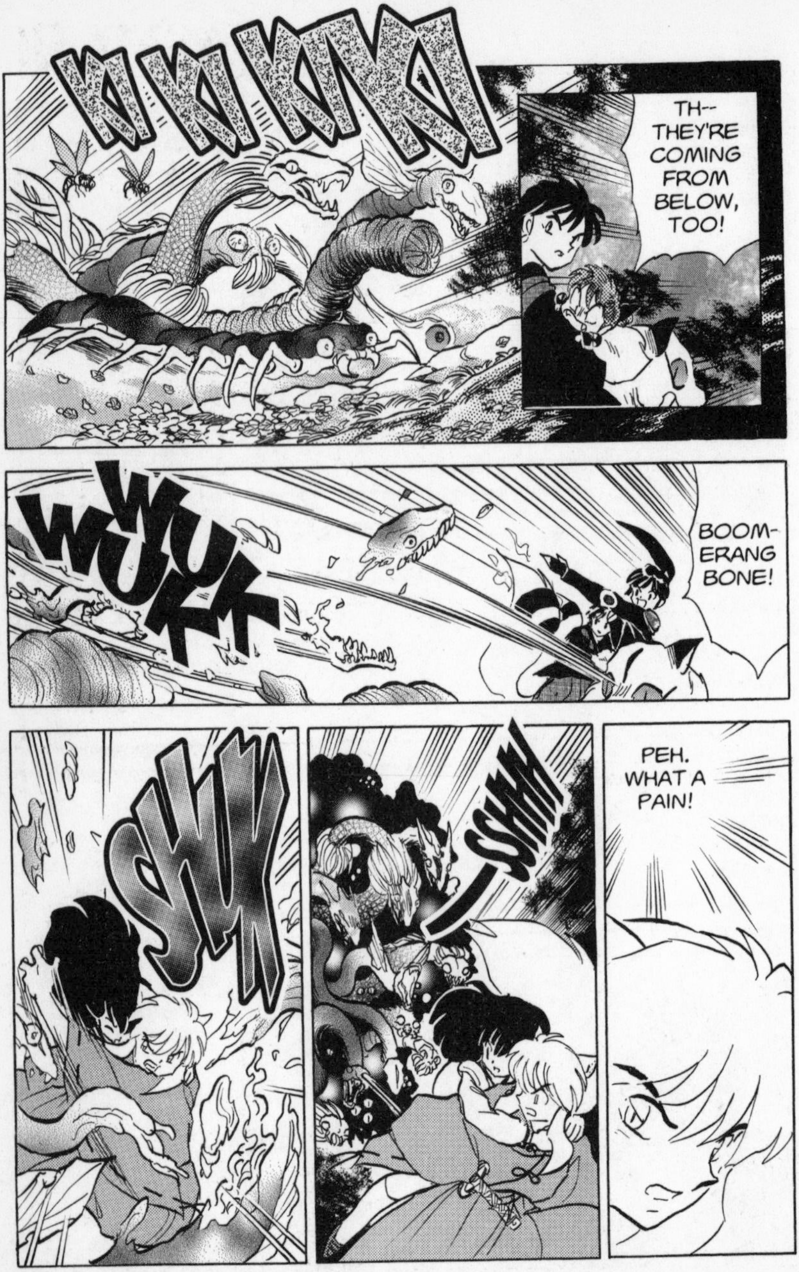
TH-- THEY'RE COMING FROM BELOW, TOO!
BOOM-ERANG BONE!
PEH. WHAT A PAIN!

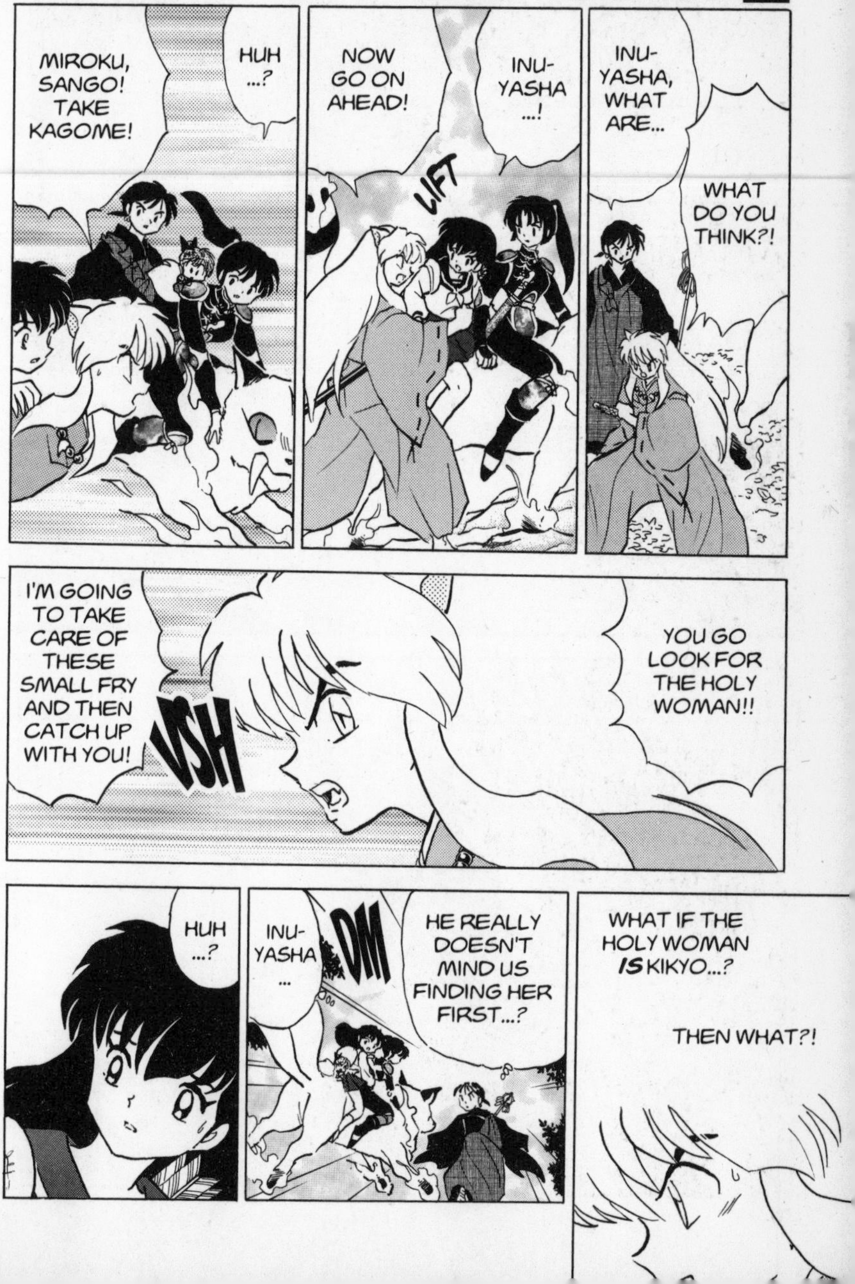
MIROKU, SANGO! TAKE KAGOME!
HUH ...?
NOW GO ON AHEAD!
INU-YASHA ...!
LIFT
INU-YASHA, WHAT ARE...
WHAT DO YOU THINK?!
I'M GOING TO TAKE CARE OF THESE SMALL FRY AND THEN CATCH UP WITH YOU!
VSH
YOU GO LOOK FOR THE HOLY WOMAN!!
HUH ...?
INU-YASHA ...
DM
HE REALLY DOESN'T MIND US FINDING HER FIRST...?
WHAT IF THE HOLY WOMAN *IS* KIKYO...?
THEN WHAT?!

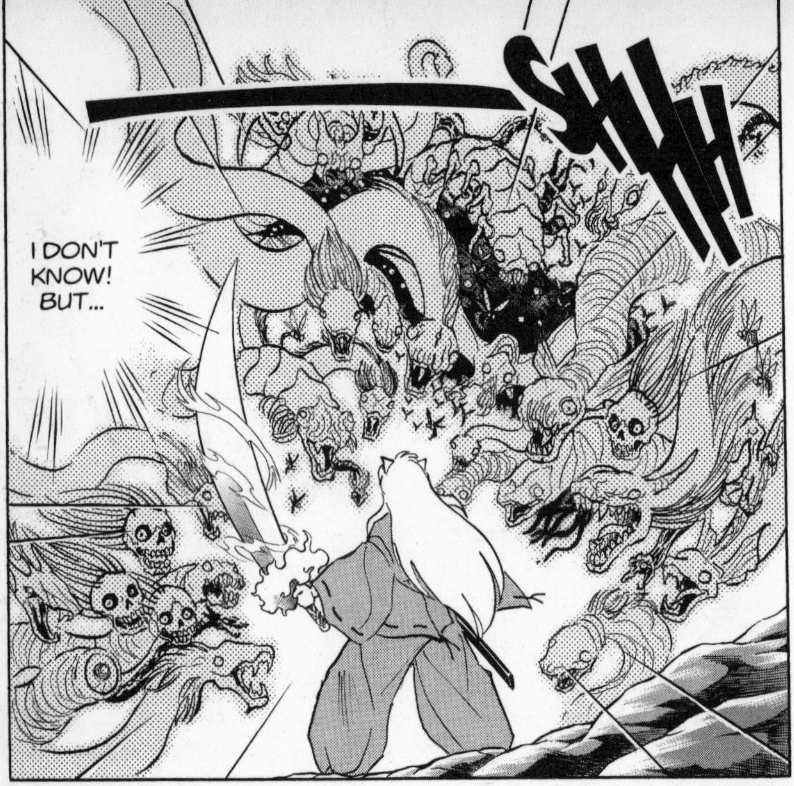
I DON'T KNOW! BUT...
SHHH
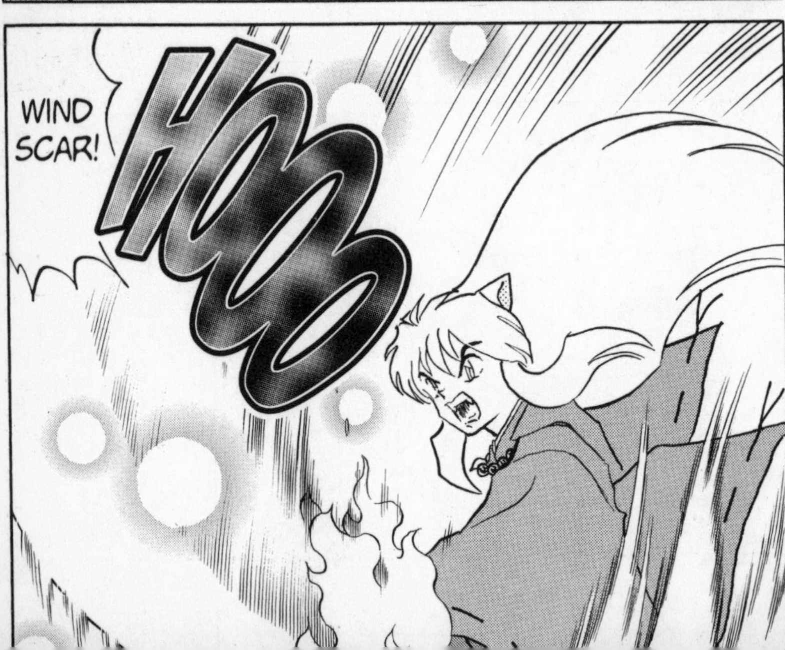
WIND SCAR!
HOOO

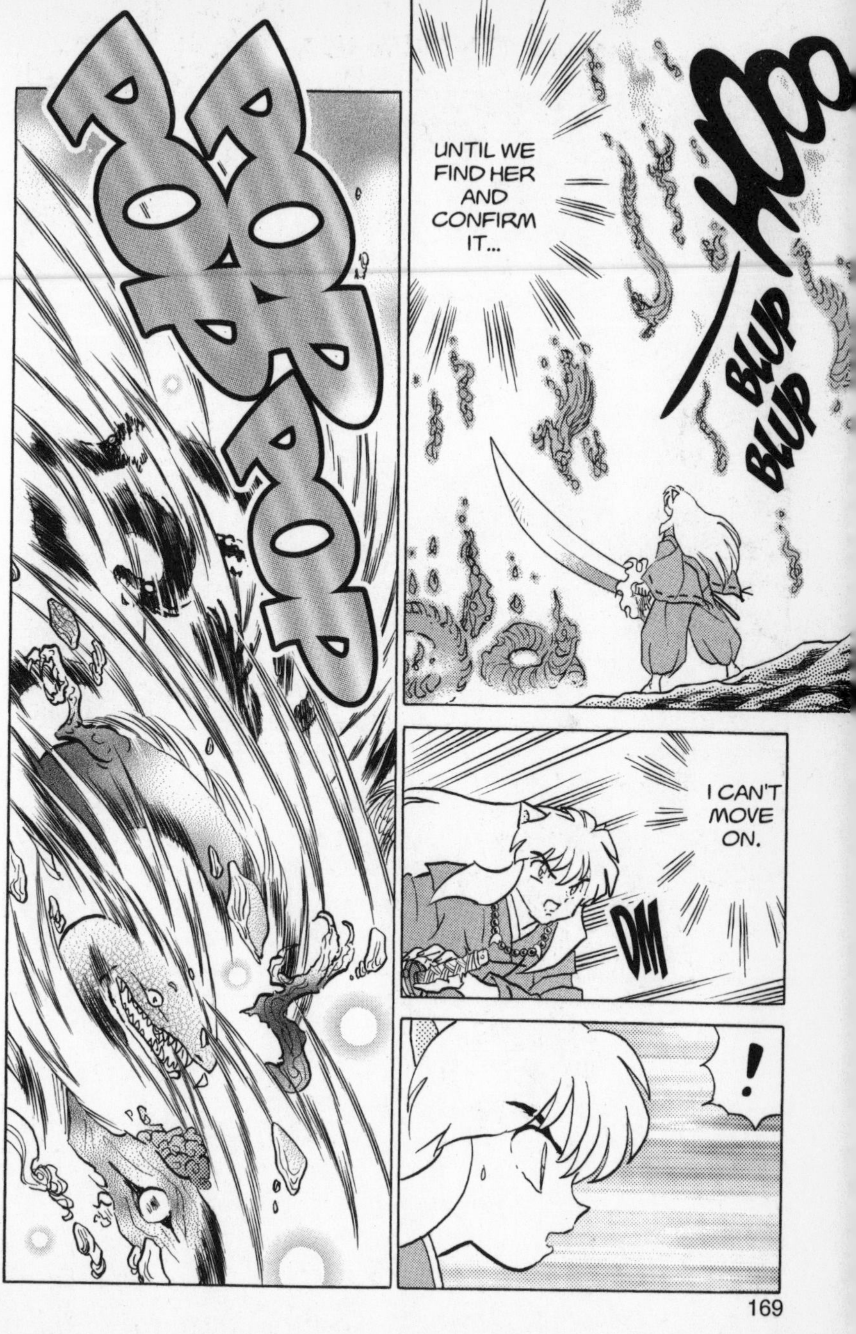
UNTIL WE FIND HER AND CONFIRM IT...
BLUP BLUP
I CAN'T MOVE ON.
DM
!

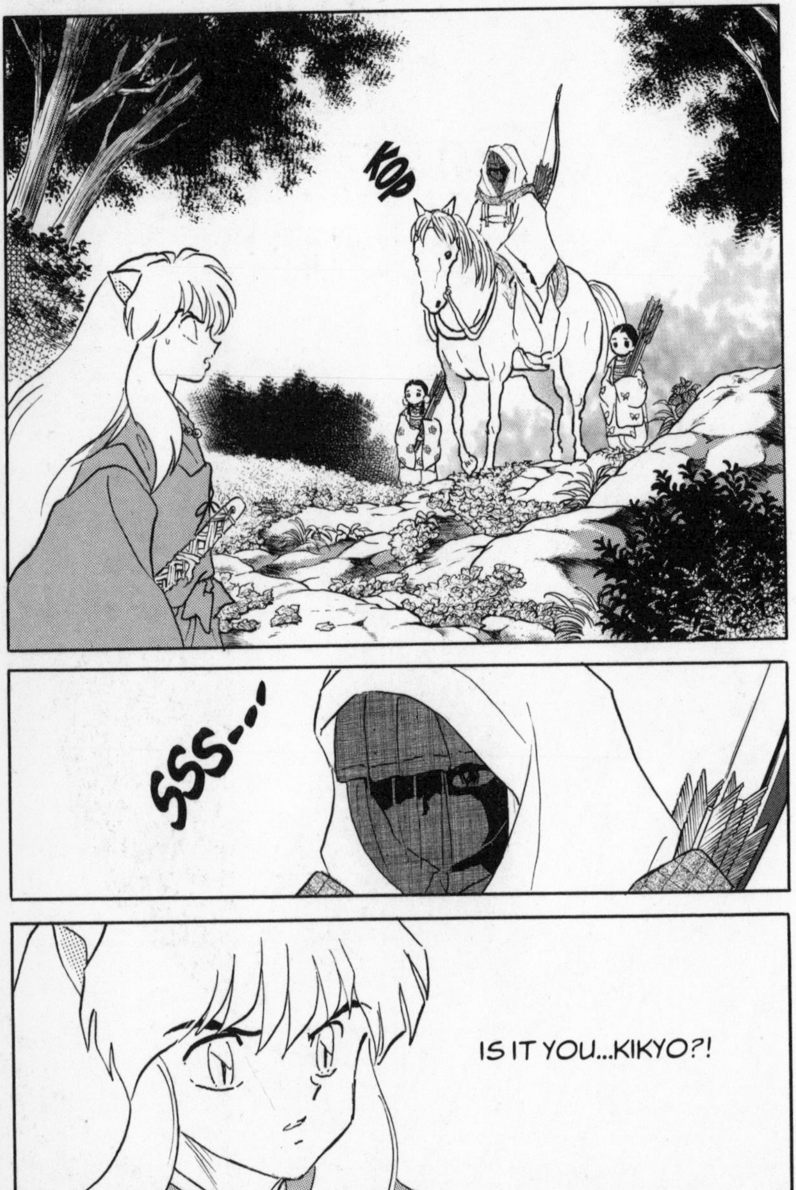
KOP
SSS...
IS IT YOU...KIKYO?!

SCROLL 10
THE WATERFALL BASIN

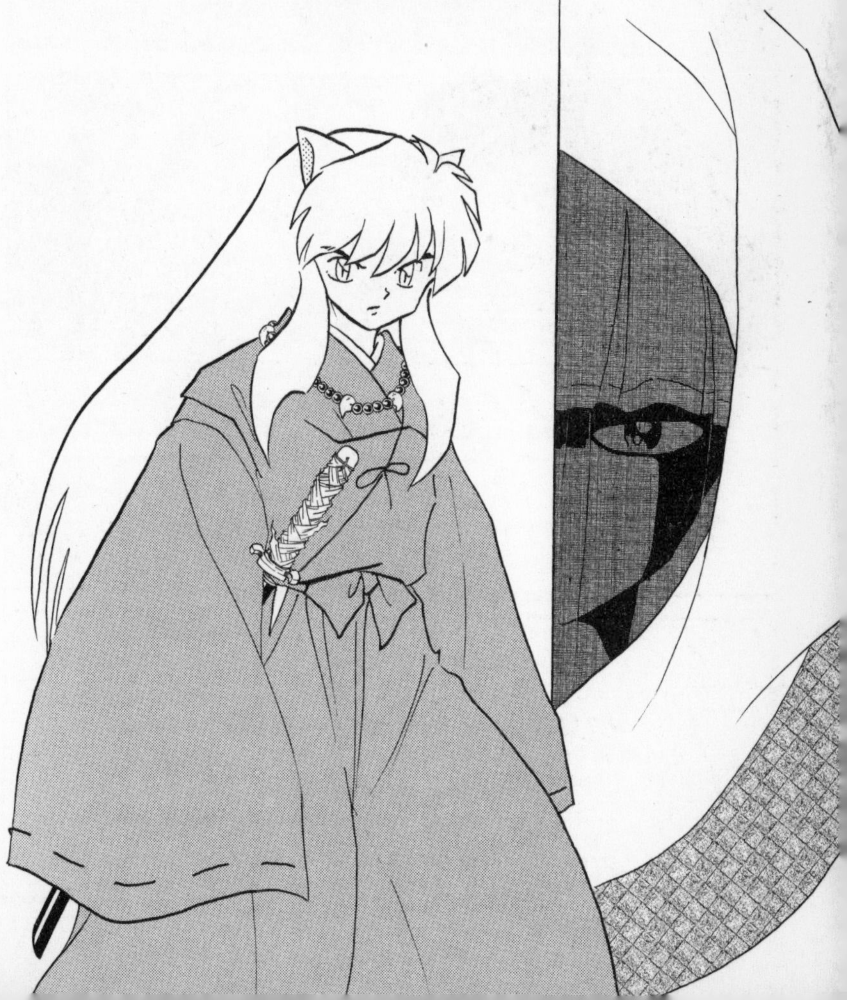

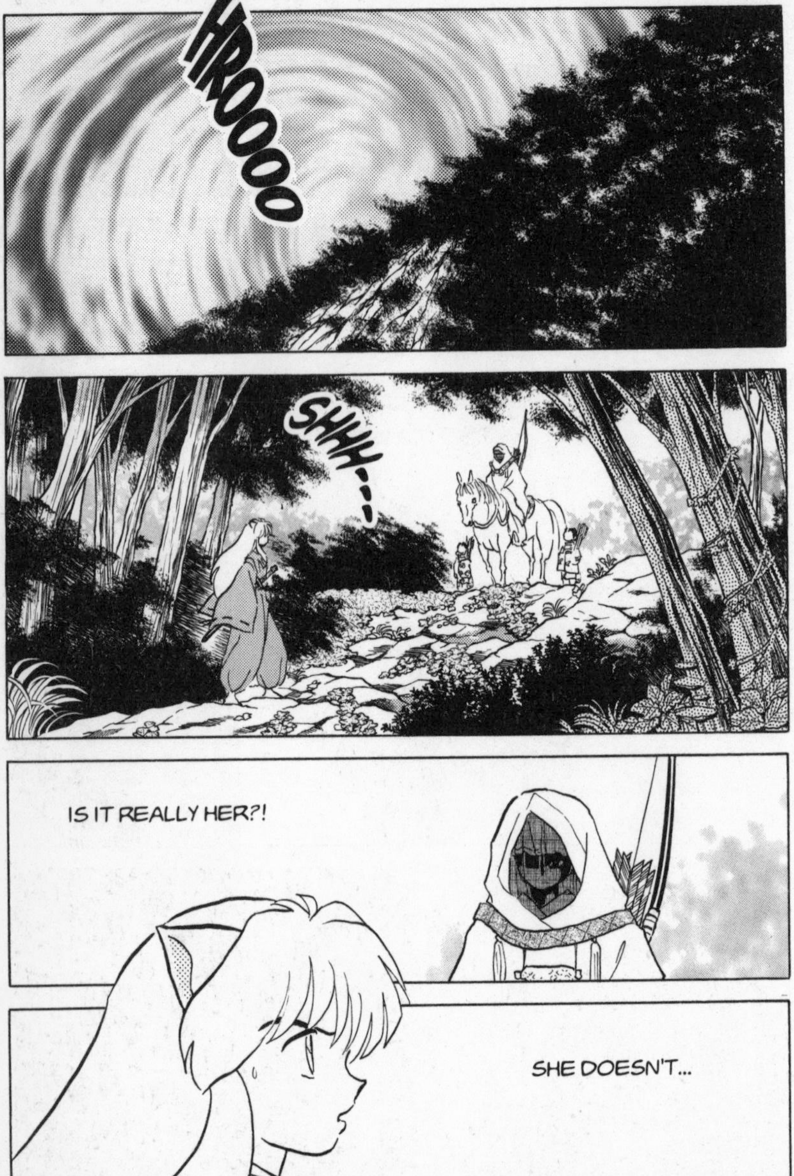
HROOOOO
SHHH...
IS IT REALLY HER?!
SHE DOESN'T...

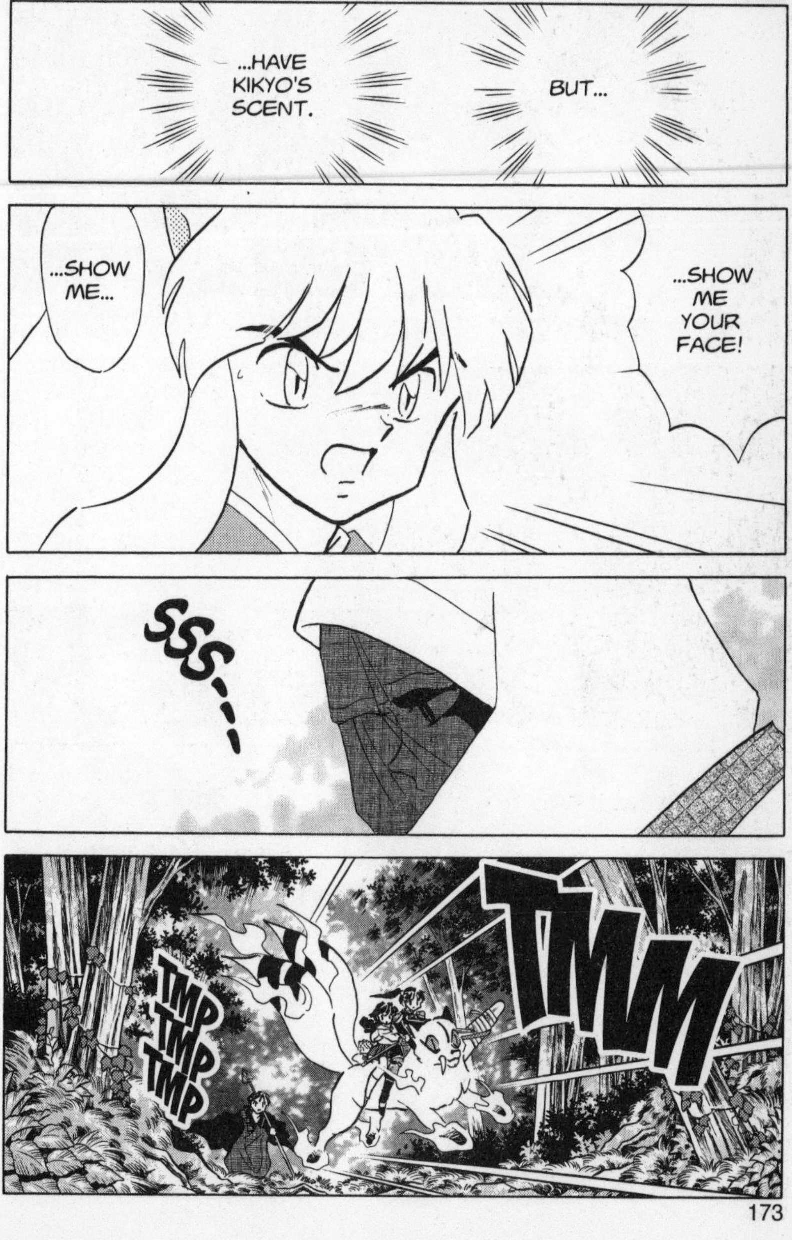
...HAVE KIKYO'S SCENT.
BUT...
...SHOW ME...
...SHOW ME YOUR FACE!
SSS...
TMP TMP TMP
TMM

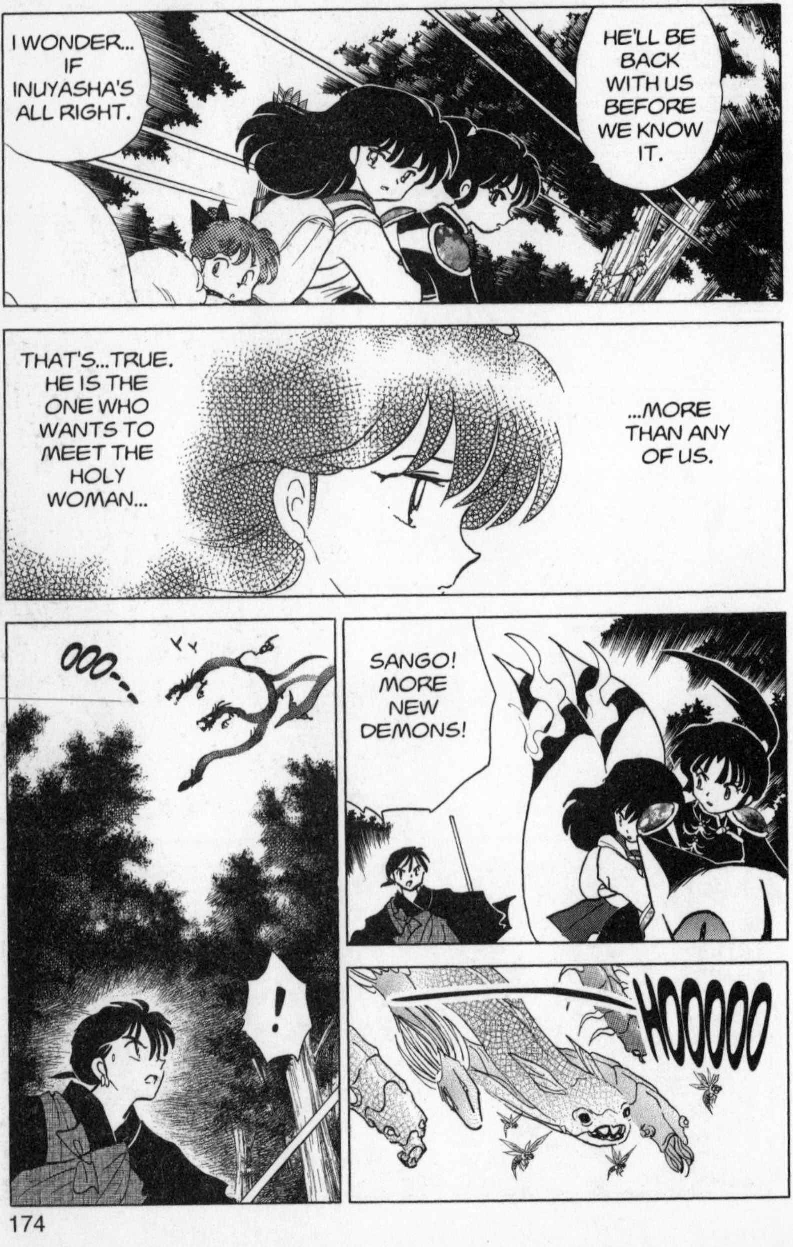
I WONDER... IF INUYASHA'S ALL RIGHT.
HE'LL BE BACK WITH US BEFORE WE KNOW IT.
THAT'S...TRUE. HE IS THE ONE WHO WANTS TO MEET THE HOLY WOMAN...
...MORE THAN ANY OF US.
OOO--
!
SANGO! MORE NEW DEMONS!
HOOOOO

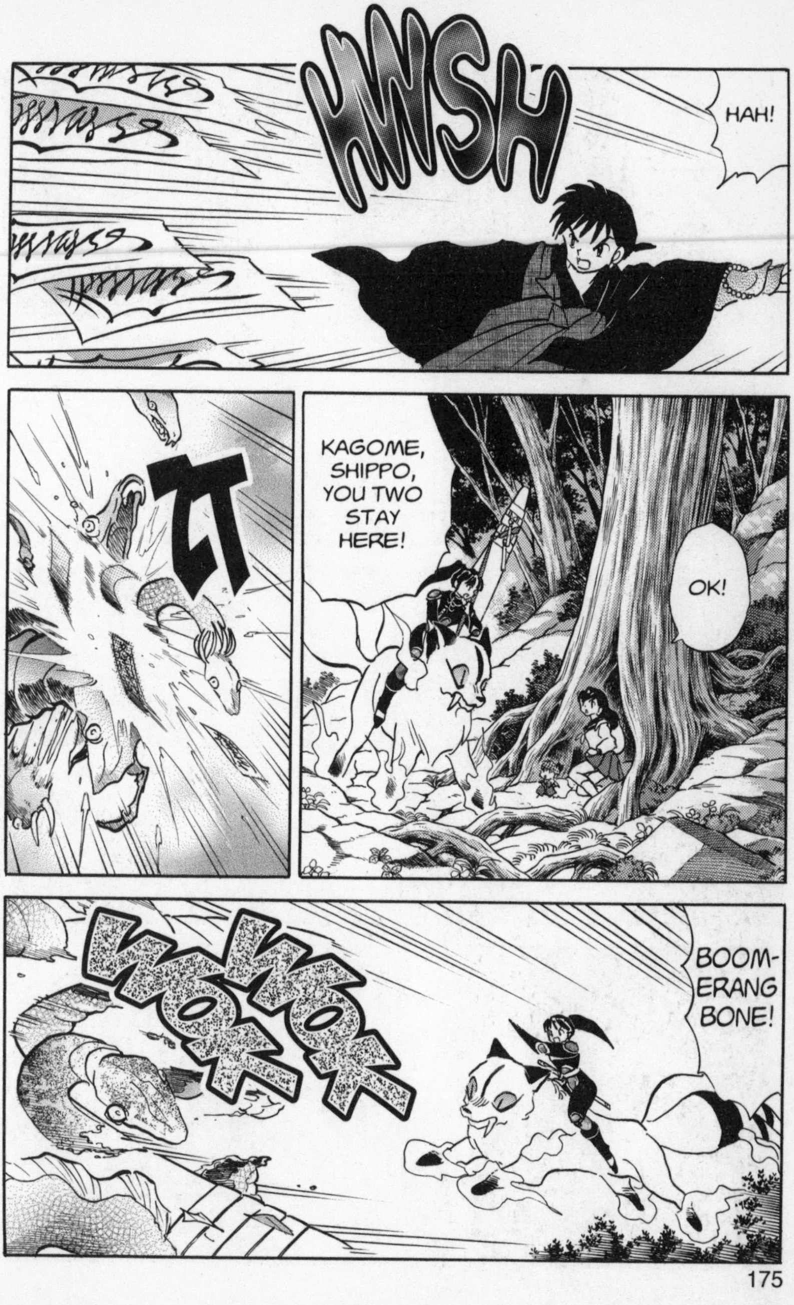
HWISH
HAH!
KAGOME, SHIPPO, YOU TWO STAY HERE!
OK!
BOOM-ERANG BONE!

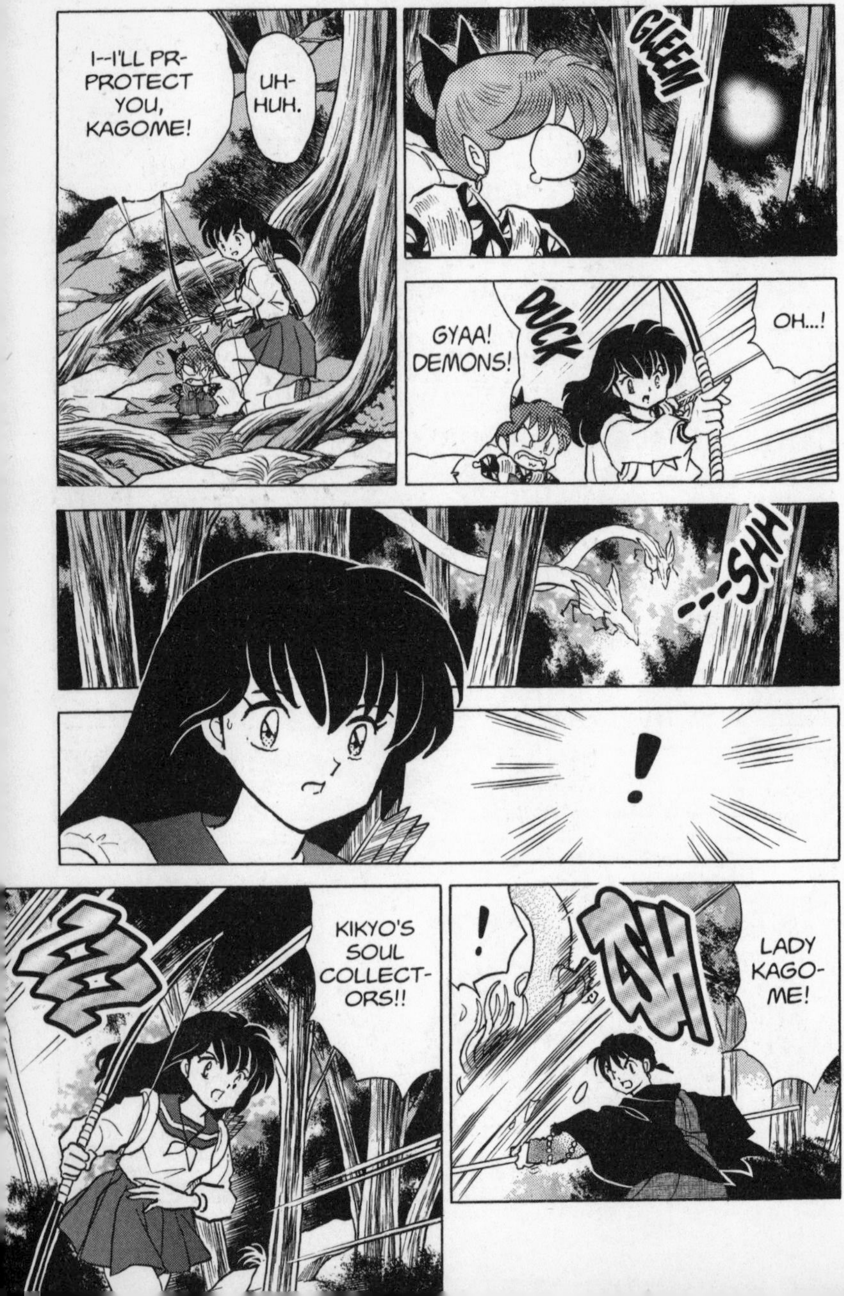
I--I'LL PR-PROTECT YOU, KAGOME!
UH-HUH.
GLEEM
GYAA! DEMONS!
DUCK
OH...!
---SHH
!
KIKYO'S SOUL COLLECT-ORS!!
!
TAH
LADY KAGO-ME!

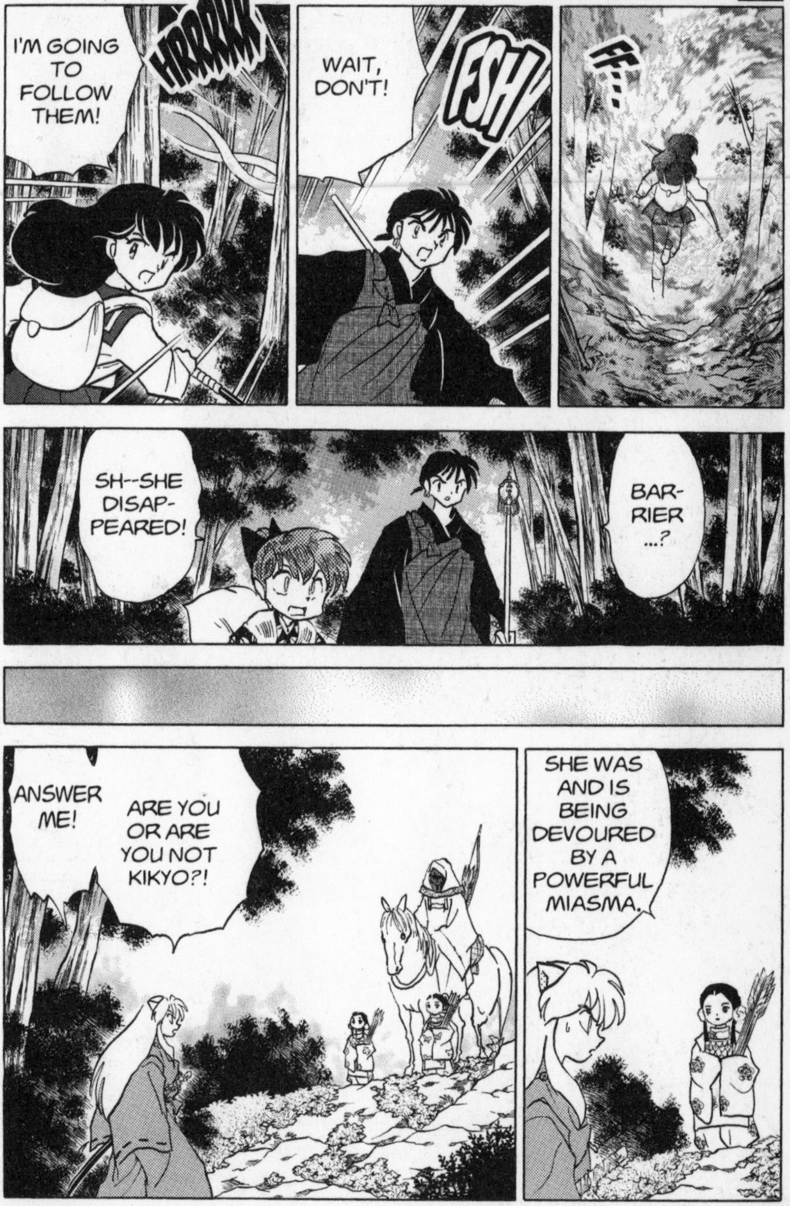
I'M GOING TO FOLLOW THEM!
HRRRRR
WAIT, DON'T!
FSH
FF...
SH--SHE DISAPPEARED!
BARRIER...?
ANSWER ME!
ARE YOU OR ARE YOU NOT KIKYO?!
SHE WAS AND IS BEING DEVOURED BY A POWERFUL MIASMA.

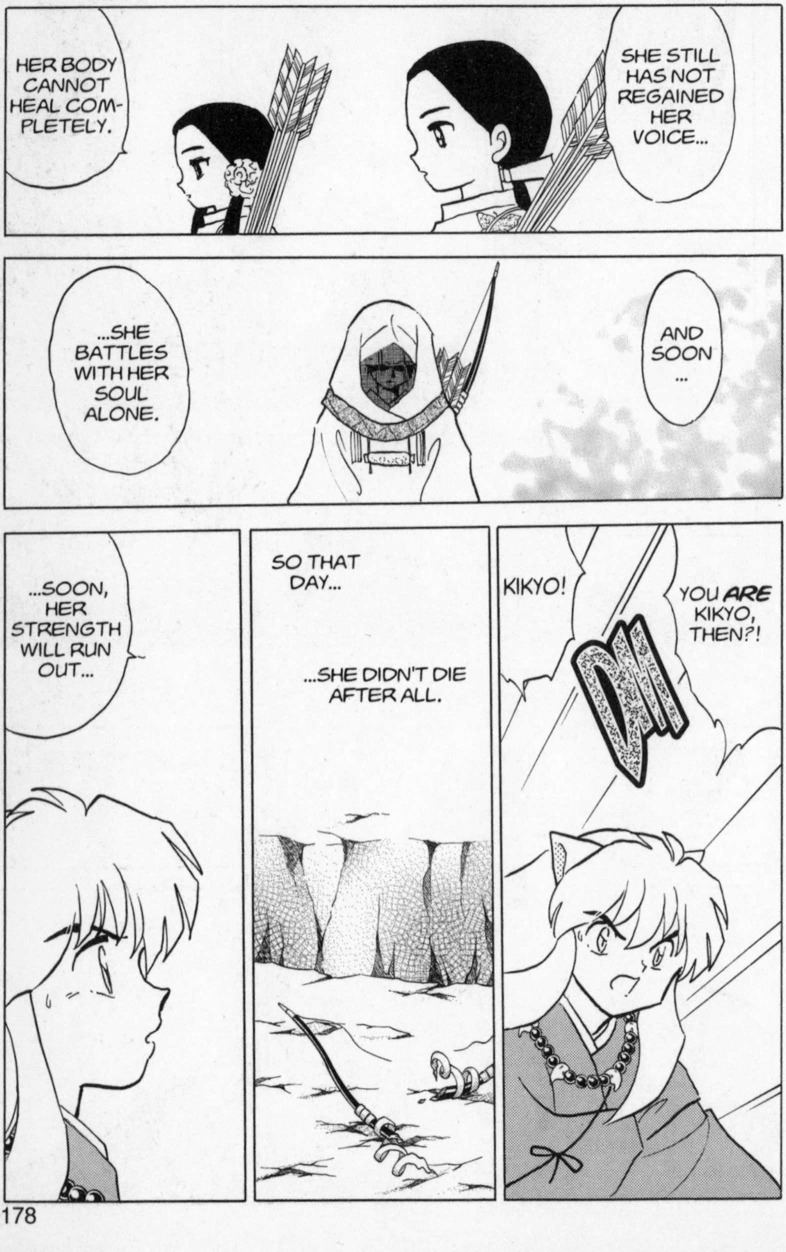
HER BODY CANNOT HEAL COM-PLETELY.
SHE STILL HAS NOT REGAINED HER VOICE...
...SHE BATTLES WITH HER SOUL ALONE.
AND SOON ...
...SOON, HER STRENGTH WILL RUN OUT...
SO THAT DAY...
...SHE DIDN'T DIE AFTER ALL.
KIKYO!
YOU ***ARE*** KIKYO, THEN?!

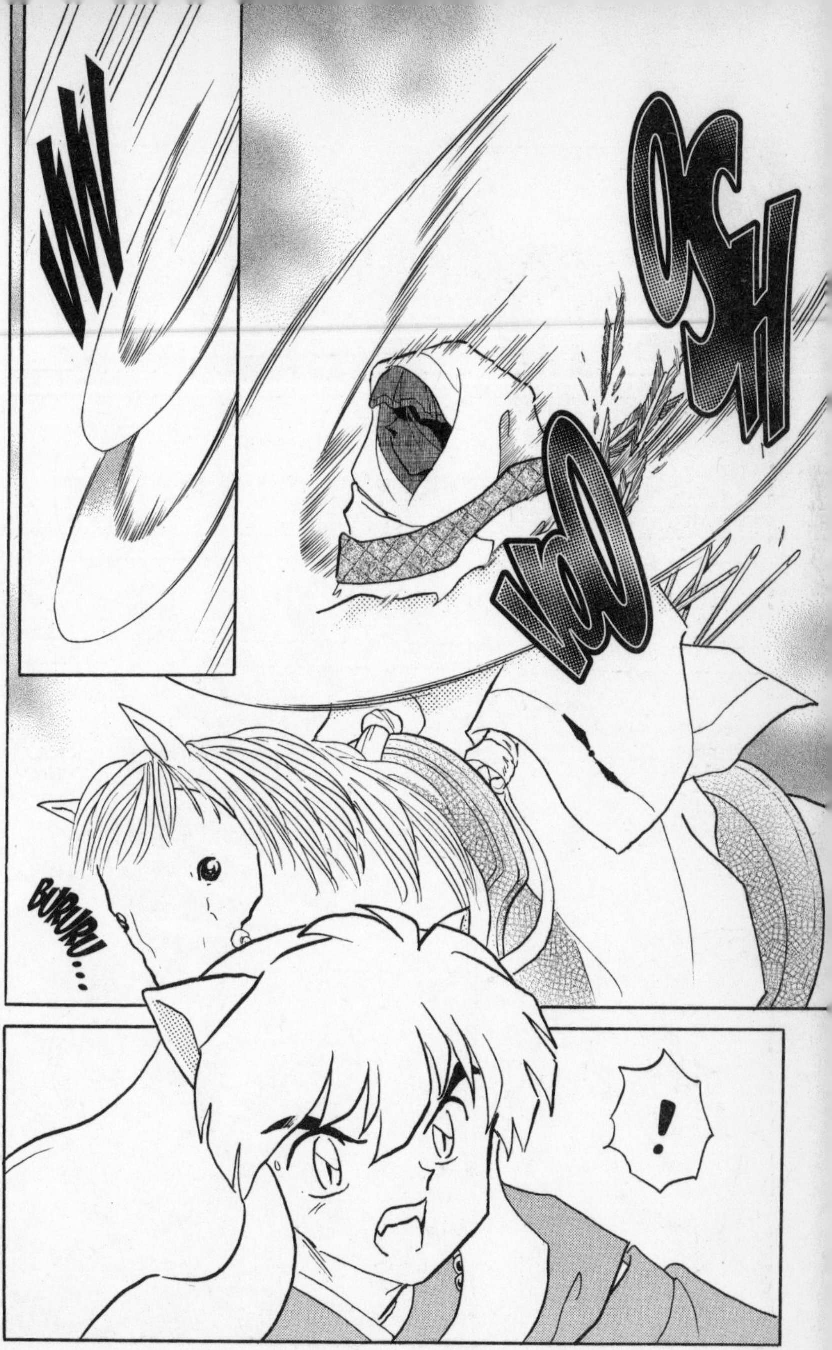
WOOSH
BURURU...
!

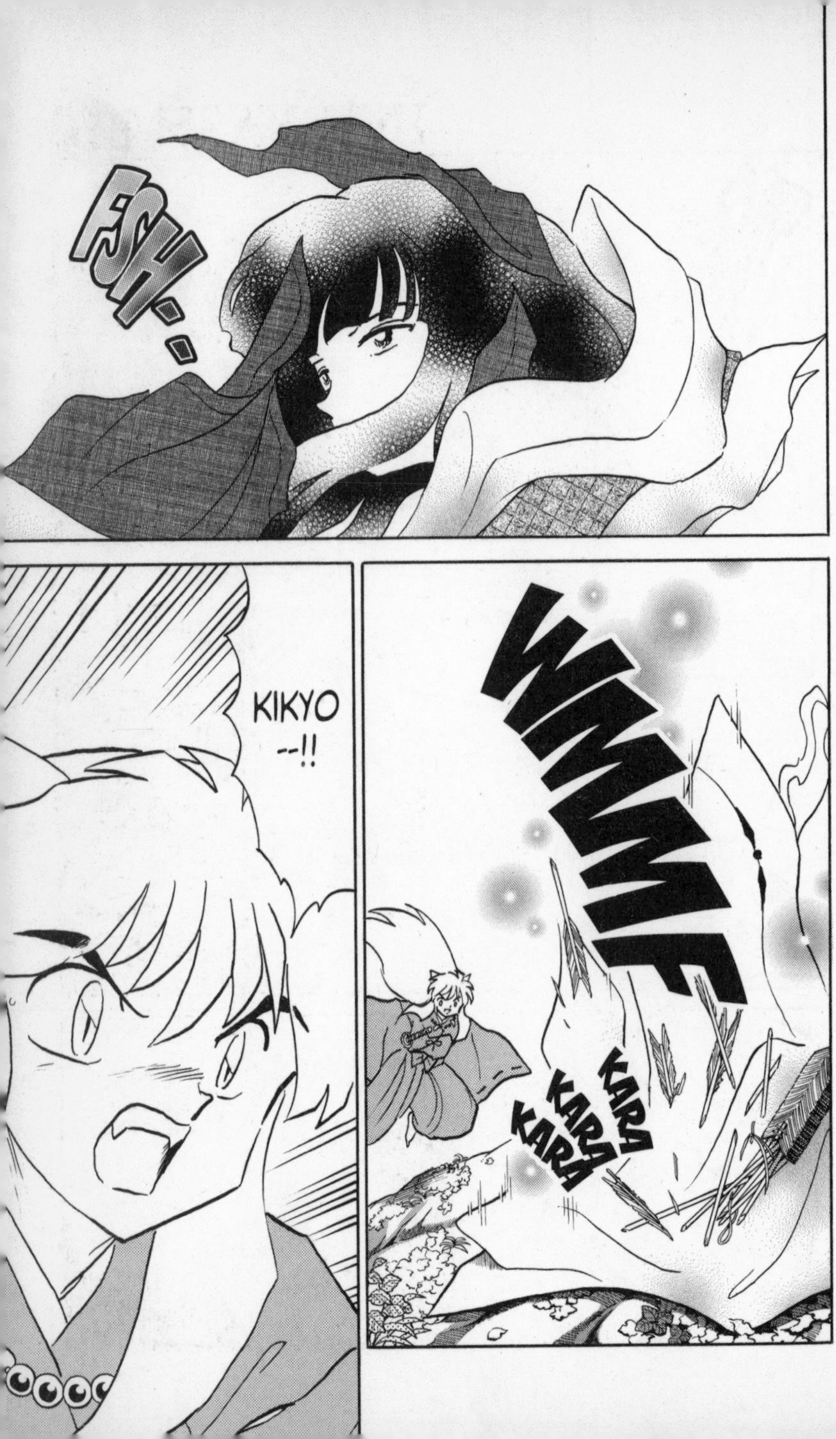
FSH...
KIKYO
--!!
WMMF
KARA
KARA
KARA

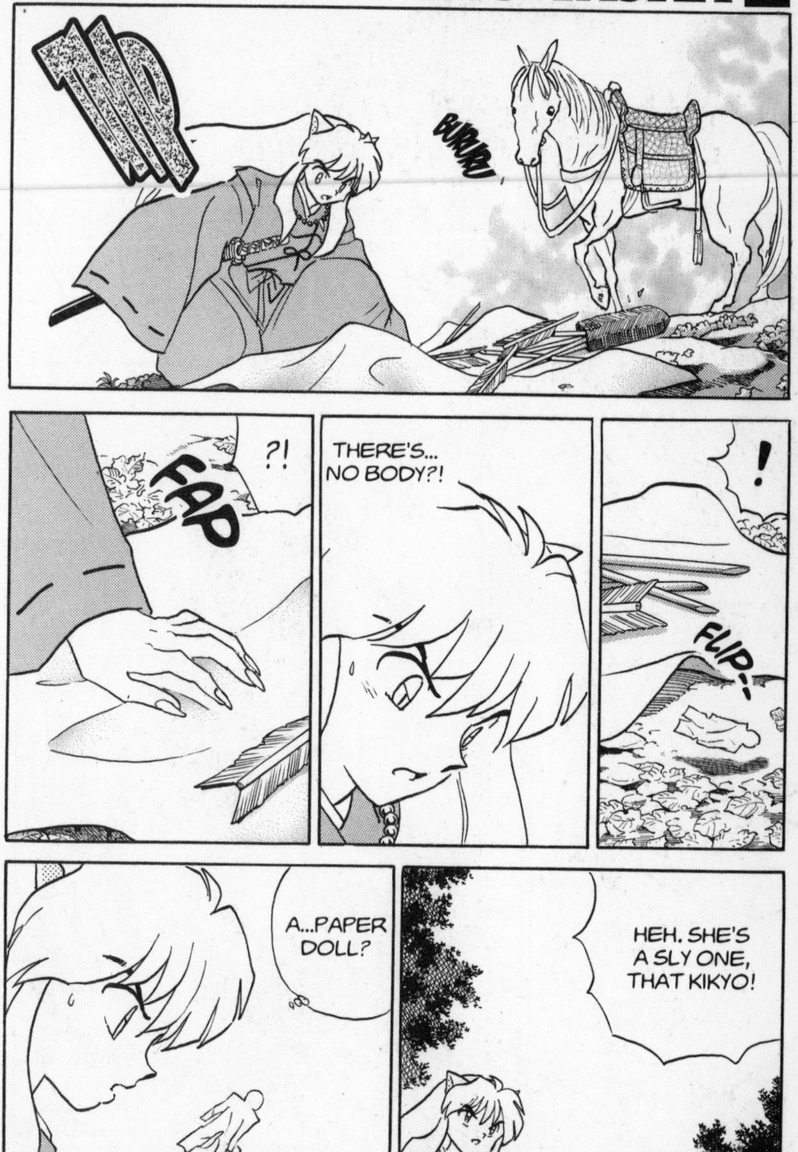
BURURU
?!
FAP
THERE'S...
NO BODY?!
!
FLIP
A...PAPER
DOLL?
HEH. SHE'S
A SLY ONE,
THAT KIKYO!

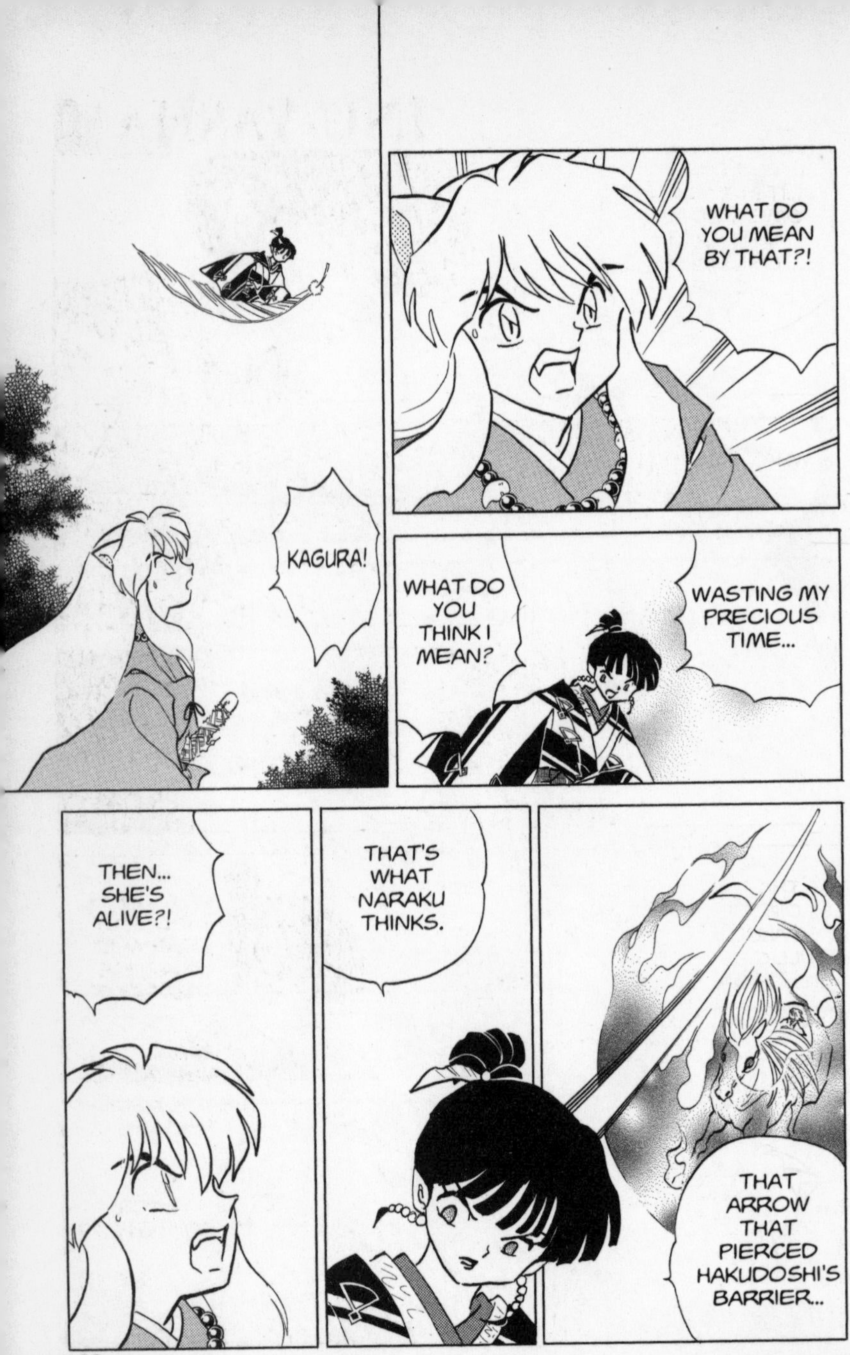
KAGURA!
WHAT DO YOU MEAN BY THAT?!
WHAT DO YOU THINK I MEAN?
WASTING MY PRECIOUS TIME...
THEN... SHE'S ALIVE?!
THAT'S WHAT NARAKU THINKS.
THAT ARROW THAT PIERCED HAKUDOSHI'S BARRIER...

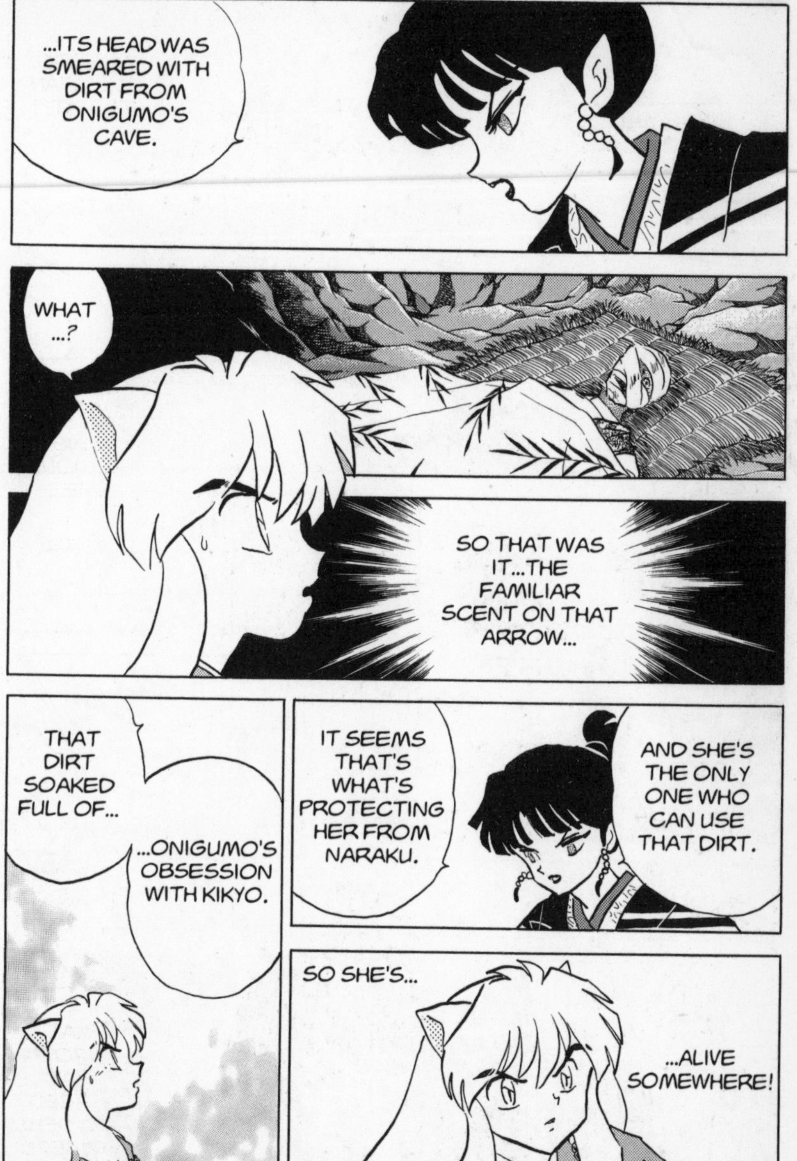
...ITS HEAD WAS SMEARED WITH DIRT FROM ONIGUMO'S CAVE.
WHAT ...?
SO THAT WAS IT...THE FAMILIAR SCENT ON THAT ARROW...
THAT DIRT SOAKED FULL OF...
...ONIGUMO'S OBSESSION WITH KIKYO.
IT SEEMS THAT'S WHAT'S PROTECTING HER FROM NARAKU.
AND SHE'S THE ONLY ONE WHO CAN USE THAT DIRT.
SO SHE'S...
...ALIVE SOMEWHERE!

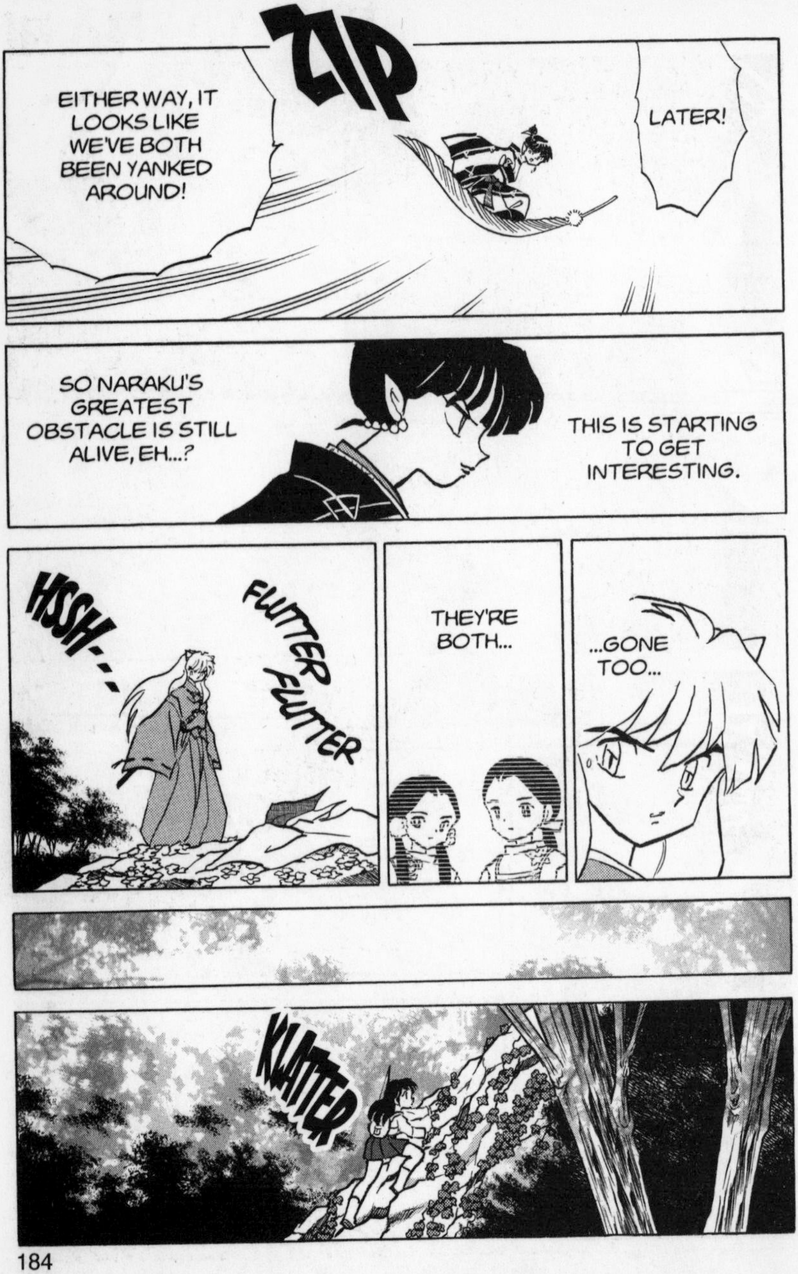
EITHER WAY, IT LOOKS LIKE WE'VE BOTH BEEN YANKED AROUND!
ZIP
LATER!
SO NARAKU'S GREATEST OBSTACLE IS STILL ALIVE, EH...?
THIS IS STARTING TO GET INTERESTING.
HSSH...
FLUTTER FLUTTER
THEY'RE BOTH...
...GONE TOO...
KLATTER

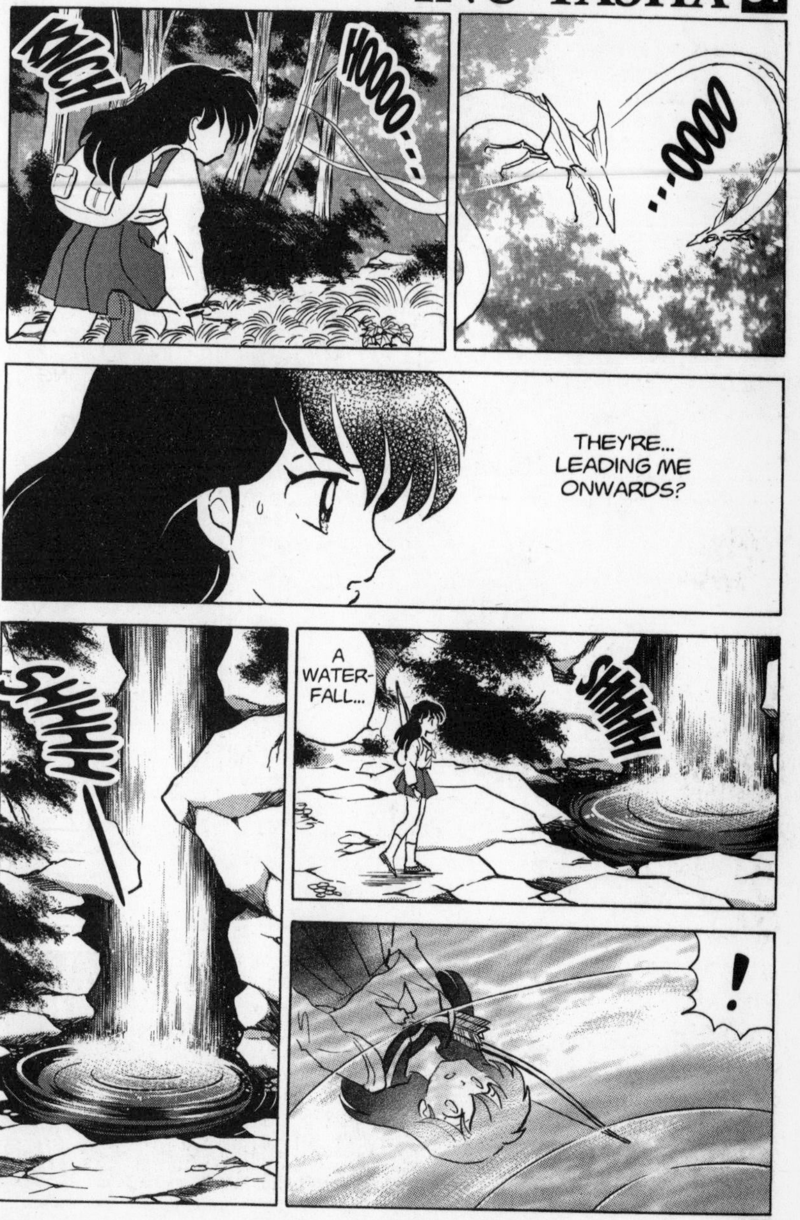
KNCH
HOOOO...
...OOOO
THEY'RE... LEADING ME ONWARDS?
SHHHH—
A WATER-FALL...
SHHHH
!

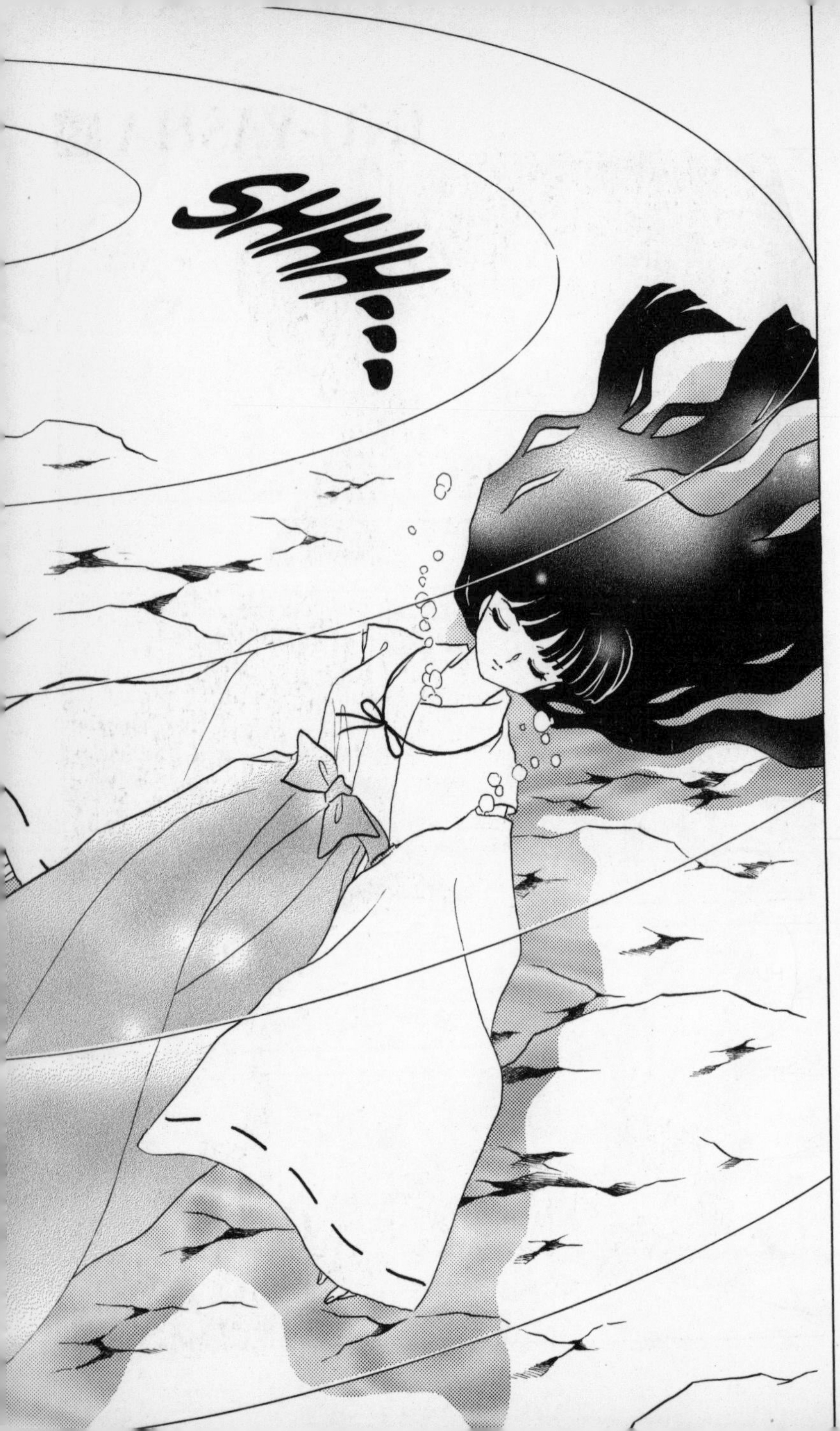
SHHH...

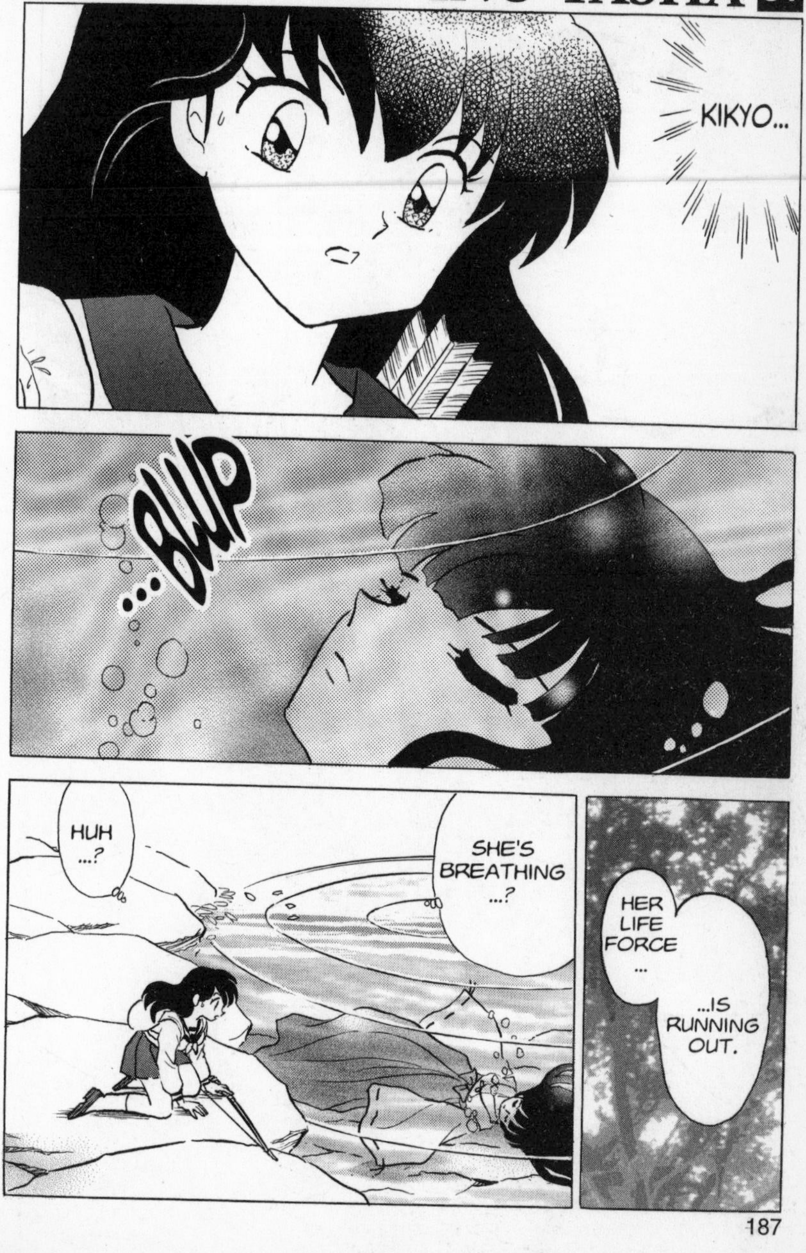
KIKYO...
...BLUP
HUH ...?
SHE'S BREATHING ...?
HER LIFE FORCE ...
...IS RUNNING OUT.

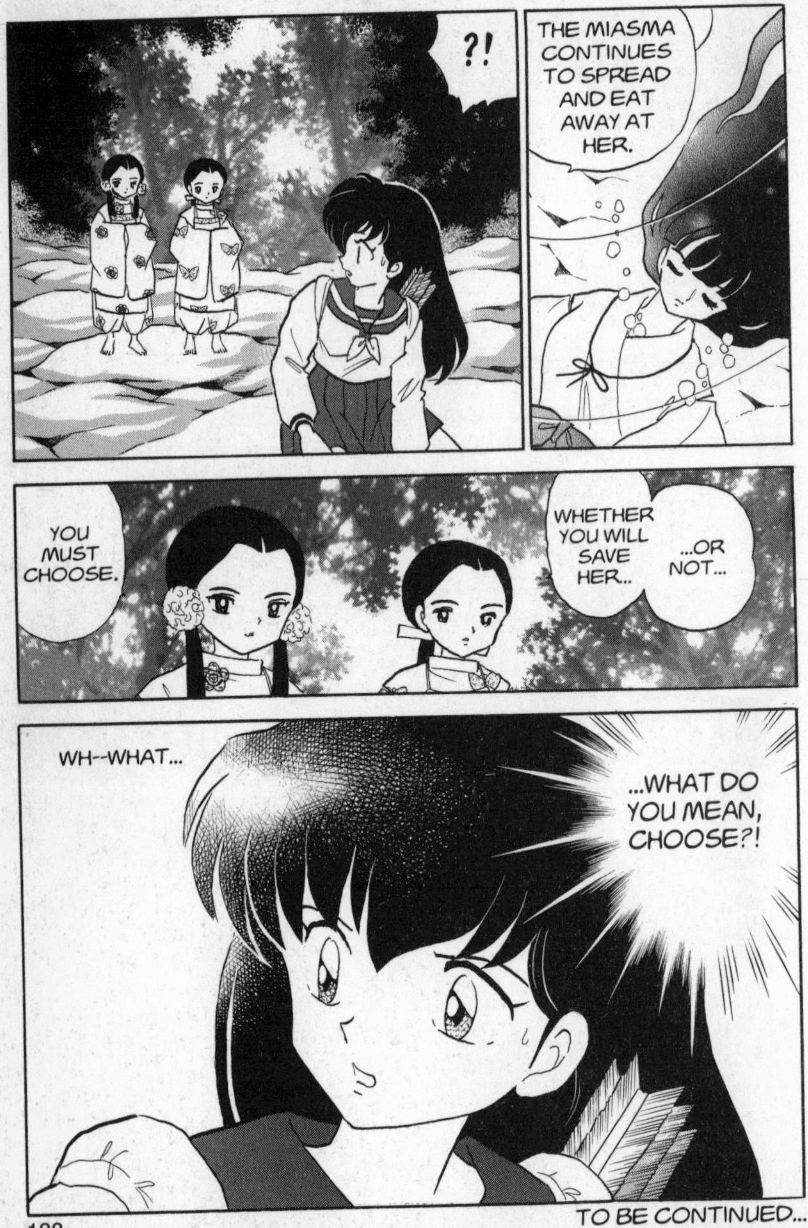
?!
THE MIASMA CONTINUES TO SPREAD AND EAT AWAY AT HER.
YOU MUST CHOOSE.
WHETHER YOU WILL SAVE HER...
...OR NOT...
WH--WHAT...
...WHAT DO YOU MEAN, CHOOSE?!

TO BE CONTINUED...

A Comedy that Redefines a

Due to an unfortunate accident, when martial artist Ranma gets splashed with cold water, he becomes a buxom young girl! Hot water reverses the effect, but when blamed for offenses both real and imagined, and pursued by lovesick suitors of both genders, what's a half-boy, half-girl to do?

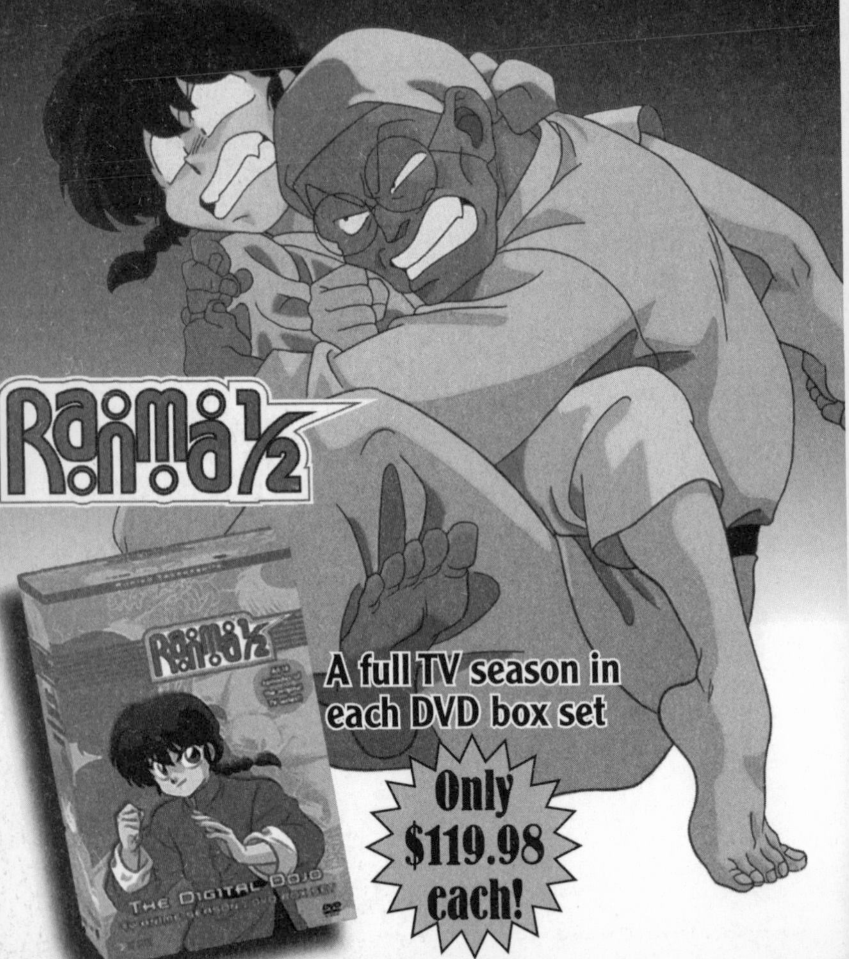

A full TV season in each DVD box set

Only $119.98 each!

LOVE MANGA?
LET US KNOW WHAT YOU THINK!

OUR MANGA SURVEY IS NOW
AVAILABLE ONLINE. PLEASE VISIT:
VIZ.COM/MANGASURVEY

HELP US MAKE THE MANGA
YOU LOVE BETTER!